P9-EEP-330

When should I travel to get the best airfare?
Where do I go for answers to my travel questions?
What's the best and easiest way to plan and book my trip?

frommers.travelocity.com

Frommer's, the travel guide leader, has teamed up with **Travelocity.com**, the leader in online travel, to bring you an in-depth, easy-to-use resource designed to help you plan and book your trip online.

At **frommers.travelocity.com**, you'll find free online updates about your destination from the experts at Frommer's plus the outstanding travel planning and purchasing features of Travelocity.com. Travelocity.com provides reservations capabilities for 95 percent of all airline seats sold, more than 47,000 hotels, and over 50 car rental companies. In addition, Travelocity.com offers more than 2,000 exciting vacation and cruise packages. Travelocity.com puts you in complete control of your travel planning with these and other great features:

Expert travel guidance from Frommer's - over 150 writers reporting from around the world!

Best Fare Finder - an interactive calendar tells you when to travel to get the best airfare

Fare Watcher - we'll track airfare changes to your favorite destinations

Dream Maps - a mapping feature that suggests travel opportunities based on your budget

Shop Safe Guarantee - 24 hours a day / 7 days a week live customer service, and more!

Whether you're traveling on a tight budget, looking for a quick weekend getaway, or planning the trip of a lifetime, Frommer's guides and Travelocity.com will make your travel dreams a reality. You've bought the book, now book the trip!

Travelocity.com
A Sabre Company

Frommer's

Here's what the critics say about Frommer's:

"Amazingly easy to use. Very portable, very complete."
—*Booklist*

♦

"The only mainstream guide to list specific prices. The Walter Cronkite of guidebooks—with all that implies."
—*Travel & Leisure*

♦

"Complete, concise, and filled with useful information."
—*New York Daily News*

♦

"The best series for travelers who want one easy-to-use guidebook."
—*U.S. Air Magazine*

Frommer's®

3rd Edition

Caribbean Ports of Call

Heidi Sarna

IDG Books Worldwide, Inc.
An International Data Group Company
Foster City, CA • Chicago, IL • Indianapolis, IN • New York, NY

ABOUT THE AUTHOR

Heidi Sarna has cruised on some 70 ships of all shapes and sizes, from 100-passenger sailing ships to 3,000-passenger megas, and she loves them all (well, OK, some more than others). She's a contributing editor to *Travel Holiday* magazine and over the past 10 years has contributed articles on cruising and travel to *Bride's, New Choices, Cigar Aficionado, Frommer's Budget Travel On-Line, Travel Weekly, Travel Counselor, Leisure Travel News, Travel Agent, Cruise & Vacation Views,* and *Porthole* magazine, as well as to other major guidebooks and the *Boston Herald, Star Ledger,* and *Washington Times* newspapers. When she's not cruising, you're bound to find her at Manhattan's West Side docks, touring and inspecting the many ships that pass through New York.

IDG BOOKS WORLDWIDE, INC.

An International Data Group Company
909 Third Ave.
New York, NY 10022

Find us online at **www.frommers.com**.

ISBN 0-7645-6116-2
ISSN 1090-2617

Editor: Matt Hannafin
Production Editors: Scott Barnes, Heather Gregory
Photo Editor: Richard Fox
Design by Michele Laseau
Staff Cartographers: John Decamillis, Roberta Stockwell, Elizabeth Puhl
Additional cartography by Nicholas Trotter
Production by IDG Books Indianapolis Production Department

SPECIAL SALES

For general information on IDG Books Worldwide's books in the U.S., please call our Consumer Customer Service department at 1-800-762-2974. For reseller information, including discounts, bulk sales, customized editions, and premium sales, please call our Reseller Customer Service department at 1-800/434-3422.

Manufactured in the United States of America

5 4 3 2 1

Contents

4	**Wrapping Up Your Cruise: Debarkation Concerns 287**

	Index 292

List of Maps

ACKNOWLEDGMENTS

A select group of experienced travel journalists and experts contributed to this book.

Kenneth Lindley, a Brooklyn-based freelance writer and a passionate, curious, and devoted traveler, didn't leave a palm tree or conch shell unturned when he explored the Caribbean islands of Bonaire, Guadeloupe, Les Saintes, and Dominica and reviewed them for this book. He also contributed the section on Caribbean history. **Arline and Sam Bleecker,** everyone's favorite husband-and-wife travel-writing team, contributed their valuable two cents to the Barbados, Cozumel, Jamaica, and St. Lucia reviews. **Brian Major,** a respected (not to mention cool) travel writer and cruise editor at *Travel Weekly,* contributed his point of view to the Martinique, Trinidad and Tobago, and BVI reviews. **Laura Dennis,** a former editor at *Travel Weekly,* has been to the Caribbean a zillion times and contributed her experiences to the Dominican Republic and Antigua reviews. **Lesley Abravanal,** a writer and editor living in Miami, provided the real scoop on that wild and crazy Pez-colored city by the sea. **Jonathan Siskin,** seasoned travel writer, broadcaster, and poet-artist, contributed to the St. Croix review. Thanks to **Dr. Christina Colon** for her help researching and verifying some of the more esoteric tidbits in the book. Special thanks to **Matt Hannafin,** the most thorough, patient, and good-hearted editorial bodhisattva in New York (who also wrote the Bequia and Nevis reviews and contributed to the St. Kitts review).

And most importantly, to my wonderful husband **Arun,** for his support, insight, and much-appreciated daily dose of "go do your work."

AN INVITATION TO THE READER

In researching this book, we discovered many wonderful places—hotels, restaurants, shops, and more. We're sure you'll find others. Please tell us about them, so we can share the information with your fellow travelers in upcoming editions. If you were disappointed with a recommendation, we'd love to know that, too. Please write to:

Frommer's Caribbean Ports of Call, 3rd edition
IDG Books Worldwide, Inc.
909 Third Ave.
New York, NY 10022

AN ADDITIONAL NOTE

Please be advised that travel information is subject to change at any time—and this is especially true of prices. We therefore suggest that you write or call ahead for confirmation when making your travel plans. The authors, editors, and publisher cannot be held responsible for the experiences of readers while traveling. Your safety is important to us, however, so we encourage you to stay alert and be aware of your surroundings. Keep a close eye on cameras, purses, and wallets, all favorite targets of thieves and pickpockets.

WHAT THE SYMBOLS MEAN

✪ Frommer's Favorites

Our favorite places and experiences—outstanding for quality, value, or both.

The following abbreviations are used for credit cards:

AE	American Express	EURO	Eurocard
CB	Carte Blanche	JCB	Japan Credit Bank
DC	Diners Club	MC	MasterCard
DISC	Discover	V	Visa
ER	enRoute		

FIND FROMMER'S ONLINE

www.frommers.com offers up-to-the-minute listings on almost 200 cities around the globe—including the latest bargains and candid, personal articles updated daily by Arthur Frommer himself. No other Web site offers such comprehensive and timely coverage of the world of travel.

The Gulf of Mexico & the Caribbean

CO. | MO. | ILL. | KY. | W. VA | VA

KS.

UNITED STATES OF AMERICA

N.C.

N.M.

White

TENN.

OK. | ARK.

Memphis

Atlanta | S.C.

Red

MISS.

ALA. | GA.

TX.

Dallas

Braços

Mississippi

LA.

Jacksonville

Cape Canave

Rio Grande

San Antonio

Houston

New Orleans

Tampa

FLA.

Fort Lauderda

Mia

Matamoros

Gulf Of Mexico

Key West

Monterrey

Saltillo

Havana

MEXICO

Tampico

Yucatan Channel

Isla de la Juventad

CAYMAN IS

Bahia de Campeche

Mérida

Playa del Carmen

Cozumel

Campeche

Yucatan Peninsula

Mexico City

Veracruz

Balsas

Belize City

Oaxaca

Coatzacoalcas

Belmopan

BELIZE

Acapulco

Gulf of Honduras

Golfo de Tehuantapec

GUATEMALA

HONDURAS

Guatemala City

Tegucigalpa

San Salvador

NICARAGUA

EL SALVADOR

Managua

Lago de Nicaragua

Golfo de los Mosquitos

San Jose

Pacific Ocean

COSTA RICA

0   300 Miles

0   300 Kilometers

N

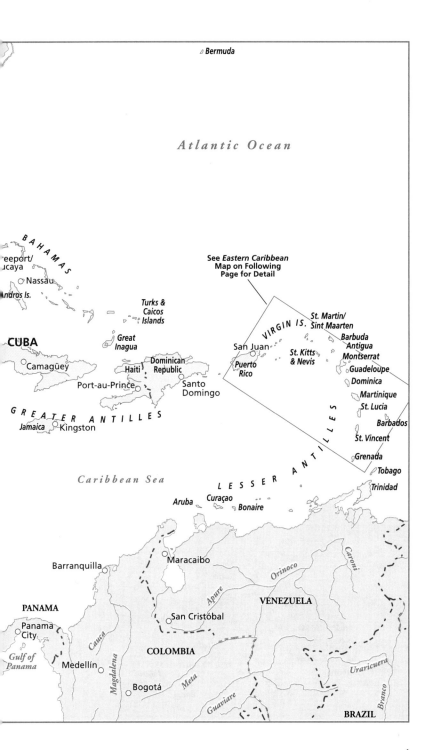

Bermuda

Atlantic Ocean

BAHAMAS

eeport/
ucaya
Nassau
ndros Is.

Turks &
Caicos
Islands

See *Eastern Caribbean
Map on Following
Page for Detail*

CUBA

Great
Inagua

VIRGIN IS.

St. Martin/
Sint Maarten

Camagüey

Haiti

Dominican
Republic

San Juan

Puerto
Rico

St. Kitts
& Nevis

Barbuda
Antigua
Montserrat
Guadeloupe
Dominica

Port-au-Prince

Santo
Domingo

Martinique
St. Lucia

GREATER ANTILLES

Barbados

Jamaica   Kingston

St. Vincent

Grenada
Tobago

Caribbean Sea

LESSER ANTILLES

Trinidad

Aruba

Curaçao
Bonaire

Barranquilla

Maracaibo

Orinoco

Caroni

PANAMA

Apure

VENEZUELA

Panama
City

San Cristóbal

Gulf of
Panama

Cauca

COLOMBIA

Medellín

Magdalena

Bogotá

Meta

Guaviare

Uraricuera

Branco

BRAZIL

The Eastern Caribbean

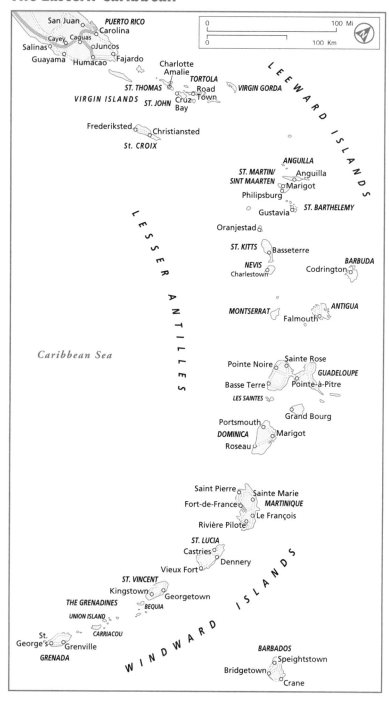

Getting Ready for Your Cruise

Ah, the Caribbean. Blue waters and white-sand beaches, amazing seafood and world-class rum, hot music and cool trade winds, and a rich history and diversity of cultures to boot. And, the islands are so close together that the region is ideal for travel by ship—you can spend a whole day on one island, maybe even stick around to sample the nightlife, then go to sleep on the ship and wake up at an entirely different island, maybe one where the language and even the whole island ecosystem is different. Such is the diversity in this part of the world.

This book is intended for the cruise vacationer, the person who's already decided to cruise and now wants to find out what there is to see and do at the ports their ship will visit. I've structured the book just for you, with attractions arranged to show which are within walking distance of the docks and which you'll have to hire a taxi to reach. I've also provided details on all the best excursions cruise lines typically offer in each port, all the best shopping you can do there, the best beaches and sports options, and some great places to go to have a meal that really gives you a taste of the island's flavor, plus places that are perfect for a cool, refreshing drink after a day of exploring.

1 The Port Experience

There are two kinds of cruisers when it comes to ports of call: those who choose a certain cruise because of its itinerary and those who don't. But even if you've been there, done that, and cruise primarily for the onboard ship life, you'll want to know how best to spend the limited time you have in whichever port you happen to land.

Here's the good news: There are no lousy Caribbean islands! Sure, depending on your likes and dislikes, you'll appreciate some more than others. Some of the ports and islands—like Key West, St. Thomas, and Nassau—are much more overrun with tourists than others, but then again, they'll appeal to shoppers, with their large variety of stores and bustling main streets. Other islands—Virgin Gorda, St. John's, Jost Van Dyke, and the Grenadines, for instance—are quieter and more natural and will appeal to those of you who'd rather walk along a deserted beach or take a drive along a lonely, winding road in the midst of pristine tropical foliage. Some ports are expensive—like Bermuda, the U.S. Virgin Islands,

St. Barts, St. Martin, and Aruba—while others are cheaper, like Cozumel, Jamaica, and the Grenadines.

At some ports, your best bet is to just head off **exploring on your own,** but at others, this could take too much time, entail lots of hassles and planning, may cost more, and might not be safe (because of poor roads or driving conditions, for instance). In these cases, the **shore excursions** offered by the cruise lines are the way to go. Under each port review in chapter 3, I'll run through a sampling of both the best excursions and the best sights and activities you can see and do on your own.

Shore excursions can be a wonderful and carefree way to get to know the islands, offering everything from **island tours** and **snorkeling and sailing excursions** (often with a rum-punch party theme) to more physically challenging pursuits like **bicycle tours, hiking, kayaking,** and **horseback-riding excursions.** Keep in mind, shore-excursion prices vary from line to line, even for the exact same tour; the prices I've listed are typical and are adult rates. Also note that in some cases the excursions fill up fast, especially on the megaships, so don't dawdle in signing up. When you receive your cruise documents after booking, or at the latest when you board your ship, you'll get a pamphlet with a listing of the excursions offered for your itinerary. Look it over, make your selections, and sign up the first or second day of your cruise. (In some cases, if a tour offered by your ship is booked up, you can try and book it independently once you get to port. The popular *Atlantis* submarine tour, for example— offered at Grand Cayman, Nassau, St. Thomas, and elsewhere—usually has an office/agent in the cruise terminals or nearby.) If there's an excursion you absolutely *need* to take and don't want to risk getting left out, a company called **Port Promotions** in Plantation, Florida, is now giving travel agents and passengers a chance to book shore excursions online at **www.portpromotions.com**.

As I mentioned, in some cases it's a great idea to go off on your own, so I'll also advise you of which islands are good for solo exploring, whether on foot or by taxi, motor scooter, ferry, or otherwise. Remember, though, if you opt to do your own independent touring, you'll be forgoing the narrative a guide gives, and may miss out on some of the historical, cultural, and other nuances of a particular island.

Most cruise ships arrive in port sometime before 10am, though this will vary slightly from line to line and port to port. You rarely have to clear Customs or Immigration, because your ship's purser will have collected your passport or documents at the start of your cruise and will have done all the paperwork for you. When local officials give the word, you just go ashore. Sometimes you can walk down the gangway right onto the pier, but if you're on a large cruise ship and the port isn't big enough, your ship will anchor offshore and ferry passengers to land via a small boat called a **tender.** In either case, you might have to wait in line to get ashore, but the waits can be longer if you have to tender in. Once ashore, even if you've come by tender, you aren't stuck there—you can return to the ship at any time for lunch, a nap, or whatever. Tenders run back and forth on a regular basis. They all look pretty much alike, though, so be sure you get on the one that's heading to your ship.

All shore excursions are carefully organized to coincide with your time in port. If you're going it on your own, you can count on finding taxi drivers at the pier when your ship docks. It's a good idea to arrange with the driver to pick you up at a certain time to bring you back to the port. In most ports you can also rent a car, moped/scooter, or bicycle.

If you opt to explore an island on your own or want to rent a car or four-wheel drive in your port of embarkation or debarkation, you may want to make rental arrangements in advance, especially during the popular winter months. To cut costs, form a car pool with another couple or two. Following are the reservations numbers and Web sites for the major rental companies. Smaller companies that rent jeeps, motor scooters, and such are listed in the individual port sections.

- **Advantage:** ☎ **800/777-5500;** www.arac.com
- **Alamo:** ☎ **800/327-9633;** www.goalamo.com
- **Avis:** ☎ **800/331-1212** in the continental United States; www.avis.com
- **Budget:** ☎ **800/527-0700;** www.budgetrentacar.com
- **Dollar:** ☎ **800/800-4000;** www.dollarcar.com
- **Hertz:** ☎ **800/654-3131;** www.hertz.com
- **National:** ☎ **800/CAR-RENT;** www.nationalcar.com
- **Payless:** ☎ **800/PAY-LESS;** www.paylesscar.com
- **Thrifty:** ☎ **800/367-2277;** www.thrifty.com
- **Value:** ☎ **800/327-2501;** www.go-value.com

With regard to **duty-free shopping** in port, the savings on duty-free merchandise can range from as little as 5% to as much as 50%. Unless there's a special sale being offered, many products carry comparable price tags from island to island. If you have particular goods you're thinking of buying, it pays to check prices at your local discount retailer before you leave home so you'll know whether you're really getting a bargain. (Note that the **U.S. dollar** is widely accepted throughout the islands as well as in Bermuda, so even though I've listed each island's official local currency, there's rarely a need to exchange U.S. dollars. Credit cards and traveler's checks are also widely accepted.)

It's also a good idea to talk with your cruise director or shore-excursion manager before you reach a port if you want to do something special (like find a special restaurant for lunch) or pursue a sport, be it scuba, golf, tennis, horseback riding, or fishing. Keep in mind that they'll most likely just tell you to sign up for one of their organized excursions (these are a money-maker for the lines, after all) and usually won't have the time or ability to help you arrange personal and private tours, especially on the megaships; personnel on the small and high-end lines, though, can and will help you in this way. You'll need to reserve spots for many of these activities before you land, because facilities might be filled by land-based vacationers or by passengers from other cruise ships. It goes without saying that if you arrive at a port of call and find the harbor filled with ships, expect the shops, restaurants, and beaches—everything, as a matter of fact—to be crowded. Call from the docks for any reservations.

Most passengers start heading back to the ship around 4pm or not much later than 5pm. By 6pm you're often sailing off to your next destination. In some cases—for instance, in Nassau, New Orleans, Key West, and the British Virgin Islands and Grenadines (for the smaller ships)—the ship may leave after midnight so passengers can stay ashore to enjoy the nightlife on the island.

Calling Home

Since the prices for calling home from a cruise ship are sky high (anywhere from $4 to $18 a minute), it's a better idea to call from land, when you're in port. I've included information on where to find phones in all the port reviews. Country codes are as follows: United States and Canada, 1; Australia, 61; New Zealand, 64; the United Kingdom, 44; and Ireland, 353.

Don't Wear the Coral!

You may be eyeing that gorgeous piece of black-coral jewelry, but did you know it's illegal to bring many products made from coral and other marine animals back to the United States? Remember, corals aren't rocks: They're living animals—a single branch of coral contains thousands of tiny coral animals (called *polyps*). Black coral in particular is a highly vulnerable species that's protected by tough international restrictions on its sale, even though you'll find it readily available throughout much of the Caribbean, including Grand Cayman and Curaçao. Of course, the shopkeeper selling it won't tell you that, and it may in fact be legal for him or her to sell it. Nonetheless, you will be in violation of U.S. and international laws if you bring these items back to the States. If caught, you could face stiff penalties and have your treasured mementos confiscated.

Sea turtles, too, are highly endangered, and sea horses, while not yet protected by laws, are currently threatened with extinction. The best way to appreciate and protect all of these natural beauties is with an underwater camera on a snorkeling expedition.

THE CRUISE LINES' PRIVATE ISLANDS

Most of the big lines have a private island or patch of island in the Bahamas that's included as a port of call on many of their Caribbean and Bahamas itineraries. Royal Caribbean, Princess, Disney, Holland America, Norwegian, and Costa each have one of these well-stocked island paradises that are off-limits to anyone but the line's passengers. While completely lacking in any true Caribbean culture, they do offer cruisers a guaranteed beach day with all the trimmings—a long stretch of beach with lounge chairs and strolling waiters selling tropical drinks, as well as water sports, shops, walking paths, hammocks, and casual picnic-style restaurants. On Disney's island, you can even rent bicycles and ride around the island.

2 Things to Know Before You Go

You've bought your ticket and you're getting ready to cruise. Here's the lowdown on what details you need to consider before you go.

PASSPORTS & VISAS

Good news in the convenience category: Visas are not generally required for American, Canadian, and European citizens visiting the Caribbean islands or ports in Mexico (although, depending on the itinerary, you may be asked to fill out tourist cards or other forms in the airplane, airport, or cruise terminal, especially if you're flying to a non-U.S. port to start your cruise). Passports aren't necessarily required either, although it's a good idea to have one. A passport speeds your way through Customs and Immigration, and you never know when entry requirements can change. Read through the documents your cruise line sends you with your tickets, and contact the line if you have any questions.

If you find you don't need a passport, you will still need **identification.** Acceptable forms of ID include an ongoing or return ticket plus an original birth certificate (or a copy that has been certified by the U.S. Department of Health) and a photo ID, such as a driver's license or an expired passport. *A driver's license is not* *acceptable as a sole form of identification.* As you would before any trip abroad, make two photocopies of your documents and ID before leaving home. Take one set with you (keeping it in a different place from your original documents) and keep one at home.

Each particular port of embarkation has its own ritual. You may be asked to turn over your ID (for instance, your passport) and sometimes your airline tickets to cruise line officials at the start of the cruise. They'll facilitate the procedures for group or individual port clearances and immigration formalities throughout the cruise, and return your documents to you at the end of the cruise.

All non-U.S. and non-Canadian citizens must have valid passports, alien-registration cards, and the requisite visas when boarding any cruise ship or aircraft departing from and/or returning to American soil. Noncitizens also need to present an ongoing or return ticket for an airline or cruise ship as proof that you intend to remain on local shores only for a brief stay.

MONEY MATTERS

Cruise ships operate on a cashless basis. Basically, this means you keep a running tab, signing for virtually everything you want to buy all week long—drinks at the bar, shore excursions, and gift-shop purchases—and paying up at the end of the cruise with cash or a credit card. Very, very convenient, yes—and also very, very easy to spend more than you would if you were doling out wads of cash each time.

Shortly before or after embarkation, a purser or check-in clerk in the terminal or on board will request the imprint of one of your credit cards. On the last day of your cruise, an **itemized account** of all you've charged throughout the cruise is slipped beneath your cabin door. If you agree with the charges, they are automatically billed to your credit-card account. If you'd rather pay in cash or if you dispute any charge, then you need to stop by the ship's cashier or purser's office, where there's usually a long line. Have fun!

At embarkation, larger ships issue you an **identification card** that you show whenever you get back on the ship after spending the day in port and that you use when you sign for something. On the newest ships, this same ID card often serves as your room key. Smaller and older ships may not have either of these ID cards, and still issue regular room keys. (Some lines, such as Windjammer and American Canadian Caribbean Line, rely on the honor system and don't even use room keys.)

The cashless system works just fine on board, but you'll likely need some dough in port. Of course, you can put any shore excursions you sign up for on your room tab, and credit cards are accepted at most port shops (as are traveler's checks), but I do recommend having some real cash on you, ideally in small denominations, for any taxi rides, tips to tour leaders, or purchases you make from craft markets and street-side hawkers.

No Vaccinations Required

The Caribbean islands do not generally require inoculations against tropical diseases, although you might want to check out the Centers for Disease Control (CDC) Web site to see what it suggests (www.cdc.gov). In early 2000, for instance, the CDC advised travelers to the rural and southeastern parts of the Dominican Republic to take malaria-prevention medications like chloroquine before traveling there.

For the most part, don't worry about **exchanging money** to local currency, since the good ole U.S. dollar is widely accepted in the Caribbean (at least in the tourist-savvy ports of call you're likely to visit) and is the legal currency of the U.S. Virgin Islands, the British Virgin Islands, and Puerto Rico. Exceptions include Guadeloupe, where you'll need to exchange your dollars for some French francs if you intend to buy anything. If you're running low on dough, there are ATM machines in nearly every cruise port covered in this guide, in some cruise terminals, and aboard many of the megaships (Remember, though, you'll get local currency from machines in the Caribbean). Expect a hefty fee for using ATMs on board cruise ships (like $5 in addition to what your bank charges you). Many lines, like Carnival and Royal Caribbean, cash traveler's checks at the purser's desk (and sometimes personal checks of up to about $200 if issued in the U.S.); with an American Express card, you can typically cash a check for up to $250. Specific currency information is included in chapter 3, "The Ports of Call."

PACKING

One of the beauties of cruising is that you only need to unpack once. Even though you'll be visiting several different countries on a typical weeklong cruise, you check in to your cabin on day one, unpack, and settle in. The destinations come to you!

Just what do you need to pack? To some extent, that depends on the kind of cruise you're taking. But overall, cruise ship life mirrors that on land. Dress codes are being relaxed, and aside from the ultra-deluxe lines and formal nights on the large ships, **casual clothes** are the norm. In fact, instead of having a combination of formal, informal, and casual nights throughout the week as in the past, many lines—Carnival and Norwegian, for instance—are just going with the two formal nights, and the rest of the week is considered casual.

DAYTIME CLOTHES

Across the board, casual daytime wear means shorts, T-shirts, bathing suits, and sundresses. Remember to bring a cover-up and sandals if you want to go right from your deck chair to lunch in one of the restaurants or to some activity being held in a public room. When in port, the same dress code works, but do respect local customs and err toward modesty (that is, something more than a skimpy bikini top if you're straying from the beach area). You might want to bring a pair of **aquasocks** if you plan on doing any snorkeling or water sports in port (if you don't have them, many cruise lines will charge you about $5 to rent a pair), and some good **walking shoes** to explore the islands as comfortably as possible.

If you plan on hitting the gym, don't forget sneakers and your workout clothes. And it can't hurt to bring along one pair of long casual pants and a long-sleeved sweatshirt, as well as a lightweight raincoat in case the weather turns dicey.

EVENING CLOTHES

Whether you like it or not, it seems cruise ship passengers are dressing down more than ever. It's the American way. Still, formal nights still survive at sea, at least a couple of nights per cruise, and, except on the ultra-casual, small-ship lines (see "Soft-Adventure Lines & Sailing Ships," below), you'll want to pack a few dressy duds. Exceptions to this are the ultra-casual Windjammer, Star Clippers, and American Canadian Caribbean lines, where shorts, T-shirts, and sandals can take you through the day and into the evening meals (although most people tend to dress up a tad more for dinner). Windstar and Club Med encourage a "smart casual" look, and have a no-jackets-required rule the entire week. Passengers aboard Clipper go casual during the day but tend to ratchet up to jackets and dresses at dinner.

Most ships have two **formal nights** on a 7-night cruise (usually the second night of the cruise for the captain's cocktail party, and the second-to-last night of the cruise). Imagine what you'd wear to a nice wedding: Men are encouraged to wear dark suits or tuxedos and women cocktail dresses, sequined jackets, or gowns (or recycled bridesmaids dresses!), or other fancy attire. If you just hate dressing up, women can get away with a blouse and skirt or pants. And, of course, accessories like jewelry and scarves can dress up an otherwise nondescript outfit.

The other nights are much more casual, and are designated either **semiformal** (or informal) or **casual.** Semiformal calls for suits or sports jackets for men and stylish dresses or pantsuits for women; casual nights call for chinos or dress pants and collared shirts for men, and dresses, skirts, or pantsuits for women.

In spite of the suggested dress codes, which are usually described in the back of a cruise line's brochure, you'll still find a wide variety of outfits being worn. Invariably, one person's "formal" is quite different from another's. So, like hemlines and everything else these days, to a large extent, anything goes. Passengers are asked not to wear jeans, baseball caps, shorts, and T-shirts for dinner in the formal dining rooms (although there are always a few who try and succeed—few people are ever turned away at the dining-room door because of what they're wearing). At the same time, despite the casual trend in America (casual Fridays and the baseball-cap, fur-coat–wearing Park Avenue set, for instance), you'll find there's a contingent of folks on board who like to get all decked out. I personally find getting dressed up for dinner a few nights a week to be part of the fun; in fact, I like to plunk myself in some heavily trafficked lounge an hour or two before dinner and do some good old-fashioned people-watching. It's a veritable fashion show!

SUNDRIES

Like hotels, many ships (especially the newest and the high-end ones) come equipped with hair dryers and supply bathroom amenities such as shampoo, conditioner, lotion, and soap (although you might still want to bring your own products— I find the ones provided often seem watered down). Some lines, like Carnival, do skimp, and provide only soap in cabins and not even hair dryers (except on *Destiny, Triumph,* and *Victory*). With the exception of the *Voyager of the Seas,* Royal Caribbean doesn't have hair dryers on its ships either. If you bring your hair dryer, curling iron, or laptop, you might want to bring an adapter, although the vast majority of ships run on 110 AC current.

Cruise Tip: Tuxedo Rentals

If you don't own a tux or don't want to bother lugging one along, you can often arrange a rental through the cruise line or your travel agent for about $75. In some cases, a rental offer arrives with your cruise tickets. If you choose this option, your suit will be waiting for you in your cabin when you arrive.

Cruise Tip: Stowing the Crown Jewels

If you want to bring good jewelry, most cabins have personal safes operated by a digital code, credit card, or, once in a while, a lock and key. If your cabin doesn't have a safe (usually it's the older ships that don't), the ship's purser can keep your valuables.

No need to pack a **beach towel,** as they're almost always supplied on board (exceptions: Windjammer and ACCL). Bird watchers will want their **binoculars** and manuals, golfers their clubs (although they can always be rented), and snorkelers their gear (which can also be rented).

If you forget to pack a personal effect or two, don't despair. Even the smallest, no-frills ships have at least one small shop on board, selling items like razor blades, toothbrushes, sunscreen, film, and other items you may need (but the stuff isn't cheap, so try to remember to bring your own).

Aside from the small ships, most vessels have a **laundry service** on board and some **dry cleaning,** too, with generally about a 24-hour turnaround time; there will be a price list in your cabin (it's not cheap, though: $1.50 to have one pair of socks washed and $3 for a T-shirt; dry-cleaning a suit will run about $9). Some ships have **self-service laundry rooms** on board—Carnival, Crystal, Princess, and Holland America, among others—so you can wash, dry, and iron your own clothes for a few dollars.

If you like reading but don't want to lug three or four hefty novels on board, there are options. Most ships of all sizes have libraries stocked with books and magazines. Some libraries are more extensive than others, of course; the *QE2*'s is huge, for example. Also, most ships stock paperback bestsellers in their shops.

Remember to save room in your luggage (or bring an empty duffel bag) for things you buy in port or in the ship's shops.

3 The Cruise Lines & Their Itineraries

Following is a quick and easy primer to the cruise lines operating in the Caribbean, with the itineraries their ships will be following for the 2001 season. Itineraries for 2002 were not even close to available at press time, but you can access them online by going to www.frommers-update.com, where we'll post them as soon as they're available (approximately February 2001).

THE MAINSTREAM LINES

These are the shopping malls of cruise ships—they're big, bustling, and attract a cross section of mostly American guests. There's lots to eat, lots to buy on board, and lots of other people sharing the experience with you. Granted, the term "mainstream" covers a lot of ground, and that's the point. These ships are generalists, if you will, attempting to offer a little something for almost everyone—all ages, backgrounds, and interests. You'll find people with no couth and lots of tattoos as well as genteel types with graduate degrees and subscriptions to *Smithsonian*. It's a mixed-bag kind of crowd, there's no doubting that.

Within the mainstream category, the more elegant and refined of the lot are commonly referred to as **premium,** a notch up in the sophistication department from others that are described as **mass-market.** Quality-wise, for the most part, they're all on equal footing and, overall, are more alike than they are different. That's why, premium or not, I've lumped them all in the same category.

Since the mainstream category is the most popular, it's the one that's seen the most growth, innovation, and investment in recent years, meaning the ships are, as a general rule, remarkably new—and also remarkably *big*. This is the category where the **megaships** reside, those hulking 1,200- to 3,200-passenger floating resorts that offer the widest variety of activities and entertainment. All the lines in this category (but particularly the "Big Three"—Carnival, Royal Caribbean, and Princess) have been pumping billions into building newer, bigger, and fancier ships, offering a wide variety of different cabins—inside (no windows), outside (with windows), suites, and cabins with private balconies and without. They'll have both formal and informal dining options, a wide array of entertainment (heavy on the Vegas-style stuff), and more activities than you can possibly squeeze into one day. Overall, the atmosphere is very social and passengers tend to enjoy mingling. These tend to be the most cutting-edge, trend-conscious ships and often the first to offer features like alternative dining and computer rooms with e-mail access.

On weeklong cruises aboard mass-market and premium ships, there are two formal nights calling for dark suits or tuxedos for men, and cocktail dresses, sequined numbers, or fancy pantsuits for women. The other 5 nights are some combination of semiformal and casual, and call for casual suits or polo shirts and slacks for men, and dresses, pantsuits, or skirts and tops for women. Guests are asked not to wear shorts and T-shirts in the formal dining rooms. Daytime is casual.

CARNIVAL CRUISE LINES

3655 NW 87th Ave., Miami, FL 33178-2428. ☎ **800/327-9501** or 305/599-2200. Fax 305/406-4740. www.carnival.com.

This 17-ship fleet of moderately priced, jumbo-size resort ships is bathed in neon and glitz. If you like Las Vegas, New Orleans, and Times Square, Carnival's brand of flamboyant fun is awesome. In fact, nobody does it better in the party department. This extraordinarily successful operation is the Coca-Cola of cruising, the line with the most recognized name in the biz. Since its establishment in 1972, it's brought the cruise experience down from a post-Victorian white-glove–and-teatime diversion to a very casual, down-to-earth, middle-American vacation getaway enjoyed by millions. The line is incredibly innovative, continually updating its onboard programs, offering things like sushi on the *Elation, Paradise, Imagination, Inspiration,* and *Jubilee,* 24-hour pizza and Caesar salad fleet-wide, and an entirely smoke-free ship, the *Paradise.*

The line's decor, like its clientele to some point, continues to evolve to a somewhat more mellow place than where it originally started, yet still each ship is an exciting collage of textures, shapes, and images. Where else but on these floating playlands would you find life-size mannequins of Hollywood stars like Marilyn Monroe and Humphrey Bogart, a San Francisco trolley car, or real oyster-shell wallpaper? The line continues to dream up interiors that stop passengers in their tracks, often spending big bucks to create rooms with stained glass, imprinted copper panels, wood inlay, buttery leathers and suedes, handmade tile mosaics and rice-paper wall coverings, gold-leaf detailing, and fossilized stone. Aboard a Carnival cruise, the destination is the ship itself, with ports playing a secondary role. The outrageousness of the decor is part of the fun, and the point—Carnival ships provide a fantasyland you can't get at home. Call it whatever you want, but don't call it dull.

Carnival Fleet Itineraries

Itineraries listed are for 2001. Visit frommers.travelocity.com for 2002 itineraries, which will be posted as soon as they become available.

CARNIVAL DESTINY   7-night E. & S. Carib: Round-trip from San Juan, visiting St. Thomas, St. Lucia, Curaçao, and Aruba. **7-night E. & S. Carib:** Round-trip from San Juan, visiting St. Thomas, Antigua, Guadeloupe, and Aruba. Itineraries alternate weekly, year-round.

CARNIVAL TRIUMPH   7-night E. Carib: Round-trip from Miami, visiting San Juan, St. Croix, and St. Thomas. **7-night W. Carib:** Round-trip from Miami, visiting Playa del Carmen/Cozumel, Grand Cayman, and Ocho Rios (Jamaica). Itineraries alternate weekly, year-round.

CARNIVAL VICTORY   7-night E. Carib: Round-trip from Miami, visiting San Juan, St. Croix, and St. Thomas. **7-night W. Carib:** Round-trip from Miami, visiting Playa del Carmen/Cozumel, Grand Cayman, and Ocho Rios (Jamaica). Itineraries alternate weekly, year-round.

CELEBRATION   4-night W. Carib: Round-trip from Galveston, visiting Playa del Carmen/Cozumel. **5-night W. Carib:** Round-trip from Galveston, visiting Playa del Carmen/Cozumel, Calica/Cancún. Itineraries alternate year-round.

ECSTASY   3-night: Round-trip from Miami, visiting Nassau. **4-night:** Round-trip from Miami, visiting Key West and Playa del Carmen/Cozumel. Both itineraries offered weekly, year-round.

FANTASY   3-night: Round-trip from Port Canaveral, visiting Nassau. **4-night:** Round-trip from Port Canaveral, visiting Nassau and Freeport. Both itineraries offered weekly, year-round.

FASCINATION   7-night E. Carib: Round-trip from San Juan, visiting St. Thomas, Sint Maarten, Dominica, Martinique, and Barbados, year-round.

IMAGINATION   4-night W. Carib: Round-trip from Miami, visiting Key West and Cozumel/Playa del Carmen. **5-night W. Carib:** Round-trip from Miami, visiting Grand Cayman, Calica/Cancún or Grand Cayman, and Ocho Rios (Jamaica). Itineraries alternate year-round.

INSPIRATION   7-night W. Carib: Round-trip from New Orleans, visiting Montego Bay (Jamaica), Grand Cayman, Playa del Carmen/Cozumel, year-round.

JUBILEE   4-night W. Carib: Round-trip from Tampa, visiting Key West and Playa del Carmen/Cozumel. **5-night W. Carib:** Round-trip from Tampa, visiting Grand Cayman and Playa del Carmen/Cozumel. Itineraries alternate year-round.

PARADISE   7-night E. Carib: Round-trip from Miami, visiting San Juan, Nassau, and St. Thomas. **7-night W. Carib:** Round-trip from Miami, visiting Cozumel/Playa del Carmen, Grand Cayman, and Ocho Rios (Jamaica). Itineraries alternate weekly, year-round.

SENSATION   7-night E. Carib: Round-trip from Tampa, visiting Grand Cayman, Playa del Carmen/Cozumel, and New Orleans, year-round.

TROPICALE   10-night Panama Canal: Round-trip from Fort Lauderdale (Nov 2000 to Jan 2001), visiting Aruba, Cartegena (Colombia), Limón (Costa Rica), and Key West, with a partial transit of Panama Canal. **7-night W. Carib:** Round-trip from Fort Lauderdale (beginning Feb 2001), visiting Belize, Playa del Carmen/Cozumel, Progreso/Mérida, and Key West.

CELEBRITY CRUISES

1050 Caribbean Way, Miami, FL 33132. ☎ **800/327-6700** or 305/539-6000. Fax 800/722-5329. www.celebrity-cruises.com.

With the most elegant big ships in the industry, Celebrity offers the best of two worlds: If you like elegance without stuffiness, fun without questionable taste, pampering without a high price, and a refined yet fun and active cruise experience, Celebrity is king. The new *Millennium,* which debuted in mid-2000, and the *Century, Galaxy,* and *Mercury,* near triplets built in the mid- to late 1990s, are bold, cutting-edge megaships, while the midsize *Zenith* and *Horizon,* virtual twins built in the early 1990s, are more understated and traditional in their designs.

Each of the ships is spacious, glamorous, and comfortable, mixing sleekly modern and vaguely art-deco styles and throwing in an astoundingly cutting-edge art collection to boot. Their genteel service is exceptional: Staff members are exceedingly polite and professional, and contribute greatly to the elegant mood. Dining-wise, Celebrity shines, offering innovative cuisine that's a cut above what's offered by all the other mainstream lines.

Like all the big-ship lines, Celebrity offers lots for its passengers to do, but its focus on mellower pursuits and innovative programming set it apart. Niceties such as roving a cappella bands who sidle up to your table to entertain during pre- or after-dinner drinks lend a warmly personal touch, while seminars on personal investing and handwriting analysis offer a little more cerebral meat than the usual fare.

Celebrity gets the "best of" nod in a lot of categories: The AquaSpas on the line's megaships are the best at sea, the art collections are fleet-wide the most compelling, the cigar bars the most plush, and the onboard activities among the most varied. Celebrity pampers suite guests with butler service, and treats all guests to in-cabin pizza delivery.

Celebrity Fleet Itineraries

Itineraries listed are for 2001. Visit frommers.travelocity.com for 2002 itineraries, which will be posted as soon as they become available.

CENTURY   7-night E. Carib: Round-trip from Fort Lauderdale, visiting San Juan, St. Thomas, Sint Maarten, and Nassau. **7-night W. Carib:** Round-trip from Fort Lauderdale, visiting Ocho Rios (Jamaica), Grand Cayman, Cozumel, and Key West. Itineraries alternate weekly, year-round.

GALAXY   7-night S. Carib: Round-trip from San Juan (late Oct to late Apr), visiting St. Croix, St. Lucia, Barbados, Antigua, and St. Thomas.

HORIZON   7-night S. Carib: Round-trip from Aruba (Nov–Apr), visiting St. Thomas, St. Kitts, St. Lucia, and Barbados.

MERCURY   7-night W. Carib: Round-trip from Fort Lauderdale (late Oct through Apr), visiting Key West, Calica, Cozumel, and Grand Cayman.

MILLENNIUM   7-night E. Carib: Round-trip from Fort Lauderdale, visiting San Juan, Catalina Island, St. Thomas, and Nassau. 7-night W. Carib: Round-trip from Fort Lauderdale, visiting Key West, Calica, Cozumel, and Grand Cayman. Itineraries alternate weekly, Nov–Mar.

ZENITH   10-night E. and S. Carib: Round-trip from Fort Lauderdale, visiting Sint Maarten, St. Lucia, Barbados, Antigua, and St. Thomas. 11- night E. and S. Carib: Round-trip from Fort Lauderdale, visiting Curaçao, La Guaira (Venezuela), Grenada, Barbados, Martinique, and St. Thomas. Itineraries alternate, Nov–Apr.

COSTA CRUISES

World Trade Center, 80 SW Eighth St., Miami, FL 33130-3097 (mailing address: P.O. Box 01964, Miami, FL 33101-9865). ☎ **800/462-6782** or 305/358-7325. Fax 305/375-0676. www.costacruises.com.

Costa's Italian-flavored mid- and megasize European-style ships offer a moderately priced, festive, international experience that you can't find on any other line. With an illustrious history stretching back almost 90 years, Costa has managed to hold on to its heritage with its mantra of "Cruising Italian Style," and that's what primarily distinguishes it from the "all-American" experiences of the competition. Its corporate offices are in both Genoa and Miami, its officers are Italian, and its ships' interiors, food, and activities are still as Italian as you can find. Although on your Caribbean routing you're likely to get a less intense dose of rampant Italianism than you would aboard the line's Mediterranean sailings, and although the line employs far fewer Italian-born stewards and crew members than in years past, the line's strength in the Italian-American market means that you'll still get quite a lot.

Costa holds a somewhat unique position in the industry with a market focus that caters heavily to Europeans while still serving substantial numbers of Americans. Its Caribbean cruises attract mostly Americans (about 80% on any given sailing), and, conversely, its Mediterranean cruises attract mostly Europeans. That said, even in the Caribbean, the passenger mix is much more international than on most other lines.

Costa Fleet Itineraries

Itineraries listed are for 2001. Visit frommers.travelocity.com for 2002 itineraries, which will be posted as soon as they become available.

COSTAATLANTICA   **7-night W. Carib:** Round-trip from Fort Lauderdale, visiting Key West, Playa del Carmen/Cozumel, Ocho Rios (Jamaica), and Grand Cayman. **7-night E. Carib:** Round-trip from Fort Lauderdale, visiting San Juan, St. Thomas, Catalina Island, and Nassau. Itineraries alternate weekly, Nov–Apr.

COSTAVICTORIA   **7-night W. Carib:** Round-trip from Fort Lauderdale, visiting Key West, Playa del Carmen/Cozumel, Ocho Rios (Jamaica), and Grand Cayman. **7-night E. Carib:** Round-trip from Fort Lauderdale, visiting San Juan, St. Thomas, Catalina Island, and Nassau. Itineraries alternate weekly, Nov–Apr.

CROWN CRUISE LINE

4000 Hollywood Blvd., Suite 385, South Tower, Hollywood, FL 33021. ☎ **877/276-9621** or 954/967-2100. Fax 954/967-2147. www.crowncruiseline.com.

The recently revived Crown Cruise Line's one and only ship, the immaculately maintained, well-designed, 800-passenger *Crown Dynasty,* is an attractive alternative to the megaships. It offers a quality, low-key, low-cost southern Caribbean experience that's a far cry from the "party hearty" atmosphere of many other mainstream Caribbean-bound ships. Built in 1993, the ship is bright and modern, with lots of windows, polished woods, and soft hues for what the company calls a "Bermuda decor." Most passengers enjoy mellow pastimes like playing cards and relaxing, snoozing, or reading a book from the comfort of a deck chair. Even announcements, which are few and far between, are only broadcast in public areas to foster a relaxing atmosphere. While most passengers eschew loud, rowdy behavior, they still enjoy a good time, and it's not unusual to see a lively group of couples sipping piña coladas in the hot tubs at sunset.

Crown Fleet Itineraries

Itineraries listed are for 2001. Visit frommers.travelocity.com for 2002 itineraries, which will be posted as soon as they become available.

CROWN DYNASTY   **7-night S. Carib:** Round-trip from Aruba (Dec–May), visiting Barbados, St. Lucia, Grenada, Bonaire, and Curaçao.

DISNEY CRUISE LINE

210 Celebration Place, Suite 400, Celebration, FL 34747-1000. ☎ **800/951-3532** or 407/566-7000. Fax 407/566-7353. www.disney.com/DisneyCruise.

The *Disney Magic* and *Disney Wonder* are the famous company's first foray into cruising, and boast mellow, even elegant interiors and a handful of truly innovative, Disney-style features, including a rotating series of restaurants on every cruise, cabins designed for families, Disney-inspired entertainment, and the biggest kids' facilities at sea. It's innovations like these that set Disney's cruises far apart from its closest peers in the Carnival, Royal Caribbean, Celebrity, and Premier lines.

In many ways, the experience is more Disney than it is cruise, so while first-timers and Disney fanatics will have a ball, old cruise hands may notice a few things missing (for instance, there's no casino or library). On the other hand, the ships, designed as more-or-less identical twins, are surprisingly elegant and well laid out, and the Disneyisms are subtly sprinkled, like fairy dust, throughout their mellow, art-deco– and art-nouveau–inspired interiors and grand, classic-liner–inspired exteriors. Head to toe, the ships are a class act.

In the spirit of Disney's penchant for organization, its 3- and 4-day cruises are designed to be combined with a land-based Disney theme park and hotel package to create a weeklong all-Disney vacation (though you can book the cruises separately). They even whisk you from Disney World to the ship in a fleet of custom Disney buses.

Disney Fleet Itineraries

Itineraries listed are for 2001. Visit frommers.travelocity.com for 2002 itineraries, which will be posted as soon as they become available.

DISNEY MAGIC   7-night E. Carib: Round-trip from Port Canaveral (weekly, year-round), visiting Sint Maarten, St. Thomas, and Castaway Cay.

DISNEY WONDER   3- and 4-night Bahamas: Round-trip from Port Canaveral, visiting Nassau and Castaway Cay, plus Freeport on 4-nighter. Itineraries alternate weekly, year-round.

HOLLAND AMERICA LINE

300 Elliott Ave. W., Seattle, WA 98119. ☎ **800/426-0327** or 206/281-3535. Fax 800/628-4855. www.hollandamerica.com.

More than any other line today (except Cunard), Holland America has managed to hang on to some of its seafaring history and tradition, offering a moderately priced, classic, casual yet refined ocean-liner-like cruise experience. The line consistently delivers a worthy and solid product for a fair price, and is unique for offering midsize-to-large ships with an old-world elegance that remains low-key and not stuffy. These ships aren't boring, but they're sedate, so it's no surprise that the line attracts predominately passengers in their fifties on up.

The line's well-maintained ships are mostly midsize, creating a cozy atmosphere, and while decors are never exhibitionistic or vulgar, the decor of the Statendam-class ships and the *Rotterdam* is stylish, sleek, and, for the most part, understated, and their excellent layouts ease passenger movement. The *Volendam,* however, has ushered in a brighter, more colorful side to HAL while still maintaining its low-key attributes—which company officials intimate is the line's new ethos. HAL's two older ships, the *Westerdam* and *Noordam,* are the most humble, with plainish one-level dining rooms and pleasing, sedate public rooms.

Holland America emphasizes tradition, and that's what sets it apart. In the public areas you'll see trophies and memorabilia, and the very names of the vessels hark back to ships in the line's past. For example, the *Statendam* commemorates an older ship that was sunk by a German U-boat before it could board its first paying passenger, and the line's flagship, the 62,000-ton *Rotterdam* (which doesn't sail in the Caribbean), is the sixth HAL ship to bear that name.

HAL Fleet Itineraries

Itineraries listed are for 2001. Visit frommers.travelocity.com for 2002 itineraries, which will be posted as soon as they become available.

MAASDAM   7-night W. Carib: Round-trip from Fort Lauderdale, visiting Playa del Carmen/Cozumel, Grand Cayman, Ocho Rios (Jamaica), and Half Moon Cay. **7-night E. Carib:** Round-trip from Fort Lauderdale, visiting Nassau, San Juan, St. John/St. Thomas, and Half Moon Cay. Itineraries alternate Apr–Oct; Nov–Mar is E. Carib only.

NOORDAM   14-night S. Carib: Round-trip from Tampa (Dec–Apr), visiting San Juan, St. John/St. Thomas, Guadeloupe, Barbados, St. Lucia, Isla de Margarita, Bonaire, Aruba, and Grand Cayman.

RYNDAM   7-night W. Carib: Round-trip from Fort Lauderdale (Oct–Apr), visiting Half Moon Cay, Grand Cayman, Playa del Carmen/Cozumel, and Key West.

VEENDAM   7-night S. Carib: Round-trip from San Juan (Oct–Mar), visiting Dominican Republic, Barbados, Martinique, Sint Maarten, and St. John/St. Thomas.

VOLENDAM   10-night S. Carib 1: Round-trip from Fort Lauderdale, visiting Bonaire, Isla de Margarita (Venezuela), St. Lucia, St. Kitts, St. John/St. Thomas, and Nassau. **10-night S. Carib 2:** Round-trip from Fort Lauderdale, visiting Antigua, St. Lucia, Barbados, Guadeloupe, St. John/St. Thomas, and Nassau. Itineraries alternate, Nov–Apr.

WESTERDAM   7-night E. Carib: Round-trip from Fort Lauderdale (Oct–Dec 2000), visiting Nassau, San Juan, St. John/St. Thomas, and Half Moon Cay. **5-night E. Carib:** Round-trip from Fort Lauderdale (Jan–Apr 2000 and Nov–Dec 2001), visiting Key West, Half Moon Cay, and Nassau. **8-night E. Carib:** Round-trip from Fort Lauderdale (Jan–Apr 2000 and Oct–Dec 2001), visiting Nassau, San Juan, Sint Maarten, St. John/St. Thomas, and Half Moon Cay.

ZAANDAM   10-night S. Carib 1: Round-trip from Fort Lauderdale, visitng Bonaire, Isla de Margarita (Venezuela), St. Lucia, St. Kitts, St. John/St. Thomas, and Nassau. **10-night S. Carib 2:** Round-trip from Fort Lauderdale, visiting Antigua, St. Lucia, Barbados, Guadeloupe, St. John/St. Thomas, and Nassau. Itineraries alternate, Nov–Apr.

NORWEGIAN CRUISE LINE

7665 Corporate Center Dr., Miami, FL 33126. ☎ **800/327-7030** or 305/436-4000. Fax 305/436-4126. www.ncl.com.

Unlike many lines that offer a similar product across the board, NCL has a varied fleet, from new to old, midsize to mega, making it difficult to generalize about the line's ships. Its two largest—the *Norwegian Sky* and the *Norway*—carry about 2,000 passengers each but are as different as night and day, the former being a brand-new megaship and the latter one of the most classic ocean liners afloat. The line's four other vessels, the *Norwegian Wind, Norwegian Sea, Norwegian Majesty,* and *Norwegian Dream* (which leaves the Caribbean in December 2000), carry about 1,500 each.

While the line strives to lure more upmarket travelers, the truth is that its product is very midmarket, and the experience not as fine-tuned and sharp as it could be. In general, the ships attract a wide variety of passengers, with some drawn by the line's popular music- or sports-theme cruises, some by the nostalgia of the *Norway,* and others simply by low prices—when NCL has empty berths to fill, it's never too proud to offer some outrageous discounts to anyone interested. Discounters always seem to have some last-minute space on NCL to sell.

Despite its shortcomings, the line is very innovative in certain areas. NCL justifiably touts its music- and sports-theme cruises, which in 1999 included the first "Sports Illustrated Afloat" cruise, an Elvis Cruise that featured a skydiving show by the Flying Elvi, and a blues cruise that featured Bo Diddley, Son Seals, and Johnny Johnson. Sports bars are also a big draw, as are alternative dining choices (a concept popular aboard megaships but much less common aboard medium-size vessels).

NCL Fleet Itineraries

Itineraries listed are for 2001. Visit frommers.travelocity.com for 2002 itineraries, which will be posted as soon as they become available.

NORWAY   7-night E. Carib: Round-trip from Miami (through Mar 2001), visiting Sint Maarten, St. John/St. Thomas, and Great Stirrup Cay (Bahamas). **2-night Bahamas:** Round-trip from Miami (beginning Apr 2001), visiting Great Stirrup Cay. **5-night W. Carib:** Round-trip from Miami (beginning Apr 2001), visiting Grand Cayman and Cozumel. Beginning Apr 2001, 2- and 5-night itineraries will alternate year-round.

NORWEGIAN MAJESTY   7-night E. Carib: Round-trip from San Juan, visiting St. Lucia, Antigua, St. Kitts, St. Croix, and St. Thomas. **7-night S. Carib:** Round-trip from San Juan, visiting Aruba, Curaçao, Tortola, and St. Thomas. Itineraries alternate weekly beginning in Dec 2000.

NORWEGIAN SEA   3-night Bahamas: Round-trip from Miami, visiting Key West and Nassau. **4-night W. Carib:** Round-trip from Miami, visiting Key West and Cozumel. Itineraries alternate year-round starting Jan 2001.

NORWEGIAN SKY   7-night E. Carib: Round-trip from Miami, visiting Eleuthera, San Juan, St. Thomas, and Great Stirrup Cay. **7-night W. Carib:** Round-trip from Miami, visiting Grand Cayman, Ocho Rios (Jamaica), Nassau, and Great Stirrup Cay. Itineraries alternate weekly, Oct–Mar.

NORWEGIAN WIND   7-night W. Carib: Round-trip from Miami (Dec–Mar), visiting Grand Cayman, Roatán (Honduras), Belize, and Cozumel.

PRINCESS CRUISES

10100 Santa Monica Blvd., Los Angeles, CA 90067-4189. ☎ **800/421-0522** or 310/553-1770. Fax 310/284-2845. www.princesscruises.com.

Princess's mostly mega fleet offers a quality, mainstream cruise experience. Its newest ships are stylish, floating resorts with just the right combination of fun, glamour, and gentility for an all-around pleasant and relaxing cruise. Although the line doesn't position any one of its ships in the Caribbean year-round (most spend their summers in Alaska and the Mediterranean), those ships it does bring in for the Caribbean season are its newest and largest. If you were to put Carnival, Royal Caribbean, Celebrity, and Holland America in a big bowl and mix them all together, you'd come up with the Princess's megas. The *Grand, Sea, Sun, Dawn,* and *Ocean Princess* (the Grand-class ships) are less glitzy and frenzied than Carnival and Royal Caribbean; not quite as cutting-edge or witty as Celebrity's *Millennium, Century,*

Galaxy, and *Mercury;* and more exciting, youthful, and entertaining than Holland America's near-megas, appealing to a wide cross section of cruisers by offering lots of choice, activities, and touches of big-ship glamour, along with lots of private balconies and plenty of the quiet nooks and calm spaces of smaller, more intimate-size vessels. You'll see: The ships feel smaller than they really are.

Overall, the Princess ships are one notch above their most aggressive mainstream competitors, Carnival and Royal Caribbean. Aboard Princess, you get a lot of bang for your buck, attractively packaged and well executed.

Princess Fleet Itineraries

Itineraries listed are for 2001. Visit frommers.travelocity.com for 2002 itineraries, which will be posted as soon as they become available.

CROWN PRINCESS   10-night Panama Canal 1: Round-trip from Fort Lauderdale, visiting Cartagena (Colombia), Puerto Limón (Costa Rica), Grand Cayman, and Cozumel. **10-night Panama Canal 2:** Round-trip from Fort Lauderdale, visiting Ocho Rios (Jamaica), Puerto Limón, Cartagena, and Aruba. Itineraries alternate, Oct–May.

DAWN PRINCESS   7-night S. Carib 1: Round-trip from San Juan, visiting Trinidad, Barbados, Antigua, Tortola, and St. Thomas. **7-night S. Carib 2:** Round-trip from San Juan, visiting St. Thomas, St. Kitts, Martinique, Isla de Margarita, and Curaçao. Itineraries alternate weekly, Oct–Apr.

GRAND PRINCESS   7-night E. Carib: Round-trip from Fort Lauderdale visiting St. Thomas, Sint Maarten, and Princess Cays weekly through spring 2001. Thereafter, alternates weekly with 7-night W. Carib: Round-trip from Fort Lauderdale, visiting Cozumel, Grand Cayman, Princess Cays, and Costa Maya (Mexico).

OCEAN PRINCESS   7-night S. Carib 1: Round-trip from San Juan, visiting Aruba, Caracas/La Guaira (Venezuela), Grenada, Dominica, and St. Thomas. **7-night S. Carib 2:** Round-trip from San Juan, visiting Barbados, St. Lucia, St. Kitts, Sint Maarten, and St. Thomas. Itineraries alternate weekly, Oct–Apr.

SEA PRINCESS   7-night W. Carib: Round-trip from Fort Lauderdale (Oct–Apr), visiting Princess Cays, Ocho Rios (Jamaica), Grand Cayman, and Cozumel.

SUN PRINCESS   10-night Panama Canal: Between San Juan and Puerto Caldera (Costa Rica), visiting St. Thomas, Dominica, Barbados, Aruba, Cartagena (Colombia), and Puntarenas (Costa Rica). North- and southbound itineraries alternate, Oct–Apr.

ROYAL CARIBBEAN INTERNATIONAL

1050 Caribbean Way, Miami, FL 33132. ☎ **800/327-6700** or 305/539-6000. Fax 800/ 722-5329. www.royalcaribbean.com

Royal Caribbean International is one of the steadiest and best-conceived cruise companies in the industry, offering fun, well-rounded, activity-packed cruises aboard a fleet of mostly similar ships designed to appeal to a wide range of people. These megas are attractive, glamorous, but not too over-the-top-glitzy ships that, except for the older *Nordic Empress,* share such similar attributes as multistory atria and mall-like shopping complexes, two-story dining rooms and showrooms, and wide-open public areas and conversely small cabins. There are lots of activities, a varied and well-executed entertainment repertoire, and enough glamour and glitz to keep things exciting, but not so much that they overwhelm the senses (except for the *Voyager* and *Explorer of the Seas,* which do). Decor-wise, these ships are a shade toned down from the Carnival brood, and while at the end of the day the onboard experience of the two fleets is similar, the Royal Caribbean ships feel and look less in-your-face than their Carnival counterparts.

Activities, daily programs, cuisine, bar service, and cabin service make for a nice package, and prices are reasonable to boot.

Royal Caribbean Fleet Itineraries

Itineraries listed are for 2001. Visit www.frommers-update.com for 2002 itineraries, which will be posted as soon as they become available.

ENCHANTMENT OF THE SEAS   7-night W. Carib: Round-trip from Miami, visiting Key West, Playa del Carmen/Cozumel, Ocho Rios, and Grand Cayman. **7-night E. Carib:** Round-trip from Miami, visiting Sint Maarten, St. John's/ St. Thomas, and Nassau. Itineraries alternate weekly, year-round.

EXPLORER OF THE SEAS   7-night E. Carib: Round-trip from Miami (year-round), visiting Labadee (Haiti), San Juan, Nassau, and St. Thomas.

GRANDEUR OF THE SEAS   7-night S. Carib: Round-trip from San Juan (year-round), visiting Aruba, Curaçao, Sint Maarten, and St. Thomas.

MAJESTY OF THE SEAS   3- and 4-night Bahamas: Round-trip from Miami, visiting Nassau, CocoCay, and (on 4-nighter only) Key West. Itineraries alternate year-round.

MONARCH OF THE SEAS   7-night S. Carib: Round-trip from San Juan (year-round), visiting St. Thomas, Antigua, Barbados, St. Lucia, and Sint Maarten.

NORDIC EMPRESS   3- and 4-night W. Carib: Round-trip from San Juan, visiting St. Thomas, Sint Maarten, and St. Croix (on 4-nighter only). Itineraries alternate, Nov–Apr.

SOVEREIGN OF THE SEAS   3- and 4-night Bahamas: Round-trip from Port Canaveral, visiting Nassau, CocoCay, and (on 4-nighter only) Key West. Itineraries alternate year-round.

SPLENDOUR OF THE SEAS   10- and 11-night Carib: Round-trip from Miami, visiting Key West (11-nighter only), Playa del Carmen/Cozumel, Grand Cayman, Ocho Rios (Jamaica), Aruba, and Curaçao. Itineraries alternate, Nov–Apr.

VISION OF THE SEAS   10-night Panama Canal: Sails between San Juan and Acapulco, visiting St. Thomas, Curaçao, and Costa Rica. **11-night Panama Canal:** Costa Rica, Curaçao, Aruba, and St. Thomas. East- and westbound itineraries alternate, Nov–Apr.

VOYAGER OF THE SEAS   7-night W. Carib: Round-trip from Miami (year-round), visiting Labadee (Haiti), Ocho Rios (Jamaica), Grand Cayman, and Cozumel.

CHEAP CRUISES, OLDER SHIPS: THE BUDGET LINES

In this category you'll find classic ocean liners, some of which have managed to stay around for almost 50 years. These ships have great appeal for ship buffs and nostalgic folks, and have retained varying amounts of their former grandeur—some have aged gracefully, others not so much. For instance, Premier's *Rembrandt* (formerly Holland America's *Rotterdam V*) is the most beautiful and intact relic left, with much of its original furniture, wall finishings, and artwork still impressing passengers (though who knows what time will bring: At press time, Premier was undecided whether or not to rename it the *Big Red Boat IV* in late 2000, paint its hull red, and rejigger its gorgeous interior). The line's *SeaBreeze* and *Big Red Boat,* on the other hand, retain only their classic exterior lines, with most of their interiors stripped of any original features.

Depending on what you like, the age of a ship can be a plus or a minus. If you appreciate relics of the past—prewar buildings over modern ones, antiques instead of IKEA—then you might like these 30-year-old-plus liners: With long, sweeping hulls, tiered decks, wood paneling, and chunky portholes, they offer a nostalgic glimpse back to a lost age of cruising. Decks, doors, railings, and bar tops are made of solid varnished wood, and cabin doors may still operate with a lock and key rather than with a computerized key-card. In comparison to the often cramped cabins on mainstream megas, cabins and closets on these ships are often quite large, owing to the fact that they formerly did long-haul sailings for a clientele traveling with steamer trunks and lots of luggage. Tall sills in most doorways require some high stepping to avoid tripping (old ships are not for wheelchair users), and there's no shortage of exposed cables, fire doors, pipes, ropes, winches, and all manner of hardware. These are ships that look like ships, and for ship buffs, they're charming. For bargain hunters, too, they're often the best deal in town, with rates at times dipping down below $100 per person per day (Although I must add, owing to the glut of cabin space throughout the industry these days, at times the rates for inside and low-category cabins on Carnival, Royal Caribbean, NCL, and even Celebrity and Princess can drop nearly as low).

Now, if you're a lover of all things fresh, new, and modern, you might want to pass on a cruise on one of the oldies. The old-timers can't hide the wear and tear accumulated from logging thousands of miles at sea. Repeatedly refurbished and restored through the years (often haphazardly and in the least expensive ways), many are a hodgepodge of design schemes and awkward spaces. Discos, spas, and gyms are often small, dark spaces in lower decks, and carpeting, wall finishes, and outside decks are often worn. All in all, you won't be seeing a lot of flash, but you will be seeing some old ships that might not be around much longer: The future of some of them will depend on compliance with a set of international safety regulations known as the **Safety of Life at Sea (SOLAS),** predominantly concerned with issues like fire prevention. Ships built after 1994 automatically incorporate SOLAS safety features, while ships built before 1994 have been required to add them by a progressive set of deadlines. The changes required could prove too costly for many of these old-timers and seal their fate forever—so enjoy them while you can.

Like the mainstream lines, weeklong cruises on these ships generally feature two formal nights, but with the exception of Premier's *Rembrandt,* you won't find too many passengers in tuxedos or fancy sequin dresses. Overall, ships in this category are somewhat more casual, with guests preferring suits or sport coats to tuxes, and pantsuits or sundresses to gowns (although it's not unheard of to see a tux and a shimmery dress). Guests are asked not to wear shorts and T-shirts in the formal dining room—although more and more people trying and succeeding. Daytime is casual.

COMMODORE CRUISE LINE

4000 Hollywood Blvd., South Tower 385, Hollywood, FL 33021. ☎ **800/237-5361** or 954/967-2100. Fax 954/967-2147. www.commodorecruise.com.

Commodore Cruise Line's *Enchanted Isle* and *Enchanted Capri* are, despite several drawbacks, two of the best bargains sailing the Caribbean: These Sputnik-era vessels may show their age, but they offer down-to-earth, fun cruises at rock-bottom rates for cruisers on a budget. Fares are cheaper mainly because the vessels lack most of the newfangled entertainment gadgets that appear on newer ships. But what the line lacks in technology, it makes up for in spunk, its officers and crew working hard to give passengers what they paid for, and then some. The cruises are casual, care-free, and fun, and the ships' small size means passengers begin to recognize each other after only a day or so at sea—much sooner than aboard larger ships.

Dubbed the "Happy Ship," *Enchanted Isle* pioneered theme cruises, and the *Isle* and *Capri* still have sock hops and "Remember When" cruises featuring music legends of the 1950s. The *Capri* has an especially active casino scene—in fact, the ship's lease is coheld by Commodore and a land-based casino concern, and you'll always see many casino regulars aboard, particularly on the 2-night cruises. Today, both ships homeport in New Orleans, giving passengers a vastly different embarkation experience than they'd get in Florida. The line attracts most of its passengers from states in this region: Louisiana, Mississippi, Texas, Arkansas, and Alabama.

Commodore Fleet Itineraries

Itineraries listed are for 2001. Visit frommers.travelocity.com for 2002 itineraries, which will be posted as soon as they become available.

ENCHANTED CAPRI   2-night Cruises to Nowhere: Round-trip from New Orleans. **5-night W. Carib:** Round-trip from New Orleans, visiting Playa del Carmen/Cozumel and Progreso/Mérida (Mexico). Itineraries alternate weekly year-round.

ENCHANTED ISLE   7-night W. Carib: Round-trip from New Orleans (year-round), visiting Playa del Carmen/Cozumel, Grand Cayman, and Montego Bay (Jamaica).

MEDITERRANEAN SHIPPING CRUISES

420 Fifth Ave., New York, NY 10018. ☎ **800/666-9333** or 212/764-4800. Fax 212/764-8593. www.msccruise.com.

A relative newcomer to the North American cruise market, Mediterranean Shipping Cruises is an Italian company that sails its three ships mostly in the Mediterranean. While the line's one Caribbean ship, the *Melody,* isn't the fanciest afloat, it is well laid out and roomy and offers a pair of great, port-packed, and low-priced 11-night itineraries catering to a mixed crowd about evenly split between Europeans and North Americans. The 1,076-passenger *Melody* once sailed as the big red *Star/Ship Atlantic* for Premier Cruise Lines, and before that as the *Atlantic* for Home Lines. It's a generally well laid-out ship and a pretty good bargain to boot, and if you and your family sailed aboard the ship before, in its Premier days, expect déjà vu: Other than painting the ship's red hull white, MSC made next to no changes to the ship's decor, which was last refurbished in early 1997. The big change that has occurred is that when the *Melody* operated as a Big Red Boat, it was child-oriented. That is no longer the case. This is now a ship for adults, with supervised children's activities provided when demand warrants (but, even if there are only a few kids on board, there will be some kind of supervised activities offered, at least for a few hours a day).

Unlike ships of the other Italian line, Costa, the *Melody* is older, smaller, and less plush, and its product less glossy and well rehearsed. To a point, the Italianness of the line adds a touch of European holiday to your Caribbean jaunt, but by no means should you expect grandeur or over-the-top elegance. At its worst, this ship is dowdy and a bit creaky. At its best, it can be fun and filled with Neapolitan flair. Above all, a cruise aboard this line is affordable.

Mediterranean Shipping Fleet Itineraries

Itineraries listed are for 2001. Visit frommers.travelocity.com for 2002 itineraries, which will be posted as soon as they become available.

MELODY **11-night W. Carib/partial Panama Canal:** Round-trip from Fort Lauderdale, visiting Montego Bay (Jamaica), Cartagena (Colombia), partial transit of Panama Canal, Puerto Limón (Costa Rica), and Key West. **11-night E. Carib:** Round-trip from Fort Lauderdale, visiting St. Thomas, Antigua, Grenada, St. Lucia, Guadeloupe, Tortola, and Nassau. Itineraries alternate Jan–Apr.

PREMIER CRUISE LINES

400 Challenger Rd., Cape Canaveral, FL 32920. ☎ **800/990-7770** or 407/783-5061. Fax 407/784-0954. www.premiercruises.com.

Its ships aren't spring chickens, but Premier's low prices and fleet of diverse oldies has something to please almost everyone, from families with kids to older folks and ship lovers, to anyone looking for a cheap cruise and a unique itinerary. The ambiance aboard all of Premier's Caribbean ships is unpretentious and undemanding, making them a good choice for first-time cruisers. The ships range in age from 36 to 43 years old, and while they can't hide their wear and tear, they continue to offer decent cruises. Along with the newly acquired *Big Red Boat II,* the *Big Red Boat I* continues to be geared to families with kids, as it has for years. For ship lovers and nostalgic types, the *Rembrandt* is the best ship in the fleet, the most elegant and spacious and closest to its original grandeur. The *SeaBreeze* and *Island Breeze/Big Red Boat III* are the least special of the five, but recent refurbishments have improved them and created more of a nautical flavor; their itineraries are some of their best features. Don't expect glamour or anything approaching cutting-edge technology. A Premier cruise is good value for the money, but keep in mind that you may have to endure elbow-to-elbow people if your ship is full, and amenities that are acceptable but not remarkable—you won't find any frills or pretense aboard. It's all a matter of being realistic about your expectations.

Premier Fleet Itineraries

Itineraries listed are for 2001. Visit frommers.travelocity.com for 2002 itineraries, which will be posted as soon as they become available.

BIG RED BOAT I **3- and 4-night Bahamas:** Round-trip from Port Canaveral, visiting Nassau and Salt Cay. Itineraries alternate year-round.

BIG RED BOAT II **7-night W. Carib:** Round-trip from Tampa (Oct–Apr), visiting Cozumel, Roatán (Honduras), Belize, and Key West.

BIG RED BOAT III (ISLAND BREEZE) **7-night W. Carib:** Round-trip from Houston (year-round), visiting Vera Cruz, Cozumel, and Playa del Carmen.

REMBRANDT **7-night E. Carib:** Round-trip from Port Canaveral (Oct–Apr), visiting St. John/St. Thomas, San Juan, and Nassau.

SEABREEZE **7-night W. Carib:** Round-trip from Fort Lauderdale (Oct–Apr), visiting Cozumel, Roatán (Honduras), Belize, and Key West.

REGAL CRUISES

300 Regal Cruise Way, Palmetto, FL 34221. ☎ **800/270-7245** or 941/721-7300. Fax 941/723-0900. www.regalcruises.com.

While the line's one ship isn't exactly regal, ship buffs will appreciate the vestiges of old-fashioned decor that remain and bargain shoppers will love the price: 1- to 12-night itineraries that can average out to less than $70 per person per day at times. Its shorter cruises encourage a party-hearty atmosphere, while its longer sailings are just the opposite. But if you're on a tight budget and are looking for a small-scale Carnivalesque cruise experience, this is a line to consider.

The 48-year-old *Regal Empress* keeps chugging along, but shows its age despite dedicated efforts to keep it in shape. (What do you expect? It's nearly half a century old!) The most noteworthy refurbishments included a $5.5 million overhaul in 1997 that placed a TV in every cabin, added verandas to some of the suites, and generally spiffed up the interior appearance. Rumor has it that, by year-end 2000, a computer room with e-mail access will be added. Impressive for the old bird! Still, the ship is a two-faced blend of the best of yesterday and the worst of today. There's more wood paneling than on most other ships in this category, but there's also Astroturf on the outside decks (beige at least, rather than the god-awful old grass-green stuff) and no shortage of chintzy chrome and mirrors in many of the public rooms. Quirks and all, though, the *Regal Empress* offers an unpretentious cruise with decent food and entertainment—especially considering its often bargain-basement prices. If you can afford it, book one of the suites or any of the Category 3 superior outside staterooms, and you'll have plenty of space to retire to if the crowds (and there's lots of them when the ship is fully booked) get to you.

Regal Fleet Itineraries

Itineraries listed are for 2001. Visit frommers.travelocity.com for 2002 itineraries, which will be posted as soon as they become available.

REGAL EMPRESS   3-night W. Carib: Round-trip from Port Manatee, visiting Key West. **4-night W. Carib:** Round-trip from Port Manatee, visiting Cancún and Playa del Carmen/Cozumel. **5-night W. Carib:** Round-trip from Port Manatee, visiting Progreso and Cozumel or Key West and Cozumel. **6-night W. Carib:** Round-trip from Port Manatee, visiting Progreso, Cozumel/Playa del Carmen, and Cancún. **7-night W. Carib:** Cancún, Playa del Carmen, Cozumel, and Key West. **10-night Panama Canal:** Round-trip from Port Manatee, visiting Grand Cayman, San Blas Islands, Puerto Limón (Costa Rica), and San Andrés (Colombia). Itineraries alternate from Nov–May.

THE ULTRALUXURY LINES

These cruise lines are the top-shelf, the best (and most expensive) of the best. Their ships, mostly small and intimate, are the sports cars of cruise ships and cater to discerning travelers who want to be pampered with fine gourmet cuisine and wines, and ensconced in spacious suites with marble bathrooms, down pillows, sitting areas, minibars, and walk-in closets. Caviar is served on silver trays, and chilled champagne poured into crystal glasses. Elegant dining rooms are dressed in the finest linens, stemware, and china, and guests dress in tuxedos and sparkling dresses and gowns on formal nights and suits and ties on informal nights. (An exception to this is Windstar Cruises, which, though luxurious and upscale, offers a much more casual kind of luxury and a more laid-back decor. Radisson Seven Seas also tends toward the casual, but not to Windstar's degree.) Exquisite French, Italian, and Asian cuisine rivals that of the best shoreside restaurants and is served in high style by doting, gracious waiters who know how to please. A full dinner can even be served to you in your cabin if you like. Luxuries like these are part of the wonderfully decadent daily routine.

Entertainment and organized activities are more dignified than on other ships—you won't see any raunchy comedy routines or bordering-on-obscene pool games—and are more limited as guests tend to amuse themselves, enjoying cocktails and conversation in a piano bar more than they would a flamboyant Vegas-style routine.

With the exception of the *QE2* and the *Crystal Harmony* (which are larger, but still quite cushy), these high-end ships are small and intimate—usually carrying just a few hundred passengers—and big on service, with almost as many staff as passengers. You're not likely to feel lost in the crowd, and staff will get to know your likes and dislikes early on. The onboard atmosphere is much like a private club, with guests trading traveling tales and meeting for drinks or dinner.

The high-end lines are discounting more than ever, so you may be able to afford something you thought was out of your price range. That said, a high-end cruise still can cost twice as much (or more) as your typical mainstream cruise. Barring specials and low-season rates, expect to pay at least $2,000 per person for a week in the Caribbean, and easily more if you opt for the penthouse suite or choose to cruise during the busiest times of the year. Besides early booking discounts, many high-end lines give discounts to repeat cruisers and those booking back-to-back cruises, and sometimes offer two-for-one deals and free airfare. Many extras are often included in the cruise rates.

Most people attracted to these types of cruises are sophisticated, wealthy, relatively social, and used to the finer things in life. While most are well traveled, they tend to stick to the five-star variety.

These ships are not geared to children at all, although every so often one or two show up. In this event, baby-sitting can sometimes be arranged privately with an off-duty crew member.

On Seabourn, Cunard, and Crystal, bring the tux and the sequined gown—guests dress for dinner on the two or three formal nights on these cruises. Informal nights call for suits and ties for men and fancy dresses or pantsuits for ladies; sports jackets for men and casual dresses or pantsuits for women are the norm on casual nights. That said, like the rest of the industry, even the high-end lines are relaxing their dress codes, heading closer to lines like Windstar, which espouses a "no jackets required" policy during the entire cruise. Men need only pack dress slacks, chinos, and nice collared shirts (short or long sleeves); women, leave the pantyhose at home—casual dresses and slacks are fine for evenings. The *Seabourn Goddesses* are also now following a no-jackets-required policy, even on formal night. Radisson is somewhere in between, so bring the suits and nice dresses, but no need to lug the tux or fancy full-length gown on board if it's not your style (in fact, on a recent *Seven Seas Navigator* cruise I saw several passengers over 60 in jeans, sneakers, and T-shirts—albeit the $50 kind—at dinner in the formal dining room on casual nights).

CRYSTAL CRUISES

2121 Ave. of the Stars, Los Angeles, CA 90067. ☎ **800/446-6620** or 310/785-9300. Fax 310/785-3891. www.crystalcruises.com.

Crystal has the two largest truly upscale ships in the industry. Carrying 960 passengers, they aren't huge, but they're big enough to offer much more than their high-end peers. Fine-tuned and fashionable, Crystal's pair of dream ships give passengers pampering service and scrumptious cuisine on ships large enough to offer lots of outdoor deck space, generous fitness facilities, four restaurants, and over half a dozen bars and entertainment venues. You won't feel hemmed in, and you likely won't be twiddling your thumbs from lack of stimulation. Service is excellent, and the cuisine is very good and on par with Seabourn and Radisson; the line's Asian food is tops. Unlike Seabourn, which tends to be more staid, Crystal's California ethic tends to keep things mingly and chatty. Passengers are social and active and like dressing for dinner and being seen.

Crystal Fleet Itineraries

Itineraries listed are for 2001. Visit frommers.travelocity.com for 2002 itineraries, which will be posted as soon as they become available.

CRYSTAL HARMONY   10-, 11-, and 12-night Panama Canal: May visit Grand Cayman, Aruba, St. Thomas, Sint Maarten, Cartagena, Puerto Quetzal, Antigua, St. Kitts, and Playa del Carmen/Cozumel. **9-, 10-, and 14-night E. Carib:** May visit St. Thomas, Key West, Aruba, Isla de Margarita (Venezuela), Antigua, Sint Maarten, Tortola, and Barbados. Itineraries sail from various home ports, Mar–May and Nov–Dec 2001.

CRYSTAL SYMPHONY   14- and 15-night Panama Canal: May visit Aruba, St. Thomas, Cartagena, Puntarenas (Costa Rica), Acapulco, and Playa del Carmen/Cozumel. 14-night itinerary between Los Angeles and Fort Lauderdale; 15-night itinerary between Los Angeles and San Juan. Both offered Dec–Jan.

CUNARD
6100 Blue Lagoon Dr., Miami, FL 33126. ☎ **800/5-CUNARD** or 305/463-3000. Fax 305/269-6950. www.cunardline.com.

It's been said Cunard is the biggest consumer of caviar on earth—get the picture? Catering to a wealthy, well-traveled clientele, the line offers an onboard experience that's high-brow British all the way. Can you say "history"? Can you say "God Save the Queen"? Cunard, about 160 years old at this writing, is a bona fide cultural icon, a tangible reminder of the days when Britannia really did rule the waves, and that's what sets it apart from the pack. From the formal, British-style service to the decor, which through artwork and memorabilia pays tribute to England and Cunard's long history, the experience is nostalgic and genteel. Activities are relatively mellow, featuring enrichment lectures, ship tours, reading, and movies. Likewise, entertainment features pianists, singers, live dance bands, and lots of conversation and cocktails. Passengers participate at their own pace. Dining is a formal affair, one of the day's main events, and guests dress the part.

Cunard currently has two ships in its fleet, the classic *QE2* and the *Caronia* (the former *Vistafjord*, only recently renamed). The *QE2* recalls the great ocean-liner days of decades ago—among other reasons, because it was built decades ago (in 1969). Both ships got face-lifts in late 1999, and at their age, they needed them. New carpeting and fabrics have perked up the 32-year-old *QE2*, which, while in good shape, can't hide a smattering of water-stained ceilings, mustiness on lower decks, and a hodgepodge of cabin decor—the wrinkles and accumulated clutter of age. The *Caronia*, too, sports its share of age-related imperfections like warped cabin ceilings and rusty bathroom fixtures, but overall manages to look pretty healthy after its recent sprucing up.

Cunard Fleet Itineraries
Itineraries listed are for 2001. Visit frommers.travelocity.com for 2002 itineraries, which will be posted as soon as they become available.

CARONIA   12- and 16-night E. Carib: Round-trip from Fort Lauderdale (Nov 2000–Jan 2001), may visit St. Croix, Dominica, Antigua, Barbados, Sint Maarten, Grenada, Bonaire, Aruba, Isla de Margarita (Venezuela), Puerto Rico, and Tortola. **14-night Carib/Amazon:** Sails between Fort Lauderdale and Manaus (Mar–Apr 2001), may visit Parintins, Santarém, and Alter do Chao (Brazil), Devil's Island (French Guiana), Barbados, St. Kitts, Dominica, Tortola, Puerto Rico, Guadeloupe, Antigua, and St. Croix.

QUEEN ELIZABETH 2   5-night E. Carib: Round-trip from Miami (Oct 2000), visiting St. Thomas. **16-night E. and S. Carib:** Round-trip from New York (Dec 2001), may visit Jamaica, Curaçao, Bonaire, Barbados, St. Thomas, Cape Canaveral (Florida), and Miami.

RADISSON SEVEN SEAS CRUISES

600 Corporate Dr., Suite 410, Fort Lauderdale, FL 33334. ☎ **800/285-1835** or 954/776-6123. Fax 954/772-3763. www.rssc.com.

Radisson Seven Seas carries passengers in style and extreme comfort. Its brand of luxury is casually elegant and somewhat subtle, and its cuisine is near the top. Its ships are spacious, and service is supreme. Unlike some high-end ships these days, extras like tips, wine with dinner, stocked minibars (stocked once), and unlimited soft drinks and mineral waters are included in the rates. Both the *Radisson Diamond* and the *Seven Seas Navigator* have all outside cabins, and well over half of them have private balconies; the *Mariner* will have balconies on every single cabin. Cuisine is some of the best at sea, and in addition to their formal restaurants, all three ships have alternative, reservations-only restaurants specializing in northern Italian food. Even if what tickles your fancy isn't on the menu, the chef will prepare it for you. In fact, you can hardly walk anywhere on the ship without staff members asking if there's something they can do for you.

These ships tend to be less stuffy, less snooty, and a bit more casual than Seabourn and Cunard. You can chuck your tux for the most part, although on formal nights they certainly aren't uncommon.

Radisson Fleet Itineraries

Itineraries listed are for 2001. Visit frommers.travelocity.com for 2002 itineraries, which will be posted as soon as they become available.

RADISSON DIAMOND 3-, 4-, 6-, and 7-night E. Carib: May visit Martinique, St. Kitts, Barbados, and St. Thomas. **7- and 9-night Panama Canal:** May visit San Blas Islands (Panama), Cartageña (Colombia), Aruba, Curaçao, and St. Thomas.

SEVEN SEAS MARINER 9-night Panama Canal: Calica and Cozumel (Mexico), Grand Cayman, Cartagena (Colombia), and Gatun Yacht Club (Panama). **9-night Bermuda:** Charleston (South Carolina), Hamilton, and Nassau. **7- and 10-night W. Carib:** May visit Grand Cayman, Cozumel and Calica, Key West, and New Orleans.

SEVEN SEAS NAVIGATOR 9-, 10-, and 12-night Panama Canal: May visit Puerto Armuelles (Panama), Cartageña (Colombia), Aruba, Grand Cayman, Roatan (Honduras), Cozumel, Calica/Cancun, and Key West. **7- and 9-night Caribbean:** Port calls not yet determined at press time.

SEABOURN CRUISE LINE

55 Francisco St., Suite 710, San Francisco, CA 94133. ☎ **800/929-9595** or 415/391-7444. Fax 415/391-8518. www.seabourn.com.

Seabourn's ships are floating pleasure palaces bathing all who enter in doting service and nearly the finest (if not *the* finest) cuisine at sea. It's a genuine aristocrat, with perfect manners. Its five small, luxurious ships have unprecedented amounts of onboard space and staff for each passenger (as do the suites aboard the larger *Seabourn Sun*), and all ships have service worthy of the grand hotels of Europe and the kind of hushed, ever-so-polite ambiance that appeals to prosperous, usually older passengers who appreciate the emphasis on their individual pleasures. If you're the type of person who responds to discretion and subdued good taste (and who has the cash to pay for it), Seabourn might be perfect for you. A travel agent faced with a "which ship is for us" query from Henry and Nancy Kissinger would definitely book them on one of Seabourn's small ships. And with the addition of the midsize

Sun to the fleet, there's now a Seabourn ship for a younger or more casual set looking for sophistication at more tempered levels (and at a more modest cost).

Seabourn Fleet Itineraries

Itineraries listed are for 2001. Visit frommers.travelocity.com for 2002 itineraries, which will be posted as soon as they become available.

SEABOURN GODDESS I & II   4-, 5-, 6-, and 7-night E. Carib: From St. Thomas and Barbados. Ports on alternating itineraries may include Mayreau, Carriacou, and Bequia (Grenadines), St. Lucia, Grenada, Dominica, St. Croix, Virgin Gorda, Antigua, Jost Van Dyke, Guadeloupe, St. Barts, St. Martin, Nevis, Martinique, St. Kitts, and Tobago.

SEABOURN LEGEND   7-, 8-, 9-, 12-, 14-, and 15-night E. and S. Carib: May visit St. Lucia, Antigua, St. Barts, Dominica, St. Martin, St. John, Grenadines, Nevis, Nassau, Cozumel, St. Croix, Puerto Rico, Dominican Republic, St. Martin, Jost Van Dyke, and Virgin Gorda. Ships sail round-trip from Fort Lauderdale, West Palm Beach, and San Juan, and between Fort Lauderdale and San Juan, San Juan and Barbados, and Barbados and West Palm Beach, Nov–Apr.

SEABOURN PRIDE   6- 11-, 12-, 14-, and 16-night E. Carib: May visit St. Barts, Puerto Rico, Cozumel, Calica, Jamaica, Dominican Republic, St. John, St. Croix, Virgin Gorda, Sint Maarten, St. Kitts, Antigua, Guadeloupe, Dominica, New Orleans, and Key West. Round-trip from Fort Lauderdale and San Juan, and between Fort Lauderdale and St. Thomas, St. Thomas and New Orleans, New Orleans and San Juan, and San Juan and Fort Lauderdale, Oct–Jan in both 2000 and 2001.

SEABOURN SUN   10-, 13-, and 14-night E. Carib: Round-trip from Fort Lauderdale (Nov–Dec 2000 and 2001), may visit St. Barts, Tortola, Barbados, Jamaica, Grand Cayman, Belize, Cozumel, New Orleans, Key West, St. Lucia, Grenada, St. Kitts, Puerto Rico, Dominica, and St. Croix.

WINDSTAR CRUISES

300 Elliott Ave. W., Seattle, WA 98119. ☎ **800/258-7245** or 206/281-3535. Fax 206/281-0627. www.windstarcruises.com.

Windstar offers a truly unique cruise experience, giving passengers the delicious illusion of adventure on board its fleet of four- and five-masted sailing ships and the ever-pleasant reality of first-class cuisine, service, and itineraries. The line's no-jackets-required policy defines its casually elegant attitude, but this is no barefoot, rigging-pulling, paper-plates-in-lap, sleep-on-the-deck kind of cruise, but a refined yet down-to-earth, yachtlike experience for a sophisticated, well-traveled crowd who despise big ships and throngs of tourists.

On board, fine stained teak, brass details, and lots of navy-blue fabrics and carpeting lend a traditional nautical ambiance. While the ships' proud masts and yards of white sails cut an ever-so-attractive profile, the ships are ultra-state-of-the-art, and the sails can be furled or unfurled at the touch of a button. The ships are so stable, in fact, that at times the bridge may actually induce a modest tilt so passengers remember they're on a sailing ship. In the Caribbean, at least once per week if at all possible, the captain shuts off the engines and moves by sail only, to give passengers a real taste of the sea. Under full sail, the calm tranquillity is utterly blissful.

Windstar Fleet Itineraries

Itineraries listed are for 2001. Visit frommers.travelocity.com for 2002 itineraries, which will be posted as soon as they become available.

WIND SPIRIT   7-night E. Carib: Round-trip from St. Thomas (Dec–Apr), visiting St. John, St. Martin, St. Barts, Tortola, Jost Van Dyke, and Virgin Gorda.

WIND STAR   7-night Belize: Round-trip from Cancún (Dec–Apr), visiting Roatán (Honduras), Goff's Cay (Belize), Half Moon Cay Reserve (Belize), San Pedro (Belize), and Cozumel.

WIND SURF   7-night E. Carib: Round-trip from Barbados (Dec–Apr), visiting Tobago, Bequia, Martinique, St. Lucia, Mayreau or Nevis, St. Martin, St. Barts, Iles des Saintes, and St. Lucia.

SOFT-ADVENTURE LINES & SAILING SHIPS

The ships in this category are like private yachts or summer camps at sea, and whether the small, motorized coastal cruisers of American Canadian Caribbean Line and Clipper or the sailing ships of Star Clippers and Windjammer Barefoot Cruises, they're a far different breed from the rest. All are small and intimate, and are often more adventure tour than they are "cruise" as we have come to know it. Leave the jackets, ties, pumps, and pearls at home: These vessels espouse an ultra-casual ethic and take passengers close up to the islands and the sea.

These ships generally visit a port every day, and because most of them have shallow drafts (the amount of the ship that rides below the waterline) they're able to sail adventurous itineraries to small, out-of-the-way ports that the big cruise ships would run aground trying to approach. Also, since all these ships depart from one or another of the Caribbean islands rather than Florida, there's little time spent at sea getting to your first port.

Passengers are generally well-traveled people who are more concerned with learning and exploring than they are about plush amenities and onboard activities of the bingo and horse-racing variety. There may not be TVs in the cabins, and you won't find a casino, but you will find fellow passengers who have booked this type of ship because they like to actually get to know the people they're traveling with. Food on board will be basic, hearty, and plentiful, but don't look for room service and midnight buffets, because there aren't any. Don't expect doting service either, but do expect very personal attention as crew and passengers get friendly fast. You'll have fun, make lots of new friends, and be able to let your hair down.

And as for dress codes, what's a dress code? Aboard most of the ships in this category you can get away with a polo shirt and khakis (or shorts) at pretty much any hour of the day, and on some—Windjammer especially—you could show up to dinner in your bathing suit and not feel out of place. These are monumentally casual ships.

AMERICAN CANADIAN CARIBBEAN LINE

461 Water St., Warren, RI 02885. ☎ **800/556-7450** or 401/247-0955. Fax 401/247-2350. www.accl-smallships.com.

This line's trio of innovative and extremely informal small ships offers an unusual cruising experience, focusing on encounters with indigenous peoples and navigating such hinterlands as the cays off the coast of Belize, remote out-islands in the Bahamas, and exotic islands near the Pacific mouth of the Panama Canal. Small and intimate, these no-frills, moderate-price ships attract a well-traveled, down-to-earth older crowd. It's a dose of real Americana—in the vessels themselves, the officers, the passengers, and the crew. ACCL offers a bare-bones experience in terms of amenities, services, and meals. It's the only line featuring a BYOB policy. Owing to the ships' tiny size, there are no quiet nooks besides your cabin for you to run and hide—you're in close quarters and constant contact with everyone else. Luckily, the ships attract a generally convivial crowd, many of whom have sailed with ACCL before.

ACCL Fleet Itineraries

Itineraries listed are for 2001. Visit frommers.travelocity.com for 2002 itineraries, which will be posted as soon as they become available.

GRAND CARIBE   11-night Panama/Panama Canal: Sails between Balboa and Colón (Dec–Mar), visiting Portobelo, San Blas Islands, Contadora, Isla del Rey, Darien, Contadora, Mogo Mogo, Isla Pacheque, and Taboga.

GRAND MARINER   11-night Virgin Islands Carib: Round-trip from St. Thomas (Dec–Jan), visiting St. John's, Tortola, Virgin Gorda, Prickly Pear, Salt Island, Anegada, Beef Island, Jost Van Dyke, and the Norman Islands. **11-night E. Carib:** Sails between Antigua and either Sint Maarten or Grenada (Jan–Mar), visiting Il Pineel and Tintamarre, Anguilla, St. Barts, Saba, St. Kitts, Nevis or Guadeloupe, Dominica, Martinique, St. Lucia, and the Grenadines. **12-night S. Carib/Orinoco:** Sails between Trinidad and Curaçao, visiting Margarita Island (Venezuela), Island of Tortuga, Los Roques, and Bonaire. **14-night S. Carib:** Sails between Panama and Belize, visiting Bocas del Toro, Bluefield's, Corn Islands, Pearl Islands, Miskitos Islands, Roatán (Honduras), Livingston (Guatemala), Punta Gorda, West Snake Cay, and Goff's Cay. Second day of cruise includes a partial transit of the Panama Canal.

NIAGARA PRINCE   10-night Belize: Round-trip from Belize City (Dec–Apr), visiting Goff's Cay, Tobacco Range, Victoria Channel Reef, Moho Cay, Laughing Bird Cay, Placencia, Punta Gorda, Livingston (Guatemala), El Gofete, Casa Guatemala, Castilo San Felipe, West Snake Cay, Punta Icacos, Lime Cay, and Water Cay. **6-night Belize:** Round-trip from Belize City (Dec–Apr), visiting Goff's Cay, Tobacco Cay, Victoria Channel Reef, Moho Cay, Lime Cay, Placencia, West Snake Cay, Punta Icacos, and Laughing Bird Cay.

CLIPPER CRUISE LINE

7711 Bonhomme Ave., St. Louis, MO 63105-1956. ☎ **800/325-0010** or 314/727-2929. Fax 314/727-6576. www.clippercruise.com.

Not your typical cruise, these down-to-earth, comfortable small ships focus on offbeat ports of call, learning, and mingling with your fellow passengers. Clipper caters to mature, seasoned, easygoing, relatively affluent and well-traveled older passengers seeking a casual (but not too casual) vacation experience, enjoying firsthand the natural beauties of the Americas and the Caribbean—it's the ideal small-ship cruise for people who've tried Holland America or Princess but want a more intimate cruise experience that's conducive to easily making new friends. You won't find any glitter, glitz, or Las Vegas gambling here; instead, the mood is perky, all-American, and unpretentious (and like many of the American-crewed small ships, cruise rates are not cheap).

The line is particularly strong in providing information on the nature, history, and culture of the ports visited, carrying one or more naturalists on every Caribbean sailing and an onboard historian as well on sailings in the Grenadines. A cruise director helps organize the days, answers questions, and assists passengers on what to do and how to do it safely during shore landings.

The line's two Caribbean ships, *Nantucket Clipper* and *Yorktown Clipper,* are small and nicely appointed, with comfortable cabins, sizable lounges and dining rooms, and an overall relaxed feel. Like other small ships, they're able to access remote coral reefs of the southern Caribbean, isolated refuges in the British Virgin Islands and Central America, and remote hideaways in the Grenadines, but they also suffer from the problems of small ships, such as instability: When a ship this size hits rough water, you know it (bring the Dramamine).

Clipper Fleet Itineraries
Itineraries listed are for 2001. Visit frommers.travelocity.com for 2002 itineraries, which will be posted as soon as they become available.

NANTUCKET CLIPPER   7-night E. Carib: Sails between Antigua and St. Martin (Dec–Feb), visiting Antigua, St. Kitts, St. Eustatius, St. Barts, Anguilla, and St. Martin.

YORKTOWN CLIPPER   7-night S. Carib: Sails between Curaçao and Trinidad (Dec 2000 and Mar 2001), visiting Curaçao, Bonaire, Isla de Margarita, Tobago, and Trinidad. Itinerary includes 1 night on land. **7-night E. Carib:** Sails between Grenada and St. Kitts (Jan–Feb 2001), visiting Grenada, Union Island, Bequia, St. Lucia, Dominica, Nevis, and St. Kitts. **7-night S. Carib/Orinoco River:** Round-trip from Trinidad (Dec 2000), visiting Tobago, Trinidad, and Orinoco River (Venezuela).

ROYAL OLYMPIC CRUISES
1 Rockefeller Plaza, Suite 315, New York, NY 10020. ☎ **800/872-6400** or 212/397-6400. Fax 212/765-9685. www.royalolympiccruises.com.

The *Stella Solaris* and new *Olympic Voyager* are the only ships in the fleet of Greek-owned, Greek-operated Royal Olympic Cruises to spend time in the Caribbean. While they're not adventurous in the same way as the rest of the ships in this category, they do offer itineraries that visit smaller, more remote ports, and their onboard program focuses on providing passengers with a real learning experience about the places visited.

In cruise service since 1973, the *Stella Solaris* offers a homey, friendly experience and a low-key atmosphere. The *Stella* is not a glamour ship and will not appeal to those seeking partying fun-in-the-sun days and glitzy nights. The typical passenger is early to bed and early to rise, and would rather watch a PBS documentary than boogie till dawn (on these ships, the disco is a ghost town). The 840-passenger *Olympic Voyager,* which debuted in June of 2000, is a brand-new, high-speed ship, but still offers a low-key, casual experience. The ships' enrichment programs far surpass others in the Caribbean. First offered in 1987, the ships' special theme itineraries are offered throughout the year; many are sold out well in advance. Especially popular are scientific theme cruises built around solar eclipses and the Mayan-theme cruises, which visit Mayan areas and have archaeologists and historians aboard to lead discussions.

Royal Olympic Fleet Itineraries
Itineraries listed are for 2001. Visit frommers.travelocity.com for 2002 itineraries, which will be posted as soon as they become available.

OLYMPIC VOYAGER   17-night S. Carib/Amazon (southbound): Round-trip from Fort Lauderdale (Jan–Apr 2001), visiting San Juan, Tortola, Barbados, Amazon River, French Guiana, Trinidad, Martinique, St. Thomas, and Boca da Valeria, Manaus, and Santarém (all in Brazil). **12-night S. Carib/Orinoco:** Round-trip from Fort Lauderdale (Jan–Apr 2001), visiting San Juan, Tortola, Orinoco River, Puerto Ordaz (Venezuela), Trinidad, Martinique, and St. Thomas. **11-night**

W. Carib/Central America: Round-trip from Fort Lauderdale (Jan–Apr 2001), visiting Montego Bay (Jamaica), Roatán and Puerto Cortes (Honduras), Santo Tomas (Guatemala), Belize City, Playa del Carmen, Cozumel, and Key West.

STELLA SOLARIS   15-night Panama Canal: Sails between Fort Lauderdale and San Diego (Dec 2000 to early Jan 2001), visiting Grand Cayman or Jamaica; Balboa (Panama), Puerto Caldera (Costa Rica), and Acapulco, Mazatlán, and Cabo San Lucas (Mexico). **58-night South America circumnavigation:** Sails round-trip from Fort Lauderdale (Jan–Mar 2001).

STAR CLIPPERS

4101 Salzedo Ave., Coral Gables, FL 33146. ☎ **800/442-0553** or 305/442-0550. Fax 305/442-1611. www.star-clippers.com.

On Star Clippers, you'll have the best of two worlds: On one hand, cruises aboard the line's 170- to 228-passenger sailing ships espouse an unstructured, let-your-hair-down, hands-on ethic—you can climb the masts (with a harness, of course), pull in the sails, crawl into the bow netting, or chat with the captain on the bridge. On the other hand, the ship offers comfortable, almost cushy public rooms and cabins. On board, ducking under booms, stepping over coils of rope, leaning against railings just feet above the sea, and watching sailors work the winches or climb the masts and the captain and his mates navigate from the open-air bridge are constant reminders that you're on a real working ship. Further, listening to the captain's daily talk about the next port of call, the history of sailing, or some other nautical subject from his forward perch on the Sun Deck, you'll feel like you're exploring some of the Caribbean's more remote stretches in a ship that belongs there—an exotic ship for an exotic locale. In a sea of look-alike megaships, the *Star Clipper* and new *Royal Clipper* stand out, recalling a romantic, swashbuckling era of ship travel.

Star Clippers Fleet Itineraries

Itineraries listed are for 2001. Visit frommers.travelocity.com for 2002 itineraries, which will be posted as soon as they become available.

ROYAL CLIPPER   7-night E. Carib 1: Round-trip from Barbados, visiting Martinique, Iles des Saintes, Antigua, St. Kitts, Dominica, and St. Lucia. **7-night E. Carib 2:** Round-trip from Barbados, visiting Martinique, St. Lucia, Bequia, Tobago Cays, Grenada, and the Grenadines. Itineraries alternate weekly, Oct–Apr.

STAR CLIPPER   7-night E. Carib 1: Round-trip from Sint Maarten (late Oct to Apr 2001), visiting St. Barts, Nevis, Guadeloupe, Dominica, Iles des Saintes, and Antigua. **7-night E. Carib 2:** Round-trip from Sint Maarten (late Oct to Apr 2001), visiting Anguilla, Sandy Cay, or Jost Van Dyke, Norman Island, Virgin Gorda, St. Kitts, and St. Barts. Itineraries alternate weekly.

WINDJAMMER BAREFOOT CRUISES, LTD.

1759 Bay Rd., Miami Beach, FL 33139 (P.O. Box 190-120, Miami Beach, FL 33119). ☎ **800/327-2601** or 305/672-6453. Fax 305/674-1219. www.windjammer.com.

When you see that the captain is wearing shorts and shades and is barefoot like the rest of the laid-back crew, you'll realize Windjammer's vessels aren't your typical cruise ships. Ultra-casual and delightfully carefree, the line's eclectic fleet of cozy, rebuilt sailing ships (powered by both sails and engines) lures passengers into a fantasy world of pirates-and-rum-punch adventure. Their yards of sails, pointy bowsprits, chunky portholes, and generous use of wood create a swashbuckling story-book look, and while passengers don't have to fish for dinner or swab the decks, they are invited to help haul the sails, take a turn at the wheel, sleep out on-deck whenever they please, and depending on the captain's ruling, crawl into the bow net. With few rules and lots of freedom, this is the closest thing you'll get to a real Caribbean adventure.

Making their way to off-the-beaten-track Caribbean ports of call, the ships are ultra-informal, and hokey yet endearing rituals make the trip feel like summer camp for adults. Add in the line's tremendous number of repeat passengers (and a few of its signature "rum swizzles") and you have a casual experience that's downright intimate.

The *Amazing Grace* is the line's supply ship, sailing 13-night routes that meet up with all the other ships of the fleet, taking passengers along for the ride. It's the only ship in the fleet that's entirely engine-powered; there are no sails.

Windjammer Fleet Itineraries

Itineraries listed are for 2001. Visit frommers.travelocity.com for 2002 itineraries, which will be posted as soon as they become available.

AMAZING GRACE   13-night E. and S. Carib: Round-trip between the Bahamas and Trinidad (year-round), visiting ports that include Antigua, Bequia, Concepción, Cooper Island, Dominica, Grand Bahama, Grand Turk, Grenada, Little Inagua, Iles des Saintes, New Providence, Nevis, Palm Island, Plana Cay, Providenciales, Puerto Plata, Montserrat, St. Barts, St. Kitts, St. Lucia, Sint Maarten, Tobago, Tortola, Trinidad, and Virgin Gorda.

FLYING CLOUD   6-night E. Carib 1: Round-trip from Tortola, visiting Salt Island, Cooper Island, Virgin Gorda, and Jost Van Dyke. **6-night E. Carib 2:** Round-trip from Tortola, visiting Cooper Island, Peter Island, Norman Island, and Virgin Gorda. Itineraries alternate year-round.

LEGACY   7-night E. Carib 1: Round-trip from Fajardo (Puerto Rico), visiting Culebra (Puerto Rico), St. Croix, St. John, St. Thomas, and Jost Van Dyke. **7-night E. Carib 2:** Round-trip from Fajardo (Puerto Rico), visiting Culebra, St. Croix, Virgin Gorda, St. John, and Vieques (Puerto Rico). Itineraries alternate year-round.

MANDALAY   13-night E. Carib: Sails between Grenada and Antigua, visiting Bequia, Carriacou, Canouan, Dominica, Guadeloupe, Iles des Saintes, Martinique, Mayreau, Nevis, Montserrat, Palm Island, St. Lucia, St. Vincent, and Tobago Cays. **6-night E. Carib:** Round-trip from Grenada, visiting the Grenadines. **6-night S. Carib:** Round-trip from Grenada, visiting Chimana Segunda, Playa Blanca, Isla Margarita, and Los Testigos. Itineraries alternate year-round.

POLYNESIA   6-night E. Carib 1: Round-trip from Sint Maarten, visiting St. Barts, Anguilla, Tintamarre, Montserrat, and Saba. **6-night E. Carib 2:** Round-trip from Sint Maarten, visiting Colombier Beach, St. Barts, St. Eustatius, Nevis, and St. Kitts. Itineraries alternate year-round.

YANKEE CLIPPER   6-night E. Carib 1: Round-trip from Grenada, visiting Carriacou, Palm Island, Bequia, St. Vincent, and Mayreau. **6-night E. Carib 2:** Round-trip from Grenada, visiting Palm Island, Union Island, Bequia, Canouan, Tobago Cays, and St. Vincent. Itineraries alternate year-round.

The Ports of Embarkation 2

The busiest of the ports of embarkation is Miami, followed by Port Everglades in Fort Lauderdale and Port Canaveral at Cape Canaveral. Tampa, on Florida's west coast, is also becoming a major port, especially for cruise ships visiting the eastern coast of Mexico, while New Orleans is popular for ships sailing to Mexico. San Juan, Puerto Rico, is both a major port of embarkation in the Caribbean and a major port of call. (See chapter 3, "The Ports of Call," for a review.)

All of these ports are tourist destinations themselves, so most cruise lines now offer special deals to extend all Caribbean/Bahamian cruise vacations in the port either before or after the cruise. These packages, for 2, 3, or 4 days, often offer hotel and car-rental discounts as well as sightseeing packages. Have your travel agent or cruise specialist check for the best deals.

In this chapter, I'll describe each port of embarkation, tell you how to get to it, and suggest things to see and do there, whether it's hitting the beach, sightseeing, or shopping. I'll also recommend a sampling of restaurants and places to stay. You'll find more detailed information about each destination in *Frommer's Florida, Frommer's Miami & the Keys, Frommer's New Orleans,* and *Frommer's Puerto Rico.*

1 Miami & the Port of Miami

Miami is the cruise capital of the world. More cruise ships, especially supersize ones, berth here than anywhere else on earth, and more than three million cruise ship passengers pass through yearly. Not surprisingly, the city's facilities are extensive and state-of-the-art, and Miami International Airport is only 8 miles away, about a 15-minute drive.

Just across the bridge from the Port of Miami and a few minutes away is **Bayside Marketplace,** downtown Miami's waterfront and restaurant shopping complex, which can be reached via regular shuttle service between each cruise terminal and Bayside's main entrance.

Industry giants Carnival and Royal Caribbean both have long-term, multimillion-dollar agreements with the port, and to accommodate the influx of new cruise ships, Miami spent $76 million on major improvements to terminals 3, 4, and 5, and added a 750-space parking facility. In fact, Terminal 5 (which was created out of the old 5 and half of Terminal 4) is now the new 250,000-square-foot home for Royal Caribbean's *Voyager of the Seas* (and subsequent Eagle-class ships), designed specially to accommodate the hulking ships and about 8,400 passengers at a time. You can't miss it: It has sail-like structures on its roof and a replica of Royal Caribbean's Viking Crown Lounge on top of the terminal as well. The renovated terminals offer enhanced facilities, like 4,000 additional passenger seats between them, a new departure area in each, VIP lounges, and airport-style conveyer belts for luggage coming on and off the ship. The port is even hoping to soon be able to issue airline boarding passes to departing passengers.

Still on the drawing board are plans for a **Maritime Park,** to be built on Watson Island, a tract of land just across the channel from port. Although still in the early planning stages, the complex would likely include two new ship terminals, a convention bureau, and entertainment facilities for passengers.

GETTING TO MIAMI & THE PORT

The Port of Miami is at 1015 N. America Way, in central Miami. It's on Dodge Island, reached via a five-lane bridge from the downtown district. For information, call ☎ **305/371-PORT.**

BY PLANE   Miami International Airport is about 8 miles west of downtown Miami and the port. If you've arranged air transportation and/or transfers through the cruise line, a representative will be at the airport and will direct you to **shuttle buses** that take you to the port. **Taxis** are also available; the fare between the airport and the Port of Miami is about $18. Some leading taxi companies include **Central Taxicab Service** (☎ 305/532-5555), **Diamond Cab Company** (☎ 305/545-5555), and **Metro Taxicab Company** (☎ 305/888-8888).

You can also take a no. 7 **Metrobus** for $1.25 (☎ **305/770-3131**) from the airport to downtown Miami (stop is at Miami Dade Community College), which will land you across the street from the bridge that leads to the port (not a good option with luggage). **SuperShuttle** (☎ **305/871-2000**) charges about $7 to $14 per person, with two pieces of luggage, for a ride within Dade County, which includes the Port of Miami. Its vans operate 24 hours a day.

BY CAR   The Florida Turnpike, a toll road, and Interstate 95 are the main arteries for those arriving from the north. Coming in from the northwest, take Interstate 75 or U.S. 27 to reach the center of Miami. Parking lots right at street level face the cruise terminals. Parking runs $8 per day. Porters can carry your luggage to the terminals.

BY TRAIN   Amtrak (☎ 800/872-7245) offers three trains daily between New York and Miami, and daily service between Los Angeles and Miami. You'll pull into Amtrak's Miami terminal at 8303 NW 37th Ave. (☎ **305/835-1206**).

EXPLORING MIAMI

Miami is no longer just a beach-vacation destination. A sizzling, multicultural mecca, Miami and its beaches offer the best in cutting-edge restaurants, unusual attractions, shopping, and luxury, boutique, kitschy, and charming hotels.

After a relaxing day on the water, take advantage of choice theater or opera, restaurants serving exotic and delicious food, the hopping, star-studded club scene, or the lively cafe culture.

VISITOR INFORMATION   Contact the **Greater Miami Convention and Visitors Bureau,** 701 Brickell Ave., Miami, FL 33131 (☎ **800/283-2707** or 305/ 539-3000), for the most up-to-date information.

Miami at a Glance

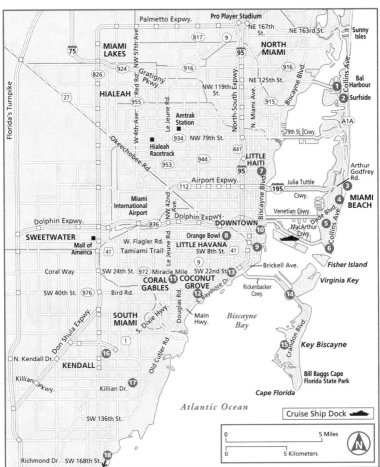

ATTRACTIONS & SHOPPING

Art Deco district **5**
Bal Harbour Shops **1**
Bass Museum of Art **5**
Bayside Marketplace **10**
CocoWalk and the
  Streets of Mayfair **12**
Coral Gables Merrick
  House & Gardens **11**
Crandon Park Beach **15**
Dadeland Mall **16**
Lincoln Road shopping **5**
Miami Seaquarium **14**
Miracle Mile **11**
Monkey Jungle **18**
Parrot Jungle and Gardens **17**
Vizcaya Museum & Gardens **13**

ACCOMMODATIONS

The Beach House **2**
Biltmore Hotel **11**
The Delano **5**
The Eden Roc **3**

Fontainebleau Hilton
  Resort & Towers **3**
The Hotel **6**
Hotel Astor **5**
Hotel Ocean **5**
Hotel Place St. Michel **11**
Indian Creek Hotel **4**
The Kent **5**
Miami Hotel Inter-Continental **10**
Park Washington Hotels **5**
Sonesta Beach Resort
  Key Biscayne **15**
The Tides **5**
Wyndham Grand Bay Hotel **12**

DINING & NIGHTLIFE

Albion's Falabella Bar **5**
Bambu **6**
Bar Room **6**
Bash **5**
Café Nostalgia **8**
Café Tu Tu Tango **12**
Casa Panza Restaurant **8**

ClubSpace **10**
crobar **5**
East Coast Fisheries
  & Restaurant **10**
Forge **3**
Groove Jet **4**
Joe's Stone Crab **6**
Joia **6**
Larios on the Beach **6**
Level **5**
Lombardi's **10**
Nemo's **6**
Norman's **11**
Pacific Time **6**
Rose Bar **5**
Rusty Pelican **15**
Soyka **7**
Spris **5**
Tantra **5**
Tiramesu **6**
Tobacco Road **9**
Van Dyke Cafe **6**
Versailles **8**

GETTING AROUND   See "Getting to Miami & the Port," above, for **taxi** information. The meter starts at $1.50, and ticks up another $2 each mile and 25¢ for each additional minute, with standard flat-rate charges for frequently traveled routes.

Bus transportation in Miami is often a nightmare. Call ☎ **305/770-3131** for public transit information. The fare is $1.25.

Metromover (☎ **305/770-3131**), a 4.4-mile elevated line, circles downtown, stopping near important attractions and shopping and business districts. It's fun if you've got time to kill. It runs daily from about 5am to midnight. The fare is 25¢.

HITTING THE BEACH

A 300-foot-wide sand beach runs for about 10 miles from the south of Miami Beach to Haulover Beach Park in the north. (For those of you who like to get an all-around tan, Haulover is a known nude beach, though it's not mandatory that you sunbathe in your birthday suit.) Although most of this stretch is lined with a solid wall of hotels, beach access is plentiful, and you are free to frolic along the entire strip. A wooden boardwalk runs along the hotel side from 21st to 46th streets—about 1¹/₂ miles.

There are lots of **public beaches** here, wide and well maintained, complete with lifeguards, toilet facilities, concession stands, and metered parking (bring lots of quarters). Lifeguard-protected public beaches include 21st Street, at the beginning of the boardwalk; 35th Street, popular with an older crowd; 46th Street, next to the Fontainebleau Hilton; 53rd Street, a narrower, more sedate beach; 64th Street, one of the quietest strips around; and 72nd Street, a local old-timers spot. On the southern tip of the beach is family favorite South Pointe Park, where you can watch the cruise ships. Lummus Park, in the center of the Art Deco district, is the best place for people-watching and model-spotting. The beach between 11th and 13th streets is popular with the gay crowd. Senior citizens prefer the beach from 1st to 15th streets.

To escape the crowds, head up to the 40-acre **Oleta River State Recreation Area** (formerly known as the North Shore State Recreation Area), 3400 NE 163rd St. at Collins and Biscayne (☎ **305/919-1844**). It costs $2 per person to get in, or $4 per car for up to eight people.

In Key Biscayne, **Crandon Park,** 4000 Crandon Blvd. (☎ **305/361-5421**), is one of metropolitan Miami's finest white-sand beaches, stretching for some 3¹/₂ miles. There are lifeguards, and you can rent cabanas with a shower and chairs. Saturday and Sunday the beach can be especially crowded. Parking nearby is $3.50.

SOUTH BEACH & THE ART DECO DISTRICT

Miami's best sight is a part of the city itself. Located at the southern end of Miami Beach, the ✪ **Art Deco District** is filled with outrageous and fanciful 1920s and 1930s architecture that shouldn't be missed. This treasure trove features more than 900 pastel, Pez-colored buildings in the art-deco, Streamline Moderne, and Spanish Mediterranean Revival styles. The district stretches from 6th to 23rd streets, and from the Atlantic Ocean to Lennox Court. **Ocean Drive** boasts many of the premier art-deco hotels.

Also in South Beach is the ✪ **Bass Museum of Art,** 2121 Park Ave. (☎ **305/ 673-7533**), with a permanent collection of Old Masters, along with textiles, period furnishings, objets d'art, ecclesiastical artifacts, and sculpture. Rotating exhibits include pop art, fashion, and photography, and attract South Beach's fashion-forward lovers of modern art.

CORAL GABLES & COCONUT GROVE

These two Miami neighborhoods are fun to visit for their architecture and ambiance. In **Coral Gables,** the old world meets the new as curving boulevards, sidewalks, plazas, fountains, and arched entrances evoke Seville.

Today the area is an epicurean's Eden boasting some of Miami's most renowned eateries. "The Gables," as the locals say, is also home to the University of Miami and the **Miracle Mile** (it's actually half a mile), a 5-block retail mecca stretching from Douglas Road (37th Avenue) to Le Jeune Road (42nd Avenue). You can even visit the boyhood home of George Merrick, the man who originally developed Coral Gables. The **Coral Gables Merrick House & Gardens,** 907 Coral Way (☎ **305/460-5361**), has been restored to its 1920s look and is filled with Merrick memorabilia. The house and garden are open for tours on Wednesday and Saturday between 1 and 4pm.

Coconut Grove, South Florida's oldest settlement, remains a village surrounded by the urban sprawl of Miami. It dates back to the early 1800s when Bahamian seamen first sought to salvage treasure from the wrecked vessels stranded along the Great Florida Reef. Mostly people come here to shop, drink, dine, or simply walk around and explore. But don't miss the ✪ **Vizcaya Museum & Gardens,** 3251 S. Miami Ave. (☎ **305/250-9133**), a spectacular 70-room Italian Renaissance–style villa.

ANIMAL PARKS

Just minutes from the Port of Miami in Key Biscayne, the **Miami Seaquarium,** 4400 Rickenbacker Causeway (☎ **305/361-5705**), is a delight. Performing dolphins such as Flipper, TV's greatest sea mammal, perform along with "Lolita the Killer Whale." You can also see endangered manatees, sea lions, tropical-theme aquariums, and the gruesome shark feeding. It's open daily from 9:30am to 6pm. Admission is $21.95 for adults and $16.95 for children 3 to 9, free for children under 3.

At **Monkey Jungle,** 14805 SW 216th St., Homestead (☎ **305/235-1611**), the trick is that the visitors are caged and nearly 500 monkeys frolic in freedom and make fun of them. The most talented of these free-roaming primates perform shows daily for the amusement of their guests. Beware of monkeys in heat, however, as they may mistake you for a possible object of their affections. The site also contains one of the richest fossil deposits in South Florida, with some 5,000 specimens. It's open daily from 9:30am to 5pm. Admission is $13.50 for adults, $8 for children 4 to 12, and free for children under 3.

In South Miami, **Parrot Jungle and Gardens,** 11000 SW 57th Ave. (☎ **305/669-7030**), is actually a botanical garden, wildlife habitat, and bird sanctuary all rolled into one. Children can enjoy a petting zoo and a playground. It's open daily from 9:30am to 6pm. Admission is $14.95 for adults, $9.95 for children 3 to 10, and free for children under 3.

ORGANIZED TOURS

BY BOAT   From September through May **Heritage Tours of Miami II** features jaunts aboard an 85-foot schooner. Tours depart from the Bayside Marketplace at 401 Biscayne Blvd. (☎ **305/442-9697**). The daily 2-hour cruises pass by Villa Vizcaya, Coconut Grove, and Key Biscayne and put you in sight of Miami's spectacular skyline. They leave at 1:30, 4, and 6pm. Tickets cost $15 for adults and $10 for children under 12. On Friday, Saturday, and Sunday evenings, there are 1-hour tours to see the lights of the city at 9, 10, and 11pm.

ON FOOT   An **Art-Deco District Walking Tour,** sponsored by the Miami Design Preservation League (☎ **305/672-2014**), leaves every Saturday at 10:30am from the Art Deco Welcome Center at 1001 Ocean Dr., South Beach. The 90-minute tour costs $10.

SHOPPING

Most cruise ship passengers shop right near the Port of Miami at **Bayside Marketplace,** a mall with 150 specialty shops at 401 Biscayne Blvd. Some 20 eateries serve everything from Nicaraguan to Italian food; there's even a Hard Rock Café. Many have outdoor seating right along the bay for picturesque views of the yachts harbored there (unfortunately, sometimes the water here is littered with debris like plastic bottles). You can also watch the street performers, enjoy the pulsating rhythms of live salsa music, or take a boat tour from here.

A free shuttle from the Hotel Inter-Continental in downtown Miami takes you to the **Bal Harbour Shops** at 9700 Collins Ave. They're Miami's version of Rodeo Drive, housing big-name stores from Chanel and Prada to Lacoste to Neiman-Marcus and Florida's largest Saks Fifth Avenue. In addition to shopping, Bal Harbour Shops is an ideal people-watching venue and a favorite hangout for foreigners looking to unload lots of cash before their trip back to their native countries.

In South Beach, **Lincoln Road,** an 8-block pedestrian mall, runs between Washington Avenue and Alton Road, near the northern tier of the Art Deco district. It's filled with popular shops such as The Gap and Banana Republic, interior-design stores, art galleries, and even vintage-clothing outlets, as well as coffeehouses, restaurants, and cafes. Despite the recent influx of commercial anchor stores, Lincoln Road still manages to maintain its funky, arty flair, attracting an eclectic, colorful crowd.

Just a short drive south of downtown, the Dadeland Mall, at the corner of U.S. Highway 1 and SW 88th Street (☎ **305/665-6226**), is the most popular shopping plaza in suburban Dade County. Its tenants include Burdines and Burdines Home Gallery, Lord & Taylor, and Saks Fifth Avenue. The food court offers many quick-bite options from fast food to sweets.

Coconut Grove, centered on Main Highway and Grand Avenue, is the heart of the city's boutique district and features two open-air shopping and entertainment complexes, **CocoWalk** and the **Streets of Mayfair.**

In Coral Gables, **Miracle Mile,** actually a half-mile stretch of SW 22nd Street between Douglas and Le Jeune roads, features more than 150 shops.

For a change of pace from the fast-paced glitz of South Beach or the serene luxury of Coral Gables, head for **Little Havana,** where pre-Castro Cubans commingle with young artists who have begun to set up performance spaces in the area. It's located just west of downtown Miami on SW 8th Street. In addition to authentic Cuban cuisine, the cafe Cubano culture is alive and well.

ACCOMMODATIONS

Thanks to the network of highways, you can stay virtually anywhere in Greater Miami and still be within 10 to 20 minutes of your cruise ship.

DOWNTOWN   Set across the bay from the cruise ship piers, the **Miami Hotel Inter-Continental,** 100 Chopin Plaza (☎ **800/327-3005** or 305/577-1000), is a bold triangular tower soaring 34 stories.

SOUTH BEACH   The art-deco, comfy-chic ✪ **Hotel Astor,** 956 Washington Ave. (☎ **800/270-4981** or 305/531-8081), originally built in 1936, reopened after a massive renovation in 1995. The Astor is only 2 blocks from the beach, but if that's still too far for you, try the upscale **Hotel Ocean,** 1230-38 Ocean Dr. (☎ **800/783-1725** or 305/672-2579). If you're on a budget, but want a cozy deco feel, try the **Park Washington Hotels**—Park Washington, Belaire, Taft, and Kenmore—a group of small, low-frills hotels next door to the Astor, at 1020 Washington Ave. (☎ **305/532-1930**). **The Delano,** 1685 Collins Ave. (☎ **800/555-5001** or 305/672-2000), is a sleek, postmodern, and self-consciously hip celebrity hot spot, but it's worth at least a peak. ✪ **The Hotel,** 801 Collins Ave. at the corner of Collins and 8th Street (☎ **305/531-5796**), formerly known as The Tiffany Hotel until the folks behind the little blue box threatened to sue, is a deco gem, not to mention the most fashionable hotel on South Beach thanks to the whimsical interiors designed by haute couturier Todd Oldham. ✪ **The Tides,** 1300 Ocean Dr. (☎ **800/688-7678** or 305/604-5000), is located right on the beach and features a retro fab yet ultra-modern nautically inspired Deco monument. **The Kent,** 1131 Collins Ave. (☎ **305/531-6771**), like The Tides, is part of Chris Blackwell's Island Outpost chain and attracts a less upwardly mobile yet no less chic crowd of young, hip travelers.

MIAMI BEACH   At the ✪ **Indian Creek Hotel,** 2727 Indian Creek Dr. at 28th Street (☎ **800/491-2772** or 305/531-2727), each room is an homage to the 1930s art-deco age. **The Eden Roc,** 4525 Collins Ave. (☎ **800/327-8337** or 305/531-0000), and the **Fontainebleau Hilton Resort & Towers,** next door at 4441 Collins Ave. (☎ **800/548-8886** or 305/538-2000), are both popular, updated 1950s resorts evoking the bygone Rat Pack era, with spas, health clubs, outdoor swimming pools, and beach access. **The Beach House,** 9449 Collins Ave., in Surfside (☎ **305/865-3551**) brings a taste of Nantucket to Miami with soothing hues, comfortable furniture, oceanfront views, and a Ralph Lauren-decorated interior.

COCONUT GROVE   Near Miami's City Hall and the Coconut Grove Marina, the ✪ **Wyndham Grand Bay Hotel,** 2669 S. Bayshore Dr. (☎ **800/327-2788** or 305/838-9600), overlooks Biscayne Bay.

CORAL GABLES   The famous ✪ **Biltmore Hotel,** 1200 Anastasia Ave. (☎ **800/228-3000** or 305/445-1926), was restored a few years ago, but despite renovations, exudes an old-world, stately glamour and is rumored to be haunted by ghosts of travel days past. There's also the **Hotel Place St. Michel,** 162 Alcazar Ave. (☎ **800/848-HOTEL** or 305/444-1666), a three-story establishment reminiscent of an inn in provincial France.

KEY BISCAYNE   The **Sonesta Beach Resort Key Biscayne,** 350 Ocean Dr. (☎ **800/SONESTA** or 305/361-2021), offers relative isolation from the rest of congested Miami.

DINING

DOWNTOWN   **Lombardi's,** in Bayside Marketplace (☎ **305/381-9580**), is a moderately priced Italian restaurant. **East Coast Fisheries & Restaurant,** 360 W. Flagler at South River Drive (☎ **305/372-1300**), is a no-nonsense retail market and restaurant, offering a terrific variety of the freshest fish available. Further up Biscayne Boulevard near the burgeoning Miami Design District is **Soyka,** 5580 NE Fourth Court (☎ **305/759-3117**), the hip downtown sibling of South Beach's News and Van Dyke cafes.

SOUTH BEACH   Join the celebs and models at **Nemo's,** 100 Collins Ave. (☎ **305/532-4550**). Take time to stroll down the pedestrian mall on Lincoln Road, which offers art galleries, specialty shops, and several excellent outdoor cafes such as **Spris,** 731 Lincoln Rd. (☎ **305/673-2020**), the **Van Dyke Cafe,** 846 Lincoln Rd. (☎ **305/534-3600**), and **Tiramesu,** 731 Lincoln Rd. (☎ **305/532-4538**). The standout culinary trendsetter on Lincoln Road, however, is **Pacific Time,** 915 Lincoln Rd. (☎ **305/534-5979**), where you can enjoy a taste of the Pacific Rim with a deliciously modern South Beach twist. Another Asian-inspired newcomer to Lincoln Road is **Bambu,** 1661 Meridian Ave. (☎ **305/531-4800**), the hot eatery co-owned by actress Cameron Diaz. At the legendary **Joe's Stone Crab,** 227 Biscayne St., between Washington and Collins avenues (☎ **305/673-0365**), about a ton of stone-crab claws are served daily during stone-crab season from October to May, and keep people waiting for up to 2 hours for a table. Even if Gloria Estefan weren't part-owner of **Larios on the Beach,** 820 Ocean Dr. (☎ **305/532-9577**), the crowds would still flock to this bistro serving old-fashioned Cuban dishes, such as *masitas de puerco* (fried pork chunks).

COCONUT GROVE   If you'd like to people-watch while you eat, head for **Café Tu Tu Tango,** 3015 Grand Ave. (☎ **305/529-2222**), on the second floor of CocoWalk. This second-floor restaurant is designed to look like a disheveled artist's loft, complete with original paintings (some half-finished) on easels or hanging from the walls.

CORAL GABLES   ✪ **Norman's,** 21 Almeria Ave. (☎ **305/446-6767**), possibly the best restaurant in the entire city of Miami, is run by its namesake, Norman Van Aken, a James Beard award–winning chef and pioneer of New World and Floribbean cuisine.

KEY BISCAYNE   The surf and turf is routine at the **Rusty Pelican,** 3201 Rickenbacker Causeway (☎ **305/361-3818**), but it's worth coming for a drink and the spectacular sunset view.

LITTLE HAVANA   One reason to visit Little Havana is to enjoy its excellent Hispanic cuisine. **Casa Panza Restaurant,** 1620 SW 8th St. (☎ **305/643-5343**), a taste of old Seville in Little Havana, is a feast for the senses with flamenco dancers, tempting tapas, and a lively atmosphere that reels in crowds on a nightly basis. At 11pm, everyone, no matter what their religion, is given a candle to pray to La Virgen del Rocio, one of Seville's most revered saints—it's a party with piety! Another place to check out is **Versailles,** 3555 SW 8th St. (☎ **305/538-8533**), a 24-hour palatial, mirrored diner serving all the Cuban mainstays in large and reasonably priced portions.

MIAMI AFTER DARK

Miami nightlife is as varied as its population. Known as Hollywood-south, Miami's sizzling nightlife is no stranger to A-list celebrities from Leonardo DiCaprio and Al Pacino to Gwyneth Paltrow, Sylvester Stallone, and part-time resident Madonna. Look for the klieg lights to direct you to the hot spots of South Beach. And while the blocks of Washington Avenue, Collins Avenue, and Ocean Drive are the main nightlife thoroughfares, you're more likely to spot a celebrity in a more off-the-beaten-path eatery such as **Tantra,** a grass-floored, Middle Eastern (aphrodisiac-inspired) eatery and late-night hangout at 1445 Pennsylvania Ave. (☎ **305/672-4765**); **Joia,** a popular, chic Italian eatery at 140 Ocean Dr. (☎ **305/674-8855**); or the **Forge,** 432 41st St. (☎ **305/538-8533**), an ornately decorated rococo-style steak house boasting one of the finest wine selections around (☎ **305/538-8533**). Another hot spot is the Cameron Diaz–co-owned **Bambu,** 1661 Meridian Ave. (☎ **305/531-4800**), an Asian eatery and celebrity magnet with a chichi private upstairs lounge. Restaurants and bars are open late—usually until 5am. Also popular are the hotel bars such as the Delano's **Rose Bar** and the Rubell-owned **Albion's Falabella Bar,** 1650 James Ave. (☎ **888/665-0008**).

As trends come and go, so do clubs, so before you head out for a decadent night of disco, make sure the place is still in business! As of press time, the clubs at which to see, be seen, and, of course, dance, were **Bar Room,** 320 Lincoln Rd. (☎ **305/604-0480**); **Groove Jet,** 323 23rd St. (☎ **305/532-2002**); **crobar,** 1445 Washington Ave. (☎ **305/531-5027**); **Level,** 1235 Washington Ave. (☎ **305/532-1525**); and **Bash,** 655 Washington Ave. (☎ **305/538-2274**).

But South Beach isn't the only place for nightlife in Miami. Not too far from the Miami River is the city's oldest bar, **Tobacco Road,** 626 S. Miami Ave. (☎ **305/0374-1198**), a nitty-gritty place, which still attracts some of the city's storied, pre–"Miami Vice" natives. **ClubSpace,** 11th Street at NE Second Ave. (☎ **305/577-1007**), occupies a very large warehouse in Downtown Miami and is vaguely reminiscent of a funky, SoHo-style dance palace. Down in Little Havana is **Café Nostalgia,** 2212 SW Eighth St. (☎ **305/541-2631**), where salsa is not a condiment but a way of life.

Other nocturnal options abound in Coconut Grove and Coral Gables and, slowly but surely, the downtown/Design District areas. Check the *Miami Herald, Miami New Times,* and **miami.citysearch.com** for specific events.

2 Fort Lauderdale & Port Everglades

Port Everglades, in Broward County, is the second-busiest cruise port in the world. It boasts the deepest harbor south of Norfolk along the eastern seaboard, an ultra-modern cruise ship terminal, and an easy access route to the Fort Lauderdale airport, less than a 5-minute drive away. The port lies some 40 miles north of Miami's center.

The port itself is fairly free of congestion. Ten modern cruise terminals offer covered loading zones, drop-off and pickup staging, and curbside baggage handlers. An 11th terminal is underway for completion in late 2001, with plans for a couple more terminals within the next 5 years or so. Terminals are comfortable and safe, with seating areas, snack bars, lots of taxis, clean rest rooms, and plenty of pay phones. Parking lots have recently been expanded to offer a total of 4,500 parking places.

For information about the port, call **Port Everglades Authority** at ☎ **954/523-3404.**

GETTING TO FORT LAUDERDALE & THE PORT

BY AIR   Small and extremely user-friendly, the **Fort Lauderdale/Hollywood International Airport** (☎ **954/359-6100**) is less than 2 miles from Port Everglades, making this the easiest airport-to-cruiseport trip in Florida—what could be easier than a 5-minute bus or cab ride? (Port Canaveral, on the other hand, is about an hour's drive from the Orlando airport.) Cruise line **buses** meet incoming flights when they know transfer passengers are on board, so make arrangements for pickup when you book your cruise. Taking a **taxi** to the port costs less than $10.

BY CAR   The port has three passenger entrances: Spangler Boulevard, an extension of State Road 84 East; Eisenhower Boulevard, running south from the 17th Street Causeway (A1A); and Eller Drive, connecting directly with Interstate 595.

Interstate 595 runs east-west, with connections to the Fort Lauderdale/Hollywood Airport, Interstate 95, State Road 7 (441), Florida's Turnpike, Sawgrass Expressway, and Interstate 75. Convenient parking is available at the port in two large garages. The 2,500-space Northport Parking Garage, next to the Greater Fort Lauderdale/Broward County Convention Center, serves terminals 1, 2, and 4. The 2,000-space Midport Parking Garage serves terminals 18, 19, 21, 22, 24, 25, and 26. Garages are well lit, security-patrolled, and designed to accommodate RVs and buses. The 24-hour parking fee is about $8.

BY TRAIN   Amtrak (☎ 800/USA-RAIL) trains from New York to Miami make various stops along the way, including Fort Lauderdale. The local station is at 200 SW 21st Terrace (☎ **954/587-6692** or 305/835-1123). Taxis are lined up to deliver you to Port Everglades for a $10 to $15 fare.

EXPLORING FORT LAUDERDALE

Fort Lauderdale Beach, a 2-mile strip along Florida A1A, gained fame in the 1950s as a spring-break playground, popularized by the movie *Where the Boys Are.* But in the 1980s, partying college kids, who brought the city more mayhem than money, began to be less welcome. Fort Lauderdale tried to attract a more mainstream, affluent crowd in an effort to transform itself into the "Venice of the Americas." The city has largely been successful.

In addition to miles of beautiful wide beaches, Fort Lauderdale has more than 300 miles of navigable natural waterways, in addition to innumerable artificial canals that permit thousands of residents to anchor boats in their backyards. You too can easily get on the water by renting a boat or hailing a private, moderately priced water taxi.

VISITOR INFORMATION   The **Greater Fort Lauderdale Convention & Visitors Bureau,** 1850 Eller Dr., Suite 303, Fort Lauderdale, FL 33316 (☎ **954/765-4466**), is an excellent resource, distributing a comprehensive guide on events and sightseeing in Broward County.

GETTING AROUND   For a taxi, call **Yellow Cab** (☎ **954/565-5400**). Rates start at $2.45 for the first mile and $1.75 for each additional mile. **Broward County Mass Transit** (☎ **954/357-8400**) runs bus service throughout the county. Each ride costs $1.15 for the first transfer and 15¢ for each additional same-day transfer.

HITTING THE BEACH

Backed by an endless row of hotels and popular with visitors and locals alike, the **Fort Lauderdale Beach Promenade** underwent a $20-million renovation not long back, and it looks marvelous. It's located along Atlantic Boulevard (Fla. A1A), between SE 17th Street and Sunrise Boulevard. The fabled strip from *Where the Boys Are* is **Ocean Boulevard,** between Las Olas Boulevard and Sunrise Boulevard. On weekends, parking at the ocean-side meters is difficult to find.

Fort Lauderdale Beach at the Howard Johnson is a perennial local favorite. A jetty bounds the beach on the south side, making it rather private, although the water gets a little choppy. High-school and college students share this area with an older crowd. The beach is at 4660 N. Ocean Dr. in Lauderdale by the Sea.

SEEING THE SIGHTS

The **Museum of Discovery & Science,** 401 SW 2nd St. (☎ **954/467-6637**), is an excellent interactive science museum with an IMAX theater. Check out the 52-foot-tall "Great Gravity Clock" in the museum's atrium.

Fort Lauderdale at a Glance

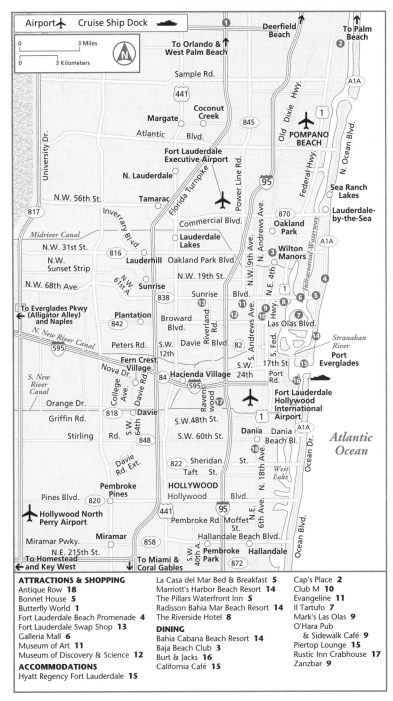

Airport ✈ Cruise Ship Dock 🚢

0 — 3 Miles
0 — 3 Kilometers
N

To Orlando &
West Palm Beach

Deerfield
Beach ①

To Palm
Beach ②

Sample Rd.

441

Coconut
Creek

Margate

845

Atlantic   Blvd.

Old Dixie Hwy.

POMPANO
BEACH

A1A

1

Fort Lauderdale
Executive Airport

N. Lauderdale

N.W. 56th St.

Tamarac

Florida Turnpike

Power Line Rd.

I-95

Federal Hwy.

Sea Ranch
Lakes

Lauderdale-
by-the-Sea

N. Ocean Blvd.

817

Inverrary Blvd.

Commercial Blvd.

870

Oakland
Park

A1A

Midriver Canal

N.W. 31st St.

816

Lauderhill   Oakland Park Blvd.

N. Andrews Ave.

③ Wilton
Manors

Intracoastal Waterway

④

N.W.
Sunset Strip

N.W. 19th St.

N.W. 9th Ave.

1

N.E. 4th Ave.

N.W. 68th Ave.

N.W. 61st A.

Sunrise

838

Sunrise   Blvd.

⑬

⑪

⑨

⑧

⑥ ⑤

Plantation

842

Broward
Blvd.

⑫

⑩ Hwy.

⑦

To Everglades Pkwy
(Alligator Alley)
and Naples

N. New River Canal

595

Peters Rd.

S.W.
12th

Davie Blvd.

Riverland
Rd.

82

S. Fed.

Las Olas Blvd.

⑭

Stranahan
River

⑮ Port
Everglades

S. New
River
Canal

Nova Dr.

Fern Crest
Village

College Ave.

Davie Rd.

84

Hacienda Village

595

S.W.
24th

Port
Rd.

⑯

Orange Dr.

818

Davie

S.W. 64th

848

Griffin Rd.

Stirling   Rd.

Ravens wood

⑰

Fort Lauderdale
Hollywood
International
Airport

1

Dania

A1A

Atlantic
Ocean

Davie Rd. Ext.

S.W.48th St.

S.W. 60th St.

Dania
Beach Bl.

⑱

N. 18th Ave.

Ocean Dr.

822

Sheridan   St.

Taft   St.

West
Lake

Pembroke
Pines

Pines Blvd.

820

HOLLYWOOD

Hollywood   Blvd.

Ocean Blvd.

Hollywood North
Perry Airport

441

95

N.E. 6th Ave.

Pembroke Rd.

Moffet
St.

Miramar Pkwy.

Miramar

858

Hallandale Beach Blvd.

N.E. 215th St.

S.W. 40th A.

Pembroke
Park

Hallandale

872

To Homestead
and Key West

To Miami &
Coral Gables

ATTRACTIONS & SHOPPING
Antique Row **18**
Bonnet House **5**
Butterfly World **1**
Fort Lauderdale Beach Promenade **4**
Fort Lauderdale Swap Shop **13**
Galleria Mall **6**
Museum of Art **11**
Museum of Discovery & Science **12**

ACCOMMODATIONS
Hyatt Regency Fort Lauderdale **15**

La Casa del Mar Bed & Breakfast **5**
Marriott's Harbor Beach Resort **14**
The Pillars Waterfront Inn **5**
Radisson Bahia Mar Beach Resort **14**
The Riverside Hotel **8**

DINING
Bahia Cabana Beach Resort **14**
Baja Beach Club **3**
Burt & Jacks **16**
California Café **15**

Cap's Place **2**
Club M **10**
Evangeline **11**
Il Tartufo **7**
Mark's Las Olas **9**
O'Hara Pub
  & Sidewalk Café **9**
Piertop Lounge **15**
Rustic Inn Crabhouse **17**
Zanzbar **9**

The **Museum of Art,** 1 E. Las Olas Blvd. (☎ **954/763-6464**), is a truly terrific small museum of modern and contemporary art.

A guided tour of the **Bonnet House,** 900 N. Birch Rd. (☎ **954/563-5393**), offers a glimpse into the lives of the pioneers of the Fort Lauderdale area. This unique 35-acre plantation-style home and estate survives in the middle of an otherwise highly developed beachfront condominium area. One-hour tours are offered Wednesday through Friday at 10:30am, 11:30am, 12:30pm, and 1:30pm, Saturday and Sunday at 12:30, 1:15, 1:45, and 2:30pm; arrive 15 minutes before the tour. $9 adults, $8 senior citizens, $7 students.

Butterfly World, Tradewinds Park South, 3600 W. Sample Rd., Coconut Creek, west of the Florida Turnpike (☎ **954/977-4400**), cultivates more than 150 species of these colorful and delicate insects. In the park's walk-through, screened-in aviary, visitors can watch newborn butterflies emerge from their cocoons and flutter around as they learn to fly. It's open from 9am to 5pm Monday through Sunday. Admission is $12.95 for adults, $7.95 for kids 4 to 12, free for kids under 4.

ORGANIZED TOURS

BY BOAT   The Mississippi River–style steamer *Jungle Queen,* Bahia Mar Yacht Center, Florida A1A (☎ **954/462-5596**), is one of Fort Lauderdale's best-known attractions. Dinner cruises and 3-hour sightseeing tours take visitors up the New River past Millionaires' Row, Old Fort Lauderdale, the new downtown, and the Port Everglades cruise ship port. Call for prices and departure times.

✪ **Water Taxi of Fort Lauderdale,** 651 Seabreeze Blvd. (☎ **954/467-6677**), is a fleet of old port boats that navigate this city of canals. The boats operate taxi service on demand and carry up to 48 passengers each. You can be picked up at your hotel and shuttled to the dozens of restaurants and bars on the route for the rest of the night. The service operates daily from 10am to midnight or 2am. The cost is $7.50 per person per trip, $14 round-trip, $16 for a full day. Opt for the all-day pass—it's worth it.

BY TROLLEY BUS   **South Florida Trolley Tours** (☎ **954/946-7320**) covers Fort Lauderdale's entire history during a 90-minute air-conditioned trolley tour. Tours cost $12 for adults; children under 12 are free. The trolleys pick up passengers from most major hotels for three tours daily, at 9:30am, 12:05pm, and 2:10pm.

ON FOOT   The **Old Ft. Lauderdale Museum of History,** 231 SW Second Ave. (☎ **954/463-4431**) is open Tuesday to Friday from noon to 5pm, Saturday from 10am to 5pm, and Sunday from noon to 5pm. On occasion, walking tours of the city's historic center are offered. You can also walk along **Riverwalk,** a 10-mile linear park along the New River that connects the cultural heart of Fort Lauderdale to its historic district.

SHOPPING

Not counting the discount "fashion" stores on Hallandale Beach Boulevard, there are three places every visitor to Broward County should know about.

The first is **Antique Row,** a strip of U.S. 1 around North Dania Beach Boulevard (in Dania, about 1 mile south of Fort Lauderdale/Hollywood International Airport) that holds about 200 antique shops. Most shops are closed Sunday.

The **Fort Lauderdale Swap Shop,** 3291 W. Sunrise Blvd. (☎ **954/791-SWAP**), is one of the world's largest flea markets. In addition to endless acres of vendors, there's a mini–amusement park, a 13-screen drive-in movie theater, and even a free circus complete with elephants, horse shows, high-wire acts, and clowns. It's open daily.

Sawgrass Mills, 12801 W. Sunrise Blvd., Sunrise (☎ **954/846-2300**), a behemoth mall shaped like a Florida alligator, covers nearly 2.5 million square feet, including more than 300 shops and kiosks, such as Saks Fifth Avenue, Levi's, Ann Taylor, Waterford Crystal, and hundreds more, offering prices 20% to 60% lower than in the Caribbean. Take Interstate 95 North to 595 West until Flamingo Road, where you'll exit and turn right. Drive 2 miles to Sunrise Boulevard.

Not for bargain hunters, swanky **Las Olas Boulevard** hosts literally hundreds of unusual boutiques. Close to Fort Lauderdale Beach, the **Galleria** mall, 2414 E. Sunrise Blvd., between NE 26th Avenue and Middle River Drive (☎ **954/564-1015**), has Neiman-Marcus, Saks, Lord & Taylor, and many other stores.

ACCOMMODATIONS

Fort Lauderdale Beach has a hotel or motel on nearly every block, and the selection ranges from run-down to luxurious.

✪ **Hyatt Regency Fort Lauderdale** at Pier 66 Marina, 2301 SE 17th St. Causeway (☎ **800/233-1234** or 954/525-6666), is a circular landmark with larger rooms than some equivalently priced hotels in town. Its famous Piertop Lounge, a revolving bar on its roof, is often filled with cruise ship patrons.

Marriott's Harbor Beach Resort, 3030 Holiday Dr. (☎ **800/222-6543** or 954/525-4000), is the only Marriott resort set directly on the beach. Its modest-size bedrooms have water views.

Radisson Bahia Mar Beach Resort, 801 Seabreeze Blvd. (☎ **800/327-8154** or 954/764-2233), is scattered over 42 acres of seacoast. A four-story row of units is adjacent to Florida's largest marina. **The Riverside Hotel,** 620 E. Las Olas Blvd. (☎ **800/325-3280** or 954/467-0671), which opened in 1936, is a local favorite. Try for a ground-floor room, which has higher ceilings and more space.

La Casa del Mar Bed & Breakfast, 3003 Grand Granada St. (☎ **800/739-0009** or 954/467-2037), a 10-room Spanish-inspired inn, appeals to the bed-and-breakfast fancier and is only a block away from Fort Lauderdale Beach. **The Pillars Waterfront Inn,** 111 N. Birch Rd. (☎ **954/467-9639**), is a small, 23-room inn, the best of its size in the region. The clean and simple accommodations have very comfortable beds. Call the **Fort Lauderdale Convention and Visitors Bureau** (☎ **954/765-4466**) for a copy of *Superior Small Lodgings,* a guide to other accommodations in the area.

A number of chains operate here, including **Best Western** (☎ 800 528-1234), **Days Inn** (☎ 800/325-2525), **Doubletree Hotels** (☎ 800/222-8733), and **Holiday Inn** (☎ 800/465-4329).

DINING

The only restaurant at Port Everglades, ✪ **Burt & Jacks,** at Berth 23 (☎ **954/522-2878**), is a collaboration between actor-director Burt Reynolds and restaurateur Jack Jackson. As you sit at this elegant restaurant, you can watch the cruise ships and other boats pass by. A waiter will arrive with steaks, lobster, veal, pork chops, and more; you choose, and your dish will arrive perfectly cooked. Reservations are required and so are jackets for men.

Bahia Cabana Beach Resort, 3001 Harbor Dr. (☎ **954/524-1555**), offers American-style meals three times a day in hearty portions. The hotel's bar, known for its Frozen Rumrunner, is the most charming and laid-back in town.

In the shadow of the Hyatt Pier 66 Hotel, **California Café,** Pier 66, 2301 SE 17th Causeway (☎ **954/728-8255**), serves avant-garde modern cuisine at affordable prices.

Cap's Place, 2765 NE 28th Court, in Lighthouse Point (☎ **954/941-0418**), is a famous old-time seafood joint, offering good food at reasonable prices. The restaurant is on a peninsula; you get a ferry ride over. Dolphin (not the mammal but a local saltwater fish also known as mahimahi) and grouper are popular, and like the other meat and pasta dishes here, can be prepared any way you want.

Evangeline, 211 Hwy. A1A at Las Olas Boulevard (☎ **954/522-7001**), as the name suggests, is a Cajun-style place. At lunch, enjoy an oyster or catfish po' boy, or rabbit gumbo for dinner. You can also try the alligator.

Il Tartufo, 2400 E. Las Olas Blvd. (☎ **954/767-9190**), is the most charming and fun Italian restaurant in Fort Lauderdale. It serves oven-roasted specialties and other Italian standards, plus a selection of fish baked in rock salt.

Mark's Las Olas, 1032 E. Las Olas Blvd. (☎ **954/463-1000**), is the showcase of Miami restaurant mogul Mark Militello. The daily changing menu is continental gourmet and might include Jamaican jerk chicken with fresh coconut salad or a superb sushi-quality tuna.

Zanzbar, 602 E. Las Olas Blvd. (☎ **954/767-3377**), serves the food and wine of South Africa, and not many places can boast that. For a taste of the country, order a sample platter for two that includes ostrich tips, cured beef strips, and savory sausages.

Garlic crabs are the specialty at the **Rustic Inn Crabhouse,** 4331 Ravenswood Rd. (☎ **954/584-1637**), located west of the airport. This riverside dining choice has an open deck over the water.

FORT LAUDERDALE AFTER DARK

From the area's most famous bar, the ✪ **Piertop Lounge,** in the Hyatt Regency at Pier 66 (☎ **954/525-6666**), you'll get a 360° panoramic view of Fort Lauderdale. The bar turns every 66 minutes. There's a dance floor and live music, including blues and jazz.

On weekends it's hard to get into **Club M,** 2037 Hollywood Blvd. (☎ **954/ 925-8396**), one of the area's busiest music bars. Although the small club used to be a local blues showcase, it now features a DJ and live bands on weekends playing blues, rock, and jazz.

O'Hara Pub & Sidewalk Café, 722 E. Las Olas Blvd. (☎ **954/524-1764**), is often packed with a trendy crowd who come to listen to live blues and jazz. Call its jazz hot line (☎ **954/524-2801**) to hear the lineup.

If you want to dance, try the **Baja Beach Club,** 3200 N. Federal Hwy. (☎ **954/ 563-8494**), perhaps the world's only dance club that anchors an entire shopping mall.

With the 1991 completion of the **Broward Center for the Performing Arts,** 201 SW Fifth Ave. (☎ **954/462-0222**), Fort Lauderdale finally got itself the venue it craved for top opera, symphony, dance, and Broadway productions. Look for listings in the *Sun-Sentinel* or the *Miami Herald* for schedules and performers or call the 24-hour **Arts & Entertainment Hotline** (☎ **954/357-5700**).

3 Cape Canaveral & Port Canaveral

Underrated Port Canaveral is Florida's most unusual and multifaceted port, with facilities that are the most up-to-date, stylish, and least congested of any port in Florida. After years of underutilization, the cruise industry is starting to give the port the

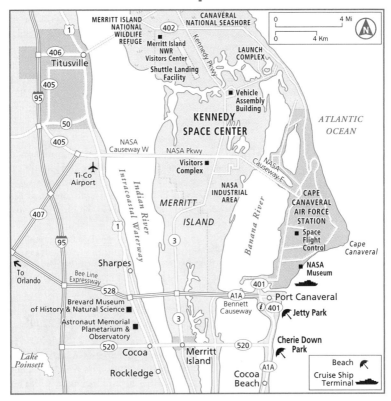

attention it's due. With the competition between a stronger Premier, an expanded Disney product, Carnival, and Royal Caribbean, Port Canaveral's 3-to-4-day-cruise market continues to remain strong and keeps this port on the map. Cruise lines appreciate the port's proximity to Cape Canaveral's Kennedy Space Center and Walt Disney World at Orlando. Many lines offer pre- or postcruise packages.

The 3,300-acre port covers an area larger than the Port of Miami. Terminal no. 9/10, completed in 1995, was built in a modern, dramatic style. Terminal no. 5, built in 1991, looks a bit like a glossy downtown hotel. The new Disney terminal, no. 8, the port's newest, was built in 1998 in an updated, Disneyfied art-deco style. The other terminals are more the traditional, industrial-looking kind. On the drawing boards is a fourth mega cruise ship terminal, no. 6/7. As you head for your cruise ship, look for shrimp- and fishnets drying in the sun. This port is the home base for the region's fishing industry.

GETTING TO CAPE CANAVERAL & THE PORT

Port Canaveral is located at the Cape Canaveral side of the Bennett Causeway on the 528 Bee Line Expressway. For information about the port, call the **Canaveral Port Authority** at ☎ **407/783-7831.**

BY AIR   The nearest airport is the **Orlando International Airport** (☎ **407/ 825-2001**), a 45-mile drive from Port Canaveral via Highway 528 (the Bee Line Expressway). Cruise line representatives will meet you if you've booked air and/or transfers through the line. **Cocoa Beach Shuttle** (☎ **800/633-0427** or 407/ 784-3831) offers shuttle service between Orlando's airport and Port Canaveral; the trip costs $20 per person each way.

BY CAR   Port Canaveral and Cocoa Beach are about 35 miles southeast of Orlando and 190 miles north of Miami. They're accessible from virtually every interstate highway along the east coast. Most visitors arrive via Route 1, Interstate 95, or Highway 528 (the Bee Line Expressway from Orlando). At the port, park in the North Lots for north terminals nos. 5 and 10 and the South Lots for nos. 2, 3, or 4. Parking costs $7 a day.

BY TRAIN   Amtrak (☎ **800/USA-RAIL**) trains make stops at Kissimmee, Sanford, and Orlando, the closest points to the port, but still about 55 to 60 miles away. You'll have to rent a car or take a taxi to the port. The **Kissimmee railway station** is at 316 Pleasant St. (☎ **407/933-1170;** corner of Dakin Street and Thurman Street). The **Orlando station** is at 1400 Sligh Blvd. (☎ **407/843-7611**), between Columbia and Miller streets.

EXPLORING CAPE CANAVERAL

Most passengers spend only a night or two in Cocoa Beach, visiting the Kennedy Space Center and going to the beach, before rushing to nearby Orlando and Walt Disney World.

VISITOR INFORMATION   Contact the **Cocoa Beach Chamber of Commerce,** 400 Fortenberry Rd., Merritt Island, FL 32952 (☎ **407/459-2200**).

GETTING AROUND   For taxis, call **Comfort Travel** (☎ **800/567-6139,** 407/784-8294, or 407/799-0442). Buses are run by the **Space Coast Area Transit Authority (SCAT)** (☎ **407/633-1878** for information and schedules). A ticket costs $1 for adults, 50¢ for senior citizens, and is free for children under 6. No buses pass close to the port.

✪ TOURING THE JOHN F. KENNEDY SPACE CENTER

Set amid many square miles of marshy wetlands favored by birds, reptiles, and amphibians, the **John F. Kennedy Space Center Visitor Complex** (☎ **407/ 452-2121**), open Monday through Friday from 8am to 5:30pm, has played an important role in the minds of people around the world as the cradle of the space age and a symbol of America's technological prowess. Even if you've never really considered yourself a science buff, you'll appreciate the sheer grandeur of the place and the achievements represented by the facilities here. A $120-million renovation of the site, completed in 1999, has sparked it with new life, making it more appealing for visitors than ever. The visitor center stands with an isolated, even eerie, dignity within the municipality of the Space Center.

The sheer scope of the site can be confusing, even baffling, without some guidance from the organization's official caretakers. Parking is free in any of the vast lots nearby. (Remember to note the location of your car!) It's best to make a stop—maps and advice are free—at a highly visible booth, Information Central, within the visitor center. It maintains the same hours (9am to 5:30pm daily except Christmas and some launch days) as the complex itself. Expect to spend a full day on-site to best experience the wealth of options.

The core of the site revolves around the visitor center, site of the **Rocket Garden,** which displays the now-obsolete shells of at least eight space rockets that during their heydays were the hottest things in the world of astrophysics. There are also hundreds of exhibitions and a timeline of photographs detailing humankind's

Wanna See a Launch?

There are only about a dozen launches from the Kennedy Space Center every year, so chances are you won't catch one. Still, you never know. Call ☎ **407/449-4322** for schedule information; it costs $10 to get on the property. During launch days, some parts of the complex, including Launch Complex 39 and its Observation Gantry, are firmly closed to everyone except NASA insiders.

exploration of space. The visitor center is also home to two IMAX theaters that show three separate films, each about 45 minutes long.

Some visitors pressed for time opt to remain entirely within the center, which does not charge admission. But for a more complete insight into the space age, take a bus tour of the complicated subdivisions that rise from the hundreds of acres of marshy flatlands nearby. Self-guided and self-timed, they depart at 15-minute intervals. Each bus is equipped with video screens portraying great moments of the space program's past. Tours make stops at three pivotal points within the complex, the Apollo Saturn V Center, Launch Complex 39, and the International Space Station Center.

The most comprehensive visitor package is the **Crew Pass.** Priced at $26 for adults, and $20 for children aged 4 to 11, free for children under 4, it includes unlimited access to any of the tour buses and entrance to any one of the ongoing IMAX movies. The Maximum Access Badge pass combines the Kennedy Space Center tour with two IMAX movies at $26 for adults and $20 for kids. The tour itself, without access to any of the IMAX theaters, costs $14 for adults and $10 for children under 11. Admission to the visitor center itself is free. Individual IMAX films are $7.50 each per adult, and $5.50 per child under 11. Most major credit cards are accepted throughout the complex.

There's a handful of fast-food, theme-parkish eateries adjacent to the visitor center. Among the cheapest and least formal of the bunch is something called The Launch Pad, serving family-friendly burgers and hot dogs. Better-recommended is Mila's, a fancy diner serving American-style platters, sandwiches, and salads.

ANOTHER SPACE-RELATED ATTRACTION

Six miles west of the Kennedy Space Center is the **U.S. Astronaut Hall of Fame,** State Rd. 405, 6225 Vectorspace Blvd., Titusville (☎ **407/269-6100**), a satellite attraction founded by the astronauts who flew the first *Mercury* and *Gemini* missions into outer space. It contains space-program memorabilia, displayed with a decidedly human and anecdotal touch. It's open daily from 9am to 5pm. Admission is $13.95 for adults, $9.95 for kids 6 to 12, and free for children 5 and under.

HITTING THE BEACH

Cocoa Beach, Merritt Island, and the surrounding landscapes are known as "The Space Coast," and most of the beaches there are called "parks." Here are my favorites.

Jetty Park, 400 E. Jetty Rd., near the port, is more like a Florida version of Coney Island than the parks described below. The area has been recently renovated. A massive stone asphalt-topped jetty juts seaward as protection for the mouth of Port Canaveral. You'll see dozens of anglers there waiting for a bite. Parking costs $1 per car.

On the border between Cocoa Beach and Cape Canaveral, **Cherie Down Park,** 8492 Ridgewood Ave., is a relatively tranquil sunning and swimming area. You'll find a boardwalk, as well as showers, picnic shelters, and a public rest room. Parking is $1 per car.

Set in the heart of Cocoa Beach, **Lori Wilson Park,** 1500 N. Atlantic Ave., has children's playgrounds and a boardwalk that extends through about 5 acres of protected grasslands. Parking is $1 per car. Next to it is **Fischer Park,** with public rest rooms and a seasonal scattering of food kiosks. Parking is $2 per car.

The region's best surfing is at **Robert P. Murkshe Memorial Park,** SR A1A and 16th streets, Cocoa Beach, which also has a boardwalk and public rest rooms.

SHOPPING

Cocoa Beach offers a wide array of shopping, but the most unique shopping experience is **Ron Jon Surf Shop,** 4151 N. Atlantic Ave., Cocoa Beach, as you're driving down Florida AIA. The wildly original art-deco building is more interesting than the merchandise, but if you're looking for a surfing souvenir, you'll find it here. The store also rents beach bikes, boogie boards, surfboards, in-line skates, and other fun stuff by the hour, day, or week. It's open 24 hours a day.

ACCOMMODATIONS

Closest to the port and the Kennedy Space Center is the ✪ **Radisson Resort at the Port,** 8701 Astronaut Blvd. (☎ **800/333-3333** or 407/784-0000). The bedrooms are comfortable, but not as wonderful as those at The Inn at Cocoa Beach (see below). Chain hotels in the area include the **Cocoa Beach Hilton,** 1550 N. Atlantic Ave. (A1A) (☎ **800/HILTONS** or 407/799-0003); the **Holiday Inn Cocoa Beach Ocean Front Resort,** 1300 N. Atlantic Ave. (☎ **800/206-2747** or 407/783-2271), more upscale and better designed than the average Holiday Inn; and the **Howard Johnson Express Hotel/Cocoa Beach,** 2082 N. Atlantic Ave. (☎ **800/654-2000** or 321/783-8855).

Between the sea and route AIA and behind Ron Jon Surf Shop, ✪ **The Inn at Cocoa Beach,** 4300 Ocean Beach Blvd. (☎ **800/343-5307** or 407/799-3460), is more of an upscale, personalized inn than a traditional hotel (it even calls itself an oversize bed-and-breakfast). A taxi from Port Canaveral to the inn will cost around $12 to $15. Call **Comfort Taxi** at ☎ **407/799-0442.**

DINING

In the heart of Cocoa Beach, **Bernard's Surf,** 2 S. Atlantic Ave. (☎ **407/783-2401**), has been a Florida institution since 1948. Specializing in steaks and seafood, the name "Bernard's Surf" should be followed by "and Turf"—it's a carnivore's paradise. The walls are adorned with pictures of astronauts who have celebrated their safe return to Earth with a filet mignon here.

Near the port is **Flamingo's,** in the Radisson Resort at the port, 8701 Astronaut Blvd. (☎ **407/784-0000**). The fish dishes here are the best around the port, made with top-notch ingredients and deftly prepared.

✪ **The Mango Tree,** 118 N. Atlantic Ave. (☎ **407/799-0513**), is the most beautiful and sophisticated restaurant in Cocoa Beach. Indian River crab cakes are perfectly flavored, and the sesame-seed-encrusted grouper with a tropical fruit salsa is yummy.

PORT CANAVERAL AFTER DARK

The Pier, 401 Meade Ave. (☎ **407/783-7549**), is the largest and busiest entertainment complex in Cocoa Beach, crowded every afternoon and evening with diners, drinkers, and sunset-watchers. Two open-air cafes, four bars, and a pair of restaurants jut 800 feet beyond the shoreline into the waves and surf. At **Marlin's Good Times Bar and Grill,** you can enjoy fish platters, drinks, or sandwiches and a view of the sea that practically engulfs you. One or sometimes two bands play live 6 nights a week.

In Cocoa Beach's Heidelberg restaurant, the smoky and noisy **Heidi's Jazz Club,** 7 N. Orlando Ave. (☎ **407/783-6806**), offers jazz and classic blues.

4 Tampa & the Port of Tampa

The Port of Tampa is set amid a complicated network of channels and harbors near the historic Cuban enclave of Ybor City and its deepwater Ybor Channel. The port's position on the western (Gulf) side of Florida makes it the logical departure point for ships headed for westerly ports of call, including the beaches and Mayan ruins of the Yucatán, the aquatic reefs of Central America, and the ports of Venezuela. The port's safe harbors have kept ships secure even during devastating tropical storms.

The bulk of the port's 400,000-plus annual passengers makes their way through the modern **Garrison Seaport cruise terminal** no. 2, which was doubled in size in 1998. The 30-acre site also includes the constantly evolving **Channelside,** a massive complex of restaurants, theaters, and shops inspired by Baltimore's Inner Harbor complex. This hub of waterfront activity and entertainment includes the Florida Aquarium and a multiscreen theater complex.

GETTING TO TAMPA & THE PORT

The **Garrison Seaport Terminal** at the Port of Tampa is located at 1101 Channelside Drive. For information, call ☎ **813/905-5044.**

BY AIR   Tampa International Airport (☎ **813/870-8700**) lies 5 miles northwest of downtown Tampa, near the junction of Florida 60 and Memorial Highway. If you haven't arranged transfers with the cruise line, the port is an easy 15-minute taxi ride away; the fare is $10 to $15 via **Central Florida Limo** (☎ **813/ 396-3730**). Travel Ways (☎ **813/643-5533**) also runs a bus service, which costs $16 per person from the airport to Garrison Terminal.

BY CAR   Tampa lies 200 miles southwest of Jacksonville, 63 miles north of Sarasota, and 254 miles northwest of Miami. It's easily accessible from Interstate 275, Interstate 75, Interstate 4, U.S. 41, U.S. 92, U.S. 301, and many state roads. The port has ample parking with good security, and costs $8 per day.

BY TRAIN   Amtrak (☎ **800/USA-RAIL**) trains arrive at the Tampa Amtrak Station, 601 Nebraska Ave., Tampa (☎ **813/221-7601**). Taxi fare to the port costs $5 to $7.

EXPLORING TAMPA

Tampa is best explored by car, as only the commercial district can be covered on foot. If you want to go to the beach, you'll have to head to neighboring St. Petersburg.

VISITOR INFORMATION   Contact the **Tampa/Hillsborough Convention and Visitors Association, Inc. (THCVA),** 400 North Tampa St., Suite 1010, Tampa, FL 33602 (☎ **800/44-TAMPA** or 813/223-2752). You can also stop by the **Tampa Bay Visitor Information Center,** 3601 E. Busch Blvd. (☎ **813/985-3601**), north of downtown in the Busch Gardens area. The office books organized tours of Tampa and the rest of Florida.

GETTING AROUND   Taxis in Tampa do not normally cruise the streets for fares; instead, they line up at public loading places. You can also call **Yellow Cab** (☎ **813/253-0121**) or **United Cab** (☎ **813/253-2424** or 813/251-5555).

The **Hillsborough Area Regional Transit/HARTline** (☎ 813/254-HART) provides regularly scheduled bus service between downtown Tampa and the suburbs. Fares are $1.15 for local services and $1.50 for express routes; exact change is required.

✪ BUSCH GARDENS

Yes, admission prices are high, but Busch Gardens remains Tampa Bay's most popular attraction. The 335-acre family entertainment park, at 3000 E. Busch Blvd. (☎ **888/800-5447** or 813/987-5171), features thrill rides, animal habitats, live entertainment, shops, restaurants, and games. The park's zoo ranks among the best in the country, with nearly 3,400 animals.

In 1996, Busch Gardens opened Montu, the world's tallest and longest inverted roller coaster. It's part of **Egypt,** the park's ninth themed area. The area includes a replica of King Tutankhamen's tomb, plus a sand-dig area for kids.

Timbuktu is a replica of an ancient desert trading center, complete with African craftspeople at work. It also features a sandstorm ride, Dolphin theater with daily shows, a boat-swing ride, a roller coaster, and an electronic-games arcade. **Morocco,** a walled city with exotic architecture, has Moroccan craft demonstrations, a sultan's tent with snake charmers, and the Marrakech Theaters. The **Serengeti Plain** is an open area with more than 500 African animals roaming freely in herds. This 80-acre natural grassy veldt can be viewed from the tram ride, the Trans-Veldt Railway, or the Skyride.

Nairobi is home to a natural habitat for various species of gorillas and chimpanzees, a baby-animal nursery, a petting zoo, reptile displays, and Curiosity Caverns, where visitors can observe animals active at night. **Stanleyville,** a prototype African village, has a shopping bazaar and live entertainment, as well as two water rides: the Tanganyika Tidal Wave and Stanley Falls. **The Congo** features white-water raft rides, as well as Kumba, the largest steel roller coaster in the southeastern United States, and Claw Island, a display of rare white Bengal tigers in a natural setting.

Bird Gardens, the original core of Busch Gardens, offers rich foliage, lagoons, and a free-flight aviary holding hundreds of exotic birds, including golden and American bald eagles, hawks, owls, and falcons. This area also features Land of the Dragons, a new children's adventure area.

Crown Colony, a multilevel restaurant overlooking the Serengeti plains, is the home of a team of Clydesdale horses, as well as the Anheuser-Busch hospitality center. Akbar's Adventure Tours, which offers a flight-simulator adventure experience, is located here.

A 1-day ticket costs $45.70 for adults, $36.75 for children ages 3 to 9; kids 2 and under are free. The park is open daily from 9am through 7pm, with extended hours in summer and during holiday periods. To get here, take Interstate 275 northeast of downtown to Busch Boulevard (Exit 33), and go east 2 miles to the entrance on 40th Street (McKinley Avenue). Parking costs $6.

MORE ATTRACTIONS

Only steps from the newly built Garrison Seaport Center, the ✪ **Florida Aquarium** (☎ 813/273-4000) celebrates the role of water in the development and maintenance of Florida's topography and ecosystems, with more than 10,000 aquatic plants and animals. An overriding theme follows a drop of water as it bubbles through Florida limestone and wends its way to the sea.

Tampa at a Glance

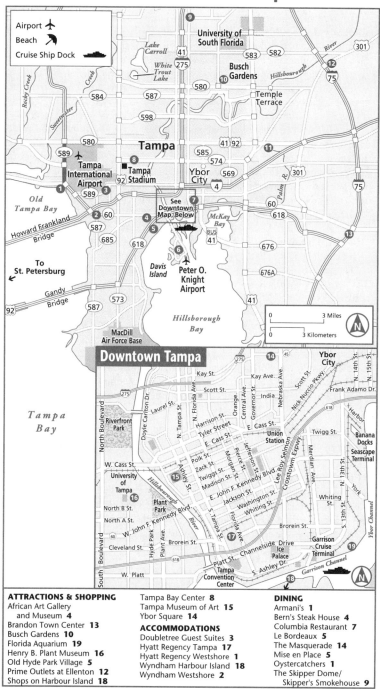

Map Legend:
- Airport ✈
- Beach ✔
- Cruise Ship Dock ⛴

Lake Carroll
White Trout Lake
University of South Florida 9
Busch Gardens 10
583 582
Hillsborough River
301
75 12
Temple Terrace
580
Rocky Creek
Sweetwater Creek
584
587
598
580
589 ✈
Tampa
585 574
41 92
11
Ybor City
Palm R.
301
Tampa International Airport 1
Tampa Stadium 8
92
589 3
569
4
75
Old Tampa Bay
2 60
587
685
618
4
5
See Downtown Map Below 7
McKay Bay
BUS 41
60
618
13
Howard Frankland Bridge
To St. Petersburg
Davis Island
6 ✈
Peter O. Knight Airport
676
676A
Gandy Bridge
92
573
587
41
Hillsborough Bay
MacDill Air Force Base

0 ——— 3 Miles
0 ——— 3 Kilometers
N

Downtown Tampa

275
14 45
Kay St.
Kay Ave.
Scott St.
Scott Ave.
India
Nebraska Ave.
Nick Nuccio Pkwy.
Scott St.
Ybor City
N. 14th St.
N. 15th St.
Frank Adamo Dr.
Tampa Bay
Riverfront Park
Doyle Carlton Dr.
North Boulevard
N. Florida Ave.
N. Tampa Ave.
Laurel St.
Harrison St.
Tyler Street
E. Cass St.
Polk St.
Zack St.
Orange
Central Ave.
Governor St.
E. Cass St.
Union Station
Lee Roy Selmon
Crosstown Expwy.
Twiggs St.
618
Harbor
Banana Docks
Seascape Terminal
W. Cass St.
University of Tampa
15
Ashley St.
Pierce St.
Morgan St.
Jefferson St.
Madison St.
Twiggs St.
E. John F. Kennedy Blvd.
Jackson St.
S. Tampa St.
Florida Ave.
Washington St.
Whiting St.
Meridan Ave.
Whiting St.
N. 13th St.
York
Ybor Channel
North B St.
16
Plant Park
Hillsborough River
North A St.
Hyde Park
Plant Ave.
W. John F. Kennedy Blvd.
Brorein St.
Brorein St.
17
Washington St.
Garrison Cruise Terminal
19
South Boulevard
60
Cleveland St.
618
Platt St.
Channelside Drive
Ice Palace
S. Ashley Dr.
Garrison Channel
W. Platt
Tampa Convention Center
18
N

ATTRACTIONS & SHOPPING
African Art Gallery and Museum 4
Brandon Town Center 13
Busch Gardens 10
Florida Aquarium 19
Henry B. Plant Museum 16
Old Hyde Park Village 5
Prime Outlets at Ellenton 12
Shops on Harbour Island 18
Tampa Bay Center 8
Tampa Museum of Art 15
Ybor Square 14

ACCOMMODATIONS
Doubletree Guest Suites 3
Hyatt Regency Tampa 17
Hyatt Regency Westshore 1
Wyndham Harbour Island 18
Wyndham Westshore 2

DINING
Armani's 1
Bern's Steak House 4
Columbia Restaurant 7
Le Bordeaux 5
The Masquerade 14
Mise en Place 5
Oystercatchers 1
The Skipper Dome/ Skipper's Smokehouse 9

51

Thirteen silver minarets and distinctive Moorish architecture make the stunning
✪ **Henry B. Plant Museum,** 401 W. Kennedy Blvd. (☎ **813/254-1891**), the focal
point of the Tampa skyline. This National Historic Landmark, built in 1891 as the
511-room Tampa Bay Hotel, is filled with European and Oriental furnishings, and
decorative arts from the original hotel collection. Definitely a worthwhile trip.

Only about a mile or so from the cruise ship docks, a visit to **Ybor City,** Tampa's
historic Latin enclave and one of only three national historic districts in Florida, is
a must. Once known as the cigar capital of the world, Ybor offers a charming slice
of the past with its Spanish architecture, antique street lamps, wrought-iron balconies, ornate grillwork, and renovated cigar factories. Stroll along Seventh Avenue,
the main artery (closed off to traffic at night), where you'll find cigar shops, boutiques, nightclubs, and the famous 100-year-old **Columbia Restaurant,** a classic
covered in tiles and lots of historic character, serving up paella, Cuban sandwiches,
seafood, and other local favorites. **Walking tours** of Ybor City are available, call the
Ybor City Museum, 1818 E. Ninth Ave. (☎ **813/247-6323**), for more info.

The **African Art Gallery and Museum,** 1711 W. Kennedy Blvd. (☎ **813/
258-0223**), features visual art by and about people of African descent. The collection includes ancient African artifacts and modern carvings and furniture.

The permanent collection of the **Tampa Museum of Art,** 600 N. Ashley Dr.
(☎ **813/274-8130**), is especially strong in ancient Greek, Etruscan, and Roman
artifacts, as well as 20th-century art. The museum grounds, fronting the Hillsborough River, contain a sculpture garden and a decorative fountain.

In St. Petersburg, the ✪ **Salvador Dalí Museum,** 1000 Third St. S. (☎ **727/
823-3767**), contains the largest assemblage of the artist's works outside Spain. The
former marine warehouse that houses this widely divergent collection is as starkly
modern as the works of art displayed within. It's open Monday to Saturday from
9:30am to 5:30pm (Thurs till 8pm), Sunday from noon to 5:30pm. The entrance
fee is $9 for adults, $7 for senior citizens, $5 for students, and free for children
under 10.

ORGANIZED TOURS

BY BUS   Swiss Chalet Tours, 3601 E. Busch Blvd. (☎ **813/985-3601**), operates guided tours of Tampa, Ybor City, and the surrounding region. Four-hour
(10am to 2pm) tours run on Monday and Thursday, and cost $40 for adults, $35
for children. Seven-hour tours (10am to 5pm) cost $70 for adults and $65 for children. You can also book full-day tours to most Orlando theme parks, including
MGM Studios, Walt Disney World, and Sea World, as well as to the Kennedy Space
Center, Cypress Gardens, Universal Studios, and Islands of Adventure.

HITTING THE BEACH

You have to start at St. Petersburg, across the bay, for a north-to-south string of
interconnected white sandy shores. Most beaches have rest rooms, refreshment
stands, and picnic areas. You can either park on the street at meters (usually 25¢ for
each half hour) or at one of the four major parking lots, located from north to south
at Sand Key Park (in Clearwater), beside Gulf Boulevard (also known as Route
699), just south of the Clearwater Pass Bridge; Redington Shores Beach Park, beside
Gulf Boulevard at 182nd Street; Treasure Island Park, on Gulf Boulevard just north
of 108th Avenue; and St. Pete Beach Park, beside Gulf Boulevard at 46th Street.

St. Petersburg Municipal Beach lies in the town of Treasure Island. **Clearwater Beach,** with its silky sands, is the place for beach volleyball. Water-sports rentals,
lifeguards, rest rooms, showers, and concessions are available. The swimming is

excellent, and there's a pier for fishing. Parking is $10 a day in gated lots (or $1.50 an hour.).

If you want to shop as well as tan, consider **Madeira Beach,** midway between St. Petersburg and Clearwater, with a boardwalk, T-shirt emporiums, and ice-cream parlors.

Honeymoon Island isn't great for swimming, but it has its own rugged beauty and a fascinating nature trail. From here, you can catch a ferry to **Caladesi Island State Park,** a 3^1/$_2$-mile stretch of sand at 3 Causeway Blvd. in Dunedin (☎ **727/469-5942** for information).

You can also go south to **Fort Desoto Park,** 3500 Pinellas Bayway S. (☎ **727/ 866-2484**), consisting of 1,136 acres and 7 miles of waterfront exposed to both the Gulf of Mexico and a brackish channel. There are fishing piers, shaded picnic areas, a bird-and-animal sanctuary, campsites, and a partially ruined fort near the park's southwestern tip. Take Interstate 275 South to the Pinellas Bayway (Exit 4) and follow the signs.

SHOPPING

On and around **Seventh Avenue in Ybor City,** you'll find lots of cigar stores selling handmade stogies as well as a variety of interesting boutiques and shops. At press time, a new shopping complex at 1600 E. 7th Ave. called Centro Ybor was about to open, with six restaurants, 30 new stores, a 20-screen movie theater, and a high-tech entertainment center called GameWorks, sponsored by Steven Spielberg's Dreamworks and Universal Studios.

Upscale stores are located in **Old Hyde Park Village,** an outdoor, European-style market at Swann and Dakota avenues near Bayshore Boulevard (☎ **813/ 251-3500**). **The Shops on Harbour Island,** 601 S. Harbour Island Blvd. (☎ **813/ 202-1830**), are set on an island off the coast of Tampa's commercial heart.

Malls include the **Brandon Town Center,** at the intersection of State Road 60 and Interstate 75, and the city's largest mall, **Tampa Bay Center,** Himes Avenue and Martin Luther King, Jr. Boulevard. You'll find substantial discounts at the **Prime Outlets at Ellenton,** 5461 Factory Shops Blvd., at the junction of Interstate 75 and Highway 301 (☎ **941/723-1150**).

ACCOMMODATIONS

TAMPA   Each handsomely furnished accommodation at the **Doubletree Guest Suites,** 11310 N. 30th St. (☎ **800/222-TREE** or 813/971-7690), contains two separate rooms, one with a wet bar and small refrigerator.

There are two Tampa Hyatts: the **Hyatt Regency Tampa,** Two Tampa City Center at 211 N. Tampa St. (☎ **800/233-1234** or 813/225-1234), which towers over Tampa's commercial center; and the ✪ **Hyatt Regency Westshore,** 6200 Courtney Campbell Causeway (☎ **800/233-1234** or 813/874-1234), at the Tampa end of the long causeway traversing Tampa Bay. At the Westshore, some Spanish-style townhouses/villas are set about a half mile from the main hotel building.

Three miles south of Tampa International Airport is **Wyndham Westshore,** 4860 W. Kennedy Blvd. (☎ **800/822-4200** or 813/286-4400), Tampa's most stylish modern hotel. The 11-story building is modeled after a butterfly.

Wyndham Harbour Island, 725 S. Harbour Island Blvd. (☎ **800/822-4200** or 813/229-5000), sits on one of Tampa Bay's most elegant residential islands.

ST. PETERSBURG   The ✪ **Don CeSar Beach Resort and Spa,** 3400 Gulf Blvd. (☎ **800/282-1116** or 727/360-1881), is the most famous landmark in town. This pink-sided Moorish/Mediterranean fantasy, listed on the National

Register of Historic Places, sits on 7^1/$_2$ acres of beachfront. Guest rooms are first-rate, usually with water views. Also in St. Pete, ✪ **Stouffer Renaissance Vinoy Resort,** 501 Fifth Ave. NE at Beach Drive (☎ **800/HOTELS1** or 813/894-1000), reigns as the grande dame of the region's hotels. Accommodations in the new wing ("The Tower") are slightly larger than those in the hotel's original core.

DINING

On the 14th floor of the Hyatt Regency Westshore Hotel, **Armani's,** 6200 Courtney Campbell Causeway (☎ **813/874-1234**), is a stylish northern Italian restaurant. Jackets are required.

The steaks at ✪ **Bern's Steak House,** 1208 S. Howard Ave. (☎ **813/251-2421**), are close to perfect. You order according to thickness and weight.

Le Bordeaux, 1502 S. Howard Ave. (☎ **813/254-4387**), presents competent French food at reasonable prices. The changing menu often includes bouillabaisse and fillet of beef with Roquefort sauce.

In Ybor City, the nearly 100-year-old ✪ **Columbia Restaurant,** 2117 Seventh Ave. E., between 21st and 22nd streets (☎ **813/248-4961**), occupies an attractive tile-sheathed building that fills an entire city block, about a mile from the cruise docks. The aura is pre-Castro Cuba. The more simple your dish is, the better it's likely to be. Filet mignons, roasted pork, and the black beans, yellow rice, and plantains are flavorful and well prepared. Flamenco shows begin on the dance floor Monday through Saturday at 7:30pm.

At lunch, ✪ **Mise en Place,** 442 W. Kennedy Blvd. (☎ **813/254-5373**), serves an array of delicious sandwiches, as well as savory pastas, risottos, and platters. More formal dinners feature free-range chicken with smoked tomato coulis, and loin of venison with asparagus, tarragon mash, and red-onion balsamic marmalade.

The best fish in Tampa is served at **Oystercatchers,** in the Hyatt Regency Westshore Hotel complex, 6200 Courtney Campbell Causeway (☎ **813/874-1234**). Pick the fish you want from a glass-fronted buffet or enjoy mesquite-grilled steaks, chicken rollatini, and shellfish.

TAMPA AFTER DARK

Nightfall now transforms **Ybor City,** Tampa's century-old Latin Quarter, into a hotbed of music, ethnic food, poetry readings, and after-midnight coffee and dessert. Thousands crowd one of its main arteries, Seventh Avenue, Wednesday through Saturday evenings when its closed to all but pedestrian traffic. **The Masquerade,** 1503 E. Seventh Ave. (☎ **813/247-3319**), set within a 1940s movie palace, is the first of the many nightclubs that pepper the streets here.

Elsewhere, **The Skipper Dome/Skipper's Smokehouse,** 910 Skipper Rd. (☎ **813/971-0666**), is a favorite evening spot, with an all-purpose restaurant and bar (with oysters and fresh shellfish sold by the dozen and half dozen). For live music, head out back to the "Skipper Dome," a sprawling deck sheltered by a canopy of oak trees.

The Tampa/Hillsborough Arts Council maintains **Artsline** (☎ **813/229-ARTS**), a 24-hour information service about current and upcoming cultural events.

5 New Orleans & the Port of New Orleans

There's power and majesty in this historic port, 110 miles upriver from the Gulf of Mexico. By some yardsticks, it's the busiest port in the nation, servicing many vessels much larger than the cruise ships that call New Orleans home. Although the bulk of business conducted here mainly involves the transport of grains, ores,

Greater New Orleans

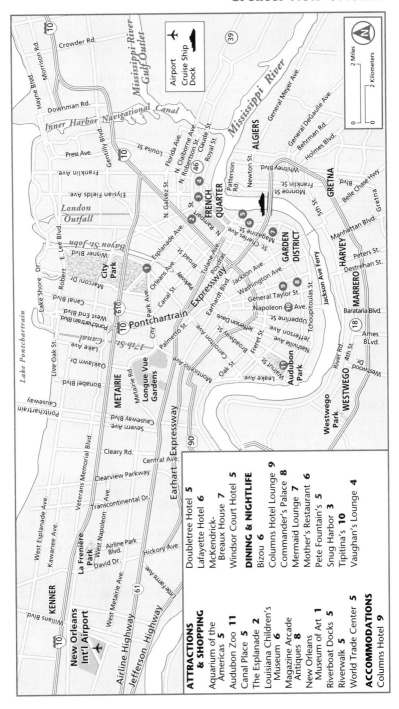

ATTRACTIONS & SHOPPING

Aquarium of the Americas **5**
Audubon Zoo **11**
Canal Place **5**
The Esplanade **2**
Louisiana Children's Museum **6**
Magazine Arcade Antiques **8**
New Orleans Museum of Art **1**
Riverboat Docks **5**
Riverwalk **5**
World Trade Center **5**

ACCOMMODATIONS

Columns Hotel **9**

Doubletree Hotel **5**
Lafayette Hotel **6**
McKendrick-Breaux House **7**
Windsor Court Hotel **5**

DINING & NIGHTLIFE

Bizou **6**
Columns Hotel Lounge **9**
Commander's Palace **8**
Mermaid Lounge **7**
Mother's Restaurant **6**
Pete Fountain's **5**
Snug Harbor **3**
Tipitina's **10**
Vaughan's Lounge **4**

mining byproducts, machinery, and building supplies, the city is poised for increased visibility as home port to a handful of cruise ships. Cruises from here are mainly bound for the western edge of the Caribbean, including the western "Mexican Riviera" and Cancún and Cozumel.

If you're boarding a cruise ship in New Orleans, it's almost certain your access will be through the Julia Street Cruise Ship Terminal on the Julia Street Wharf. Originally developed as part of the 1984 Louisiana World's Exposition, the cruise ship area was inaugurated in 1993, then doubled in size in 1996, and now one of the terminals is being expanded again to accommodate Carnival's *Inspiration,* which will make New Orleans its year-round home port in September of 2000. The docks lie near the commercial heart of town, a 10-minute walk from the edge of the French Quarter, or a short and convenient streetcar ride away.

GETTING TO NEW ORLEANS & ITS PORT

The port is at 1350 Port of New Orleans Place. For information, call the **Port of New Orleans** at ☎ **504/522-2551.**

BY AIR   New Orleans International Airport (☎ **504/464-0831**) is about 15 miles northwest of the port. Cruise line representatives meet all passengers who have booked transfers through the line. For those who haven't, a taxi to the port costs about $21 and takes about 20 minutes. **Airport Shuttle** (☎ **504/592-0555**) runs vans at 10- to 12-minute intervals from outside the airport's baggage claim to the port and other points in town. It costs $10 per passenger each way; free for children under 6.

BY CAR   Highways I-10, U.S. 90, U.S. 61, and Louisiana 25 (the Lake Pontchartrain causeway) lead directly to New Orleans. You can park your car in long-term parking at the port, but only for blocks of 1 week. Reserve parking directly with your cruise ship operator. You must present a boarding pass or ticket before parking.

BY TRAIN   Amtrak (☎ **800/USA-RAIL**) trains stop at the **Union Passenger Terminal** at 1001 Loyola Ave., in the central business district. Taxis are outside the passenger terminal's main entrance; the fare to the port is $6.

EXPLORING NEW ORLEANS

In many respects, the **French Quarter** *is* New Orleans, and many visitors never leave its confines. It's the oldest part of the city and still the most popular for sightseeing. But if you venture outside the French Quarter, you'll be able to feel the pulse of the city's commerce, see river activities that keep the city alive, stroll through spacious parks, drive or walk by the impressive homes of the Garden District, and get a firsthand view of the bayou/lake connection that explains why New Orleans grew up here in the first place.

VISITOR INFORMATION   Contact the **Greater New Orleans Convention and Visitors Bureau,** 1520 Sugar Bowl Dr., New Orleans, LA 70112 (☎ **504/566-5011;** www.neworleanscvb.com), for brochures, pamphlets, and information. Once you arrive, stop at the **New Orleans Welcoming Center,** 529 St. Ann St. in the French Quarter (☎ **800/672-6124**).

GETTING AROUND   Taxis are plentiful. If you're not near a taxi stand, call **United Cabs** (☎ **504/522-9771**), and a cab will come within 5 to 10 minutes. The meter begins at $2.10, and rises $1.20 per mile thereafter.

Streetcar lines run the length of St. Charles Avenue. They operate 24 hours a day and cost $1.25 per ride (you must have exact change). A transfer from streetcar to bus costs 25¢. Board at the corner of Canal and Carondelet streets in the French Quarter. A VisiTour Pass, which gives you unlimited rides on all streetcar and bus lines, sells for $5 for 1 day, $12 for 3 days.

Where the trolleys don't run, a **city bus** will. For route information, call ☎ **504/248-3900** or pick up a map at the Visitor Information Center (address above). Most buses charge $1.25 (plus 25¢ for a transfer) per ride, although some express buses charge $1.50.

A **Vieux Carré Minibus** takes you to French Quarter sights. The route is posted along Canal and Bourbon streets. The minibus operates weekdays between 5am and 6:30pm and weekends 8am to 6:30pm and costs $1.25.

From Jackson Square (at Decatur Street), you can take a 2¼-mile horse-drawn carriage ride through the French Quarter. **Royal Carriage Tour Co.** (☎ **504/943-8820**) offers group tours for $10 per person in open-topped surreys suitable for up to 10 passengers at a time, daily from 9am to midnight. Private rides for up to four passengers in a Cinderella carriage go for $50 a pop.

A **ferryboat** departs at frequent intervals from the foot of Canal Street, carrying cars ($1) and passengers (free) across the river to the Algiers section of town. A round-trip passage takes about 25 minutes.

SEEING THE SIGHTS

At the well-designed ✪ **Aquarium of the Americas,** 1 Canal St., at the Mississippi River (☎ **504/861-2537**), a 400,000-gallon tank holds a kaleidoscope of species from the deep waters of the nearby Gulf of Mexico.

You'll need at least 3 hours to visit the ✪ **Audubon Zoo,** 6500 Magazine St. (☎ **504/861-2537**), home to 1,500 animals in natural habitats. In a Louisiana swamp replication, alligators and other reptiles slither and hop among native birds and clusters of marsh grasses.

Despite its massive Doric columns and twin staircases, local architects nonetheless refer to **Beauregard-Keyes House,** 1113 Chartres St. (☎ **504/523-7257**), as a "Louisiana raised cottage." Built in 1826, it's one of the most impressive and socially prestigious structures in town.

Incorporating seven historic buildings connected by a brick courtyard, the ✪ **Historic New Orleans Collection,** 533 Royal St. (☎ **504/523-4662**), evokes New Orleans of 200 years ago. The oldest building in the complex escaped the tragic fire of 1794. The others hold exhibitions about Louisiana's culture and history.

Housed in a former granary 4 blocks from the river, the **Louisiana Children's Museum,** 420 Julia St. (☎ **504/523-1357**), divides its exhibits into activities for children over and under the age of 12. The Lab demonstrates principles of physics and math, motion, and inertia. Younger children can play in a simulated supermarket.

Musée Conti Wax Museum, 917 Conti St. (☎ **504/525-2605**), is the bayou equivalent of Madame Tussaud's, featuring pivotal figures in Louisiana history and legend. Look for the replicas of the notorious politico Huey Long, jazz meister Pete Fountain, Andrew Jackson, and Jean Lafitte. It's open daily from 10am to 8pm.

The collections of the **New Orleans Historic Voodoo Museum,** 724 Dumaine St. (☎ **504/523-7685**), celebrate the occult and the mixture of African and Catholic rituals first brought to New Orleans by slaves from Hispaniola. A gift shop and voodoo parlor are stocked with apothecary ingredients. Staff there can also provide you with psychic services. Admission is $7 for adults, $5.50 for college students and seniors, and $4.50 for high-school kids. It's open daily from 10am to

8pm. A **guided voodoo-and-cemetery walking tour** of the French Quarter departs from the museum daily at 10:30am and 1pm; tour of the undead departs at 8pm. These group tours (and others), as well as private customized tours, are led by a gal calling herself **Bloody Mary** (☎ **504/486-2080**), a folk historian and acclaimed storyteller. The walking tours are all $15 and include museum admission.

The collections of the **New Orleans Museum of Art (NOMA),** Lelong Avenue (☎ **504/488-2631**), span the centuries, with one floor devoted to ethnographic and non-Western art.

The ✪ **Old Absinthe House/Tony Moran's Restaurant,** 240 Bourbon St. (☎ **504/523-3181**), is the oldest bar in New Orleans, built in 1806 by two Spanish partners. Upstairs is a restaurant, Tony Moran's, open only for dinner (closed Sun).

The **World Trade Center of New Orleans,** 2 Canal St. (☎ **504/529-1601**), one of the tallest buildings in town, has the ✪ **Viewpoint** observation platform on its 31st floor. Check out the freighters, cruise ships, tug boats, submarines, and aircraft carriers that ply the swift-flowing waters of New Orleans's harbor. A cocktail lounge spins slowly on the 33rd floor.

ORGANIZED TOURS

ON FOOT   Friends of the Cabildo (☎ **504/523-3939**) lead 2-hour walking tours of Vieux Carré (the French Quarter). They leave from the Museum Store at 523 St. Ann St. every Tuesday through Sunday at 10am and 1:30pm, and Monday at 1:30pm, except holidays. Donations are expected: $10 per adult, and $8 for seniors over 65 and children ages 13 to 20 (kids under 12 are free).

Magic Walking Tours (☎ **504/588-9693**) offers theme tours associated with the city's cemeteries, its Garden District, and its voodoo traditions. Two-hour tours cost $13 per person ($10 for seniors and students).

You can see historic interiors on a **Hidden Treasures Tour** (☎ **504/529-4507**); $20 per person by reservation.

BY BOAT   The paddle wheeler *Creole Queen* (☎ **504/524-0814**), departs from the Poydras Street Wharf, adjacent to the Riverwalk mall, every day at 10:30am for a 2¹/₂-hour waterborne tour. Riverwalk is at the end of Canal Street; the wharf is about 2 blocks east. There's a buffet restaurant and a cocktail lounge on board. Daytime cruises cost $21 with lunch for adults, $14 with lunch for children ($15 and $8, respectively, without lunch). Evening cruises, which sail from 8pm to 10pm, with live jazz and dinner, run $45 for adults and $22 for children ($21 and $13 without dinner).

Another steam-powered stern-wheeler is the *Natchez* (☎ **504/569-1414**), departing daily from the Toulouse Street Wharf, next to the French Quarter's Jackson Street Brewery. Cruises begin at 11:30am and 2:30pm and feature live jazz and an optional Creole-style luncheon buffet. The cost with lunch is $21.75 for adults and $13.75 for children 6 to 12 ($15.75 and $7.75 without lunch); free for children under 6. Evening jazz cruises depart at 7pm, and with a buffet dinner cost $45.50 for adults and $22.75 for children ($25.50 and $12.75 without dinner).

The riverboat *John James Audubon* (☎ **504/586-8777**) departs from the Canal Street dock and travels the Mississippi between the Audubon Zoo and the aquarium. The cruise costs $14.50 for adults, $7.25 for children.

BY BUS   A 2-hour **Gray Line** bus tour, 1300 World Trade Center of New Orleans (☎ **800/535-7786** or 504/587-0861), offers a fast overview of the city. Tours cost $22 for adults and $10 for children, and require advance booking.

The French Quarter

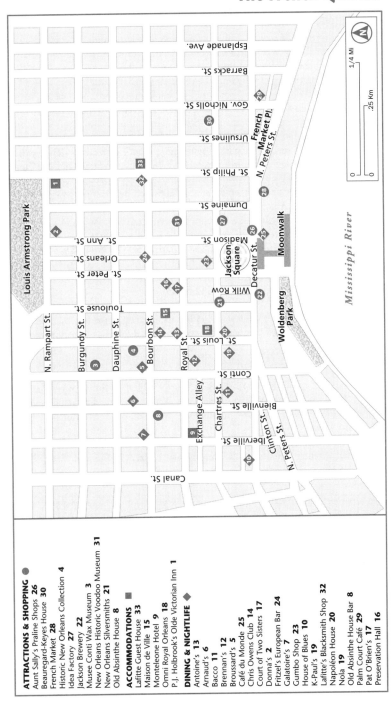

Esplanade Ave.

Barracks St.

Gov. Nicholls St. **29**

30

Ursulines St.

French Market Pl.

St. Philip St. **33**

1 **32**

Dumaine St. **28**

Louis Armstrong Park

2

St. Ann St. **31** **27** Madison St. **26** **25**

Orleans St. **24** **23** Moonwalk

St. Peter St.

Jackson Square

Wilk Row **16** **17**

Toulouse St. **21** **22**

N. Rampart St.

Burgundy St. **15**

Dauphine St. **3** **14** **13** **18** **20**

Bourbon St. **4** St. Louis St. **19**

Royal St. **5** **12**

Conti St. **6**

Chartres St. **11**

Bienville St. **8**

Exchange Alley **7**

Iberville St. **9**

Clinton St.

N. Peters St.

Woldenberg Park

Canal St. **10**

Mississippi River

Decatur St.

N. Peters St.

1/4 Mi

.25 Km

0 / 0

SHOPPING

Shopping here is, in a word, fun. Antique stores are especially well stocked, and gift shops seem to sell more than just a cheap array of T-shirts and souvenir items (although there are plenty of those, too).

Major shopping venues include the triple-tiered mall **Canal Place,** where Canal Street meets the Mississippi Wharves. **The Esplanade,** 1401 W. Esplanade, boasts a constantly busy food court and more than 150 retailers. **The French Market,** whose main entrance is on Decatur Street across from Jackson Square, is big on Louisiana kitsch and cookware. The **Jackson Brewery,** adjacent to Jackson Square, is a transformed suds factory filled with more than 125 retailers. **Riverwalk** is a covered mall that runs along the wharves between Poydras Street and the Convention Center.

You'll find a row of art galleries along **Julia Street,** between the Mississippi River and Camp Street. A jumble of antiques and flea market–style emporiums sit along a 6-block stretch of **Magazine Street,** between Audubon Park and Canal Street. There's also **Magazine Arcade Antiques,** 3017 Magazine St. (☎ **504/895-5451**).

For crafts, try the **Idea Factory,** 838 Chartres St. (☎ **504/524-5195**), where they stock a colorful array of wooden letterboxes, trays, paper-towel holders, and wall brackets. You'll find new and antique silver flatware at **New Orleans Silversmiths,** 600 Chartres St. (☎ **504/522-8333**).

You can see pralines being made at **Aunt Sally's Praline Shops, Inc.,** 810 Decatur St. (☎ **504/944-6090**). They'll ship anything home for you, and sell you items such as cookbooks, packaged Creole food, and Louisiana memorabilia.

ACCOMMODATIONS

Seekers of Southern charm and grace head for the **Columns Hotel,** 3811 St. Charles Ave. (☎ **800/445-9308** or 504/899-9308), a former private residence from 1883 now converted into a small hotel. One of the stateliest remaining examples of belle-époque Italianate architecture, it's listed on the National Register of Historic Places.

Conveniently located near both the embarkation piers for cruise ship passengers and the French Quarter, the **Doubletree Hotel,** 300 Canal St. (☎ **504/ 581-1300**), is at the edge of the city's business district. Rooms are comfortable and clean.

The ✪ **Omni Royal Orleans,** 621 St. Louis St. (☎ **800/THE-OMNI** in the U.S. and Canada, or 504/529-5333; fax 504/529-7037), is a most elegant hotel located smack in the center of the Quarter. The lobby is a small sea of marble, and the rooms are sizable and comfortable. Truman Capote and William Styron both stayed here.

✪ **Lafayette Hotel,** 600 St. Charles Ave., at Lafayette Square (☎ **800/ 827-5621** or 504/524-4441), resembles an upscale turn-of-the-century hotel in London. From old-world architecture, French doors, and wrought-iron balconies to marble floors, polished mahogany, and English botanical prints, the ambiance is consistently luxurious.

Lafitte Guest House, 1003 Bourbon St. (☎ **800/331-7971** or 504/581-2678), is a meticulously restored elegant French manor house furnished with splendid antiques. The three-floor brick structure in a residential section of Bourbon Street was built in 1849. Its wrought-iron balconies and Victorian antiques are as alluring as each of its individually decorated bedrooms, which come in various sizes.

In the heart of the French Quarter, you can follow in the footsteps of Tennessee Williams (who often stayed in room no. 9) and head for ✪ **Maison de Ville,**

727 Toulouse St. (☎ **800/634-1600** or 504/561-5858), located on its original 1742 site. It was here that Williams wrote *A Streetcar Named Desire.* Though the hotel is just steps from honky-tonk Bourbon Street, it has an air of Southern gentility.

One of the best guest houses for value is **The McKendrick-Breaux House,** 1474 Magazine St. (☎ **888/570-1700** or 504/586-1700), built at the end of the Civil War by a wealthy plumber and Scottish immigrant. Located in the lower Garden District, it has been completely restored to its original charm. Each room is furnished with antiques, family collectibles, and fresh flowers.

About 7 blocks from the cruise ship terminal is the grande dame of the French Quarter, the atmospheric **Monteleone Hotel,** 214 Royal St. (☎ **800/535-9595** or 504/523-3341). Decor and floor layouts are slightly different in each of the 597 rooms.

Three streets from Bourbon in the French Quarter, ✪ **P. J. Holbrook's Olde Victorian Inn,** 914 N. Rampart St. (☎ **800/725-2446** or 504/522-2446), is a beautifully restored 1840s home, with antiques and reproductions. Some rooms have balconies, and most come with fireplaces. P. J. herself exemplifies Southern hospitality.

Only blocks from the French Quarter, ✪ **Windsor Court Hotel,** 300 Gravier St. (☎ **800/262-2662** or 504/523-6000), rents 224 beautifully furnished bedrooms, all but 50 of which are suites. From its $8-million art collection to the harpist floating celestial music over the afternoon tea drinkers, the Windsor Court provides an experience more like visiting an English country house than sojourning in Louisiana.

DINING

Don't ask what's new at **Antoine's,** 713 St. Louis St. (☎ **504/581-4422**), established in 1840. Oysters Rockefeller, first served here in 1899, is still available. Tournedos of beef and ramekins of crawfish cardinal remain perennial favorites, and rightly so. The only radical menu change occurred in the 1990s, when French menu terms were given English translations.

The legendary **Arnaud's,** 813 Bienville St. (☎ **504/523-5433**), lies within three interconnected, once-private houses from the 1700s. The five belle-époque dining rooms are lush with Edwardian embellishments. Menu items include shrimp Arnaud, snails *en casserole,* oysters stewed in cream, rack of lamb diablo, roasted duck à l'orange, and classic bananas. The dark balcony around the main dining room is where proper New Orleans gentlemen used to dine with their mistresses while their wives dined below, unaware.

A great New Orleans bistro, **Bacco,** 310 Chartres St. (☎ **504/522-2426**), stands adjacent to the De La Poste Hotel, right in the heart of the French Quarter. In an elegant setting of pink Italian marble floors and Venetian chandeliers, you can feast on wood-fired pizzas, regional seafood, and such specialties as porcini roasted duck and crabmeat and pappardelle.

Bizou, 701 St. Charles Ave. (☎ **504/524-4114**), is hardly the most glamorous place in New Orleans, but its cuisine, a rejuvenation of Creole and French traditional cookery, has the exuberance of a spring day. Try the crawfish cakes with Creole mustard and baby greens in a Tabasco-infused white butter.

Broussard's, 819 Conti St. (☎ **504/581-3866**), has thrived here since 1920. It's a quieter, more dignified version of Antoine's, less heavily patronized by out-of-towners, and more authentic to the "Nawlins" ethic. Dishes include fillets of pompano Napoléon-style (with scallops and a mustard-caper sauce, served in puff pastry with a side order of shrimp).

At the corner of Washington Avenue and Coliseum Street in the Garden District, **Commander's Palace,** 1403 Washington Ave. (☎ **504/899-8221**), still reigns as one of the city's finest dining choices. The cuisine is haute Creole. Try anything with shrimp or crawfish, or the Mississippi quail.

✪ **Galatoire's,** 209 Bourbon St. (☎ **504/525-2021**), feels like a bistro in turn-of-the-century Paris, and still basks in its legendary reputation. Menu items include trout (*meunière* or *amandine*), remoulade of shrimp, oysters en brochette, a savory Creole-style bouillabaisse, and a good eggplant stuffed with a purée of seafood.

K-Paul's Louisiana Kitchen, 416 Chartres St. (☎ **504/524-7394**), is one of Louisiana's most famous restaurants. There are two dining rooms, one of which takes reservations and another that doesn't (at this one you may be seated at a communal table with other diners). Try fiery gumbos, Cajun popcorn shrimp, roasted rabbit, and the delicious spicy blackened fish (especially tuna). For the rare vegetarian, the breaded, vegetable-stuffed eggplant is just amazing.

Brennan's, 417 Royal St. (☎ **504/525-9711**), is the place for the legendary "Breakfast at Brennan's," a multicourse affair that's changed very little over the years. It includes traditional dishes like eggs Hussarde, eggs Sardou, and trout Nancy (fillet of fresh trout sautéed and topped with lump crabmeat, sprinkled with capers and lemon-butter sauce). Turtle soup is a famous local dish, and Brennan's makes one of the best. Desserts include bananas Foster (sautéed in liqueur, brown sugar, cinnamon, and butter; drenched in rum; set ablaze; and served over vanilla ice cream). It's a little overwhelming. A friend ate there recently and afterward stumbled to the nearest phone, canceled his lunch and dinner reservations, and went back to the hotel for a nap.

The ambiance is more of a draw than the food at the **Court of Two Sisters,** 613 Royal St. (☎ **504/522-7261**), but what an ambiance it is. You enter through a huge courtyard filled with flowers, fountains, and low-hanging willows, with a wishing well at its center. You can dine outside amid the greenery or in the Royal Court Room. The daily jazz brunch buffet features more than 80 dishes (meat, fowl, fish, vegetables, fresh fruits, homemade bread, and pastries) and a strolling jazz band.

The **Gumbo Shop,** 630 St. Peter St. (☎ **504/525-1486**), is a cheap and convenient place to get solid, classic Creole food. The menu reads like a textbook list of traditional local food: red beans and rice, shrimp Creole, crawfish étouffée. The seafood gumbo with okra is a meal in itself, and do try the jambalaya. Other dishes include crawfish and penne pasta, filet mignon, salads, po' boys (from regular ham and cheese to Cajun sausage), and homemade desserts such as Southern pecan pie with ice cream.

If you don't mind facing the world's toughest waitresses, head for **Mother's Restaurant,** 401 Poydras St. (☎ **504/523-9656**), at the corner of Tchoupitoulas. Customers have been flocking to this crowded place since 1938. Homemade biscuits and red-bean omelets are featured at breakfast, giving way at lunch to po' boys. For dinner you can get everything from soft-shell crabs to jambalaya.

Napoléon House, 500 Chartres St. (☎ **504/524-9752**), at the corner of St. Louis Street, would have been the house of the lieutenant himself if some locals' wild plan to bring him here in exile had panned out. A landmark 1797 building, this place is a hangout for drinking and good times, but also serves food. The specialty is Italian muffuletta, with ham, Genoa salami, pastrami, Swiss cheese, and provolone.

At **Nola,** 534 St. Louis St. (☎ **504/522-6652**), Cajun New Orleans mingles gracefully with Hollywood. Try such intriguing dishes as slow-roasted duck with a sweet and spicy glaze, along with a buttermilk corn pudding.

✪ **Café du Monde,** at 800 Decatur St., right on the river (☎ **504/581-2914**), is basically a 24-hour coffee and donuts stop (Okay, coffee and beignets—a square, really yummy French doughnut-type thing, hot and covered in powdered sugar), but it's *the* place for people-watching (if you don't want to wait for a table, you can always get a bag of beignets to go).

NEW ORLEANS AFTER DARK

Life here in "The Big Easy" is conducive to all manner of nighttime entertainment, usually raucous. Visitors reel from club to club in the neighborhoods around Bourbon and St. Louis streets. There's a reason why jazz was born in this town.

Do what most people do: Start at one end of **Bourbon Street** (say, around Iberville), walk down to the other, and then turn around and do it again. Along the way, you'll hear R&B, blues, and jazz pouring out of dozens of bars, be beckoned by touts of the numerous strip clubs, and see one tiny little storefront stall after another sporting hand-lettered signs that say OUR BEER IS CHEAPER THAN NEXT DOOR. It's a scene. Base and immoral? Maybe, but it's loads of fun. Grab yourself a big $2 beer or one of the famous rum-based Hurricanes (preferably in a yard-long plastic cup shaped like a Roswell alien) and join the party.

Preservation Hall, 726 St. Peter St., just off Bourbon (☎ **504/523-8939**), is a deliberately shabby little hall with very few places to sit and no air-conditioning. Nonetheless, the place is usually packed with people in to see the house band, a bunch of mostly older musicians who have been at this for *eons*. Don't request "When the Saints Go Marching In" 'cause the band won't play it—even classics get to be old smelly hats when you've played them 45,000 times.

Chris Owens Club, 500 Bourbon St. (☎ **504/523-6400**), is a one-woman cabaret act. New Orleans legend and mistress of ceremonies Ms. Owens sings along with whatever band happens to be accompanying her that night. On nights when Owens is indisposed, the venue becomes a dance club.

On a small stage in ✪ **Fritzel's European Bar & Cuisine,** 733 Bourbon St. (☎ **504/561-0432**), musicians will improvise, boogie, and generally shake, rattle, and roll. It's one of the better places on Bourbon. Very late at night, musicians from other clubs might hop onstage to jam.

Lafitte's Blacksmith Shop, 941 Bourbon St. (☎ **504/523-0066**), is a French Quarter pub housed in an 18th-century Creole blacksmith shop that looks like only faith keeps it standing. Tennessee Williams used to hang out here.

Established in 1933, the quite touristy **Pat O'Brien's,** 718 St. Peter St., just off Bourbon (☎ **504/525-4823**), is famous for its twin piano players, raucous high jinx, singers, and gargantuan Hurricanes. There's also an outdoor courtyard.

If you're looking to get away from the Bourbon scene and hear some real brass-band jazz, head up to ✪ **Donna's,** 800 N. Rampart St., at the top of St. Ann Street (☎ **504/596-6914**). This joint is often packed, especially for the more famous acts—the Marsalis family has been known to play here from time to time—though when I was there in late 1998 to see a fella named Tuba Fats and his band, the patrons were almost outnumbered by the musicians. There's no better place to hear that authentic sound that made New Orleans famous. Cover varies, but is always reasonable. Owner Donna is often tending bar.

Elsewhere in town, Pete Fountain, the Dixieland clarinet maestro, runs **Pete Fountain's** in the plush third-floor interior of the New Orleans Hilton, 2 Poydras St. (☎ **504/561-0500**). If he's not on tour, Fountain usually performs several nights a week.

Jazz, blues, and Dixieland pour out of the nostalgia-laden bar and concert hall **Tipitina's,** 501 Napoleon Ave. (☎ 504/891-8477); there's a second location at 233 Peter's St. (☎ 504/895-8477).

At the **Mermaid Lounge,** 1100 Constance St. (☎ 504/524-4747), in the Warehouse District, anything goes, and music ranges from rockabilly to jazz. It's open Wednesday through Saturday, and sometimes Tuesday night, if the mood strikes. The joint keeps going at least until 2am, but if it's jumping, the owners will keep it open later.

House of Blues, 225 Decatur St. (☎ 504/529-2583), is one of the city's largest live-music venues. You stand and move among the several bars that pepper the club. There's also a restaurant.

Follow the footsteps of Michael Jordan and U2 to the Victorian Lounge at the **Columns Hotel,** 3811 St. Charles Ave. (☎ 504/899-9308), and try one of the staff's justly celebrated Bloody Marys. A young local crowd is attracted to this bar on the fringe of the Garden District, where a jazz trio entertains on Tuesday nights.

At **Palm Court Café,** 1204 Decatur St. (☎ 504/525-0200), you'll find an equal appreciation of good jazz and international food.

One block beyond Esplanade, on the periphery of the French Quarter, **Snug Harbor,** 626 Frenchman St. (☎ 504/949-0696), is a jazz bistro, a classic spot to hear modern jazz in a cozy setting. Sometimes R&B combos and blues are added to the program. There's a full dinner menu as well.

Vaughan's Lounge, 800 Lesseps St. (☎ 504/947-5562), is a genuine New Orleans joint.

6 San Juan & the Port of San Juan

In addition to being the embarkation port for a number of ships, San Juan is also a major port of call. See chapter 3, "The Ports of Call," for all information.

The Ports of Call 3

What is the Caribbean, anyway? *Webster's New Geographical Dictionary* has it as "an arm of the Atlantic Ocean, bounded by the West Indies on the north and east, northern South America on the south, and Central America on the West," but that's a pretty dry description for such a multifaceted place. The Caribbean is in fact a pastiche of cultures, history, great wealth, great poverty, and a natural beauty that runs the gamut from dense rain forest to dry, almost desertlike landscape. Your cruise may take you to bustling Nassau with its frantic shopping scene, peaceful Bequia with its idyllic bayside restaurants, Cozumel with its rowdy bars and proximity to ancient Mayan ruins, Grand Cayman with its ritzy homes and amazing "Stingray City" experience, or Dominica with its incredible rain forest beauty. Wherever you end up, there are incredible experiences waiting, of enough variety to suit practically any taste. In the pages that follow I'll fill you in on the best things to do in every port, whether it's riding a raft down a tropical river, piloting your own jeep over sand dunes, or catching some nachos and beer under a shade tree.

First, to give you a little background, let's talk history.

1 A Brief History of the Caribbean

Caribbean history reads like a Hollywood blockbuster—brutal conquests, devastating plagues, swashbuckling pirates, new frontiers, monumental sea battles, slave insurrections, and violent revolutions. Grab your popcorn.

PRE-COLUMBIAN CULTURES   Every schoolchild learns that in 1492 Columbus sailed the ocean blue. He was a johnny-come-lately, of course—people had been living in the Caribbean for hundreds, even thousands, of years before Europeans arrived. Three major groups, all originally from South America, were there when Columbus arrived.

The least advanced of the native peoples, the **Ciboney,** were probably the first to arrive. Living primarily in rock shelters and caves, they formed small family groups; collected shellfish, wild fruits, and herbs; and hunted turtles and reptiles. Their rudimentary tools were made of stone.

The more advanced **Arawak** and **Carib** peoples had frequent contact with each other and shared many of the same material technologies. They farmed, hunted, and fished, and used similar methods to make canoes, build huts, weave cloth, and make pottery. Both peoples cultivated root plants—yucca, yams, arrowroot, peanuts, peppers, and gourds—and seed crops like maize, beans, and squash. Pineapple and guava, shellfish, fish, iguanas, birds, and snakes provided additional sustenance. Men generally hunted and fished, while women farmed, cooked, wove cloth, and made household pottery and baskets.

The Arawak, by all accounts, were peaceful, gentle, and friendly. Women enjoyed considerable status, religion was based on the belief that spirits inhabited both humans and natural objects, and islands were divided into provinces ruled by chiefs.

Carib authority was less centralized. Independent villages elected war chiefs for each island. Men lived together in communal houses and kept their wives, who they treated as servants, in separate huts. Because they resisted efforts to enslave them, the Carib were vilified as bloodthirsty savages by the Spanish. In fact, the word "cannibal" comes from the Spanish name for the tribe (*caribal*). There is no evidence that the Carib practiced cannibalism—the Spanish may have made the claim to justify their assault on the tribe. The Carib were more aggressive than the Arawak, who they frequently raided, but when the French and English settled the Lesser Antilles in the 1630s, the Carib were friendly and provided food to the starving adventurers—they became violent only after the Europeans attacked them.

EUROPEAN "DISCOVERY" OF THE ISLANDS   On October 12, 1492, Columbus became the first European to reach the New World, landing on Watling's Island in the Bahamas. This exploratory first voyage was followed in 1493 by a second and much larger expedition to establish a permanent foothold on the islands. Along with 1,500 men, Columbus this time brought horses, sheep, cattle, and hogs, as well as plants grown in Europe such as wheat, barley, grapes, and sugarcane. Landing first on Dominica, the fleet passed through and named the islands of the Lesser Antilles before arriving in Hispaniola in November 1494. Before returning to Spain, Columbus sighted Jamaica and explored Cuba.

ENSLAVEMENT OF THE INDIANS   The Spanish Crown distributed land on the islands to individual settlers, who were expected to cultivate it for four years. In return they received the use of the property in perpetuity. By the time Columbus returned on his third voyage in 1498, the system had been distorted considerably. Disdaining work, the Spanish settlers took over Indian communities and lived off the slave labor of the indigenous population. In the face of settler revolt, Columbus placated the colonists by distributing to them the Indian communities. Under this system, settlers forced the Indians to work without wages. Without this slave labor, the colonial economies certainly would have failed. Unfortunately, the Spanish not only enslaved the local population, but obliterated it with disease.

DISEASE & DECIMATION   Prior to the 15th century, the peoples of Europe and Africa rarely mingled, and the indigenous peoples of the Americas existed in total isolation. Consequently, a distinctive disease environment developed on each continent. Until the Europeans and Africans arrived, a host of illnesses—among them smallpox, measles, typhus, yellow fever, malaria, and tuberculosis—were unknown in the New World. The native peoples had no natural immunity to these diseases, and when exposed to them, they died in staggering numbers. In 1492, as many as six million Arawak and Carib Indians lived in the Caribbean. Within 20 years, almost all were dead. Europeans and African slaves gave each other diseases as well, and as many as a third of both races died during their first two years on the islands.

GOLD FEVER The Spanish, of course, were interested in one thing only—gold. Wherever gold was found, settlers rushed in, but the meager gold supply on any given island was quickly exhausted. Undaunted, the Spanish would move on to another island, with Indian slaves in tow. Eventually, the Spanish searched farther, into Mexico, Panama, and Peru, where they hit the jackpot: the unparalleled treasures of the Aztec and Inca.

Once the enormous value of the gold and silver in Mexico and Peru became clear, the Spanish forgot about the Antilles; they were "useless" except for the slaves they provided. King Ferdinand authorized slaving expeditions to the Lesser Antilles and the Curaçao group in 1511. By 1520, the northern (or Leeward) islands from the Virgins to Barbuda, except for St. Kitts and Nevis, were depopulated. The inhabitants of the Curaçao group, Barbados, St. Lucia, and Tobago were also forcibly removed, and on the remaining islands the Carib retreated to the mountainous interiors, where they resisted would-be enslavers with considerable skill.

TREASURE SHIPS & PIRATES Aside from providing slaves, the islands remained valuable because Spanish treasure fleets had to pass by them on their way from Mexico and Peru to Seville, the sole port in Spain authorized to receive the gold, silver, and other riches from the New World. Rulers of other European states, envious of Spain's wealth, encouraged their subjects to plunder it. Piracy became an accepted business, and thousands of buccaneer ships, sailing from ports in France, Britain, and the Netherlands, attacked Spanish ships and ports in the Caribbean and along the coast of Central America. **Sir Francis Drake** took the greatest booty, capturing an entire year's yield of Peruvian silver in 1573. To protect its treasure fleets from pirates, Madrid closed its American empire to outside trade and limited ocean crossings to Europe—only two heavily guarded convoys made the trip each year. While great forts were built on islands along the fleet route, other settlements had to fend for themselves. Spain's focus on Peru and Mexico precluded state development of the Caribbean colonies, and for three centuries, most inhabitants of the forgotten islands earned modest livings as farmers and ranchers.

COLONISTS FROM NORTHERN EUROPE For 150 years, the British, French, and Dutch pillaged the riches produced by Spain's colonies in Mexico and Peru, attacking Spain's treasure-loaded ships as they sailed through the waters of the Caribbean. The northern Europeans finally established permanent colonies on the islands in the 1620s. They initially concentrated on the smaller, still unoccupied islands of the eastern Caribbean, but after 1650 they moved west into the Greater Antilles. The success of these efforts often depended on events in Europe, and islands, like chips in a poker game, often changed hands during wars on the Continent. Governments, more interested in European affairs and with no money to spend on colonial development, played only a limited role in the initial settlement and economic development of the islands. Individual adventurers, often acting for groups of merchants, established the first Dutch, French, and British colonies. Governments gave adventurers exclusive licenses to exploit specific areas in return for a share of the profit.

In 1618, Dutch raiders provided the vanguard assault. During the 17th century, the Netherlands led all other European nations in manufacturing, commerce, and finance capitalism, and it soon dominated trade with the Far East, Africa, and the Caribbean. The **Dutch West India Company,** chartered in 1621, had a state-granted 25-year monopoly in the Americas. Between 1625 and 1635, Dutch maritime forces changed the balance of power in the Caribbean, making it possible for Dutch traders to control most of the region's commerce for decades. The Dutch established colonies on Sint Maarten, St. Eustatius, Saba, Curaçao, Aruba, and Bonaire. Once the West India Company's fortunes waned and its monopoly expired after investors became underwhelmed by the venture's take, individual traders filled the void. The company reorganized to focus on the trade in West African slaves and goods to colonies of other powers.

New waves of British and French marauders followed the Dutch to the Caribbean. Tropical products such as **tobacco** and **sugar** were fetching high prices in Europe, and few investments at home promised comparable profits. The prospect of economic gain was the primary lure, but adventurers, fame-seekers, and religious nationalists had their own motives for going to the Caribbean. The British and French claimed many of the same islands, but speaking in very general terms, the British settled St. Kitts, Barbados, Nevis, Antigua, Montserrat, Anguilla, the British Virgin Islands, and Jamaica, while the French established colonies on Guadeloupe, Martinique, St. Christophe (the French name for St. Kitts), and what is today Haiti. The Danish (St. Thomas, St. John, and St. Croix) and Swedish came in much smaller numbers.

ENORMOUS SUGAR PROFITS   The Caribbean enjoyed relative peace and prosperity for much of the 1700s, and the region's economy—especially the sugar industry—grew rapidly. During the 18th century, the islands produced 80 to 90% of the sugar consumed in Western Europe. Demand encouraged planters to develop large-scale plantations and ushered in a new era of slavery. Profits and associated tax revenues convinced British and French politicians that sugar and slavery were essential to their national economies.

SLAVERY ON AN UNPRECEDENTED SCALE   Economically, socially, and politically, slavery dominated the sugar islands to an extent never matched in human history. By the 1750s, almost nine out of 10 people on all the islands where sugar was grown were slaves. Conditions were brutal: Heat, disease, and back-breaking work killed Caribbean slaves before they could reproduce. Sugar estates could operate only by constantly importing enormous numbers of new slaves from Africa. Except for the Spanish, all the colonial powers encouraged and were directly involved in the trade. The genocide began even before the human cargo from Africa arrived on the islands. The trip across the Atlantic—the Middle Passage, as it was known—claimed the lives of millions. Shackled together, surviving on tainted water and food of minimal nutritional value, and exposed to disease, 20% of the slaves died aboard ship. As many as another third, already weakened by confinement and malnutrition, perished in their first few years on the islands. And three out of four babies born to slaves died before the age of 5.

ENGLAND & FRANCE COMPETE FOR DOMINANCE   From 1740, Great Britain and France fought throughout the world to gain commercial and colonial supremacy. The Caribbean was a major theater of battle, but the struggle was world-wide in scope, affecting Europe, North America, Africa, and India as well. Caribbean islands, often used as bargaining chips, changed flags frequently as the balance of world power shifted from France to England or from England to France. But the swing of the pendulum affected local Caribbean societies and economies only superficially. Battles were fought by soldiers, not civilians. Crops and plantations were largely unscathed, and planters essentially maintained power over island politics regardless of which flag happened to be flying at any particular time. Slaves, of course, remained slaves whether an island was designated as British or French.

French islands were vulnerable to attack from the British, and British islands were easily attacked by the French, as both powers were loath to spend huge sums of money for their protection. The British maintained two permanent ports in the region; France had none, electing instead to send ships from Europe for specific purposes. The French fleets arrived fresh from the dockyard and in good shape, while the British ships quickly rotted under tropical conditions. Once they arrived in the region, however, the French fleets quickly ran out of food, while British ships obtained provisions from their permanent naval stations. Disease also played a role: Any victory had to be won almost immediately, as a long siege led to staggering death rates from illnesses.

SLAVE RESISTANCE   During the height of the slave era, blacks outnumbered whites ten to one on most islands. Individual slaves frequently ran away, and groups of slaves planned escapes and uprisings. Slaves rebelled much more frequently in the Caribbean than in the United States, and thousands joined in widespread insurrection on dozens of occasions, destroying plantations and killing slave owners. But only the 1791 revolt on Saint-Domingue, led by **Toussaint L'Ouverture,** culminated in permanent liberation, the establishment of an independent Haiti in 1804. Maroons—escaped slaves who banded together and formed their own independent communities—sought refuge in mountains and areas of dense brush and broken terrain. But as planters cut down forests to create new cane estates, maroons fled to Dominica and St. Vincent, two lush, mountainous islands designated as Carib territory. Slaves on flatter, drier islands had no hiding places at all.

ABOLITION OF SLAVERY & INFLUX OF INDENTURED SERVANTS
Slavery dominated every aspect of the Caribbean islands—it made sugar plantations possible, shaped social and familial relations, and dominated the laws and politics of the region. The abolition of slavery, therefore, represented a cataclysmic change in island life. In 1833, pressured by large segments of the British population who increasingly found the system morally repugnant, cruel, and economically inefficient, and by slave rebellions that became more frequent, England permanently ended slavery in its Caribbean colonies. Inspired by the success of British abolitionists, French intellectuals pressed for emancipation, winning the fight in 1848. The Dutch abolished slavery in 1863. Many freed slaves moved off the plantations to squat on vacant land, and the loss of free labor temporarily crippled sugar production. To fill the labor void, planters recruited indentured workers, primarily from India but also from China, Indochina, and West Africa.

INDEPENDENCE & ECONOMIC CHALLENGES   From the end of the 19th century, the United States succeeded the European powers as the main economic and political force in the Caribbean. Under the centralized political systems in place until the 1950s, laws governing the region continued to be made in London, Paris, and the Hague, but after almost a century of economic decline on the islands, it was American capital that provided the means to rebuild the sugar, coffee, and banana industries. And American military power, protecting American commercial interests in the region, intervened in Cuba, Haiti, and the Dominican Republic.

In the years between the two world wars, island-wide political movements developed, paving the way for independence. Since World War II, some islands have become integral parts of larger states in constitutional arrangements that give their peoples management of local affairs. Puerto Rico and the Virgin Islands entered into relationships with the United States, the French Antilles were integrated into France, and the Dutch West Indies became an autonomous part of the Kingdom of the Netherlands. The major British colonies have become totally independent states, while smaller islands remaining within the British sphere enjoy home rule.

The Caribbean islands have different languages, political systems, and cultural traditions, but all face similar economic problems as they search for new sources of income to replace the declining sugar industry. Tourism is now the region's main industry.

2 Antigua

Rolling, rustic Antigua (An-*tee*-gah) in the British Leewards claims to have a different beach for every day of the year. This may be an exaggeration, but its numerous sugary-white, reef-protected beaches are reason enough to visit, even if just for a day. Antigua is also known for its **English Harbour,** home of Nelson's Dockyard National Park, one of the Caribbean's major historical attractions.

Some British traditions (including a passion for cricket) linger on, although the nation became independent in 1981. Some 4,000 years ago, Antigua was home to a people called the Ciboney, who later disappeared completely and mysteriously from the island. When Columbus showed up in 1493 (he named the island after the Santa Maria La Antigua cathedral in Seville, Spain), the Arawaks had already settled on the island. They were joined in the mid–17th century by the English, who eventually won out after many conflicts.

On Antigua you'll find isolated and conservative (but very glamorous) resorts, poorly maintained highways, and some of the most interesting historic naval sites in the British maritime world. Antigua is politically linked to the sparsely inhabited and largely underdeveloped island of Barbuda, about 30 miles north.

Sleepy **St. John's,** the capital, springs to life when cruise ships come to town. It's a large, neatly laid-out town, 6 miles from the airport and less than a mile from Deep Water Harbour Terminal. Protected in the throat of a narrow bay, St. John's is full of cobblestoned sidewalks, weather-beaten wooden houses, corrugated iron roofs, and louvered Caribbean verandas. The streets were built wide to let the trade winds keep them cooler. The port is the focal point of commerce, industry, and government, as well as visitor shopping.

Frommer's Favorite Antigua Experiences

- **Taking a four-wheel-drive island tour:** Drive down rain-forest trails and make a stop at the beach. Sounds fun, huh? (See "Shore Excursions," below.)
- **Visiting Harmony Hal:** The place to go for mouth-watering cuisine, works of art, shopping, refreshing breezes, and some of the island's best people-watching. (See "On Your Own: Beyond Walking Distance," below.)

COMING ASHORE   Most cruise ships dock at Heritage Quay (pronounced *key*) in St. John's, the island's capital. Heritage Quay and Redcliffe Quay (about a

Frommer's Ratings: Antigua					
	Poor	Fair	Good	Excellent	Outstanding
Overall Experience				✓	
Shore Excursions			✓		
Activities Close to Port			✓		
Beaches & Water Sports				✓	
Shopping		✓			
Dining/Bars				✓	

Atlantic Ocean

Hodges Bay
Jabberwock Beach
Dutchman's Bay
Dickenson Bay
Cedar Grove
Long Island
Runaway Bay
Deepwater Harbor
Galley Bay
Fort James
V.C. Bird Airport
Guiana Island
Hawksbill Beaches
Five Islands
St. John's
Parham
Pineapple Beach
Long Bay
Indian Town Point
Devil's Bridge
Jennings
Betty's Hope Plantation
Willikies
Jolly Harbor
Bolans
Megaliths
All Saints
Harmony Hall
Driftwood Beach
Boggy Peak
Urlings
Potworks Dam
Freetown
Half Moon Bay
Johnson's Point
Fig Tree Dr.
Old Road
Falmouth
Falmouth Bay
English Harbour
Willoughby Bay
Morris Bay
Turner's Beach
Carlisle Bay
Pigeon Point
Nelson's Dockyard National Park
Shirley Heights
Mamora Bay
Rendezvous Bay
Caribbean Sea

0   5 Miles
0   5 Kilometers

Airport ✈   Beach ☂   Mountain ▲▲   Cruise Ship Dock ⛴

10-minute walk from the dock) are the main shopping centers. Cruise passengers will find duty-free stores, restaurants, taxis, and other services in both quays. On busy port days, ships will also use the Deep Water Harbour Terminal in St. John's. From there, passengers take a short taxi ride to Heritage Quay. Occasionally, smaller vessels drop their anchors at English Harbour; everyone else reaches it via taxi or a shore excursion from St. John's.

Credit-card **phone booths** are located on the dock and throughout both quays and at Deep Water Harbour. Passengers can also head to **Parcel Plus** (☎ 268/562-7587) at 14 Redcliffe St. (in Redcliffe Quay), which offers 10 booths in an air-conditioned setting. You can also check your e-mail from here. The cost is about $8 for a half hour, $11 for 1 hour. **Cable & Wireless** (☎ 268/480-4237) has an office on the corner of Long and Thames streets, where prepaid phone cards can be purchased. Prices start at $4. Phone cards can also be purchased from stores around the quay and from the pilot office at Deep Water Harbour.

CURRENCY   The **Eastern Caribbean dollar (EC$)** is used on these islands; however, you'll find that nearly all prices, except those in certain tiny restaurants, are given in U.S. dollars. The exchange rate is EC$2.70 to $1 U.S. (EC$1 is worth about 37¢). It's always a good idea to ask if you're not sure which currency a price tag refers to. The U.S. dollar is readily accepted by most shopkeepers and cab drivers. Unless otherwise specified, rates quoted in this section are given in U.S. dollars.

LANGUAGE   The official language is English, spoken with a bit of an island lilt.

INFORMATION   Head to the **Antigua and Barbuda Department of Tourism** at Nevis Street and Friendly Alley in St. John's (☎ **268/462-0480**). You'll get just the basics from the staff here. Open Monday to Thursday from 8am to 4:30pm and Friday from 8am to 3pm.

The **Department of Tourism** has an office in New York (☎ **888/268-4227** or 212/541-4117). The E-mail address is info@antigua-barbuda.org. The official Web site for Antigua and Barbuda is www.interknowledge.com/antigua-barbuda/. Other sites worth browsing include www.antiguanice.com and http://AntiguaToday.com/.

CALLING FROM THE U.S.   When calling Antigua from the United States, you need to dial only a "1" before the numbers listed throughout this section.

GETTING AROUND

BY TAXI   Taxis meet every cruise ship. They don't have meters, so even though rates are fixed by the government it's always wise to settle on a fare and the currency before taking the ride. One of the best ways to explore the island is by private taxi, since drivers also double as tour guides. Hourly rates are about $20 for up to four people in a cab. The standard tip for a driver is between 10% and 15%.

The rate from St. John's to Nelson's Dockyard, Pigeon Point, and Shirley Heights is about $20. To Half Moon Bay and Harmony Hall from St. John's, a cab costs about $23. From St. John's to Dickenson Bay, the fare is $10. The fare for a luncheon tour, which includes Nelson's Dockyard, Fig Tree Drive, and a stop for lunch, is $77.

BY BUS   The fare for buses is cheap (around $1) but the service is irregular. It is geared to locals rather than tourists. Unless you are a looking for a local adventure or being merely thrifty, buses are not recommended for the average visitor. However, if you want to give it a whirl, the West Bus Station is located near St. John's market. Buses from this locale head to the villages in the southern part of the island and English Harbour.

RENTAL CARS   Driving is on the left in this former British colony, and renting a car is not recommended. The roads are narrow and seriously potholed, and there is a definite lack of signage. If you do opt to rent a car, Avis, Dollar, Hertz, and Thrifty have outlets in St. John's. A local permit, which costs $20, is required.

SHORE EXCURSIONS

✪ **Four-Wheel-Drive Island Tour** ($55–$64, 3 hours hours): A tour of the whole island via four-wheel drive will take you along rain-forest trails and to the ruins of forts, sugar mills, and plantation houses, and is a great way to get a feel for Antigua. The tour includes a stop at the beach for some swimming.

Nelson's Dockyard at English Harbour ($37–$39, 3 hours): This is the major excursion on the island. On the way, you get to view some of the island's lush countryside. That still leaves you plenty of time in the day for shopping or hitting the beach.

Catamaran Tour ($39–$49, 3 hours): The boat takes you along the coast of Antigua, making a stop for swimming, sunbathing, and snorkeling.

A Cruise on the *Jolly Roger* ($33–$39 adults, 3 hours): Antigua's famous "pirate ship," the *Jolly Roger,* is one of the island's most popular attractions. You're taken for a fun-filled day of sightseeing and snorkeling, plus dancing on the poop deck and a limbo contest. Lunch (a choice of grilled lobster, chicken, or steak) and drinks are served.

TOURING THROUGH LOCAL OPERATORS

Jolly Roger **Cruise:** If your ship doesn't offer this excursion, you can book it independently. Call ☎ **268/462-2064** at least a day or two ahead to make a booking. The ship berths at Redcliffe Quay, within walking distance of the cruise ship docks in St. John's. The lunch cruises depart at 10am and return at 2pm.

ON YOUR OWN: WITHIN WALKING DISTANCE

If you don't want to go to **English Harbour,** you can stay in St. John's to shop and explore. All of its minor attractions can be reached on foot from the cruise ship dock. The people in town may impress you, if not the town itself. They're helpful, have a sense of humor, and will guide you in the right direction if you've lost your way.

The Museum of Antigua and Barbuda sells a self-guided walking tour that focuses on the historical buildings of St. John's, particularly the ones in Redcliffe Quay. The tour wraps up in Redcliffe Tavern with a rum punch. The brochure costs $1.

The **market** in the southern part of St. John's is colorful and interesting, especially on Friday and Saturday mornings, when vendors are busy selling their fruits and vegetables, and gossiping. The partially open-air market lies at the lower end of Market Street.

The Anglican **St. John's Cathedral,** on Church Street (between Long and Newgate streets), has had a disastrous history. Originally built in 1681, it was replaced in 1720 by an English brick building, which was destroyed by an earthquake in 1843. The present pitch-pine interior dates from 1846. The church was going through a restoration in 1974 when another earthquake hit. The twin-spired landmark dominates St. John's skyline.

The **Museum of Antigua and Barbuda,** at the corner of Market and Long streets (☎ **268/462-1469**), traces the history of the nation from its geological birth to the present day. Housed in the old Court House building dating from 1750, exhibits include a wattle-and-daub house model, African-Caribbean pottery, and utilitarian objects of daily life. It's open Monday to Friday from 8:30am to 4pm, Saturday from 10am to 1pm. Admission is free, but a minimum donation of $2 is requested.

ON YOUR OWN: BEYOND WALKING DISTANCE

One of the major attractions of the eastern Caribbean, **Nelson's Dockyard National Park** (☎ **268/460-1379**) sits 11 miles southeast of St. John's on one of the world's safest harbors, and is open daily from 9am to 5pm. (Admission is $5 per person to tour the dockyard; children under 12 are free.) The centerpiece of the national park is the only existing example of a Georgian naval base. English ships used the harbor as a refuge from hurricanes as early as 1671, and Admiral Nelson made it his headquarters from 1784 to 1787. The dockyard played a leading role in the era of privateers, pirates, and great sea battles in the 18th century. The dockyard still plays a pivotal role in Antigua's sailing scene and is the venue for the island's annual Sailing Week. The admission price includes the Dockyard Museum, Dow's Hill Interpretation Center, Shirley Heights, the Blockhouse, and the park.

The restored dockyard is sometimes known as a Caribbean Williamsburg, and in the heart of it is the **Dockyard Museum** (☎ **268/460-8181**). Housed in a building from 1855, museum exhibits illustrate the history of the dockyard, from its beginning as a British Navy stronghold to its development as a national park. Nautical memorabilia as well as island artifacts are on display. The museum is open daily from 9am to 5pm.

For a quick bite, head to the **Dockyard Bakery** (☎ **268/460-1474**), which features homemade rolls, pastries, and other goodies. It is located right behind the museum.

The park itself is well worth exploring. It's filled with sandy beaches and tropical vegetation, including various species of cactus and mangroves that shelter a migrating colony of African cattle egrets. Nature trails expose the vegetation and coastal scenery. You'll also find archaeological sites that date back to before the Christian era. Tours of the dockyard last 15 to 20 minutes, but tours along nature trails can last anywhere from 30 minutes to 5 hours.

For an eagle's-eye view of English Harbour, take a taxi up to the top of **Shirley Heights,** directly to the east of the dockyard. Still standing are Palladian arches, once part of a barracks. The **Blockhouse** was put up as a stronghold in case of siege. The nearby **Military Cemetery** contains an obelisk monument to the men of the 54th Regiment.

Take a taxi from English Harbour $2^1/_2$ miles east to the **Dow's Hill Interpretation Center** (☎ **268/460-2777**), which offers a multimedia journey through six periods of the island's history. You'll learn about the Amerindian hunters, the British military, and the struggles connected with slavery. It's open from 9am to 5pm daily, and admission, including the multimedia show, is $5 for adults, free for children under 12. A stone's throw from the center is the **Belvedere,** which provides a panoramic view of the park, and a footpath leads to **Fort Berkley,** a fine specimen of old-time military engineering at the entrance to English Harbour. The path starts just outside the dockyard gate; the fort is about half a mile away.

In Brown's Bay Mill, near Freetown, the partially restored ✪ **Harmony Hall** (☎ **268/460-4120**) 1843 plantation house and sugar mill overlooks Nonsuch Bay, making it an ideal lunch stopover or shopping expedition. The sister establishment to Jamaica's Harmony Hall displays Antigua's best selection of Caribbean arts and crafts and sponsors regular exhibitions. Lunch, served daily from noon to 3pm, features fresh lobster, pasta dishes, and other specialties. You can also take a boat trip to nearby Green Island from here. If you want to go on the boat trip, call before you arrive or send an e-mail to harmony@candw.ag. Harmony Hall is special and worth the effort to reach it.

Go to **Betty's Hope Plantation,** south of Pares village (☎ **268/462-1469**), to see the only operational 18th-century sugar mill in the Caribbean. Restoration work on the former plantation started in the 1980s. On-site are twin mills and a visitor center.

On the way back to your cruise ship from English Harbour, ask your taxi driver to take you along the 20-some-mile circular route down **Fig Tree Drive,** across the main mountain range of Antigua. Although rough and very potholed in places, it's the island's most scenic drive. The drive passes through lush tropical settings and fishing villages along the southern coast. Nearly every hamlet has a little battered church and lots of goats and children running about. There are also the ruins of several old sugar mills. However, don't expect fig trees—*fig* is the Antiguan word for bananas.

SHOPPING

Most shops in St. John's are clustered on St. Mary's Street or High Street, lying within an easy walk of the cruise ship docks. There are many duty-free items for sale here, including English woolens and linens. You can also purchase Antiguan specialties, such as original pottery, local straw work, Antigua rum, hand-printed local designs on fabrics, floppy foldable hats, and shell curios.

Specialty shops in Redcliffe Quay worth exploring include **Jacaranda** on Redcliffe Street (☎ 268/462-1888), for batik clothing, spices, bath products, and works by Caribbean artists; **The Map Shop** on St. Mary's Street (☎ 268/462-3993), for old and new map prints, sea charts, and Caribbean literature; and **The Goldsmitty** on Redcliffe Street (☎ 268/462-4601), for handmade jewels such as black opal and topaz created by Hans Smit.

If you need some additional formal wear during your cruise, visit **Noreen Philips** on Redcliffe Street (☎ 268/462-3127). Noreen, a former model, designs all the clothing in her shop. There is a fine selection of evening gowns and bags, hats, belts, and costume jewelry, as well as casual outfits. If needed, Noreen can also design something specifically for you in a few hours.

If you are looking for woven goods, stop by the **Workshop for the Blind** on All Saint's Road, by St. John's market (☎ 268/462-0663). Items such as breadbaskets and straw hats are for sale.

Located at the cruise dock, **Heritage Quay,** Antigua's first shopping-and-entertainment center, is a multimillion-dollar complex featuring some 40 duty-free shops and a vendors' arcade where local artists and craftspeople display their wares. Shops feature artwork, china and crystal, Swiss-made watches, and a great selection of swimwear. Restaurants offer a range of cuisine and views of St. John's Harbour. A food court serves visitors who prefer local specialties in an informal setting.

Redcliffe Quay, near Heritage Quay, was a slave-trading quarter that filled up with grog shops and a variety of merchants after abolition. Now it has been redeveloped and contains a number of the most interesting shops in town, selling batiks and accessories, casual and dressy clothing, works of art, herbs and spices, and jewelry.

To find a truly authentic Caribbean souvenir, head to **Sofa** (☎ 268/463-0610), which stands for Sculpture Objets Functional Art, and is housed in a renovated shed in Falmouth Harbour. You'll find an eclectic collection of Caribbean products, including hot sauces, arts and crafts, and items for the home, office, and garden.

BEACHES

On Antigua, it's all about the beaches, and there is certainly an endless supply (tourism folks claim there are 365). All the beaches are public, and there are quite a few that are truly spectacular, including the secluded stretches at Rendezvous Bay and Darkwood Beach. The beach at Galley Bay resort is also stunning. The most well known are Dickenson Bay, Half Moon Bay, and Pigeon Point.

Closest to St. John's is the beach at **Fort Bay,** located about 5 to 10 minutes by taxi from the cruise ship dock (the cab fare is about $7). Both locals and tourists visit this beach, where it is not uncommon to find people playing volleyball or beach cricket.

Further north is **Dickenson Bay** and **Runaway Bay,** where you will get the full resort beach experience—hotels, restaurants, water sports, and more.

One of the island's most attractive beaches can be found on the northwest coast at **Galley Bay** resort. Surfers are fond of this stretch. Also on this part of the coast are four beaches at **Hawksbill,** site of the Hawksbill Beach Resort. For those looking to go au naturel, try the fourth and final beach. It is quite secluded, and clothing is optional.

Port Tip: Beach Safety

Be careful if you have your heart set on a deserted beach. You could be the victim of a mugging. Don't bring valuables. Also, readers increasingly complain of beach vendors hustling everything from jewelry to T-shirts. The beaches are open to all, so hotels can't restrain these bothersome peddlers.

Good spots on the less-developed southwest coast are the unspoiled **Darkwood Beach** and **Carlisle Bay.** While at Darkwood, stop by O.J.'s (no, not that one!) Beach Bar & Restaurant for a cool drink and a bite to eat. To get there, follow the signposts after the beach. **Carlisle Bay,** where the legendary Curtain Bluff Resort is located, is an ideal spot for swimming.

Pigeon Point is about a 5-minute drive from English Harbour on the southeast coast; try the snorkeling here. Also on the southeast is **Half Moon Bay,** which boasts a loyal following and is known for its pink sands.

One of the better-kept secrets is **Jabberwock Beach** in Hodges Bay on the north coast. It is a favorite with locals. Another quiet and secluded beach is located at **Rendezvous Bay** on the south coast.

Taxis will take you from the cruise ship dock in St. John's to your choice of beach, but remember to make arrangements to be picked up at an agreed-upon time. A typical fare to Pigeon Point (about 25 min.) from St. John's is $20 per car. To Hawksbill and Galley Bay (about 10 min.), the fare is $12. Confirm all fares with the driver before setting out.

SPORTS

GOLF   The 18-hole, par-70 **Cedar Valley Golf Club,** Friar's Hill Road (☎ 268/462-0161), is 3 miles east of St. John's, a 5-minute, $10 taxi ride from the cruise dock. The island's largest golf course offers panoramic views of Antigua's northern coast. It costs $65 to play, which covers greens fees and use of a cart. Club rentals cost $15.

SCUBA DIVING   You can arrange a dive through **Dockyard Divers** in Nelson's Dockyard at English Harbour (☎ 268/460-1178). Capt. Tony Fincham and his team take divers to explore Antigua's south coast. A two-tank dive is priced at $63.

GREAT LOCAL RESTAURANTS & BARS

Most cruise passengers dine in St. John's, English Harbour, or Shirley Heights. Reservations usually aren't needed for lunch unless it's a heavy cruise-ship-arrival day. In that case, call from the dock when you come ashore.

The **local beer** of Antigua is Wadadli. The **local rum** is Cavalier.

IN ST. JOHN'S   **Big Banana Holding Company,** on Redcliffe Quay (☎ 268/462-2621), makes the best pizza on the island in what used to be a slave quarters (you can get a great frothy coconut or banana crush, too, as well as overstuffed baked potatoes, fresh-fruit salad, or lobster salad). **Hemingway's,** on St. Mary's Street (☎ 268/462-2763), named after Papa himself, has an upper veranda that overlooks Heritage Quay. Tasty salads, sandwiches, burgers, sautéed fillets of fish, pastries, ice cream, and an array of brightly colored tropical drinks are on the menu. **Redcliffe Tavern,** on Redcliffe Quay (☎ 268/461-4557), is a bustling resorted warehouse that uses machinery from old factories as part of the decor. There is a good selection of lunch entrees, including pineapple stuffed with crab and spicy jerk chicken with plantains, as well as salads, sandwiches, and finger foods.

AT ENGLISH HARBOUR   Admiral's Inn, in Nelson's Dockyard (☎ **268/ 460-1027**), is housed in a 1788 building and features a menu that changes daily but usually features pumpkin soup and a choice of four or five main courses, such as local red snapper, grilled steak, or lobster.

AT SHIRLEY HEIGHTS   Shirley Heights Lookout (☎ **268/460-1785**) is the best alternative to the Admiral's Inn. In the 1790s the building was the lookout station for unfriendly ships heading toward English Harbour; today, it offers such favorites as grilled lobster in lime butter and garlic-flavored shrimp. You can order less expensive hamburgers and sandwiches in the pub downstairs. This is the place to be on Thursday and Sunday nights for live music, the island's best barbecue, and to watch the sun sink into the Caribbean.

AT HARMONY HALL   The restaurant at **Harmony Hall (☎ **268/460-4120**) is worth the trek. Caribbean cuisine with a Mediterranean twist is served in a restored sugar mill that offers sweeping views of Nonsuch Bay.

3 Aruba

Aruba, in the Dutch Leewards, is one of the most popular destinations in the Caribbean. Until its wide white-sand beaches were "discovered" in the 1970s, though, Aruba was an almost forgotten outpost of Holland, mostly valued for its oil refineries and salt factories. Aruba became a self-governed part of the Netherlands in 1986 and has its own royally appointed governor and an elected parliament. Today it's favored for the bizarre lunar landscapes of its desertlike terrain, spectacular beaches, constant sunshine, and gambling.

Just 20 miles long and 6 miles at its widest point, Aruba is shaped more or less like an elongated triangle; one side faces west and is home to the hotels and beaches, and along the southern side are the airport, capital city of Oranjestad, and an oil refinery. It's Aruba's northern half that is wild and woolly—a dry, windswept collage of cacti, rock, and the island's signature divi-divi trees.

The capital, **Oranjestad,** isn't a picture-postcard port, but it has glittering casinos, lots of shopping, and one of the Caribbean's finest stretches of beach. With only 17 inches of rainfall annually, Aruba is dry and sunny almost year-round, and trade winds keep it from becoming unbearably hot. The air is clean and exhilarating, like that of Palm Springs, California. Aruba also lies outside the path of hurricanes that batter islands to the north.

Its population of about 90,000 is culturally diverse, with roots in Holland, Portugal, Spain, Venezuela, India, Pakistan, and Africa.

Frommer's Favorite Aruba Experiences
• **Renting a jeep or doing a jeep tour:** There's more to Aruba than a 7-mile strip of oceanfront high-rise hotels and wide white-sand beach, and this is the way to see it. (See "Shore Excursions" and "On Your Own: Touring by Rental Jeep," below.)
• **Taking an *Atlantis* submarine trip:** A real submarine takes you down 150 feet to see the undersea world (see "Shore Excursions," below).

COMING ASHORE   Cruise ships arrive at the Aruba Port Authority, a modern terminal with a tourist information booth and the inevitable duty-free shops. From the pier it's just a 5-minute walk to the major shopping districts of downtown Oranjestad. If you opted not to take one of the shore excursions, you can make your way around on your own, allowing some time for Aruba's famous beach (just a

5- to 10-minute taxi ride away) in between luncheon stopovers and shopping. Still a large cargo port, Aruba is now separating its cruise and cargo facilities and beefing up passenger terminal services.

CURRENCY   The currency is the **Aruba florin (AFl),** which is divided into 100 cents. Silver coins are in denominations of 5, 10, 25, and 50 cents and 1 and 2$^1/_2$ florins. The 50-cent piece, the square "yotin," is Aruba's best-known coin. The exchange rate is AFl1.77 to U.S.$1 (1 AFl is worth about 56¢). Unless otherwise stated, prices quoted in this section are in U.S. dollars.

LANGUAGE   The official language here is Dutch, but nearly everybody speaks English. The language of the street is often Papiamento, a patois. Spanish is also widely spoken.

INFORMATION   For information, go to the **Aruba Tourism Authority,** 172 L. G. Smith Blvd., Oranjestad (☎ **297/8-21019**). It's open Monday to Saturday from 9am to 5pm.

CALLING FROM THE U.S.   When calling Aruba from the United States, you need to dial the international access code (011) before the numbers listed throughout this section.

GETTING AROUND

BY RENTAL CAR   It's easy to rent a car or four-wheel-drive vehicle and explore Aruba (I don't recommend renting a scooter or motorcycle, though, unless you plan on keeping to the paved roads only). You won't have much trouble finding your way around, but if you really want to explore Aruba's rough, moonlike hinterland, you need to rent a jeep. The rental agencies are just outside the airport's main terminal. Try **Budget Rent-a-Car,** 1 Kolibristraat (☎ **800/472-3325** in the U.S., or 297/8-28600); **Hertz,** 142 L. G. Smith Blvd. (☎ **800/654-3001** in the U.S., or 297/8-24545); **Avis,** 14 Kolibristraat (☎ **800/331-1084** in the U.S., or 297/8-23496).

BY TAXI   Taxis don't have meters, but fares are fixed. Tell the driver your destination and ask the fare before getting in. The main office is on Sands Street between the bowling center and Taco Bell. A **dispatch office** is located at Bosabao 41 (☎ **297/8-22116**). A ride from the cruise terminal to most of the beach resorts, including those at Palm Beach, costs about $8 to $16 per car, plus a small tip. A maximum of five passengers is allowed. It's next to impossible to locate a taxi on some parts of the island, so when traveling to a remote area or restaurant, ask the taxi driver to pick you up at a certain time. Some English-speaking drivers are available as guides. A 1-hour tour (and you don't need much more than that) is offered for about $40 for a maximum of four passengers.

Frommer's Ratings: Aruba					
	Poor	Fair	Good	Excellent	Outstanding
Overall Experience					✓
Shore Excursions			✓		
Activities Close to Port				✓	
Beaches & Water Sports					✓
Shopping				✓	
Dining/Bars				✓	

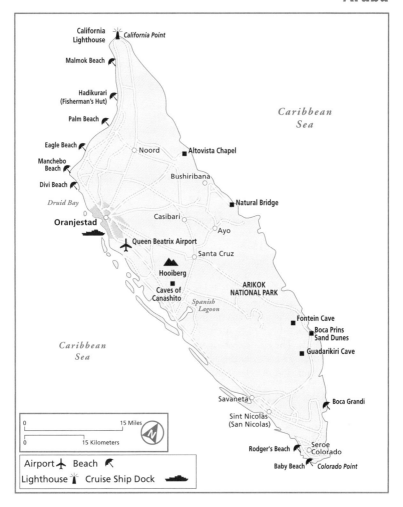

BY BUS Aruba has excellent bus service, with regular daily service from 6am to midnight. The round-trip fare between the beach hotels and Oranjestad is about $2. Try to have exact change. Buses stop across the street from the cruise terminal on L. G. Smith Boulevard and will take you to any of the hotel resorts or the beaches along the West End.

SHORE EXCURSIONS

✪ **Four-Wheel-Drive Backcountry Aruba Tour** ($54, 4 hours): Just like the solo tour described below, but this version does the tour in a convoy of four-passenger sports utility vehicles (with you behind the wheel). A stop is made for lunch and some swimming. If you don't have the gumption to go it alone but you're still looking for some adventure, this is a great alternative.

✪ *Atlantis* **Submarine Journey** ($74 adults, $37 children 4 to 16; 2 hours): One of Aruba's most diverting pastimes, an underwater journey on the submarine

Atlantis is a great opportunity for nondivers to witness firsthand the underwater life of a coral reef. Passengers submerge to about 150 feet without ever getting wet. The submarine departs from the Oranjestad harbor front every hour on the hour, Tuesday to Sunday from 10am to 2pm. Each tour includes a 25-minute transit by catamaran to Barcadera Reef, 2 miles southeast of Aruba, a site chosen for its huge variety of underwater flora and fauna. At the reef, participants transfer to the submarine for a 1-hour underwater tour and lecture. Book this through your cruise ship or make advance reservations with *Atlantis*. The company's offices are at Seaport Village Marina (opposite the Sonesta) in Oranjestad.

Aruba Bus Tour ($26, 3 hours): This city and countryside air-conditioned bus tour takes passengers along part of Aruba's wild and woolly windward coastline to the Natural Bridge (a rocky "bridge" cut by the sea and wind) and the Casibari rock formations, as well as along Aruba's bustling hotel strip.

TOURING WITH LOCAL OPERATORS

Catamaran Cruise/Snorkeling: De Palm Tours, L. G. Smith Blvd. 142, in Oranjestad (☎ **800/766-6016** or 781/821-1012 in the U.S., or 297/8-24400 in Aruba), combines boat rides with snorkeling. For $40 per person, they'll take you on a 1$^1/_2$-hour "fun cruise" aboard a catamaran, after which passengers stop for 3 hours at the company's private De Palm Island for snorkeling. Lunch and an open bar aboard are included in the price. If there are enough takers, the tour leaves daily at 10am and returns at 4pm, just in time to return to the cruise ship. De Palm also offers a 1-hour glass-bottom-boat cruise that visits two coral reefs and the German shipwreck *Antilla.* The cruise costs about $20 per person and operates Tuesday and Wednesday. (Many lines offer this tour in two separate parts; the cruise and snorkeling is one tour, and the glass-bottomed boat ride to the *Antilla* is another.)

ON YOUR OWN: WITHIN WALKING DISTANCE

Bustling **Oranjestad,** the capital and port, attracts shoppers rather than sightseers. The town has a very Caribbean flavor, with both Spanish and Dutch architecture. The main thoroughfare, Lloyd G. (L. G.) Smith Boulevard, runs from the airport along the waterfront and on to Palm Beach, changing its name along the way to J. E. Irausquin Boulevard. Most visitors cross the road heading for **Caya G. F. Betico Croes,** where they find the best shopping.

   After a shopping trip, you might return to the harbor, where fishing boats and schooners, many from Venezuela, are moored. Nearly all newcomers to Aruba like to take a picture of **Schooner Harbor.** Colorful boats are docked along the quay, and boat people display their wares in open stalls. The local patois predominates. A little farther along, fresh seafood is sold directly from the boats at the fish market. On the sea side, you'll find **Wilhelmina Park,** named after Queen Wilhelmina of the Netherlands. A tropical garden has been planted here along the water, and there's a sculpture of the Queen Mother.

   Aside from shopping, Aruba's major attraction is **Palm Beach,** among the finest beaches in the Caribbean. Most of Aruba's high-rise hotels sit in a Las Vegas–style strip along the pure white sand.

ON YOUR OWN: TOURING BY RENTAL JEEP

   The best way to see all of Aruba and its intriguing terrain—a dry, windswept collage of cacti, rock, and the island's signature divi-divi trees—is to ✪ **rent a four-wheel-drive jeep.** You can rent a convertible Suzuki Samurai or nonconvertible four-wheel drive for about $60 to $75 per day, and share the expense with another couple to cut costs. Car-rental companies, which are located on L. G. Smith Boulevard and Kolibristraat, as well as at the airport, will give you a map highlighting the best routes to reach the attractions.

Here's a good route to follow: Following the system of roads that circle the perimeter of the island, start your journey clockwise from the airport. Head back past the hotel strip and on to the island's northwestern-most point. Here, the **California Lighthouse,** named for a ship that wrecked in the area nearly a century ago, affords sweeping 360° views of the island. (Tour the island counterclockwise, and you'll hit the Lighthouse in time to watch the magnificent sunset melt into the sea.)

By the time you reach the Lighthouse, you've already entered Aruba's twilight zone. From here on, your four-wheel-drive adventure will take you into the island's moonlike terrain, past huge heaps of giant boulders and barren rocky coastlines. The smooth, well-maintained road system that links together the hotel strip and Oranjestad transforms itself into a single band of rubble, and the calm, bright turquoise sea turns rough and rowdy.

Reaching the **Alto Vista Chapel,** about 5 miles or so from the Lighthouse, chances are a thin film of red dust has already coated you and the jeep. But don't let that stop you from having a peek inside the quaint pale-yellow church that sits atop a small hill. From its solitary perch, enjoy breathtaking views.

Farther along on the northern coast, you'll approach the hulking ruins of the **Bushiribana Gold Smelter** amid a desolate stretch of parched landscape. Don't bother stopping for a closer look at its graffitied walls, though; its impact is more powerful from a distance.

Just beyond it is the **Natural Bridge,** one of Aruba's most popular attractions. Over the centuries, the crashing ocean surf and whipping wind crafted this "bridge" out of the vulnerable coral rock. The **Thirst Aid Station** restaurant sits nearby, and with its campy colored lights and used-car-lot metallic fringes strung across the ceiling, you may find it to be an interesting site in itself (it's also one of the few places to grab a couple of cold drinks and a sandwich before hitting the road again).

Just before the Gold Smelter and Natural Bridge, keep a look out for **secluded beach coves.** While some are littered with plastic bottles and debris, just as many are pristine patches of paradise. Often just 50 to 100 feet from the road, the craggy coast opens up to random wedges of protected beach and shallow water, perfect for a dip.

Next, veer off towards the center of the island to check out the bizarre **Ayó and Casibari rock formations.** Somewhat of a mystery even to geologists, it's as though the random piles of massive boulders have been dropped from the sky. If you can handle the gusting winds, climb to the top of the mound for great views. Be sure to look for the ancient **Amerindian drawings** painted on the rocks at Ayó.

In the center of the island, **Hooiberg** is affectionately known as "The Haystack." It's Aruba's most outstanding landmark. On a clear day, you can see Venezuela from atop this 541-foot hill.

Farther east along the desolate northern coast is a series of caves punched into the cliff sides of the area's mesas. Have a look inside the graffiti-covered, bat-inhabited **Guadirikiri, Fontein,** and **Tunnel of Love caves;** rent flashlights for $6 apiece (there's no admission charge).

Heading southeast toward Aruba's behemoth oil refinery is **Baby Beach,** at the island's easternmost point. Like a great big bathtub, this shallow bowl of warm turquoise water is protected by an almost complete circle of rock, and is a great place for a peaceful dip after a sweaty day behind the wheel.

Before returning to the ship, in San Nicolas you might want to grab a cool drink at Aruba's most famous local dive, **Charlie's Bar and Restaurant** at Blvd. Veen Zeppenveldstraat 56 (Main Street). Charlie's dates from 1941 and qualifies through its decor and history as one of the most authentic and raffish bars in the West Indies. It's also perhaps the most overly decorated bar, sporting an array of memorabilia and local souvenirs.

SHOPPING

Aruba is a shopper's paradise. An easy walk from the cruise terminal, Oranjestad's half-mile-long **Caya G. F. Betico Croes** compresses six continents into one main, theme-park-like shopping street. While this is not technically a free port, the duty is only 3.3%, and there's no sales tax. You'll find the usual array of jewelry, liquor, Swiss watches, German and Japanese cameras, English bone china and porcelain, French perfume, British woolens, Indonesian specialties, Madeira embroidery, and Dutch, Swedish, and Danish silver and pewter. Delft blue pottery is an especially good buy, as are Edam and Gouda cheeses from Holland. Stamp collectors can purchase colorful and artistic issues at the post office in Oranjestad.

The **Alhambra Moonlight Shopping Center,** L. G. Smith Boulevard, next to the Alhambra Casino, blends international shops, outdoor marketplaces, cafes, and restaurants, and sells everything from fine jewelry, chocolates, and perfume to imported craft items, leather goods, clothing, and lingerie.

The Seaport Village/Seaport Market, overlooking Oranjestad's harbor, at L. G. Smith Blvd. 82, is Aruba's densest concentration of shopping options, with several bars and cafes, two casinos, and at least 200 purveyors of fashion, gift items, sporting goods, liquors, perfumes, and photographic supplies.

BEACHES

The western and southern shores, known as the **Turquoise Coast,** attract sun seekers to Aruba. An $8 taxi ride from the cruise terminal will get you to **Palm Beach** and **Eagle Beach,** the two best beaches on the island. The latter is closer to Oranjestad. Aruba's beaches are open to the public, so you can spread your towel anywhere along this 7-mile stretch of uninterrupted sugar-white sand, which also includes **Manchebo Beach** and **Druid Bay Beach.** But you will be charged for using the facilities at any of the hotels on this strip.

In total contrast to this leeward side, the northern, or windward, shore is rugged and wild.

SPORTS

GOLF   Aruba's long-awaited **Tierra del Sol Golf Course** (☎ 297/8-67800) opened in 1995. Designed by the Robert Trent Jones II Group, this 18-hole, par-71, 6,811-yard course is on the northwest coast, near the California Lighthouse. It was designed to combine the beauty of the island's indigenous flora, such as the swaying divi-divi tree, with lush greens. The course is managed by Hyatt Resorts Caribbean. Greens fees are $120 in winter, including golf cart, or $75 after 3pm. Off-season, the fees drop to $75, or $55 after 3pm. The course is open daily from 6am to 7pm.

SCUBA DIVING & SNORKELING   Scuba divers can explore stunning marine life, with endless varieties of coral, as well as tropical fish in infinite hues. At some points visibility is up to 90 feet. Most divers head for the German freighter *Antilla,* which was scuttled in the early years of World War II off the northwestern tip of

Aruba, near Palm Beach. **Red Sails Sports,** Palm Beach (☎ **297/8-61603**), is the island's best water-sports center, offering sailing, windsurfing, waterskiing, and scuba diving. The resort scuba-diving course is tailored for cruise ship passengers. Certified divers pay $36 and up for one-tank excursions.

WINDSURFING   Divi Winds Center, J. E. Irausquin Blvd. 41 (☎ **297/8-23300,** ext. 623), at the Tamarind Aruba Beach Resort, is the island's windsurfing headquarters. Equipment rents for about $15 per hour. The resort is on the tranquil (Caribbean) side of the island, away from the fierce Atlantic waves (still the winds are strong). You can also arrange Sunfish lessons or rent snorkeling gear. The operation has another location at the Hyatt.

GAMBLING

Although most cruise ships have their own casinos, you can also try your luck ashore at roulette, craps, blackjack, Caribbean stud poker, baccarat, and the ubiquitous one-armed bandits. Aruba's gaming establishments are second only to San Juan in the Caribbean. Most casinos here are open day and night, thus drawing both cruise ship passengers and land-based vacationers. They're mainly located in the big hotels on Palm Beach, an $8 to $12 taxi ride from the cruise terminal.

The casino at the **Holiday Inn Aruba Beach Resort,** L. G. Smith Blvd. 230 (☎ **297/8-67777**), wins the prize for all-around gambling action. It keeps its doors open daily from 9am to 4am.

Closer to Oranjestad, the **Crystal Casino** at the Aruba Sonesta Resort & Casino at Seaport Village (☎ **297/8-36000**) is open 24 hours. It evokes European casinos with its luxurious furnishings, ornate moldings, marble, brass, gold leaf, and crystal chandeliers.

Casino Masquerade, at the Radisson Aruba Caribbean Resort & Casino, J. E. Irausquin Blvd. 81 (☎ **297/8-66555**), is the newest casino in Aruba. Located in the center of the high-rise hotel area, it's open daily from 10am to 4am.

The **Casablanca Casino** occupies a large room adjacent to the lobby of the Wyndham Hotel and Resort, J. E. Irausquin Blvd. (☎ **297/8-64466**). **Casino Copacabana,** in the island's most spectacular hotel, Hyatt Regency Aruba, L. G. Smith Blvd. 85 (☎ **297/8-61234**), evokes France's Côte d'Azur. These two are open throughout the day, accommodating cruise ship passengers.

Outdrawing them all, however, is the **Royal Cabaña Casino,** at the La Cabaña All-Suite Beach Resort & Casino, J. E. Irausquin Blvd. 250 (☎ **297/ 8-79000**), the third largest casino in the Bahamian-Caribbean region. It's known for its three-in-one operation, combining a restaurant, showcase cabaret theater, and nightclub. The casino, the largest on Aruba, has 33 tables and games plus 320 slot machines.

More than just a casino, the **Alhambra,** L. G. Smith Blvd. 47 (☎ **297/8-35000**), offers a collection of boutiques, along with an inner courtyard modeled after an 18th-century Dutch village. The desert setting of Aruba seems appropriate for this Moorish-style building, with its serpentine mahogany columns, repeating arches, and sea-green domes. The casino and its satellites are open daily from 10am until very late at night.

The **Aruba Palm Beach Resort & Casino,** J. E. Irausquin Blvd. 79 (☎ **297/ 8-23900**), opens its slots at 9am and its other games at 1pm. **Americana Aruba Beach Resort & Casino,** J. E. Irausquin Blvd. 83 (☎ **297/8-64500**), opens daily at noon for slots, blackjack, and roulette; however, other games aren't available until 8pm, when most cruise ships have departed.

GREAT LOCAL RESTAURANTS & BARS

If there are a lot of cruise ships in port, call from a pay phone in the cruise ship terminal to make a reservation. If there aren't many ships around, chances are you can just walk in. All restaurants listed are in Oranjestad.

Boonoonoonoos, Wilhelminastraat 18 (☎ **297/8-31888**), is in an old-fashioned Aruban house on the capital's main shopping street, and features dishes from throughout the Caribbean. ✪ **Chez Mathilde,** Havenstraat 23 (☎ **297/8-34968**), Oranjestad's French restaurant, is expensive, but most agree that it's worth the price, especially those who order the chef's bouillabaisse, made with more than a dozen different sea creatures. **The Paddock,** 13 L. G. Smith Blvd. (☎ **297/8-32334**), is a cafe and bistro with a Dutch aesthetic and ambiance and a menu of sandwiches, salads, fish, and more. **The Waterfront Crabhouse,** Seaport Market, L. G. Smith Boulevard (☎ **297/8-36767**), is a seafood restaurant set at the end of a shopping mall.

4 The Bahamas: Nassau & Freeport

Only 36 of the some 700 islands of the Bahamas are inhabited, and only a few of those—Grand Bahama (where Freeport is), New Providence (where Nassau is), Abaco, Eleuthera, Andros, Cat Island, and San Salvador—are known to most travelers. Arawak Indians inhabited the islands until, in 1492, Christopher Columbus first set foot in the New World on the Bahamian island of San Salvador, opening the door to centuries of repression and dominance. The rest, of course, is history, and the Caribbean islands were never to be the same again. British settlement of the Bahamas began in 1647, and the islands became a British colony in 1783. In 1973, the Bahamas became an independent commonwealth, and today, of course, they're a major tourist destination, being so close to Miami (Nassau is only 90 miles away).

CURRENCY   The legal tender is the **Bahamian dollar (B$1),** which is on par with the U.S. dollar. Both U.S. and Bahamian dollars are accepted on an equal basis throughout the Bahamas. There is no restriction on the amount of foreign currency tourists can bring into the country. Most stores accept traveler's checks.

LANGUAGE   The language of the Bahamas is English. Bahamians speak it with a lilt and with more British than American influence. They also pepper their colorful speech with words left from the indigenous Arawak tongue (like *cassava* and *guava*), as well as African words and phrases.

CALLING FROM THE U.S.   When calling Nassau from the United States, you need to dial only a "1" before the numbers listed throughout this section.

NASSAU

Nassau is the capital of the Bahamas, and it has that nation's best shopping, best entertainment, and best beaches. It's big. It's bold. It's one of the busiest cruise ship ports in the world. It's got the old, it's got the new, there's probably something borrowed here, and there's a whole heckuva lot of blue seas. One million visitors a year make their way onto its shores to enjoy its bounty.

With its adjoining **Cable Beach** and **Paradise Island** (linked by bridge to the city), Nassau has luxury resorts set on powdery-soft beaches; all the water sports, golf, and tennis you could want; and so much duty-free shopping that its stores outdraw its museums. Yet historic Nassau hasn't lost its British colonial charms—it just boasts up-to-date tourist facilities to complement them.

Nassau

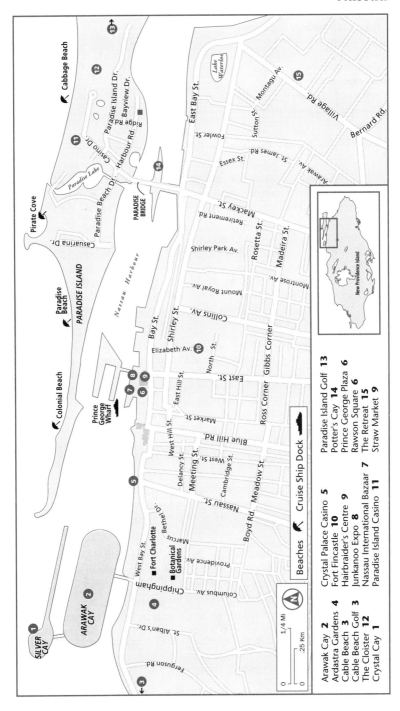

New Providence Island

Beaches — **Cruise Ship Dock** —

Arawak Cay **2**
Ardastra Gardens **4**
Cable Beach **3**
Cable Beach Golf **3**
The Cloister **12**
Crystal Cay **1**

Crystal Palace Casino **5**
Fort Fincastle **10**
Hairbraider's Centre **9**
Junkanoo Expo **8**
Nassau International Bazaar **7**
Paradise Island Casino **11**

Paradise Island Golf **13**
Potter's Cay **14**
Prince George Plaza **6**
Rawson Square **15**
The Retreat **15**
Straw Market **9**

0   1/4 Mi
0   .25 Km

Frommer's Ratings: Nassau

	Poor	Fair	Good	Excellent	Outstanding
Overall Experience				✓	
Shore Excursions			✓		
Activities Close to Port				✓	
Beaches & Water Sports			✓		
Shopping				✓	
Dining/Bars			✓		

Many people come on 3- to 4-day cruises leaving from Miami, Fort Lauderdale, and Port Canaveral. In recent years, the government has spent millions of dollars increasing its facilities, so now about a dozen cruise ships can pull into dock at one time.

Frommer's Favorite Nassau Experiences
- **Dining on fresh conch at Arawak Cay:** The small man-made island across West Bay Street is the place to go for the freshest stuff, washed down with coconut milk laced with gin (see "Great Local Restaurants & Bars," below).
- **Getting your hair braided:** For a new look, get your hair braided in the local style at the Hairbraider's Centre on Prince George Dock (see "On Your Own: Within Walking Distance," below).

COMING ASHORE   The newly expanded cruise ship docks near Rawson Square are at the very center of the city and its main shopping area. The Straw Market, at Market Plaza, is nearby, as is the main shopping artery of Bay Street. The Nassau International Bazaar is at the intersection of Woodes Rogers Walk and Charlotte Street.

Your best bet for making long-distance **phone calls** is the Bahamas Telecommunications Co. phone center on East Street, which runs perpendicular to Rawson Square. Walk about 4 blocks on East Street, and it'll be on your right-hand side.

INFORMATION   You can get help from the Information Desk at the **Ministry of Tourism's** office, Bay Street (☎ **242/356-7591**), open Monday to Friday from 9am to 5pm. A smaller information booth can be found at Rawson Square near the dock. For info before you go, call the Tourist Office in the United States (☎ **800/327-7678**) or log on to the Web site www.bahamas.com.

GETTING AROUND
Unless you rent a horse and carriage, the only way to really see old Nassau is on foot. All the major attractions and the principal stores are within walking distance. You can even walk to Cable Beach or Paradise Island.

BY TAXI   Taxis are practical, at least for longer island trips, and are required to have working meters, so you probably won't be cheated. That said, on a recent trip, my drivers never wanted to use their meters and insisted on flat fees. The official fare is $2 at flag fall and 30¢ for each quarter mile for the first two passengers; additional passengers pay $2. Five-passenger cabs can be hired for $23 to $25 per hour. For a radio taxi, call ☎ **242/323-5111.**

BY MINIBUS   The least expensive means of transport is by the medium-size buses called jitneys that the locals take. The fare is 75¢; exact change is required.

BY FERRY   Ferries run from the end of Casuarina Drive on Paradise Island across the harbor to Rawson Square for $2 per person. These "water taxis" operate during the day at 20-minute intervals between Paradise Island and Prince George Wharf. The one-way fare is $3 per person.

BY HORSE-DRAWN CARRIAGE   The elegant, traditional way to see Nassau is in a horse-drawn surrey. Negotiate with the driver and agree on the price before you get in. The average charge for a 20- to 25-minute tour is $10 per person. The maximum load is three adults plus one or two children under the age of 12. The surreys are available daily from 9am to 4:30pm, except when horses are rested—usually from 1 to 3pm May through October, and from 1 to 2pm November through April. You'll find the surreys at Rawson Square, off Bay Street.

BY MOTOR SCOOTER/MOPED   Motor scooters have become a favorite mode of transportation. For a rental, contact **Ursa Investment,** Prince George Wharf (☎ **242/326-8329**). Mopeds cost about $20 per hour or $50 for a full day.

BY RENTAL CAR   If you want to rent a car, try **Avis** (☎ **800/331-1212** in the U.S., or 242/326-6380), **Budget** (☎ **800/527-0070** in the U.S., or 242/377-7405), and **Hertz** (☎ **800/654-3131** in the U.S., or 242/377-8684), and remember to drive on the left, British-style.

SHORE EXCURSIONS

There's a lot you can do on your own in Nassau, and it's easy to get around by taxi and on foot. Your ship will probably offer several organized island tours, as well as snorkeling and a range of waterborne sightseeing tours via glass-bottomed boat and submarine and/or booze cruises aboard a catamaran. Here are some of the best ones.

Heart of Nassau and Ardastra Gardens ($25, 2$^{1}/_{2}$ hours): You're taken along Bay Street, the main shopping district, and later treated to the famous marching flamingo review in the gardens. Other stops include the Queen's Staircase and Fort Charlotte.

Fort Fincastle Tour ($21, 2 hours): This tour takes you to a great view, the Queen's Staircase, and some of the most beautiful homes of Nassau, then across the bridge to view the highlights of Paradise Island, including the Cloisters and its side gardens.

Crystal Cay Tour ($21, 3 hours): The country's most popular attraction has a network of aquariums, an Underwater Observation Tower, landscaped park areas, lounges, and a restaurant. The tour is more expensive if you opt to rent snorkeling equipment. (*Note:* It's almost as easy to go on your own.)

TOURING THROUGH LOCAL OPERATORS

Goombay Guided Walking Tours: These free tours, arranged by the Ministry of Tourism (☎ **242/326-9772**), leave from the Tourist Information Booth on Rawson Square. Make an advance reservation, as schedules can vary. Usually the tours leave the booth at 10am and again at 2pm, except on Thursday and Sunday afternoons. These tours last for about 45 minutes and include descriptions of some of the city's most venerable buildings, with commentaries on the history, customs, and traditions of Nassau.

Walking Around Underwater: Hartley's Undersea Walk, East Bay Street (☎ **242/ 393-8234**), takes you on a 3$^{1}/_{2}$-hour cruise on the yacht *Pied Piper.* At one point you don a breathing helmet and spend about 20 minutes walking along the ocean bottom through a "garden" of tropical fish, sponges, and other undersea life. Entire families can make this walk. You don't even have to be able to swim. Trips are operated Tuesday to Saturday at 9:30am and 1:30pm.

Day Cruises: Nassau Cruises Ltd., at the Paradise Island Bridge (☎ **242/363-3577**), maintains a trio of luxurious three-deck motorized yachts, *Calypso I, Calypso IV,* and *The Islander,* all of which depart from a point just west of the toll booth at the Paradise Island Bridge. Daytime trips leave every day for the secluded beaches of Blue Lagoon Island, a 4-mile sail east of Paradise Island. The day sails leave at 10am and 11:30am and come back from the island at 1:30, 3, and 4:30pm. The day pass is $20 for adults and $10 for children, and pays for the boat ride only. The all-inclusive day pass is $50 for adults and $25 for children (3 to 12), and covers transportation, the boat ride, lunch, two daiquiris for adults, and all nonmotorized water sports.

ON YOUR OWN: WITHIN WALKING DISTANCE

The best way to see some of the major public buildings of Nassau is to take a walk, which gives you not only an overview of the historical monuments, but a feel for the city and its history. Later you can concentrate on specific outlying sights, notably Ardastra Gardens and Coral Island Bahamas.

Begin your stroll around Nassau at **Rawson Square** in the center, home of the Straw Market stalls. I also enjoy the native market on the waterfront, a short walk through the Straw Market. This is where Bahamian fishermen unload a variety of fish and produce—crates of mangoes, oranges, tomatoes, and limes, plus lots of crimson-lipped conch. For a look, it's best to go any Monday-to-Saturday morning before noon.

"Lady, get your hair braided!" You'll be aggressively solicited to have your hair braided in the local style at the ✪ **Hairbraider's Centre,** Prince George Dock. The government sponsors this open-air pavilion where all sorts of braiding experts gather. If you're looking for a new look, here's your chance. If you're not, a polite "no thanks" does the trick.

Potter's Cay, under the Paradise Island Bridge, provides a chance to observe local life as nowhere else. Sloops from the Out Islands pull in here, bringing their fresh catch along with plenty of conch. Freshly grown herbs and vegetables are also sold here, along with limes (the Bahamians' preferred seasoning for fish) and tropical fruits such as *paw-paw* (papaya), pineapple (usually from Eleuthera), and bananas. Little stalls sell conch in several forms: raw, marinated in lime juice, as spicy deep-fried fritters, and in conch salad and conch soup.

The Cloister, in front of the Ocean Club, Ocean Club Drive, Paradise Island (☎ 242/363-3000), is a real 14th-century cloister, built in France by Augustinian monks and reassembled here stone by stone. Huntington Hartford, the A&P stores heir, purchased the cloister from the estate of William Randolph Hearst at San Simeon in California, but the dismantled parts arrived unlabeled and unnumbered on Paradise Island. The deconstructed cloister baffled the experts until artist and sculptor Jean Castre-Manne set about to reassemble it. It took him 2 years, and what you see today presumably bears some similarity to the original. The gardens, extending over the rise to Nassau Harbour, are filled with tropical flowers and classic statuary.

Crystal Cay marine park, on Silver Cay just off West Bay Street, between downtown Nassau and Cable Beach (☎ 242/328-1036), has a network of aquariums, landscaped park areas, lounges, a gift shop, and a restaurant, but its outstanding feature is the Underwater Observation Tower. You descend a spiral staircase to a depth of 20 feet below the surface of the water, where you view coral reefs and abundant sea life in their natural habitat. The tower rises 100 feet above the water to two viewing decks. Graceful stingrays, endangered sea turtles, and Caribbean sharks swim in Shark Tank, which has both an overhead viewing deck and a below-water viewing area. Nature trails with lush tropical foliage, waterfalls, exotic trees, and wildlife further enhance this setting. You can get here via a scenic 10-minute ferry ride from the Prince George Dock.

Fort Fincastle, Elizabeth Avenue (☎ **242/322-2442**), which can be reached by climbing the Queen's Staircase, was constructed in 1793 by Lord Dunmore, the royal governor. From here you can take an elevator ride to the top and walk on an observation floor (a 126-foot-high water tower and lighthouse) for a view of the harbor. Although the ruins of the fort can hardly compete with the view, you can walk around on your own or take a guided tour. You don't have to ask for a guide, since very assertive young men wait to show you around. Frankly, there isn't that much to see except some old cannons.

It's quite likely you'll miss the Junkanoo parade beginning at 2am on Boxing Day (Dec 26), but you can relive the Bahamian Junkanoo carnival at the **Junkanoo Expo,** Prince George Wharf (☎ **242/356-2731**), in the old Customs Warehouse. All the glitter and glory of Mardi Gras comes alive in this museum, with its fantasy costumes used for the holiday bacchanal.

ON YOUR OWN: BEYOND WALKING DISTANCE

A flock of pink flamingos parading in formation is the main attraction at the lush, 5-acre ✪ **Ardastra Gardens,** Chippingham Road, near Fort Charlotte, about a mile west of downtown Nassau (☎ **242/323-5806**). These Marching Flamingos have been trained to obey the drillmaster's oral orders with long-legged precision and discipline. They perform daily at 11am, 2pm, and 4pm. Other exotic wildlife to be seen here are very tame boa constrictors, kinkajous (honey bears) from Central and South America, green-winged macaws, peafowl, blue-and-gold macaws, capuchin monkeys, and more. You can get a good look at the flora of the gardens by walking along the signposted paths, as many of the more interesting and exotic trees bear identification plaques. Guided tours of the gardens and the aviary are given Monday to Saturday at 10:15am and 3:15pm.

A true oasis in Nassau, the 11 acres of unspoiled gardens at **The Retreat,** Village Road (☎ **242/393-1317**), are even more intriguing than the Botanical Gardens. They are home to about 200 species of exotic palm trees, as well as the headquarters for the Bahamas National Trust. Half-hour tours of the acres are given Tuesday to Thursday at noon.

GAMBLING

Many cruise ship passengers spend almost their entire time ashore at one of the casinos on Cable Beach or Paradise Island.

All gambling roads eventually lead to the extravagant **Paradise Island Casino,** in the Atlantis, Casino Drive (☎ **242/363-3000**). For sheer gloss, glitter, and showbiz extravagance, this mammoth 30,000-square-foot casino, with adjacent attractions, is the place to go. It's the only casino on Paradise Island, and is superior to the Crystal Palace Casino, below. No visit to the Bahamas would be complete without a promenade through the Bird Cage Walk, an assortment of restaurants, bars, and cabaret facilities. Doric columns, a battery of lights, and a mirrored ceiling vie with the British-colonial decor in the enormous gaming room. Some 1,000 slot machines operate 24 hours a day, and from midmorning until early the following morning, the 59 gaming tables are all seriously busy.

The glitzy **Crystal Palace Casino,** West Bay Street, Cable Beach (☎ **242/ 327-6200**), screams 1980s with its pink and purple rainbow decor. It's the only casino on New Providence Island and is run by Nassau Marriott Resort. Although some savvy gamblers claim you get better odds in Las Vegas, this 35,000-square-foot casino nevertheless stacks up well against all the major casinos of the Caribbean. The gaming room features 750 slot machines in true Las Vegas style, along with 69 gaming tables. An oval-shaped casino bar extends onto the gambling floor, and a Casino Lounge, with its bar and bandstand, offers live entertainment. Open Sunday to Thursday from 10am to 4am, Friday and Saturday 24 hours.

SHOPPING

In 1992, the Bahamas abolished import duties on 11 categories of luxury goods, including china, crystal, fine linens, jewelry, leather goods, photographic equipment, watches, fragrances, and other merchandise, but even though prices are duty-free, you can still end up spending more on an item in the Bahamas than you would back home. If you're contemplating buying a good Swiss watch or some expensive perfume, it's best to look in your hometown discount outlets before making serious purchases here. While the advertised 30% to 50% reductions off stateside prices might be true in some cases, they're not in most. There are few great bargains here.

The principal shopping area is a stretch of **Bay Street,** the main drag, and its side streets. Here's you'll find chain stores like **Colombian Emeralds, Soloman's Mines,** and **Fendi.** There are also shops in the hotel arcades. In lieu of street numbers along Bay Street, look for signs advertising the various stores.

The crowded aisles of the **Straw Market** in Straw Market Plaza on Bay Street seems to be on every shopper's itinerary. Even those who don't want to buy anything come here to look around. You can watch the Bahamian craftspeople weave and plait straw hats, handbags, dolls, place mats, and other items, including straw shopping bags. You'll also find earrings and other inexpensive items. Most shopkeepers are willing to bargain, though a few won't budge. Give it a shot. Note, though, that some of the items here are not locally made, but imported from Asia. Be careful. The **Bahamas Plait Market,** Wulff Road, and **The Plait Lady,** the Regarno Building, Victoria and Bay streets, are both far superior to the Straw Market, offering good choices for 100% Bahamian-made products. **Island Tings,** Bay Street between East Street and Elizabeth Avenue, and **Seagrape,** West Bay Street, both offer Bahamian arts and crafts, plus jewelry and other items.

The tired-looking **Nassau International Bazaar,** running from Bay Street down to the waterfront near the Prince George Wharf, is composed of some 30 shops selling goods from around the globe. The alleyways here have been cobbled and storefronts are garreted, evoking the villages of old Europe. **Prince George Plaza,** Bay Street, can be crowded with cruise ship passengers. Many fine shops here sell Gucci and other quality merchandise. You can also patronize an open-air rooftop restaurant overlooking the street.

If you've fallen under the junkanoo spell and want to take home some steel drums, stop by **Pyfroms** on Bay Street. If you'd rather listen than play, try **Cody's Music and Video Center** on East Bay Street, corner of Armstrong Street, which specializes in contemporary music of the Bahamas and the Caribbean. The father of owner Cody Carter was mentor to many of the country's first Goombay and junkanoo artists.

Pipe of Peace, on Bay Street between Charlotte and Parliament streets, is called the "world's most complete tobacconist." You can buy both Cuban and Jamaican cigars here. (However, the Cuban cigars can't legally be brought back to the United States.)

Stamp collectors should stop by the **Bahamas Post Office Philatelic Bureau,** in the General Post Office, at the top of Parliament Street on East Hill Street, for beautiful Bahamian stamps, while **Coin of the Realm,** on Charlotte Street, just off Bay Street, is the place for coin collectors. **The Girls from Brazil** on Bay Street is the best outlet for swimwear in Nassau, and **Mademoiselle, Ltd.,** on Bay Street at Frederick Street, specializes in all kinds of resort wear as well as locally made batik garments by Androsia.

BEACHES

On New Providence Island, sun lovers flock to **Cable Beach,** one of the best-equipped in the Caribbean, with all sorts of water sports and easy access to shops, casinos, bars, and restaurants. The area was named for the telegraph cable laid in 1892 from Jupiter, Florida, to the Bahamas. Cable Beach runs for some 4 miles and is relatively wide. Waters can be rough and reefy, and then turn calm and clear. The beach is about 5 miles from the port and can be reached by taxi (for about a steep $10 a person) or bus no. 10 (for 75¢).

Western Esplanade, which sweeps westward from the British Colonial hotel, is closer and more convenient for those arriving by cruise ship, but is inferior to Cable Beach. It has rest rooms, changing facilities, and a snack bar.

Paradise Beach on Paradise Island is a fine beach and convenient to Nassau—all visitors have to do is walk or drive across the bridge or take a boat from the Prince George Wharf (see "Getting Around," above). Admission to the beach is $3 for adults, $1 for children, including use of a shower and locker. An extra $10 deposit is required for towels. Paradise Island has a number of smaller beaches as well, including **Pirate's Cove Beach** and **Cabbage Beach,** both on the north shore. Bordered by casuarinas, palms, and sea grapes, Cabbage Beach's broad sands stretch for at least 2 miles. It's likely to be crowded with guests of the island's megaresorts. Escapists find something approaching solitude on the northwestern end, accessible only by boat or foot.

SPORTS

GOLF   South Ocean Golf Course, Southwest Bay Road (☎ 242/362-4391), is the best course on New Providence Island and one of the best in the Bahamas. It's located 30 minutes from Nassau on the southwest edge of the island. This 18-hole, 6,706-yard, par-72 beauty has some first-rate holes with a backdrop of trees, shrubs, ravines, and undulating hills. The lofty elevation offers some panoramic water views. It's best to phone ahead in case there's a tournament scheduled. **Cable Beach Golf Course,** Cable Beach, West Bay Road (☎ 242/327-6000), is a spectacular 18-hole, 7,040-yard, par-72 championship golf course, although not as challenging as South Ocean. Under the management of Radisson Cable Beach Hotel, this course is often used by guests of the other nearby hotels. **Paradise Island Golf Club,** Paradise Island Drive (☎ 242/363-3925), is a superb 18-hole championship course at the east end of Paradise Island. The 14th hole of the 6,771-yard, par-72 course has the world's largest sand trap: The entire left side over the hole is white-sand beach.

HORSEBACK RIDING   On the southwest shore, 2 miles from the Nassau Airport, **Happy Trails Stables,** Coral Harbour (☎ 242/362-1820), offers a 1-hour 20-minute horseback trail ride for $60 per person, including free round-trip transportation from your hotel. The weight limit for riders is 200 pounds. Children must be 8 or older. Reservations are required, especially during the holiday season.

SCUBA DIVING & SNORKELING   Bahama Divers, East Bay Street (☎ 242/393-5644), offers a half day of snorkeling at offshore reefs, and a half-day scuba trip with preliminary pool instruction for beginners. Participants receive free transportation to the boats. Children must be 8 or older to go snorkeling. Reservations are required, especially during the winter season. **Stuart Cove's Dive South Ocean,** Southwest Bay Street, South Ocean (☎ 800/879-9832 in the U.S., or 242/362-4171), is about 10 minutes from top dive sites, including the coral reefs, wrecks, and an underwater airplane structure used in filming James Bond thrillers. The Porpoise Pen Reefs and steep sea walls are also on the diving agenda. All prices for boat dives include tanks, weights, and belts. A special feature is a series of shark-dive experiences.

WATER SPORTS   Sea Sports, at the Nassau Marriott Resort & Crystal Palace Casino on West Bay Street (☎ 242/327-6200), offers a full water-sports program. You can rent Hobie Cats, Sunfish, Windsurfers, and kayaks, and arrange for parasailing and waterskiing. **Sea & Ski Ocean Sports,** at the Radisson Grand Resort on Casino Dr. (☎ 242/363-3370), offers scuba-diving and snorkeling trips, parasailing, and windsurfing.

GREAT LOCAL RESTAURANTS & BARS

The **local beer** in Bermuda is Kalik. The **local rum** is Bacardi.

✪ **ON ARAWAK CAY**   You'll get all the conch you can possibly eat on Arawak Cay, a small man-made island across West Bay Street. The Bahamian government created the cay to store large tanks of freshwater, of which New Providence Island often runs out. You don't go here to see the water tanks, however, but to join the locals in sampling their favorite food. The conch is cracked before your eyes (not everybody's favorite attraction), and you're given some hot sauce to spice it up. The locals wash it down with their favorite drink, coconut milk laced with gin (an acquired taste, to say the least). This ritual is a local tradition, and you'll feel like a real Bahamian if you participate.

IN NASSAU   Bahamian Kitchen, Trinity Place, off Market Street, next to Trinity Church (☎ 242/325-0702), is one of the best places for good, down-home Bahamian food at modest prices. Specialties include lobster Bahamian style, fried red snapper, and curried chicken. **Café Kokomo,** in the garden of the Parliament Hotel, 18 Parliament St. (☎ 242/322-2836), serves well-prepared Bahamian seafood in a verdant setting. If you like your dining with a view, there's no better place than the second-floor, open-air terrace of the **Poop Deck,** Nassau Yacht Haven Marina, East Bay Street (☎ 242/393-8175), overlooking the harbor and Paradise Island.

Far removed from the well-trodden tourist path, the **Shoal Restaurant and Lounge,** Nassau Street (☎ 242/323-4400), is a steadfast local favorite and ranks near the top for authentic flavor.

Green Shutters Restaurant, 48 Parliament St., 2 blocks south of Rawson Square (☎ 242/325-5702), is an English pub transplanted to the tropics. It offers three imported English beers along with pub-grub favorites such as steak-and-kidney pie, bangers and mash, shepherd's pie, and fish-and-chips. **Gaylord's,** Dowdeswell Street at Bay Street (☎ 242/356-3004), is the only Indian restaurant in the country, and as such, is now a culinary staple of Nassau, serving a wide range of Punjabi, tandoori, and curry dishes. **Caribe Café Restaurant and Terrace,** in the British

Colonial Beach Resort, 1 Bay St. (☎ **242/322-3301**), serves typical faves like beef burgers and freshly made salads.

AT CABLE BEACH   **Café Johnny Canoe,** in the Nassau Beach Hotel, West Bay Street (☎ **242/327-3373**), serves burgers and all kinds of steaks, seafood, and chicken dishes. The best items on the menu are blackened grouper and barbecued fish. **Tequila Pepe's,** in the Radisson Cable Beach Hotel, West Bay Street (☎ **242/327-6000**), serves buffet-style Tex-Mex dishes: fajitas, tacos, burritos, tamales, and chimichangas.

ON PARADISE ISLAND   **The Cave,** at the Atlantis, Casino Drive (☎ **242/363-3000**), is a burger-and-salad joint located near the beach of the most lavish hotel and casino complex on Paradise Island. It caters to the bathing-suit-and-flip-flops crowd. To reach the place, you pass beneath a simulated rock-sided tunnel illuminated with flaming torches. **Seagrapes Restaurant,** in the Atlantis, Casino Drive (☎ **242/363-3000**), serves buffet-style tropical food, including Cuban, Caribbean, and Cajun dishes.

FREEPORT/LUCAYA

Bold and brassy Freeport/Lucaya on Grand Bahama Island is the second most popular tourist destination in the Bahamas. Its cosmopolitan glitz and the frenzy of its gambling and shopping scenes might be too much for some visitors, but there's also plenty of sun, surf, and excellent golf, tennis, and water sports. For orientation's sake, note that Freeport is technically the landlocked section of town whereas Lucaya lies right next door, along the waterfront. Though originally intended as two separate developments, they've grown together over the years.

Frommer's Favorite Freeport/Lucaya Experiences

- **Catching a concert at Count Basie Square:** Right in the center of Port Lucaya, a vine-covered bandstand hosts the best live music on the island, performed nightly. And it's free (see "On Your Own: Beyond Walking Distance," below).
- **Visiting the Star Club:** Built in the 1940s, this place has hosted many famous guests over the years, and is now the only 24-hour bar on the island (see "Great Local Restaurants & Bars," below).
- **Taking the Lucaya National Park Tour:** About 12 miles from Lucaya, the park has one of the loveliest, most secluded beaches on Grand Bahama (see "Shore Excursions," below).

COMING ASHORE   Unlike some ports of call where you land in the heart of everything, on Grand Bahama Island you're deposited in what cruisers call the middle of nowhere—the west central part of the island. You'll want to take a $10 taxi ride (for two passengers) over to Freeport and its International Bazaar, center of most of the action. As you'll quickly learn after leaving the dreary port area, everything on this island is spread out. Grand Bahama doesn't have the compactness of Nassau.

CALLING HOME FROM THE BAHAMAS   There are long-distance phones in the terminal.

INFORMATION   Information is available from the **Grand Bahama Tourism Board,** International Bazaar in Freeport (☎ **800/823-3136** or 242/352-8044). Another **information booth** is located at Port Lucaya (☎ **242/373-8988**). It's open from 9am to 5:30pm Monday to Saturday. For info before you go, call the **Bahamas Tourism Board** in New York City (☎ **212/758-2777**) or visit its Web site at www.bahamas.com.

Frommer's Ratings: Freeport/Lucaya					
	Poor	Fair	Good	Excellent	Outstanding
Overall Experience					✓
Shore Excursions			✓		
Activities Close to Port				✓	
Beaches & Water Sports			✓		
Shopping				✓	
Dining/Bars			✓		

GETTING AROUND

Once you get to Freeport by taxi you can explore the center of town on foot. If you want to make excursions into the West End or East End of the island, you'll either need a car or have to rely on taxis or the highly erratic public transportation.

BY TAXI   The government sets the taxi rates. The meter starts at $2, and 30¢ is charged for each additional quarter mile for two passengers. Most taxis wait at the cruise ship dock to pick up passengers, or you can call **Freeport Taxi Company** (☎ 242/352-6666) or **Grand Bahama Taxi Union** (☎ 242/352-7101).

BY RENTAL CAR   Roads are generally good on Grand Bahama Island, and it's easy to drive around. For car rentals, try **Avis** (☎ 800/331-2112 in the U.S., or 242/352-7666); **Hertz** (☎ 800/654-3001 in the U.S., or 242/352-9277); or the local **Star Rent-a-Car,** Old Airport Road (☎ 242/352-5953).

BY MOTOR SCOOTER OR BICYCLE   You can rent them at any of the major hotels such as **Princess Country Club,** West Sunrise Highway (☎ 242/352-6721). A two-seat scooter requires a $100 deposit and rents for about $40 per day; bicycles require a $50 deposit and cost about $12 for a half day, $20 for a full day.

BY BUS   Public bus service runs from the International Bazaar to downtown Freeport and from the Pub on the Mall to the Lucaya area. The typical fare is 75¢ to $1.

SHORE EXCURSIONS

Because most things to do here are in Freeport, the excursion offerings are weak and you can often manage better on your own. Many cruise ships tout a sightseeing trip where you spend about 30 minutes at the Garden of the Groves and then are led like cattle around the International Bazaar. The latter is better explored on your own. The 3-hour trip costs about $23 per passenger.

Lucaya National Park Tour: Not all lines offer this, but if you see it offered, an excursion to the lush, 40-acre park on Sunrise Highway is a worthwhile and relaxing afternoon. The park, about 12 miles from Lucaya, has one of the loveliest, most secluded beaches on Grand Bahama.

TOURING THROUGH LOCAL OPERATORS

Booze Cruise: Many lines offer booze cruises, but you can also arrange your own with **Superior Watersports** in Freeport (☎ 242/373-7863), which offers fun cruises on its *Bahama Mama,* a 72-foot catamaran with two semisubmersibles that dive 5 feet.

Freeport/Lucaya

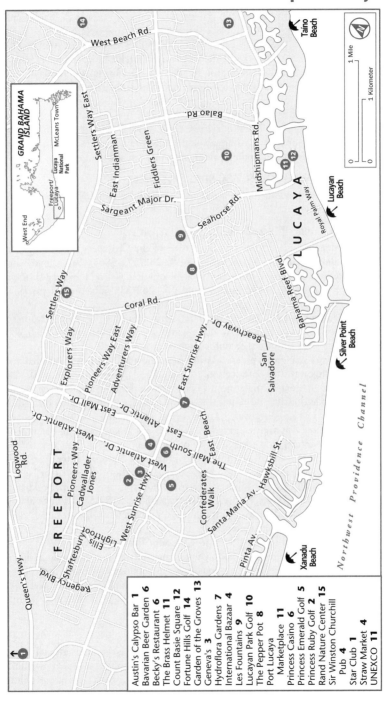

GRAND BAHAMA ISLAND

West End

Freeport/Lucaya

Lucaya National Park

McLeans Town

FREEPORT

Queen's Hwy.

Logwood Rd.

Regency Blvd.

Shaftesbury

Ellis

Lightfoot

Pioneers Way

Cadwallader Jones

West Atlantic Dr.

West Sunrise Hwy.

Explorers Way

Pioneers Way East

Adventurers Way

East Mall Dr.

East Atlantic Dr.

Settlers Way

Coral Rd.

Settlers Way East

East Indianman

Fiddlers Green

Sargeant Major Dr.

Seahorse Rd.

Balao Rd.

Midshipmans Rd.

East Sunrise Hwy.

Beachway Dr.

San Salvadore

Confederates Walk

The Mall South

East Beach

Santa Maria Av.

Hawksbill St.

Pinta Av.

Xanadu Beach

Silver Point Beach

LUCAYA

Bahama Reef Blvd.

Royal Palm Way

Lucayan Beach

Taino Beach

Northwest Providence Channel

1 Mile

1 Kilometer

Austin's Calypso Bar **1**
Bavarian Beer Garden **6**
Becky's Restaurant **6**
The Brass Helmet **11**
Count Basie Square **12**
Fortune Hills Golf **14**
Garden of the Groves **13**
Geneva's **3**
Hydroflora Gardens **7**
International Bazaar **4**
Les Fountains **9**
Lucayan Park Golf **10**
The Pepper Pot **8**
Port Lucaya
  Marketplace **11**
Princess Casino **6**
Princess Emerald Golf **5**
Princess Ruby Golf **2**
Rand Nature Center **15**
Sir Winston Churchill
  Pub **4**
Star Club **1**
Straw Market **4**
UNEXCO **11**

95

Swimming with Dolphins: You get to see porpoises up close with **The Dolphin Experience,** operated by the Underwater Explorers Society (UNEXSO), in Port Lucaya opposite Lucayan Beach Casino (☎ **800/992-3483** or 242/373-1250). UNEXSO conducts this unique dolphin/human familiarization program in which participants observe these intelligent, friendly animals close up and hear an interesting lecture by a member of the animal-care staff. This is not a swim-with-the-dolphins type of program, but all ages can step onto a shallow wading platform and interact with the animals. The encounter onshore costs $39. An "Assistant Trainer" program costs $179 and is an all-day interactive experience in which a maximum of four people, aged 16 or older, can learn about dolphins and marine mammals in a behind-the-scenes experience, including swimming with them and feeding them.

ON YOUR OWN: WITHIN WALKING DISTANCE

There's nothing within walking distance of the port; you have to head over to Freeport/Lucaya.

ON YOUR OWN: BEYOND WALKING DISTANCE

The prime attraction is the 11-acre **Garden of the Groves,** at the intersection of Midshipman Road and Magellan Drive (☎ **242/373-5668**). Seven miles east of the International Bazaar, this scenic preserve of waterfalls and flowering shrubs has some 10,000 trees. The **Palmetto Café** (☎ **242/373-5668**) serves snacks and drinks, and a Bahamian straw market sits at the entrance gate.

Hydroflora Garden, on East Beach at Sunrise Highway (☎ **242/352-6052**), is an artificially created botanical wonder, featuring over 150 specimens of indigenous Bahamian plants. A special section is devoted to bush medicine.

Filled with mangrove, pine, and palm trees, the 40-acre **Lucaya National Park,** Sunrise Highway (for information, contact Rand Nature Centre at ☎ **242/352-5438**), is about 12 miles from Lucaya. The park contains one of the loveliest, most secluded beaches on Grand Bahama. A wooden path winding through the trees leads to this long, wide, dune-covered stretch. You can enter two caves, exposed when a portion of ground collapsed. The pools there are composed of 6 feet of freshwater atop a heavier layer of salt water.

Located 2 miles east of Freeport's center, the **Rand Nature Centre,** East Settlers Way (☎ **242/352-5438**), is the regional headquarters of the Bahamas National Trust, a nonprofit conservation organization. Forest nature trails highlight native flora and bush medicine in this 100-acre pineland sanctuary. Wild birds abound. Other features include native animal displays, a replica of a Lucayan Indian village, an education center, and a gift shop.

If your ship is in port late, head to ✪ **Count Basie Square** for one of the free nightly concerts. Count Basie had a grand home on Grand Bahama, and in the center of the waterfront restaurant-and-shopping complex of Port Lucaya there's a square named in his honor. There's a vine-covered bandstand where steel bands, small junkanoo groups, and even gospel singers from a local church are likely to perform, their music wafting across the 50-slip marina.

SHOPPING

There's no place for shopping in the Bahamas quite like the **International Bazaar,** at East Mall Drive and East Sunrise Highway. It's one of the world's most unusual shopping marts—Bahamian kitsch in poured concrete and plastic, 10 acres of born-to-shop theme-park tastelessness—but in the nearly 100 shops you're bound to find something that is both a discovery and a bargain. Many items sold in the shops here could run about 40% less than in the United States, but don't count on it. Buses marked INTERNATIONAL BAZAAR take you right to the much-photographed Toril Gate, a Japanese symbol of welcome.

The bazaar blends architecture from 25 countries into several theme areas: the Ginza in Tokyo for Asian goods; the Left Bank of Paris, or a reasonable facsimile, with sidewalk cafes where you can enjoy a café au lait and perhaps a pastry under shade trees; a Continental Pavilion for leather goods, jewelry, lingerie, and gifts at shops with names such as Love Boutique; India House for exotic goods such as taxi horns and silk saris; Africa for carvings or a colorful dashiki; and a Spanish section for Latin-American and Iberian serapes and piñatas.

At the **Straw Market,** beside the International Bazaar, you'll find items with a special Bahamian touch—colorful baskets, hats, handbags, and place mats—all of which make good gifts and souvenirs of your trip.

The **Port Lucaya Marketplace** on Seahorse Road, the first of its kind in the Bahamas, was named after the original settlers of Grand Bahama. This is a shopping-and-dining complex set on 6 acres. Free entertainment, such as steel-drum bands and strolling musicians, adds to a festival atmosphere. The complex rose on the site of a former Bahamian straw market, but the craftspeople and their straw products are back in full force after having been temporarily dislodged. Full advantage is taken of the waterfront location. Many of the restaurants and shops overlook a 50-slip marina, home of a "fantasy" pirate ship featuring lunch and dinner/dancing cruises. A variety of charter vessels are also based at the Port Lucaya Marina, and dockage at the marina is available to visitors coming by boat to shop or dine. A boardwalk along the water makes it easy to watch the frolicking dolphins and join in other activities at the **Underwater Explorers Society (UNEXSO).**

Merchandise in the shops of Port Lucaya ranges from leather to lingerie to wind chimes. Traditional and contemporary fashions are featured for men, women, and children. Some of the better shops are **Coconits by Androsia,** an outlet of the famous batik house of Andros Island; **Jeweler's Warehouse,** a place for bargain hunters looking for good buys on discounted, close-out 14-karat gold and gemstone jewelry; the **UNEXSO Dive Shop,** selling swimsuits, wet suits, underwater cameras, shades, hats, souvenirs, state-of-the-art divers' equipment, and computers; **Colombian Emeralds International,** offering a wide array of precious gemstone jewelry and one of the island's best watch collections; **Sea Treasures,** in the Spanish Section, with gold and silver jewelry inspired by the sea and handcrafted on the island; and **Bahamas Coin and Stamp Ltd.,** Arcade, specializing in Bahamian coin jewelry, ancient Roman coins, and relics from sunken Spanish galleons.

BEACHES

Grand Bahama has some 60 miles of white-sand beaches rimming the blue-green waters of the Atlantic. The mile-long **Xanadu Beach,** at the Xanadu Beach Resort, is the premier beach in the Freeport area. Most beaches are in the Lucaya area, site of the major resort hotels. The resort beaches, with a fairly active program of water sports, tend to be the most crowded in winter.

Other island beaches include **Taíno Beach,** lying to the east of Freeport, plus **Smith's Point** and **Fortune Beach,** the latter one of the finest on Grand Bahama. Another good beach, about a 20-minute ride east of Lucaya, is **Gold Rock Beach,** a favorite picnic spot with the locals, especially on weekends.

SPORTS

GENERAL WATER SPORTS **Paradise Watersports,** at the Xanadu Beach Resort and Marina (☎ 242/352-2887), offers a variety of activities. With snorkeling trips, you cruise to a coral reef on a 48-foot catamaran. You can also rent paddleboats and go waterskiing, parasailing, or on a glass-bottom boat ride.

GOLF This island boasts more golf links than any other in the Bahamas. They're all within 7 miles of one another, and you usually don't have to wait to play. All courses are open to the public year-round, and you can rent clubs from any of the pro shops on the island. Go on your own or sign up for an organized golf excursion if your ship offers them. **Fortune Hills Golf & Country Club,** Richmond Park, Lucaya (☎ 242/373-4500), was designed as an 18-hole course, but the back nine were never completed. You can replay the front nine for a total of 6,916 yards from the blue tees. Par is 72. The club is 5 miles east of Freeport. **Lucayan Park Golf & Country Club,** at Lucaya Beach (☎ 242/373-1066), is the best-kept and most manicured course on Grand Bahama. The course was recently made over and is quite beautiful. It's known for its entrance and a hanging boulder sculpture. Greens are fast, and there are a couple of par-5 holes more than 500 yards long. Total distance from the blue tees is 6,824 yards, 6,488 from the white tees. Par is 72. Even if you're not a golfer, sample the food at the club restaurant. It offers everything from lavish champagne brunches to first-rate seafood dishes. **Princess Emerald Course,** The Mall South (☎ 242/352-6721), is one of two courses owned and operated by the Bahamas Princess Resort & Casino. The Emerald Course was the site of the Bahamas National Open some years back. The course has plenty of trees along the fairways, as well as an abundance of water hazards and bunkers. The toughest hole is the ninth, a par-5 with 545 yards from the blue tees to the hole. The championship **Princess Ruby Course,** on West Sunrise Highway (☎ 242/352-6721), was designed by Joe Lee in 1968 and recently hosted the Michelin Long Drive competition. It's a total of 6,750 yards if played from the championship blue tees.

HORSEBACK RIDING **Pinetree Stables,** North Beachway Drive, Freeport (☎ 242/373-3600), is the best in the Bahamas, superior to rivals on New Providence Island (Nassau).

SCUBA DIVING & SNORKELING One of the premier facilities for diving and snorkeling throughout the Bahamas and Caribbean is the **Underwater Explorers Society (UNEXSO),** at Lucaya Beach (☎ 242/373-1244). It has daily reef trips, shark dives, wreck dives, and night dives. This is also the only facility in the world where divers can swim alongside dolphins in the open ocean (see "Touring Through Local Operators," above). It offers a popular 3-hour learn-to-dive course every day as well as dives for the experienced and snorkeling trips.

PARASAILING **Clarion Atlantik Beach Resort,** on Royal Palm Way (☎ 242/373-1444), is the best center on the island for parasailing.

GAMBLING

Even though there are casinos aboard almost all ships, many passengers head immediately for a land-based casino once they hit shore. Most of the day-life/nightlife in Freeport/Lucaya revolves around the **Princess Casino,** the Mall at West Sunrise Highway (☎ 242/352-7811), a glittering, giant, Moroccan-style palace.

GREAT LOCAL RESTAURANTS & BARS

The **local beer** in Bermuda is Kalik. The **local rum** is Bacardi.

If you'd like to see what's left of the Bahamas "the way it was," head for the ✪ **Star Club,** on Bayshore Road (☎ 242/346-6207) in the West End. Built in the 1940s, it was the first hotel on Grand Bahama, and hosted many famous guests over the years. It's been a long time since any guests have checked in, but the place is still going strong and is open daily until at least 2am. Sometimes people leaving the casinos late at night come over here to eat grouper fingers, play pool, or listen to the taped music. The "club" is still run by the family of the late Austin Henry Grant, Jr., a former Bahamian senator and West End legend. You can order Bahamian chicken in the bag, burgers, fish-and-chips, or "fresh sexy" conch prepared as chowder, fritters, and salads. But come here for the good times, not the food. You can also drop in next door at **Austin's Calypso Bar,** a real Grand Bahama dive if there ever was one. Austin Grant, the owner, will tell you about the good ol' days.

Geneva's, Kipling Lane, the Mall at West Sunrise Highway (☎ 242/352-5085), is another place where the food is the way it was before the hordes of tourists invaded. **Les Fountains,** East Sunrise Highway (☎ 242/373-9553), offers a great all-you-can-eat buffet as well as chicken, steak, and lobster, and dishes prepared at the jerk grill outside. **The Pepper Pot,** East Sunrise Highway at Coral Road (☎ 242/ 373-7655), a 5-minute drive east of the International Bazaar in a tiny shopping mall, serves take-out portions of the best carrot cake on the island, as well as a savory conch chowder, the standard fish and pork chops, chicken souse (an acquired taste), cracked conch, sandwiches and hamburgers, and an array of daily specials. **The Brass Helmet,** in the Port Lucaya Marketplace, directly above UNEXSO Dive Shop (☎ 242/373-2032), serves Bahamian staples, including cracked conch and grouper, plus an array of steaks, lobster, and a variety of pastas. **Becky's Restaurant,** at the International Bazaar, offers authentic Bahamian cuisine prepared in the time-tested style of the Out Islands.

Sir Winston Churchill Pub, East Mall (next to the Straw Market and the International Bazaar; ☎ 242/352-8866), is mainly a pizzeria, and also serves a selection of pastas, salads, and sandwiches. At the International Bazaar, the **Bavarian Beer Garden** features at least a dozen kinds of imported beer, recorded oom-pah-pah music, such German fare as knockwurst, bockwurst, and sauerkraut, and a selection of pizzas.

5 Barbados

No port of call in the southern Caribbean can compete with Barbados when it comes to natural beauty, attractions, and fine dining. With all it offers, you'll think the island is much bigger than it is. But what really puts Barbados on world tourist maps is its seemingly endless stretches of pink-and-white sandy beaches, among the best in the entire Caribbean Basin.

This Atlantic outpost was one of the most staunchly loyal members of the British Commonwealth for over 300 years, and although it gained its independence in 1966, British-isms still remain—the accent is Brit, driving is on the left, and Queen Elizabeth is still officially the head of state.

Originally operated on a plantation economy that made its aristocracy rich, the island is the most easterly in the Caribbean, floating in the mid-Atlantic like a great coral reef and ringed with beige-sand beaches. Cosmopolitan Barbados has the densest population of any island in the Caribbean, a sports tradition that avidly pursues cricket, and a loyal group of return visitors who appreciate its many stylish, medium-size hotels. Overall, service is usually extremely good. Topography varies from rolling hills and savage waves on the eastern (Atlantic) coast to densely populated flatlands, rows of hotels and apartments, and sheltered beaches in the southwest.

The people in Barbados are called *Bajans,* and you'll see this term used everywhere.

Frommer's Favorite Barbados Experiences

- **Renting a car for a Barbados road trip:** Seventeenth-century churches, tropical flowers, snorkeling, great views, and more are just a rental car ride away (see "On Your Own: Beyond Walking Distance," below).
- **Visiting Gun Hill Signal Station:** If you've got less time, hire a taxi or rent a car and go to Gun Hill for panoramic views of the island (see "On Your Own: Beyond Walking Distance," below).
- **Diving deep on a submarine:** Sightseeing submarines make several dives daily (see "Shore Excursions," below).

COMING ASHORE   The cruise ship pier, a short drive from Bridgetown, the capital, is one of the best docking facilities in the southern Caribbean. You can walk right into the modern cruise ship terminal, which has car rentals, taxi services, sightseeing tours, and a tourist information office, plus shops and scads of vendors (see "Shopping," below). You'll also find credit-card telephones, fax facilities, and phone cards and stamps for sale.

If you want to go into Bridgetown, about a mile from the port, instead of to the beach, you can take a hot, dusty walk of at least 30 minutes, or catch a taxi. The one-way fare ranges from $4 on up. There's also a bus running until noon for $1.

Credit-card **phone booths** with AT&T access are located in the cruise ship terminal. Also, in downtown Bridgetown there's a phone center (B.E.T.) on the corner of Hinck Street.

CURRENCY   The **Barbados dollar (BD$)** is the official currency, available in $100, $20, $10, and $5 notes and $1, 25¢, and 10¢ silver coins, plus 5¢ and 1¢ copper coins. The exchange rate is BD$1.98 to $1 U.S. (BD$1 is worth about 51¢). Unless otherwise specified, prices in this section are given in U.S. dollars. Most stores take traveler's checks or U.S. dollars, so don't bother to convert them if you're here for only a day.

LANGUAGE   English is spoken with an island lilt.

INFORMATION   The **Barbados Tourism Authority** is on Harbour Road (P.O. Box 242), Bridgetown, Barbados, W.I. (☎ **888/barbados** or 246/427-2623). Its cruise terminal office, which is very well run, is always open when a cruise ship is in port.

CALLING FROM THE U.S.   When calling Barbados from the United States, you need to only dial a "1" before the telephone numbers listed throughout this section.

Frommer's Ratings: Barbados					
	Poor	Fair	Good	Excellent	Outstanding
Overall Experience				✓	
Shore Excursions			✓		
Activities Close to Port			✓		
Beaches & Water Sports			✓		
Shopping			✓		
Dining/Bars			✓		

Barbados

Airport ✈ **Beach** 🏖 **Church** ✝
Lighthouse 🗼 **Cruise Ship Dock** 🚢

North Point

Archer's Bay
River Bay

Stroud Bay
Cuckold Point

ST. LUCY
Harrison Point
Fairfield
Gay's Cove
Maycock's Bay 1B
Pico Teneriffe
Coleton 1C
Half Moon Fort
Morgan Lewis Beach

Six Men's Bay
Greenland 2
Heywoods Beach
St. Andrew's Church
Speightstown
ST. PETER
ST. ANDREW
SCOTLAND
Mullins Beach
Turner's Hall Woods
Chalky Mount
Cattlewash
Gibbs Beach

Gold Coast
Lower Carlton 1 2A
Bathsheba Tent Bay

Church Point
ST. JAMES
ST. JOSEPH 3
Martin's Bay
FOLKSTONE UNDERWATER PARK 1
2 3A
Congor Rocks
Welchman Hall
3
Consett Bay
Holetown 1A
Blackmans
ST. JOHN
CULPEPPER ISLAND
Sunset Crest
4
Ragged Point Lighthouse
Paynes Bay
ST. THOMAS
3B
Three Houses
Kitridge Point
Lazaretto
2A 2
Prospect
Locust Hall
Bushy Park
Bottom Bay
Paradise Beach
Warrens 3
5 6
Sandford
5
Brighton Beach
ST. MICHAEL
ST. GEORGE
4
ST. PHILIP
Black Rock
4 4B
Marchfield
Long Bay 7
3
5
Beachy Head
Deep Water Harbour
Queen's Park
CHRISTCHURCH
Crane Beach
6
Bridgetown
6
7
Carlisle Bay
Needham's Point
Hastings
St. Lawrence
Tom Adams Hwy.
Rockley Beach
Worthing
Maxwell
7
Grantley Adams International Airport
Sandy Beach
Oistins
Casuarina Beach
Long Bay
South Point
Silver Sands Beach

Atlantic Ocean

East Coast Rd.
Hackleton's Cliff

Errol Barrow Hwy.
Spring Garden Hwy.

Charles Duncan O'Neale Hwy.

Caribbean Sea

0   5 Miles
0   5 Kilometers

Caribbean Islands
Barbados

Flower Forest of Barbados **3**
Francia Plantation **5**
Gun Hill Signal Station **6**
Harrison's Cave **4**
Sam Lord's Castle **7**
St. James Church **1**
Welchman Hall Gully **2**

GETTING AROUND

BY TAXI   They're not metered, but their rates are fixed by the government. Even so, drivers may try and get more money out of you, so make sure you settle on the rate before getting in. Taxis are identified by the letter *Z* on their license plates, and you'll find them just outside of the terminal.

BY BUS   Blue-and-yellow public buses fan out from Bridgetown every 20 minutes or so onto the major routes; their destinations are marked on the front. Buses going south and east leave from Fairchild Street, and those going north and west depart from Lower Green and the Princess Alice Highway. Fares are about BD$1.50 (U.S.75¢) and exact change is required; you can use U.S. currency, but you're likely to get change back in local BD$.

Privately owned **minibuses** run shorter distances and travel more frequently. These bright yellow buses display destinations on the bottom-left corner of the windshield. In Bridgetown, board at River Road, Temple Yard, and Probyn Street. Fare is about BD$1.50 (U.S.75¢).

BY RENTAL CAR   While it's a good way to see the island if you've got an adventurous streak and an easygoing attitude, before you decide to rent a car, keep in mind that driving is on the left side of the road, and the signs are totally inadequate (boy, could I tell you stories!). There are several car-rental agents at the cruise terminal (be sure you take a look at the car before signing on the dotted line).

SHORE EXCURSIONS

It's not easy to get around Barbados quickly and conveniently, so a shore excursion is a good idea here.

Harrison's Cave ($37–$54 adults and $29–$40 children, 3–4 hours): Most cruise lines offer a tour to Harrison's Cave in the center of the island (see "On Your Own: Beyond Walking Distance," below, for details).

Atlantis **Submarine Adventure** ($83–$89, 2 hours): The *Atlantis* transports passengers through Barbados's undersea world, where you can watch the fishies and other colorful marine life through 28-inch windows.

✪ **Barbados Highlights Bus Tour** ($29–$38, 3 hours): Tours take passengers by bus to Gun Hill Signal Station, St. John's Church, and Sam Lord's Castle Resort (see "On Your Own: Beyond Walking Distance," below, for details).

Insider Tips: Barbados

- The rough seas on the island's East Coast make it dangerous for swimming.
- Be sure to try the tasty local delicacy, flying fish. You can even get it in burger form.
- Being that this is a British-flavored island, in restaurants, custom has it that you won't get your bill until you ask for it.
- Rental cars all have an *H* on their license plates (meaning "hired"), so everyone will know you're a tourist (which will explain to them while you're probably driving so dang slow!).

TOURING THROUGH LOCAL OPERATORS

Island Tours/Eco Tours ($56 per person, 6 to 8 hours): Since most cruise lines don't really offer a comprehensive island tour, many passengers deal with one of the local tour companies. **Bajan Tours,** Glenayre, Locust Hall, St. George (☎ **246/ 437-9389**), offers an island tour that leaves between 8:30am and 9am, and returns to the ship before departure. It covers all the island's highlights. On Friday company conducts a heritage tour, focusing mainly on the island's major plantations and museums. On Tuesday and Wednesday it offers an Eco Tour, which takes in the natural beauty of the island. Call ahead for information and to reserve a spot.

If you can afford it, **touring by taxi** is far more relaxing than the standardized bus tour. Nearly all Bajan taxi drivers are familiar with their island and like to show off their knowledge to visitors. The standard rate is about $20 per hour per taxi (for one to four passengers). You might want to try contacting taxi driver and owner Aaron Francis (☎ 246/431-9059). He's a gem—friendly, reliable, and knowledgeable.

ON YOUR OWN: WITHIN WALKING DISTANCE

About the only thing you can walk to is the cruise terminal. The modern, pleasant complex has an array of duty-free shops and retail stores, plus many vendors selling arts and crafts, jewelry, liquor, china, crystal, electronics, perfume, and leather goods.

ON YOUR OWN: BEYOND WALKING DISTANCE

I don't recommend wasting too much time in Bridgetown—it's hot, dry, and dusty, and the honking horns of traffic jams only add to its woes. So, unless you want to go shopping, you should spend your time exploring all the beauty the island has to offer instead. The tourist office in the terminal is very helpful if you want to go somewhere on your own.

Welchman Hall Gully, St. Thomas (Highway 2 from Bridgetown; ☎ **246/ 438-6671**), is a lush tropical garden owned by the Barbados National Trust. The gully is 8 miles from the port and features some plants that were here when the English settlers landed in 1627. It can be reached by bus from the terminal.

All cruise ship excursions visit **Harrison's Cave,** Welchman Hall, St. Thomas (☎ **246/438-6640**), Barbados's top tourist attraction. Here you can see a beautiful underground world from aboard an electric tram and trailer. If you'd like to go on your own, a taxi ride takes about 30 minutes and costs just under $20.

A mile from Harrison's Cave is the **Flower Forest,** Richmond Plantation, St. Joseph (☎ **246/433-8152**). This old sugar plantation stands 850 feet above sea level near the western edge of the "Scotland district," in one of the most scenic parts of Barbados. The forest is 12 miles from the cruise terminal; one-way taxi fare is about $15.

A fine home still owned and occupied by descendants of the original owner, the **Francia Plantation,** St. George (☎ **246/429-0474**), stands on a wooded hillside overlooking the St. George Valley. You can explore several rooms. The plantation lies about 20 miles from the port; one-way taxi fare is about $20.

The **Gun Hill Signal Station,** Highway 4 (☎ **246/429-1358**), one of two such stations owned and operated by the Barbados National Trust, is strategically placed on the highland of St. George and commands a wonderful panoramic view from east to west. Built in 1818, the station is 12 miles from the port; the one-way taxi ride costs about $18.

Sam Lord's Castle Resort, Long Bay, St. Philip (☎ 246/423-7350), was built in 1820 by one of Barbados's most notorious scoundrels, Samuel Hall Lord. Legend says he made his money by luring ships onto the jagged, hard-to-detect rocks of Cobbler's Reef and then "salvaging" the wreckage. You can explore the architecturally acclaimed centerpiece of this luxury resort, which has a private sandy beach. It's a $12 taxi ride from the cruise terminal.

If it's wildlife you want, head for the **Barbados Wildlife Reserve,** in St. Peter Parish on the northern end of the island. It's not exactly Animal Kingdom, but on this 4-acre site you'll see turtles, rabbits, iguanas, peacocks, green monkeys, and a caged python.

Maybe it's the party-life you crave. If so, don't miss the **Mount Gay Rum Tour** in Bridgetown. You'll get a 45-minute soup-to-nuts introduction about rum in an air-conditioned rum shop (they say, of the more than 1,200 rum shops on the island, it's the only one with A/C). The tour costs $6 a person.

TOURING BY RENTAL CAR

If you're patient with the lack of road signs, rent a car and spend the day exploring the island's interior. Worthwhile sites include the 17th-century **St. James' church** near Holetown, a humble yet awesome building made of limestone and surrounded by tropical poinsettia, frangi-pani, bougainvillea, and hibiscus plants. Next store is the **Folkestone Marine Park and Visitors Centre.** Tour the small museum there and then head over to the adjacent beach and do some **snorkeling** (rentals are right there); just offshore are schools of brightly colored fish. Don't miss out on panoramic views of the island from the quaint **Gun Hill Signal Station** and check out the fascinating limestone caverns and the stalactites and stalagmites of **Harrison's Cave. St. John's Church,** built on a cliff 800 feet above the sea, is also not to be missed. Lunch along the way at beachside cafes along Barbados's Gold Coast, like the Fisherman's Pub and Beach Bar on Orange Street, in Speightstown, and enjoy some fried fresh fish or curried chicken. Remember, driving is on the left and cars can be rented at the cruise terminal (ask to see the car first before paying).

SHOPPING

The shopping-mall–size **cruise terminal** contains an array of duty-free shops and retail stores, plus a plethora of vendors selling arts and crafts, jewelry, liquor, china, crystal, electronics, perfume, and leather goods. Check out the clever Christmas tree ornaments made of seashells by local artist Daphne Hunt and her three daughters (they go for $6 to $12 apiece). For rum cake, an island specialty, the family-owned **Calypso Island Bakery** has a shop in the terminal. The shrink-wrapped cakes last up to 6 months and make great gifts! There's also a convenience store in the terminal. In general, though, you'll find a wider selection of stuff to buy and better prices in Bridgetown. Last time I was there, T-shirts in the terminal were going for $15 apiece, a roll of film $5, and a liter of J&B (yellow label) was anywhere from $10.75 to $15.15 (U.S.).

Good duty-free buys include cameras, watches, crystal, gold jewelry, bone china, cosmetics and perfumes, and liquor (including locally produced Barbados rum and liqueurs), along with tobacco products and British-made cashmere sweaters, tweeds, and sportswear. **Cave Shepherd,** Broad Street, Bridgetown, is the largest department store on Barbados and the best place to shop for tax-free merchandise.

Among Barbados handcrafts, you'll find lots of **black-coral jewelry,** but beware: Did you know black coral is endangered, and it's illegal to bring it into the United

States? I suggest looking, but not buying. Local clay potters turn out different products, some based on designs centuries old. Check out the **Potters House** and **Earthworks,** both on Edghill Heights, in St. Thomas parish. Crafts include wall hangings made from grasses and dried flowers, straw mats, baskets, and bags with raffia embroidery. Bajan leather work includes handbags, belts, and sandals.

Some standout stores include **Articrafts,** on Broad Street in Bridgetown, for Bajan arts and crafts, straw work, handbags, and bamboo items; **Best of Barbados,** in the Southern Palms, St. Lawrence Gap, Christ Church, which sells only products designed and/or made on Barbados (coasters, mats, T-shirts, pottery, dolls and games, cookbooks, and other items); **Colours of De Caribbean,** the Waterfront Marina, Bridgetown, for tropical clothing, jewelry, and decorative objects; **Cotton Days,** Lower Bay Street, St. Michael, for casually elegant one-of-a-kind garments, suitable for cool nights and hot climes; **The Shell Gallery,** Carlton House, St. James, for the best collection of shells in the West Indies, featuring the shell art of Maureen Edghill, the finest artist in the field; and **Walker's Caribbean World,** St. Lawrence Gap, for many locally made items, as well as handcrafts from the Caribbean Basin.

BEACHES

Beaches on the island's western side—the luxury resort area called the **Gold Coast**—are far preferable to those on the surf-pounded Atlantic side. All Barbados beaches are open to the public, even those in front of the big resort hotels and private homes. The government requires that there be access to all beaches, via roads along the property line or through the hotel entrance.

ON THE WEST COAST (GOLD COAST)   Take your pick of the west-coast beaches, which are about a 15-minute, $8 taxi ride from the cruise terminal. **Payne's Bay,** with access from the Coach House or the Bamboo Beach Bar, is a good beach for water sports, especially snorkeling. There's a parking area here. This beach can get rather crowded, but the beautiful bay makes it worth it. Directly south of Payne's Bay, at Fresh Water Bay, is a trio of fine beaches: **Brighton Beach, Brandon's Beach,** and **Paradise Beach.**

Church Point lies north of St. James Church, opening onto Heron Bay, site of the Colony Club Hotel. Although this beach can get crowded, it's one of the most scenic bays in Barbados, and the swimming is ideal. Retreat under some shade trees when you've had enough sun. You can also order drinks at the Colony Club's beach terrace.

Snorkelers in particular seek out the glassy blue waters by **Mullins Beach.** There are some shady areas, and you can park on the main road. Order food and drink at the Mullins Beach Bar.

ON THE SOUTH COAST   Depending on traffic, south-coast beaches are usually easy to reach from the cruise terminal. Figure on about an $8 taxi fare. **Sandy Beach,** reached from the parking lot on the Worthing main road, has tranquil waters opening onto a lagoon. This is a family favorite, with lots of screaming and yelling, especially on weekends. Food and drink are sold here.

Windsurfers are particularly fond of the trade winds that sweep across **Casuarina Beach,** even on the hottest summer days. Access is from Maxwell Coast Road, across the property of Casuarina Beach Hotel. This is one of the wider beaches on Barbados. The hotel has food and drink.

Silver Sands Beach is to the east of the town of Oistins, near the very southern-most point of Barbados, directly east of South Point Lighthouse and near the Silver

Rock Hotel. This white sandy beach is a favorite with many Bajans, who probably want to keep it a secret from as many tourists as possible. (Tough luck, Bajans!) Windsurfing is good here, but not as good as at Casuarina Beach. You can buy drinks at Silver Rock Bar.

ON THE SOUTHEAST COAST   The southeast coast is known for its big waves, especially at **Crane Beach,** a white sandy stretch set against a backdrop of cliffs and palms. Prince Andrew owns a house overlooking this spectacular beach, and the Crane Beach Hotel towers above it from the cliffs. Crane Beach often appears in travel-magazine articles about Barbados. It offers excellent body surfing, but this is real ocean swimming, not the calm Caribbean, so be careful. At $17.50 from the cruise pier, the one-way taxi fare is relatively steep, so share a ride with some friends.

SPORTS

GOLF   The 18-hole championship golf course of the west-coast **Sandy Lane Hotel,** St. James (☎ **246/432-1311**), is open to all. Greens fees are $135 in winter and $110 in summer for 18 holes, or $100 in winter and $80 in summer for nine holes. Carts and caddies are available. Make reservations the day before you arrive in Barbados or before you leave home. The course is a 20- to 25-minute taxi ride from the cruise terminal. The one-way fare is about $13.

HORSEBACK RIDING   Maintained by Swedish-born Elizabeth Roachford and her four daughters, **Caribbean International Riding Centre,** Cleland Plantation, Farley Hill, St. Andrew (☎ **246/422-7433**), offers riding for equestrians of all experience levels. A 1-hour escorted trek through tropical forests and beaches, followed by a relaxing cool drink in the clubroom and a free transfer back to the cruise terminal, is $70; the 2-hour version of this tour is $90. The most scenic tour goes through the Gully Ride and continues out to a cliff with a panoramic view of almost the entire east coast of Barbados. Advance reservations are required. It's about a 20-minute, $10 taxi ride from the port. Closer to the port is the **Brighton Riding Stables** (☎ **246/425-9381**); it has a kiosk just outside of the terminal. Less than 5 minutes from the terminal, you'll be able to see your ship as you gallop along Brighton Beach. It's not the prettiest beach, but this is a convenient way to get in some horseback riding without spending the whole day getting to the stables and back. The ride is $45 per hour, including transportation to and from the terminal.

SCUBA DIVING & SNORKELING   The clear waters off Barbados have a visibility of more than 100 feet most of the year, providing great views of lobsters, moray eels, sea fans, gorgonias, night anemones, octopuses, and more than 50 varieties of fish, as well as wrecks and coral. **The Dive Shop,** Pebbles Beach, Aquatic Gap, St. Michael (☎ **246/426-9947**), offers the best scuba diving on Barbados and also offers snorkeling trips. Sign up for scuba at a booth next to the dock. Visitors with reasonable swimming skills who have never dived before can also take a resort course. The Dive Shop provides transportation to and from the cruise terminal.

WINDSURFING   Experts say that Barbados windsurfing is as good as any this side of Hawaii. In fact, it's a very big business between November and April, when thousands of windsurfers from all over the world come here. **Silver Sands** is rated the best spot in the Caribbean for advanced windsurfing (skill rating 5 to 6). **Barbados Windsurfing Club,** at the Silver Sands Hotel in Christ Church (☎ **246/428-6001**), gives lessons and rents boards. To reach the club, take a taxi from the cruise terminal; it's a $10 one-way fare.

GREAT LOCAL RESTAURANTS & BARS

IN BRIDGETOWN OR SOUTH OF BRIDGETOWN   **Brown Sugar,** Aquatic Gap, St. Michael (☎ 246/426-7684), is an alfresco restaurant in a turn-of-the-century bungalow. The chefs prepare some of the tastiest Bajan specialties on the island. Of the main dishes, Creole-broiled pepper chicken is popular, as are the stuffed crab backs. There's a great lunch buffet for less than $15 per person. **Rusty Pelican,** in downtown Bridgetown overlooking the Careenage, has great atmosphere and Bajan flying fish to boot. Also in town, try **Mustors,** on McGregor Street. It's a favorite with locals and serves authentic Barbadian lunch fare. Wherever you eat, be sure to try a daily Bajan special, a jumbo sandwich, or flying fish. For pub grub, the hopping **Whistling Frog Pub** works (located at Time Out at the Gap Hotel, next to the Turtle Beach resort).

ON THE WEST COAST   The beachside **Lone Star,** north of Old Town near the Royal Pavilion on the island's west side, is a new place serving up great seafood. For pizza cravings, check out **Pizzaz** in Holetown.

6 Bequia

Bequia (meaning "Island of the Cloud" in the original Carib, and inexplicably pronounced *Beck*-wee) is the largest island in the St. Vincent Grenadines, with a population of 5,000. Sun-drenched, windswept, peaceful, and green (though arid), it's a popular stop for small-ship lines such as Clipper, ACCL, Star Clippers, Windjammer, and the more upscale Seabourn and Windstar, which join the many yachts in Admiralty Bay throughout the yachting season.

Very much a tourism-oriented island, Bequia is nevertheless anything but touristy. You'll find a few of the requisite cheesy gift shops in the main town, Port Elizabeth, but none of the typical cruise-port giants like Little Switzerland. Instead, the town offers one of the most attractive settings in the Caribbean, with restaurants, cozy bars, a produce market, and craft shops, mostly strung out along the Belmont Walkway, a path that skirts so close to the calm waters of the bay that at high tide you have to skip across rocks to avoid getting your feet wet. Many ships spend the night here or make late departures, allowing passengers to take in the nightlife.

The island's rich seafaring tradition today manifests itself in fishing, sailing, boatbuilding (though most handmade boats you'll see are scale models made for the yachting set), and even whaling, though this is whaling of more of a token, almost ritualistic sort (only about one whale is taken in any given year).

Frommer's Favorite Bequia Experiences
- **Strolling along the Belmont Walkway:** In the evenings this walkway at water's edge makes for a terrifically romantic stroll as you make your way from one nightspot to the next. You might even pick up the company of one of the friendly port dogs, who seem more interested in companionship than panhandling (see "On Your Own: Within Walking Distance," below).
- **Visiting Brother King's Old Hegg Turtle Sanctuary:** Founded in 1995 and dedicated to raising and releasing Hawksbill turtle hatchlings, the sanctuary is run on a shoestring budget and a lot of energy and faith. You'll see hundreds of turtles in the main swimming pool and in their own little cubbyholes, and hear about the sanctuary's conservation efforts (see "On Your Own: Beyond Walking Distance," below). Donations are gladly accepted.
- **Visiting the Lower Bay and Princess Margaret Beach:** South of Port Elizabeth, this stretch of sand is frequently described by cruisers as "the best beach I've ever

experienced." It's a little chunk of paradise, backed by waving palms and fronted by yachts bobbing at anchor in the distance (see "Beaches," below).

COMING ASHORE   Ships dock right in the center of the island's main town, Port Elizabeth, a stone's throw from the restaurants, bars, and shops that line the waterfront.

CURRENCY   The **Eastern Caribbean dollar (EC$)** is used on Bequia; however, U.S. dollars are accepted by all businesses. The exchange rate is EC$2.70 to U.S.$1 (EC$1 is worth about 37¢). It's always a good idea to ask if you're not sure which currency a price tag refers to. Unless otherwise specified, rates quoted in this section are given in U.S. dollars.

LANGUAGE   The official and daily-use language is English.

INFORMATION   There's a small tourist information booth right on the beach by the cruise dock, but frankly, you can almost see everything there is to do from the same spot. It's a pretty small island. For information before you go, contact the Grenadines Tourist Bureau (☎ **784/458-3286**) or the St. Vincent & The Grenadines Department of Touurism (☎ **212/687-4981** in the U.S. or 784/457-1502, www.svgtourism.com).

CALLING FROM THE U.S.   To place a call to Bequia you need only dial a "1" before the numbers listed in this section.

GETTING AROUND

Ships dock right in Port Elizabeth, putting you within walking distance of any town sights. The popular Princess Margaret Beach is within walking distance as well.

BY TAXI   You'll find plenty of taxis lined up right at the cruise dock to take you around the island. The fare is approximately $15 per hour, or $5 per person per hour for groups of three persons or more.

BY MINIBUS   The entire island of Bequia is served by a fleet of small, unofficial **dollar cab** minibuses that cruise regular routes, picking up passengers when flagged down (there are also some obvious "bus stops" scattered around). Tell the driver where you want to go and he'll tell you a price.

BY RENTAL CAR   Rentals are available at **Handy Andy's Rentals,** on the Main Road in Port Elizabeth, to the right of the dock if you're facing inland (☎ **784/458-3722**; fax 784/457-3402). Day rental of a small golf-cart-type vehicle is $65. A Jeep Wrangler rents for $75.

BY MOTORCYCLE/BICYCLE   Handy Andy's (see above) also rents Honda 250XR motorbikes for $45 and Cannondale mountain bikes for $15.

Frommer's Ratings: Bequia					
	Poor	Fair	Good	Excellent	Outstanding
Overall Experience				✓	
Shore Excursions		✓			
Activities Close to Port				✓	
Beaches & Water Sports				✓	
Shopping		✓			
Dining/Bars				✓	

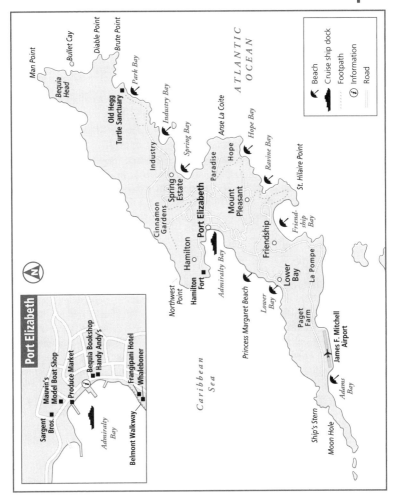

SHORE EXCURSIONS

Bequia is very much a "relax and have a drink" kind of island, rather than one with a lot of definable, tourable attractions. Aside from a standard island tour, most excursions offered are sailing trips around the island and to neighboring Mustique.

Island Tour ($35, 3 hours): The typical island tour is by taxi, meaning you can arrange one easily once you get ashore if your ship doesn't offer one officially. Tours generally visit beautiful Industry Bay on the island's east coast, the Old Hegg Turtle Sanctuary, and a model-boat shop, and at some point stop for a complimentary drink in Spring Bay.

Sail & Snorkel Catamaran Trip ($85, 5–6 hours): Your typical booze cruise, though moderation is suggested if you're going to do any snorkeling. The trip sails around Bequia's coast, where you'll see the "Moonhole," a residential community set among odd rock formations, as well as the old whaling station on Petit Nevis, a small island off the coast.

Full-Day Sailing Excursion to Mustique (7–8 hours, $85): Sail aboard a schooner to exclusive (read: rich people own it) Mustique, just southeast of Bequia, for strolling, shopping, snorkeling, or simply lying on the beach. Complimentary drinks are included aboard ship.

Half-Day Excursion to Mustique (3–4 hours, $65): Same excursion as above, but you travel between islands by powerboat rather than sailing ship.

ON YOUR OWN: WITHIN WALKING DISTANCE

In theory, almost the entire island of Bequia is within walking distance, but only for serious walkers. I decided to test this theory out by walking from Port Elizabeth first to Hamilton Fort, just north of town, then backtracking through the port and down to the tiny old whaling village of **Paget Farm,** near the airport on Bequia's southern tip. As the crow flies it's not much of a distance, but curving roads and hilly terrain made it a real journey that took about 4 to 5 hours round-trip, with no stops. If your ship is in port late and you're in good shape, it's a great way to see the island (including lovely **Friendship Bay,** on the east coast) and meet some of the local people along the way. Bring water.

For those wanting something less strenuous, strolling around Port Elizabeth itself is close to idyllic. The **Belmont Walkway** runs south from the docks right at the water's edge (meaning at high tide parts of it are actually *under* water), fronting many restaurants, shops, and bars. In the evenings this area is particularly romantic.

Heading north from the docks along the Main Road you'll find a homey **produce market** that also stocks some tourist items. Across the street, **Mauvin's Model Boat Shop** is one of the most visible reminders of the island's boatbuilding tradition, though now the money seems to lie in crafting scale models of real boats for sale to the yachting crowd. Farther along the Main Road, **Sargent Bros. Model Boat Shop** is a larger shop offering the same types of merchandise. The workshop is a little more accessible here, so you can easily see the craftsmen creating their wares (all the work is done by hand; no power tools are employed at all), and see models in various stages of construction. At both shops, the models are amazing, lovingly constructed and signed by the craftsman—and they're not what you'd call cheap: Prices start around $250 for a tiny model, and can go up as high as $10,000 for something really fabulous.

If you continue walking along the Main Road, you'll pass through an area with many boating supply stores and a few bars and food stands obviously geared to the local fishing and sailing trades. It's a quiet, pretty walk, even though it may well be the most "industrial" part of the island. Eventually you'll come upon a concrete walkway hanging above the water along the coast. From here the going gets rough—many sections of the walkway have been cracked and heaved drastically off-kilter by hurricanes, and it's patched here and there with planks and other makeshift materials. At the end of the walkway the road starts curving uphill and inland through a quiet residential area, and thus all the way up to **Hamilton Fort,** perched above Admiralty Bay and offering a lovely view of Port Elizabeth, though that's about all it offers—a few tiny fragments of battlements and five plugged canons are all that remain of the old fort. A taxi can take you here as well by another route, if you want to avoid the walk (a good idea unless you're in decent shape and very sure-footed).

ON YOUR OWN: BEYOND WALKING DISTANCE

At Park Beach on the island's northeast coast, 2 miles east of Port Elizabeth, **Brother King's Old Hegg Turtle Sanctuary** offers a chance to see conservation in action.

Since Bequia is an extremely dry island and is very conscious of water conservation, it consequently has few public washrooms, so you'd be well advised to use your ship's bathroom facilities before coming ashore.

Founded in 1995 by the eponymous King and dedicated to raising and releasing Hawksbill turtle hatchlings, the sanctuary is a real labor of love. A main concrete swimming pool and small plastic kiddy pools allow maturing hatchlings to socialize. Brother King and his assistants are on-hand to tell you about their conservation efforts, and will gladly accept donations to help keep the place going.

Aside from this and the activities in Port Elizabeth, most of the island's other attractions are **beaches,** so turn to that section, below.

SHOPPING

You'll find most shopping worth doing right within walking distance of the docks in Port Elizabeth. Heading south from the pier, one of the first businesses you'll come to is the **Bequia Bookshop** (www.caribbeanbookshop.com), selling books on the island's and region's culture and history, books of poetry and prose by local authors, yachting guides, and a selection of other fiction and nonfiction titles, as well as truly beautiful scrimshaw pocket knives, pendants, money clips, necklaces, and pins, all made from polished camel bone rather than the traditional whale bone. Presumably, camels are not yet endangered.

Sam McDowell, the artist who creates these scrimshaw items, opens his **Banana Patch Studio** for visitors by appointment. Located in the little village of Paget Farm on the southern part of the island, near the airport, the studio displays Sam's scrimshaw and whaling-themed paintings as well as his wife Donna's shellwork. Call or fax ☎ 784/458-3865 for an appointment.

There are several generic gift shops farther along, some fronting off the Belmont Walkway, including **Solana's,** for Caribelle batiks, T-shirts, etc., and **The Crab Hole,** for batiks and jewelry.

Heading in the other direction, north from the docks, you'll find the two model-boat shops described above, as well as a couple of open-air souvenir/crafts stalls, a produce market, and **Kennie's Music Shop,** for island sounds on CD and cassette.

BEACHES

Beaches are one of the big draws on Bequia, and are all open to the public. Tops on the list is **Princess Margaret Beach,** a golden-sand stretch lying just south of Port Elizabeth. To get there, take the Belmont Walkway to its end; from there, take the dirt path over the hill. **Lower Bay** beach is a little farther down along the same stretch of coast.

On the northeast coast, the beach at **Industry Bay** is windswept and gorgeous, a scene straight out of a romance novel. Trees on the hills surrounding the bay grow up to a certain height and then level out, growing sideways due to the constant wind off the Atlantic. The small, three-room Crescent Beach Hotel lies along this stretch. Along the southeast coast is **Friendship Bay,** an area that draws many European visitors.

There are no clothing-optional beaches on Bequia. Also, do not under any circumstances pick or eat the small green apples you'll see growing in some spots. These are manchineel, and are extremely poisonous.

A Quiet Grenadine Day on Union Island

Some small ships stop for a day at quiet, tranquil (very quiet, very tranquil) Union Island, the southernmost port of entry in the St. Vincent Grenadines. Think of your stop here as a "recovery day" rather than a whiz-bang exciting day in port: There are few facilities (none whatsoever in Chatham Bay, where ships usually tender passengers to land), few people, and few opportunities to do anything more than swim, snorkel, and do a little beachcombing. You'll likely see hundreds of conch-shell pieces along the beach, since a number of local fishermen are based here. (You can always tell if the conch was naturally thrown up on the beach or caught, since those caught have a small gash in the shell—the method the fishermen use to sever the muscle by which the conch beast holds onto its shell home.) Some enterprising fishermen set out the best shells they find on small tables, offering them to tourists for a couple bucks—you miss out on the personal thrill of finding them yourself, but they are some mighty nice shells.

Snorkeling is decent in Chatham Bay, though the waters don't yield the diversity you'll see elsewhere in the eastern Caribbean.

SPORTS

Besides walking (see above) and biking (mountain bikes are available to rent from Handy Andy's Rentals right by the cruise dock), the sports here, like the rest of life on the island, center around the water. **Dive Bequia** (☎ 784/458-3504, bobsax@caribsurf.com) and **Sunsports** (☎ 784/458-3577, www.sunsport@caribsurf.com), both located along Belmont Walkway, right by the docks, specialize in diving and snorkeling. Windsurfing is also available at **De Reef Aquasports,** on the beach in Lower Bay.

GREAT LOCAL RESTAURANTS & BARS

The coastal stretch along the Belmont Walkway is chockablock with restaurants and bars. The local beer of St. Vincent and the Grenadines is Hairoun, which is decent but not up to the level of St. Lucia's Piton. The local rum is Sunset.

De Bistro (☎ 784/457-3428), sporting a sign that reads NEW YORK, LONDON, PARIS, BEQUIA, is a very casual, open-air bar/restaurant located right next to Handy Andy's Rentals, near the dock. It serves the usual casual food: burgers, sandwiches, fish, pasta, and beer.

The ✪ **Frangipani Hotel Restaurant and Bar,** a little farther down the walkway (☎ 784/458-3255), is in a beautiful area right on the water. Lunch served throughout the day includes sandwiches, salads, and seafood platters. Dinner specialties include conch chowder, baked chicken with rice-and-coconut stuffing, and an array of fresh fish. On Thursday nights the bar hosts an excellent steel band. It's a lovely scene, with yachters, locals, cruisers, and a coterie of friendly local dogs all getting to know one another over drinks or settling down for the restaurant's special barbecue.

Farther along, the **Whaleboner Bar & Restaurant** (☎ 784/458-3233) serves a nice thin-crust pizza (with toppings like lobster, shrimp, and generic "fish"), sandwiches, fish-and-chips, and cold beer, either indoors or at tables in their shaded, ocean-view front yard. It's a perfect casual resting-up spot after walking around the island.

The **Gingerbread Restaurant & Bar,** also right along the waterfront (☎ **784/ 458-3800**), has a beautiful balcony dining room, and it's downstairs cafe serves coffee, tea, and Italian ice cream at outside tables. ✪ **Plantation House,** farther along still, is the premier dining spot on the island, serving informal lunches and more formal dinners of the cordon-bleu, roast-breast-of-duck, and conch-chowder variety. Service and cuisine are both first-rate.

Up the Main Road in the opposite direction from the Belmont Walkway, heading left when you walk off the cruise ship dock, you'll find the **New York Sports Bar,** which, really, needs no explanation.

7 Bonaire

Ever wonder what's going on under all that water you've been cruising on for days? There's no better place to find out than the island of Bonaire—"Divers Paradise," as the slogan on the island's license plates says. Avid divers have known about this unspoiled treasure for years, and consistently rank the island's pristine aquamarine waters, stunning coral reefs, and vibrant marine life among the best in the Caribbean, if not the world, for both diving and snorkeling.

But if diving's not for you, you'll be happy to know the island offers numerous other adventure activities such as mountain biking, kayaking, and windsurfing. If these options still sound too strenuous, why not just marvel at the sun-basking iguanas, fluorescent lora parrots, blue-tailed lizards, wild donkeys, graceful flamingos, and feral goats? As for flora, you're likely to see more cacti in Bonaire than anywhere outside the deserts of Mexico and the Southwest. Sprawling bushes of exotic succulents and permanently windswept divi-divi trees also abound.

If you'd rather just bake in the sun, Bonaire's beaches are intimate and uncrowded. In fact, the entire island is cozy and manageable. In no time at all, you'll feel it's your very own private resort. Shaped like a boomerang, Bonaire is 24 miles long and 3 to 7 miles wide—large enough to require a motorized vehicle if you want to explore, but small enough that you won't get lost.

Relying on your high-school French, you might think Bonaire ("good air") is a French island. It's not. Fifty miles north of Venezuela and 30 miles west of Curaçao, this untrampled refuge is the "B" of the ABC Netherlands Antilles chain (Aruba and Curaçao are the "A" and the "C"). The name "Bonaire" actually comes from the Caiquetio word "bonay," which means "low country." Members of the Arawak tribe who sailed from the coast of Venezuela a thousand years ago, the Caiquetios were Bonaire's first human inhabitants.

Europeans arrived 500 years later in 1499, when Alonso de Ojeda and Amerigo Vespucci claimed the island for Spain. Finding little of commercial value and seeing no future for large-scale agriculture, the Spanish enslaved the Indians and moved them to plantations on other islands, leaving Bonaire essentially unpopulated. In 1526, cattle were brought to the island, and within a few years, Bonaire was a center for raising large herds of other animals, including sheep, goats, pigs, horses, and donkeys. Wild donkeys and goats still roam the outback today. Prisoners from Spanish colonies in South America made up most of the human population. In 1633, when the Dutch took possession of the ABC islands, Bonaire became a plantation of the Dutch West Indies Company. Slaves brought from Africa provided the labor. Bonaire soon became a thriving producer of salt, used to preserve meat and fish before refrigeration, and remained so for three centuries. With the discovery of oil in Venezuela early in the 20th century, Aruba and Curaçao became refining centers,

A Passion to Preserve

Certain natural advantages make Bonaire ideal for diving. Rainfall is negligible, minimizing the runoff of sediment into the reef, and the island, south of the hurricane belt, is unscathed by storms. What makes Bonaire truly unique, though, is its inspired, visionary plan to preserve and nurture its marine resources. Twenty years ago, the Bonaire Marine Park was established to protect the island's entire coastal waters. Spear fishing is forbidden, divers are prohibited from wearing gloves (they're less likely to touch the ancient and fragile coral that way), anchoring has given way to a system of permanent moorings, and divers must prove they can control their buoyancy in mandatory orientation dives. Don't even think about collecting shells or coral—it's prohibited. The net result of these efforts? One of the healthiest underwater ecosystems on the planet and a veritable environmental showcase.

and Bonaire, too, got a piece of the pie. You can see oil storage tanks on the northeast coast. During World War II, the island served as an internment camp for 461 German and Dutch Nazis. Tourism, the island's major industry today, developed after the war, as self-rule was granted (the island remains a Dutch protectorate). The people of Bonaire are a mix of African, Dutch, and South American ancestries. You'll also meet expatriates from the United States, Britain, and Australia.

Frommer's Favorite Bonaire Experiences

- **Scuba diving:** Diving in Bonaire is said to be easier than anywhere else on Earth. The island's leeward coast has more than 80 dive sites, and whether you're diving from a boat or right from shore, you'll see spectacular coral formations and as many types of fish as anywhere in the Caribbean. If you're not certified to dive, fret not: By taking a half-day resort course, you can see firsthand what divers rave about. And if you'd rather just stick to snorkeling, be assured that abundant marine life is perfectly visible through the crystal-clear water.
- **Mountain biking along the western coast:** Bike along the coast on a road carved through lava and limestone, and bordered with cactus. The road north from the island's capital and main town, Kralendijk (*Crawl*-en-dike), is relatively flat and passes several uncrowded beaches—perfect for cooling off. If you're looking for more of a challenge, pedal uphill to Bonaire's oldest town, Rincon.
- **Exploring Washington-Slagbaai National Park:** This preserve is home to a variety of exotic wildlife and vegetation and offers spectacular coastal views. At times you might think you're in Arizona—with all the towering cacti, iguanas, and thousands of jittery lizards—but the humidity, flamingos, and beaches make it clear you're not.
- **Making new friends at the Donkeys Sanctuary:** Miss your pooch back home? Why not lavish your love on some deserving surrogates? More than 40 wild donkeys, most of them injured or orphaned by cars, call this oasis near the airport home. An entourage of hoofed critters greets you as you enter the gate, then accompanies you around the tidy, brightly colored grounds. The souvenir shop has donkey shirts, donkey bags, and donkey art. After recuperation and rehabilitation, the residents return to their rambling ways in the wild. If you're moved by the animals' unconditional affection, you can adopt one. As a new parent, you'll receive photos and letters from your adoptee twice a year.

Bonaire

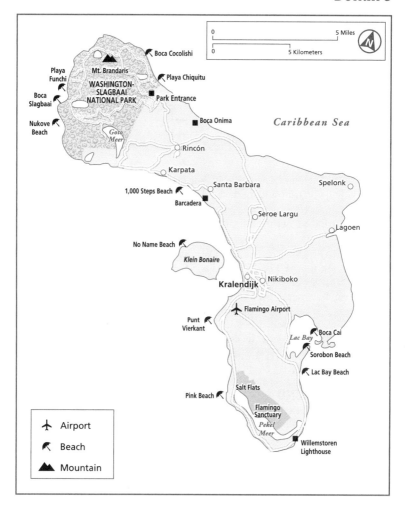

COMING ASHORE   Cruise ships dock in the port of Kralendijk, the island's capital, commercial center, and largest town (pop. about 2,500). The dock leads to Wilhelmina Park, a pleasant public space named after a former Dutch queen. Queen Beatrix Way, the brick-paved path along the waterfront, is lined with open-air restaurants and bars. Most of the town's shopping is 1 block inland on Kaya Grandi.

Your best bet for making long-distance **phone calls** is the 24-hour central phone-company office (Telbo) on Kaya Libertador Simón Bolívar, next to the tourism office.

CURRENCY   Bonaire's official currency is the Netherlands Antilles florin (NAf), also known as the **guilder.** Each florin is divisible by 100 cents. Don't waste your time exchanging money, though—the U.S. dollar is as widely accepted as the local currency. Change may be a mixture of dollars and florins. The exchange rate is 1.77 florins to $1 U.S. (NAf 1 = 56¢). If you need cash, there are several ATMs along Kaya Grandi.

Frommer's Ratings: Bonaire

	Poor	Fair	Good	Excellent	Outstanding
Overall Experience			✓		
Shore Excursions				✓	
Activities Close to Port		✓			
Beaches & Water Sports					✓
Shopping		✓			
Dining/Bars			✓		

LANGUAGE   Almost everyone in Bonaire speaks English, which, along with Dutch, is a required course in the local schools. Papiamentu is the local patois and language of the street, a rich blend of Dutch, Spanish, Portuguese, French, English, Caribbean Indian, and several African languages. Given the island's proximity to Venezuela, you're likely to hear Spanish as well.

INFORMATION   The **Tourism Corporation Bonaire** is located at Kaya Libertador Simón Bolívar 12 in Kralendijk (☎ **599/717-8322** or 599/717-8649; fax 599/717-8408; E-mail info@TourismBonaire.com). If you want information before you leave home, contact **Adams Unlimited,** 10 Rockefeller Plaza, Suite 900, New York, NY 10020 (☎ **800/BONAIRE** or 212/956-5912; fax 212/956-5913; E-mail lisa@adams-pr.com). The **Tourism Corporation** maintains an excellent Web site at **www.infobonaire.com** with links to scores of other helpful sites.

CALLING FROM THE United States   When calling Bonaire from the United States, you need to dial "011" before the numbers listed throughout this section.

GETTING AROUND

BY RENTAL CAR   Highway signs are in Dutch, and sometimes English, with easy-to-understand international symbols. Driving is on the right, the same as in the States and most of Europe. A valid driver's license is acceptable for renting and driving a car. The island has about 15 car-rental agencies, including **Avis,** at Flamingo Airport (☎ **800/230-4898** in the U.S., or 599/717-5795); **Hertz,** with offices at the airport (☎ **599/717-7221**) and at the Harbour Village Bonaire resort (☎ **800/654-3131** in the U.S., or 599/717-6020); **National,** with offices at Kaya Nikiboko Zuid 114 (☎ **599/717-7907**) and the airport (☎ **888/CAR-RENT** in the U.S., or 599/717-7940); and Flamingo Car Rental, Kaya Grandi 86 (☎ **599/717-5588**). Depending on the season and availability, rates can be as low as $40 per day. If you want a four-wheel-drive vehicle, expect to pay $60 to $65.

BY TAXI   Taxis greet cruise ship passengers at the pier. Although the cars are unmetered, the government establishes rates, and drivers should produce a price list upon request. Most cabs can be hired for a tour of the island, with as many as four passengers allowed to go along for the ride. Negotiate a price before leaving. You can get more information from the **Taxi Central Dispatch** office (☎ **599/717-8100**).

BY SCOOTER OR MOPED   If you plan to venture not too far, scooters and mopeds are practical, open-air alternatives. They can be rented from **Hot Shot Scooters,** Kaya Bonaire 4C (☎ **599/717-7166**), or **Macho! Scooter Rentals** at the Plaza Resort Bonaire, J. A. Abraham Blvd. 80 (☎ **599/717-2500**). Mopeds are about $18 a day; two-seat scooters run about $32.

You Paid What?

47,000 hotels, 700 airlines,
50 rental car companies. And a few
million ways to save money.

Travelocity.com™
A Sabre Company

Go Virtually Anywhere.

AOL Keyword: Travel

Will you have enough stories to tell your grandchildre

<u>Yahoo! Travel</u>

Do You
YAHOO!
?

BY BICYCLE   For getting around town or exploring the nearby coast, try bicy-cling. The coastal terrain is essentially flat, but the sun can be brutal even before noon. Plan your excursion as early in the day as possible. You can rent a 21-speed mountain bike for $15 to $20 from **Cycle Bonaire,** Kaya L. D. Gerharts 11D (☎ **599/717-7558**).

SHORE EXCURSIONS

✪ **Scuba Excursion for Certified Divers** ($69, 3 hours): Dive in the island's famous Bonaire Marine Park.

✪ **Bike Tour** ($64, 3–4 hours): This scenic ride along mostly flat and downhill ter-rain affords riders views of Bonaire's many species of birds, cacti, and other flora and fauna, including pink flamingos. The ride takes you along the island's northern shoreline.

✪ **Snorkeling** ($39–$69 adults, $24–$39 children, 3 hours): Snorkeling off the coast of Bonaire is some of the best you'll find in the Caribbean. A variety of snor-keling tours include spending time at the uninhabited "No Name Beach," Ebo's Reef, and Karel's Hills, all located offshore from Klein Bonaire.

TOURING THROUGH LOCAL OPERATORS

Bonaire has several large, full-service tour operators, including **Discover Bonaire** at Kaya Gobernador N. Debrot 79 (☎ **599/717-5252**), **Baranka Tours,** next door at Kaya Gobernador N. Debrot 79A (☎ **599/717-2200**), and **Bonaire Tours** at Kaya L. D. Gerharts 22 (☎ **599/717-8778**). Each conducts snorkeling, fishing, kayaking, mountain-biking, sailing, nature-touring, and windsurfing excursions. Options vary from day to day. **Chogogo Tours** (☎ **599/717-4435**) and **Klaus Bakker Bonaire Nature Tours** (☎ **599/717-7714**) offer fewer choices but cater to individuals and smaller groups.

ON YOUR OWN: WITHIN WALKING DISTANCE

You can walk the length of Kralendijk in an hour or less. Residents readily admit the town is sleepy, but they like it that way, thank you. The tourist office has **walking-tour maps,** but because Bonaire has always been off the beaten track, Kralendijk's highlights are modest and few. You'll probably want to stroll along the seafront with its views and restaurants, and along Kaya Grandi, the island's major shopping district. Just south of the town dock is **Fort Oranje,** a tiny fortress that boasts a cannon dating from the time of Napoléon. The town has some charming Dutch Caribbean architecture—gabled roofs you might see in Amsterdam, but in cheerful Caribbean colors, especially sunny ochre and terra-cotta. If your ship arrives early enough, you can visit the **waterfront produce market.**

Insider Tip

Many addresses in Bonaire make no mention of a town. How do you find out where to go? Here's a rule of thumb: If the street name is a country or Caribbean island, the place you're looking for is in Kralendijk (often referred to as "Playa" by locals). If it's a musical instrument, go to Nikiboko. Rincon features fruit, vegetable, and flower names. Female names and fish species can mean only one thing—Antriol. A Caribbean tribe? Head for Noord Salina.

ON YOUR OWN: BEYOND WALKING DISTANCE

As a day visitor, you'll probably choose to explore either the northern or southern part of the island. The **coastal road** north of Kralendijk is said to be one of the most beautiful in the Antilles. Turquoise, azure, and cobalt waters stretch to the horizon on your left, while pink-coral and black-volcanic cliffs loom on your right. Towering cacti, intimate coastal coves, strange rock formations, and panoramic vistas add to the beauty. The north also boasts **Washington-Slagbaai National Park,** an impressive, 13,500 acre preserve that occupies the northwestern portion of the island, and **Rincon,** Bonaire's "other" town and oldest settlement.

SOUTH OF KRALENDIJK   Soon after leaving Kralendijk, on the coast road, you'll pass **Santa Barbara,** an area of large homes built in several different architectural styles—Dutch Caribbean, ranch, and even Santa Fe adobe. Many are owned by Dutch nationals, who get tax breaks for building residences of a certain size. Given the size, colors, and styles of the homes, you might think you're in the Southern California town of the same name.

A few minutes farther north, across from the Bonaire Caribbean Club, you'll find **Barcadera,** an old cave once used to trap goats. Take the stone steps down to the cave and examine the stalactites.

Just past the Radio Nederland towers is **1,000 Steps beach and dive site.** The view from the top of the steps is particularly lovely: picturesque coves, craggy coastline, and tropical waters of changing hues. Actually, there are only 67 steps, but they're said to feel like a thousand when you're schlepping diving gear.

At the Kaya Karpata intersection, you'll see a mustard-colored building on your right. It's what's left of the aloe-processing facilities of **Landhuis Karpata,** a 100-year-old former plantation. Here you can learn about the cultivation, harvesting, and processing of aloe, once a major export crop.

Minutes after turning right on Kaya Karpata, you'll arrive in **Rincon,** the original Spanish settlement on the island. (Amerigo Vespucci, back in 1499, claimed Bonaire for Spain; Rincon was founded in 1527.) The town eventually became the home of African slaves who worked the island's plantations and salt pans. Nestled in a valley away from either coast, Rincon was hidden from marauding pirates, who plagued the Caribbean for decades. Today, the quiet and picturesque village is home to Bonaire's oldest church—a handsome ochre-and-white structure—and to **Prisca's,** an island institution serving the best local ice cream. Prisca, the founder, has passed on, but her daughter keeps the family tradition alive, serving creamy-yet-light homemade ice cream. Try the rum raisin, peanut, pistachio, or *ponche crema* (a little like eggnog). The shop is located in a pistachio-colored building on Kaya Komkomber (that's Papiamentu for "cucumber").

The pride of Bonaire, located on the island's northern tip, is **Washington-Slagbaai National Park,** one of the first national parks in the Caribbean. Formerly two separate plantations that produced aloe and charcoal, and raised goats, it now showcases the island's geology, animals, and vegetation. The park boasts more than 190 species of birds, thousands of kadushi, yatu, and prickly pear cactus, herds of wild goats, foraging donkeys, flocks of flamingos, and what seems like billions of lizards. The scenery includes stark, desertlike hills, quiet beaches, secluded caverns, and wave-crashed cliffs. You can either take the shorter 15-mile route around the park, marked with green arrows, or the longer 22-mile track, marked with yellow arrows. You'll have plenty of opportunities to hike, swim, or snorkel along either way. Admission is $5 per person, and the park is open from 8am to 5pm daily except for major holidays. Guide booklets and maps are available at the gate, where there's also a small museum. The dirt roads can be rugged, so if it's rained recently you may need a jeep.

On your way back to Kralendijk, take the Kaminda Onima, which traces the island's northeastern coast. You'll pass **Onima,** the site of 500-year-old Caiquetio Indian inscriptions. Some of the red and brown drawings depict turtles and rain; others appear to have religious significance. You should be able to recognize snakes, human hands, and suns among the roughly 75 inscriptions.

Before returning to Kralendijk, consider calling on **Sherman Gibbs.** You'll find his monument to the beauty of common objects on Kaminda Tras di Montaña, the road leading back to Kralendijk. Eccentric is one way to describe Mr. Gibbs; genius is another. If you're familiar with the Watts Tower in Los Angeles, you know "junk" can be transformed into something beautiful. Sherman combines old detergent bottles, boat motors, buoys, car seats, and just about anything else that strikes his fancy to create a wondrously happy sanctuary. The wind and old fan blades power his TV. As ingenuous and gentle as his seven iguanas, he's an island treasure.

SOUTH OF KRALENDIJK   Just minutes south of town, dazzlingly bright **salt pyramids** dominate the horizon. These hills, looking more like alpine snowdrifts than sodium mounds, are the product of a process that starts when the tide forces seawater into lakes and ends when evaporation crystallizes the salt. After years of neglect, the salt flats are once again flourishing, providing the United States and the Caribbean with salt for chemicals, industry, water softening, and ice control. Watch for the white, blue, and red obelisks along the coast that once guided boats to the salt depots.

Farther from the road, abandoned saltworks have been set aside as a **flamingo sanctuary.** Bonaire is one of the world's few nesting places for pink flamingos, a species that until recently was seriously threatened by extinction. Thanks to the reserve, the island's flamingo population during the breeding season now swells to roughly 10,000, rivaling the human population of 14,000. The sanctuary is completely off-limits to the public because the birds are extremely wary of humans and disturbances of any kind. But even from the road you can spot a pink haze on the horizon, and with binoculars you can see the graceful birds feeding in the briny pink and purple waters.

At the island's southern tip, restored **slave huts** stand as mute but damning monuments to the inhumanity of the island's slave era. Each hut, no bigger than a large doghouse, provided rude nighttime shelter for six slaves brought from Africa by the Dutch West Indies Company to cut dyewood, cultivate maize, and harvest solar salt. On Friday afternoons, the slaves trekked 7 hours in the oppressive heat to their homes and families in Rincon for the weekend, returning to the salt pans on Sunday evenings.

Willemstoren Lighthouse, Bonaire's first, was built in 1837. On the eastern side of the island's southern tip, the structure is fully automated today and usually closed to visitors. It's classically picturesque, and the setting implores you to contemplate the power and majesty of the sea. You may notice odd little bundles of driftwood, bleached coral, and rocks in the area. Although they look like something out of *The Blair Witch Project,* they're actually markers constructed by fishermen to designate where they've left their boats.

A few minutes up the east coast, you'll find **Lac Bay,** a lagoon that's every bit as tranquil as the nearby windward sea is furious. The calm, shallow waters and steady breezes make the area ideal for windsurfing, and various fishes come here to hatch their young. Deep inside the lagoon, mangrove trees with Edward Scissorhands roots lunge out of the water; if it weren't for the relentlessly cheerful sun, they might seem sinister. Animal lovers will relish sightings of wild donkeys, goats, and flamingos along the way.

SHOPPING

Don't expect to be caught up in a duty-free frenzy in Bonaire. You'll be able to hit every store in Kralendijk before lunch, and you'll probably find greater selections and prices at other ports. The island is a great place to buy some items, though. Consider top-of-the-line dive watches and underwater cameras. Or how about fine jewelry with fish and other marine themes?

You'll find most shops on Kaya Grandi, the adjacent streets, or in small malls. For Tag-Heuer dive watches, Cuban cigars, Lladró porcelain, Daum crystal, and Kosta Boda glass, try **Littman Jewelers** at Kaya Grandi 33. In the centrally located **Harborside Mall,** Little Holland has silk neckties, Nautica menswear, blue Delft porcelain, and an even more impressive array of Cuban cigars. If you're an aficionado, you'll love the acclimatized **Cedar Cigar Room** with its Montecristos, H. Upmanns, Romeo & Julietas, and Cohibas. **Sparky's,** in the same mall, carries perfume and other cosmetics, including Lancôme, Esteé Lauder, Chanel, Calvin Klein, and Ralph Lauren. **Maharaj Gifthouse,** at Kaya Grandi 21, has jewelry, gifts, and more blue Delft porcelain. **Boolchand's,** at Kaya Grandi 19, has a peculiarly wide range of items, including underwater cameras, electronic goods, watches, sunglasses, and shoes.

Benetton, at Kaya Grandi 49, has smart casual wear at discounts of 20% to 30%. If batik shirts, pareos, bathing suits, or souvenir T-shirts are what you want, you can't go wrong at **Best Buddies,** Kaya Grandi 32, **Boutique Vita,** Kaya Grandi 16, **Bye-Bye Bonaire,** Harborside Mall, or **Island Fashions,** Kaya Grandi 5. Probably the best place for dressier women's clothing, including Hermès scarves, Oscar de la Renta resort wear, and Kenneth Cole shoes, is **The Shop at Harbour Village** at Kaya Gobernador N. Debrot 72. You can also find sunglasses, jewelry, and perfume with Cartier, Fendi, Donna Karan, and Givenchy labels.

A personal favorite is **Cultimara Supermarket** at Kaya L. D. Gerharts 13. On a hot day, nothing beats this behemoth's frozen-food section. The store offers free coffee, a wide assortment of Dutch cheeses and chocolates, straight-from-the-oven breads and pastries, and various products from the Caribbean, Europe, South America, and the United States. And nothing will have greater snob appeal back home than a T-shirt with the Cultimara logo.

BEACHES

Bonaire's intimate and uncrowded beaches, almost all of them on the island's calm-watered west coast, come in a rainbow of colors. The sand at **Pink Beach,** south of Kralendijk near the slave huts, has a pinkish tint when wet. Busy on weekends, the beach is yours alone during the week. North of Kralendijk, **Nukove Beach** is a small white-sand cove carved out of a limestone cliff. A narrow sand channel cuts through an otherwise impenetrable wall of elkhorn coral, giving divers and snorkelers access to the sea. The island's northernmost beach, **Boca Cocolishi** ("seashell bay" in Papiamentu), is another of several beaches in Washington-Slagbaai Park. Algae makes the water here purplish, and the sand, formed by small pieces of coral and mollusk shells, is black. The water's a bit rough for anything more than wading, but it's a perfect spot to picnic. The water's even more treacherous at **Playa Chiquitu,** but the cove, sand dunes, and crashing waves make for an incomparable setting. Two other beaches in the national park are worth mentioning. On one side of **Playa Funchi,** flamingos nest in the lagoon; on the other, there's excellent snorkeling. Nearby **Boca Slagbaai,** once a plantation harbor, is also a favorite place to snorkel and dive. The water at **Lac Bay Beach** is only 1 to 2 feet deep, making it especially popular with families. Across the bay, white-sand **Sorobon Beach** is the island's only nude beach. It's part of the Sorobon Beach Resort, which means as a nonguest you'll have to pay for the privilege of disrobing.

SPORTS

FISHING   Accessibility, calm waters, and abundant fish make Bonaire an attractive fishing destination. The catch, which varies by season, can include marlin, sailfish, dorado, wahoo, amberjack, yellowfin, and bonito. **Big Game Sportfishing,** Kaya Warawara 3 (☎ **599/717-6500**), **Piscatur Fishing,** Kaya J. Pop 3 (☎ **599/717-8774**), and **Multifish Charters,** Kaya Playa Lechi (☎ **599/717-7033**) all offer deep-sea, reef, and bonefishing options. A half day (6 hours) with a maximum of six people runs between $325 and $350, including just about everything. Make arrangements in advance.

KAYAKING   For a peaceful, relaxing time, kayak through the mangroves in Lac Bay. You can proceed at your own pace in the calm waters, taking time to observe hundreds of baby fish and the bizarrely shaped tree roots. Bring protection from the sun and the ravenous mosquitoes. Divers and snorkelers have the added option of towing a lightweight sea kayak behind them as they explore the waters of the leeward coast. Guided trips and kayak rentals are available from **Discover Bonaire,** Kaya Gobernador N. Debrot 79 (☎ **599/717-5252**), and, in Sorobon, from **Jibe City** (☎ **599/717-5233**). A half-day guided tour through the mangroves is about $45, including a guide, kayak, and transportation. Kayak rental alone is $10 an hour, $15 for a two-seater. Discover Bonaire's guided kayak dive course for certified divers is about $60, including a kayak, tank, and dive instructor; other diving equipment costs extra.

MOUNTAIN BIKING   Bonaire has miles of roads, paved and unpaved, flat and hilly. The truly athletic can even follow goat paths. Take a water bottle, a map, and plenty of sunscreen. Discover Bonaire (see above) conducts guided bike tours through the *kunuku* (outback) and Washington-Slagbaai Park.

SCUBA DIVING   Veteran divers marvel at the variety and richness of Bonaire's marine ecosystem—brain, elkhorn, staghorn, mountainous star, gorgonian, and black coral; anemones, sea cucumbers, and sea sponges; parrot fish, surgeonfish, angelfish, groupers, blennies, frogfish, and yellowtails; morays and sea snakes; and water as clear as glass. Novices find the relaxed professionalism and personal attention of the island's dive masters calming and reassuring. The leeward coast and the area encircling **Klein Bonaire,** the small, uninhabited island across from Kralendijk, is studded with more than 80 dive sites. Because you'll only have time for one or two dives, put your trust in the dive shop operators. Tell them what you'd like to see, and they'll suggest a perfect site only minutes away. A resort course for beginners, which includes instruction, a skill session, and a boat dive with a dive master, could be the best $120 you'll ever spend; head-to-toe equipment is part of the price. Part of the Harbour Village Bonaire resort, **Great Adventures at Harbour Village,** Kaya Gobernador N. Debrot 72 (☎ **800/868-7477** in the U.S. and Canada, or 599/717-7500), is the island's poshest operation. It's upscale but unpretentious and friendly. In addition to two of the island's most beautiful boats, it boasts a first-class photo shop where you can rent underwater cameras or arrange video dives. **Sand Dollar Dive & Photo,** part of Sand Dollar Resort, Kaya Gobernador N. Debrot 79 (☎ **599/717-8738**), is popular with return visitors and offers comparable services. The resort's "Sand Penny" program for children is a godsend for parents who want to dive without worrying about the kids. **Habitat Dive Center** at Captain Don's Habitat, Kaya Gobernador N. Debrot 103 (☎ **800/ 327-6709** in the U.S., or 599/717-8290), is the Harley-Davidson of dive shops: Its logo sports a skull and sword, and divers here sometimes look like bikers in wet suits. These amiable fanatics are disciples of one of the island's true icons, Captain Don Stewart. Originally from California, Captain Don sailed into Kralendijk in 1962 and never looked back. He's a passionate proponent of marine ecology and was instrumental in the establishment of the Marine Park. If you're looking to feed anemones, tickle fish, or be manicured by cleaner shrimp, reserve a dive with **Dee Scarr's Touch the Sea,** P.O. Box 369 (☎ **303/816-1723** in the U.S., or 599/717-8529). An environmentalist and author, Dee takes two to four certified divers at a time for personalized, "nonstressful" interaction with marine creatures. Make arrangements in advance.

SNORKELING   Thanks to the shallow-water coral reefs, you can experience Bonaire's awesome marine environment, even if you're not a certified diver, by snorkeling. Bonaire's **Guided Snorkeling Program,** the world's first, includes a slideshow introduction to reef fishes, corals, and sponges, an in-water demonstration of snorkeling skills, and a guided tour of one of several sites. The cost is $25 per person. Equipment rental is about $10 more. You can arrange a tour through any of the dive shops listed above as well as through **Buddy Dive Resort,** Kaya Gobernador N. Debrot 85 (☎ **800/934-DIVE** from the U.S. or 599/717-5080); **Bon Bini Divers,** at the Lions Dive Hotel Bonaire, Kaya Gobernador N. Debrot 90 (☎ **800/327-5424** from the U.S. or 599/717-5424); and **Dive Inn,** Kaya C. E. B. Hellmund (☎ **599/717-8761**).

TENNIS   Several of the island's resorts, including Plaza Resort Bonaire and Sand Dollar Resort, open their tennis courts to nonguests for a fee. The best facilities are at **Harbour Village Bonaire.** This tennis center, managed by Peter Burwash International, the world's largest tennis management firm, offers clinics, custom racquet services, and the expertise of a resident pro. Court fees are $15 per hour; private lessons are $50 an hour. Make sure you have appropriate tennis shoes, and be forewarned that "clean, decent" attire is required.

WINDSURFING   Lac Bay's shallow waters, steady breezes, and protection from the stronger-winded east coast assure a safe and enjoyable windsurfing adventure for beginners and pros. There are two equipment-rental centers in Sorobon: **Jibe City** (☎ **599/717-5233**) and **Bonaire Windsurf Place** (☎ **599/717-2288**). Boards and sails are $55 per day with discounts if you rent two or more. Special beginner's lessons are $45, including equipment.

GREAT LOCAL RESTAURANTS & BARS

IN KRALENDIJK   Kralendijk offers a variety of culinary options at generally reasonable prices. **Zeezicht Bar and Restaurant,** Kaya Corsou 10 (☎ **599/717-8434**), is a local favorite on the downtown waterfront. Seviche, conch sandwiches, and a gumbo of conch, fish, shrimp, and oysters are on the menu. Mermaids, fishing nets, and pirates adorn the walls. Also on the waterfront, open-air **Shamballa's,** Kaya Grandi 7 (☎ **599/717-8286**), offers Mexican entrees and seafood. **Mi Poron,** Kaya

Caracas 1 (☎ 599/717-5199), is great for traditional Bonairean cuisine, such as stews (*stobás*) of chicken (*galiña*), beef (*baka*), goat (*kabritu*), conch (*karko*), or fish (*piska*). Every order comes with plantains and *funchi* (polenta). Housed in an old, traditional Bonairean home, the restaurant is also a museum.

Bon Awa, Kaya Nikiboko Zuid 8 (☎ 599/717-5157), a simpler alternative for local cuisine, has outside tables, killer hot sauce, and outstanding homemade ice cream. Looking for deli picnic sandwiches or pizza? Try **The Sandwich Factory,** Kaya Prinses Marie Plaza (☎ 599/717-7369). If you're on your way to the national park, ask for free day-old bread to feed the iguanas. Jutting out into the sea, **La Balandra** at Harbour Village Bonaire (☎ 599/717-7500) has a splendid view of the beach and features smoked marlin salad and other seafood. If you're there for lunch, you'll spot iguanas basking in the sun on the rocks below. Also on the water, **The Green Parrot** at the Sand Dollar Resort (☎ 599/717-5454) has seafood, burgers, and salads.

OUTSIDE KRALENDIJK   Ten minutes from Kralendijk on the way to Sorobon, the **Kontiki Beach Club,** Kaminda Sorobon 64 (☎ 599/717-5369), has a lovingly decorated bar, rattan furniture, and an outdoor terrace. Order one of the interesting seafood dishes and try a fresh juice, cold shake, or homemade ice cream.

8 British Virgin Islands: Tortola & Virgin Gorda

With small bays and hidden coves that were once havens for pirates, the British Virgin Islands are among the world's loveliest cruising regions. This British colony has some 40 islands in the northeastern corner of the Caribbean about 60 miles east of Puerto Rico, most of them tiny rocks and cays. Only **Tortola, Virgin Gorda,** and **Jost Van Dyke** are of significant size. The other tiny islets have names like Fallen Jerusalem and Ginger. Norman Island is said to have been the prototype for Robert Louis Stevenson's *Treasure Island,* and Blackbeard inspired a famous ditty by marooning 15 pirates and a bottle of rum on the rocky cay known as Deadman Bay. Yo ho ho.

Columbus came this way in 1493, but the British Virgins apparently made little impression on him. Although the Spanish and Dutch contested it, Tortola was officially annexed by the English in 1672. Today, these islands are a British colony, with their own elected government and a population of about 17,000.

The vegetation is varied and depends on the rainfall. Palms and mangos grow in profusion in some parts, whereas other places are arid and studded with cacti.

Smaller cruise lines such as Seabourn, Windstar, and Windjammer Barefoot Cruises call at Tortola and the more scenic Virgin Gorda and Jost Van Dyke. Unlike the rigid programs at St. Thomas and other major docking ports, visits here are less structured, and each cruise line is free to pursue its own policy.

CURRENCY   The **U.S. dollar** is the legal currency, much to the surprise of arriving Britishers who find no one willing to accept their pounds.

LANGUAGE   English is spoken here.

CALLING FROM THE U.S.   When calling the BVIs from the United States, you need only dial a "1" before the numbers listed throughout this section.

TORTOLA

Road Town, the colony's capital, sits about midway along the southern shore of 24-square-mile Tortola. Once a sleepy village, it's become a bustling center since

Wickhams Cay, a 70-acre landfill development and marina, brought in a massive yacht-chartering business.

The island's entire **southern coast** is characterized by rugged mountain peaks. On the northern coast are beautiful bays with white sandy beaches, banana trees, mangoes, and clusters of palms.

If your ship isn't scheduled to visit Virgin Gorda but you want to, you can catch a boat, ferry, or launch here and be on the island in no time, since it's only a 12-mile trip.

Frommer's Favorite Tortola Experiences

- **Visiting Bomba's Surfside Shack:** The oldest, most memorable bar on Tortola may not look like much, but it's the best party on the island (see "Great Local Restaurants & Bars," below).
- **Spending a day at Cane Garden Bay:** It's the best beach on the island, with palm trees, sand, and a great local restaurant (shack) for lunch and drinks (see "Beaches," below).
- **Hiking up Sage Mountain:** It's one of the best ways to learn about Tortola's natural character. Organized shore excursions usually include hiking trips to Sage Mountain, the highest point in the entire Virgin Islands (1,780 ft.), beginning with a ride along mountain roads in an open-air safari bus.
- **Take an island tour:** Open-air safari buses take you on a scenic journey around the extremely hilly island (see "Shore Excursions," below). Take the ship's organized tour, or hop in a taxi from the pier and for about $15 per person you get a 2- to 3-hour island tour, including beach stops.

COMING ASHORE   Visiting cruise ships anchor at Wickhams Cay 1 in Road Town. You'll be brought ashore by tender. The pier, built in the mid-1990s, is a pleasant 5-minute walk to Main Street. You should have no trouble finding your way around town.

INFORMATION   The **B.V.I. Tourist Board Office** (☎ 284/494-3134) is at the center of Road Town near the ferry dock south of Wickhams Cay 1. Pick up a copy of the *Welcome Tourist Guide.* It's open Monday to Friday from 9am to 5pm.

GETTING AROUND

BY TAXI   Open-air and sedan-style taxis meet every arriving cruise ship. To call a taxi in Road Town, call **B.V.I Taxi Assn.** (☎ 284/494-2322) or **Wheatley's** (☎ 284/494-3357). Two other local taxi services, Quality Taxi and the Waterfront Taxi Assn., are within walking distance of the cruise pier.

BY BUS   Scato's Bus Service (☎ 284/494-5873) picks up passengers (mostly locals) who hail it down. Fares for a trek across the island are about $1 to $3.

Frommer's Ratings: Tortola					
	Poor	Fair	Good	Excellent	Outstanding
Overall Experience				✓	
Shore Excursions			✓		
Activities Close to Port			✓		
Beaches & Water Sports			✓		
Shopping		✓			
Dining/Bars			✓		

The British Virgin Islands

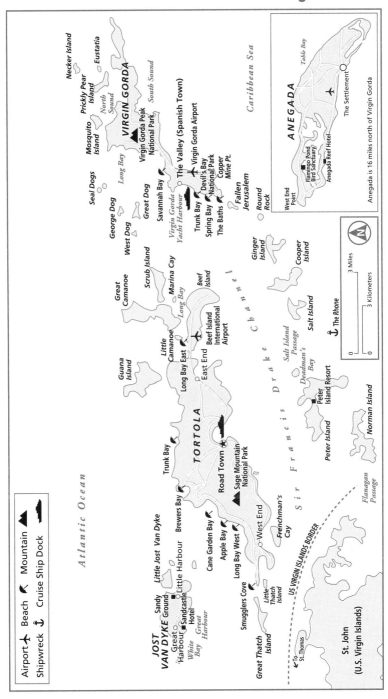

Airport ✈ Beach ⚓ Mountain ▲
Shipwreck ⚓ Cruise Ship Dock ⚓

Atlantic Ocean

JOST VAN DYKE

Little Jost Van Dyke
Sandy Ground
Great Harbour
Little Harbour
Sandcastle Hotel
White Bay
Great Harbour
Little Thatch Island
Great Thatch Island

Smugglers Cove
Long Bay West
Apple Bay
Cane Garden Bay
Brewers Bay
Trunk Bay
West End
Frenchman's Cay

TORTOLA

Road Town
Sage Mountain National Park

US VIRGIN ISLANDS BORDER

To St. Thomas

St. John (U.S. Virgin Islands)

Guana Island
Little Camanoe
Long Bay East
East End
Beef Island International Airport

Great Camanoe
Scrub Island
Marina Cay
Long Bay
Beef Island

S i r F r a n c i s D r a k e C h a n n e l

Flanagan Passage

Norman Island

Peter Island
Peter Island Resort
Deadman's Bay
Salt Island Passage
Salt Island

Ginger Island
Cooper Island

⚓ The Rhone

3 Miles
3 Kilometers
0
0

Round Rock

Fallen Jerusalem

The Baths
Spring Bay
Trunk Bay
Devil's Bay National Park
Copper Mine Pt.
Virgin Gorda Yacht Harbour
Savannah Bay
The Valley (Spanish Town)
Virgin Gorda Airport
Virgin Gorda Peak National Park

VIRGIN GORDA

Great Dog
West Dog
George Dog
Seal Dogs

Long Bay
North Sound
South Sound
Mosquito Island
Prickly Pear Island
Eustatia
Necker Island

Caribbean Sea

ANEGADA

Table Bay
Flamingo Pond Bird Sanctuary
Anegada Reef Hotel
West End Point
The Settlement

Anegada is 16 miles north of Virgin Gorda

125

BY RENTAL CAR   I don't recommend driving here, as the roads are bad and driving is on the left. But if you're intent on it, there's a **Hertz** at West End near the Jolly Roger restaurant (☎ **284/495-4405**).

Shore Excursions

✪ **Island Tour** ($30–$34, 3¹/₂ hours): Hop on an open-air safari bus and embark on a scenic journey around the island, enjoying some panoramic views and good photo ops, and ending with a stop at Cane Garden Bay Beach for swimming, sunbathing, and just plain old relaxing.

Mount Sage & Cane Garden Bay tour ($34, 4 hours): Start with a hike up Sage Mountain and end with an 1¹/₂ hours at Cane Garden Bay beach.

Lambert Beach Resort ($20, 5 hours): After a drive along the lovely north and south coasts you spend an afternoon at the Lambert Beach Resort, where you'll find a bar and Turtle's Restaurant.

Touring Through Local Operators

Bus Tours/Snorkeling/Glass-Bottom Boat Tours: Since the shore excursions here are very modest, you might consider calling **Travel Plan Tours,** Romasco Place, Wickham's Cay, Road Town (☎ **284/494-2872**), which will take one to three people on a 3-hour guided tour of the island, a snorkeling excursion, or a glass-bottom boat tour.

Taxi Tours: You can take a 2- to 3-hour taxi tour for about $45 for up to three people. For a taxi in Road Town, call ☎ **284/494-2322**.

On Your Own: Within Walking Distance

Besides the handful of shops on Main and Upper Main streets in Road Town, there's also a **Botanic Garden** right in the middle of town, across from the Police Station. The Garden is open daily from 8am to 6pm and features a wide variety of flowers and plants, including a section on medicinal plants.

On Your Own: Beyond Walking Distance

You have mainly nature to look at on Tortola. The big attraction is **Mount Sage National Park,** which rises to 1,780 feet (the highest point in the BVIs and USVIs) and covers 92 acres. It was established in 1964 to protect the remnants of Tortola's original forests not burned or cleared during its plantation era, and is both the oldest national park in the British Virgin Islands and the best present-day example of the territory's native moist forests. You'll find a lush forest of mango, papaya, breadfruit, and coconut trees; many of the plants and trees are labeled, and there are also birchberry, mountain guava, and guavaberry trees here, all of which have edible fruit. This is a great place to enjoy a picnic while overlooking neighboring islets and cays. Any taxi driver can take you to the mountain. Before going, stop at the tourist office (see above) and pick up a brochure with a map and an outline of the park's trails. The two main hikes are the Rain Forest Trail and the Mahogany Forest Trail. For a quiet beach day, head to **Smuggler's Cove,** a picture-perfect, secluded spot with white sand and calm turquoise water.

Shopping

Shopping on Tortola is a minor activity compared to other Caribbean ports. Still, you'll find most stores are on Main Street in Road Town. Only British goods are imported without duty, and they are the best buys, especially English china. You'll also find West Indian art, terra-cotta pottery, wicker and rattan home furnishings, Mexican glassware, dhurrie rugs, baskets, and ceramics.

Some good shops to visit include **Pusser's Company Store,** Main Street, Road Town, for Pusser's rum, fine nautical artifacts, and a selection of Pusser's sports and travel clothing and upmarket gift items; and the **Sunny Caribee Herb and Spice Company,** also on Main Street, for Caribbean spices, seasonings, teas, condiments, and handcrafts. You can buy two world-famous specialties here: West Indian Hangover Cure and Arawak Love Potion.

BEACHES

Most of the beaches are a 20-minute taxi ride from the cruise dock. Figure on about $15 per person one-way (some will charge less, like $5 per person if you've got a group), but discuss it with the driver before setting out. You can also ask him to pick you up at a designated time.

The finest beach is at ✪ **Cane Garden Bay,** which compares favorably to the famous Magens Bay Beach on the north shore of St. Thomas. It's on the northwest side of the island, across the mountains from Road Town, but it's worth the effort to get there, and is so special you might take a taxi here in the morning and not head back to your cruise ship until departure time. Plan to have lunch here at **Rhymer's** (☎ **284/495-4639**), where the chef will cook some conch or whelk, or perhaps some barbecue spareribs. The beach bar and restaurant is open daily from 8am to 9pm, serving breakfast, lunch, and dinner, with main courses ranging from $12 to $20. Showers are available. Rhymer's rents towels, as well as Sunfish and Windsurfers.

Surfers like **Apple Bay,** also on the northwest side, but you'll have to watch out for sharks (no joke: on a recent trip a friend saw one while surfing and its dorsal fins were visible from the shore). A hotel here called Sebastians caters to the surfing crowd that visits in January and February, but the beach is ideal year-round. **Brewers Bay,** site of a campground, is on the northwest shore near Cane Garden Bay and is good for beach strolling and swimming. Both snorkelers and surfers come here. **Smugglers Cove** (sometimes known as Lower Belmont Bay) is at the extreme western end of Tortola, opposite the offshore island of Great Thatch and very close to St. John's in the U.S. Virgin Islands. A wide crescent of white sand wrapped around calm, sky-blue water, the soft and sandy bottom grows deep very slowly. Snorkelers also like this beach.

Long Bay Beach is on Beef Island, at the far eastern end of Tortola near the island's airport. To get to this mile-long, typically uncrowded stretch of white sandy beach, cross the Queen Elizabeth Bridge, and then take a left on a dirt road before the airport. From Long Bay you'll have a good view of Little Camanoe, one of the rocky offshore islands around Tortola. Here you'll find Long Bay Beach Resort, which has a nice beach restaurant and bar.

Marina Cay, off Tortola's East End, is known for its good snorkeling beach. I also recommend the beach at **Cooper Island,** across Drake's Channel. Underwater Safaris (see "Sports," below) leads snorkel expeditions to both sites.

SPORTS

HORSEBACK RIDING   **Shadow's Ranch,** Todman's Estate (☎ **284/494-2262**), offers rides through Mount Sage National Park or down to the shores of Cane Garden Bay. Call for details Monday to Saturday from 9am to 4pm. They're located about 15 miles from the cruise dock; taxi fare is $12.

SCUBA DIVING *Skin Diver* magazine has called the wreckage of the HMS *Rhône,* which sank in 1867 near the western point of Salt Island, the world's most fantastic shipwreck dive. It teems with marine life and coral formations, and was featured in the motion picture *The Deep. Chikuzen* is another intriguing dive site off Tortola, although it's no *Rhône.* It's a 270-foot steel-hulled refrigerator ship that sank off the island's east end in 1981. The hull, still intact under about 80 feet of water, is now home to a vast array of tropical fish, including yellowtail, barracuda, black-tip sharks, octopus, and drum fish. **Baskin in the Sun** (☎ **800/233-7938** in the U.S., or 284/494-2858), a PADI five-star facility on Tortola, is a good choice for divers. It has two different locations: at the Prospect Reef Resort, near Road Town, and at Soper's Hole, on Tortola's West End. Baskin's most popular trip is the supervised "Half-Day Scuba Diving," catering to beginners, but there are trips for more advanced levels as well. Daily excursions are scheduled to the HMS *Rhône,* as well as "Painted Walls" (an underwater canyon formed of brightly colored coral and sponges), and the "Indians" (four pinnacle rocks sticking out of the water, which divers follow 40 feet below the surface). **Underwater Safaris** (☎ **800/537-7032** in the U.S., or 284/494-3235) takes you to all the best sites. It offers a complete PADI and NAUI training facility, and is associated with The Moorings yacht charter company. Underwater Safaris' Road Town office is a 5-minute or about $4 taxi ride from the docks.

GREAT LOCAL RESTAURANTS & BARS

On Cappoon's Bay, ✪ **Bomba's Surfside Shack** (☎ **284/495-4148**) is the oldest, most memorable bar on Tortola, sitting on a 20-foot-wide strip of unpromising coastline near the West End. It's the "junk palace" of the island, covered with Day-Glo graffiti and laced with wire and rejected odds and ends of plywood, driftwood, and abandoned rubber tires. Despite its makeshift appearance, the shack's got a sound system that can get a great party going any time of the day. The Sunday and Wednesday night barbecues are about $7 per person. It's open daily from 10am to midnight (or later, depending on business).

Standing on the waterfront across from the ferry dock, **Pusser's Road Town Pub** (☎ **284/494-3897**) serves Caribbean fare, English pub grub, and good pizzas. The drink to have here is the famous Pusser's Rum, the same blend of five West Indian rums that the Royal Navy served to its men for more than 300 years. Honestly, it's not the world's greatest rum, but sometimes you just have to do things for the experience. **Capriccio di Mare,** Waterfront Drive (☎ **284/494-5369**), is the most authentic-looking Italian cafe in the Virgin Islands, serving fresh pastas with succulent sauces, well-stuffed sandwiches, and the best pizzas on the island. For a great *roti* (curries wrapped in flat bread) sans atmosphere, try **Roti Palace,** in Road Town, which is sparsely furnished and not too attractive. **Callaloo,** at the Prospect Reef Resort (☎ **284/494-3311**), sits within a very romantic setting if it's a balmy day and the tropical breezes are blowing. Begin with the conch fritters or shrimp cocktail, and don't pass on the house salad, which has a zesty papaya dressing. Main dishes include fresh fish. At **Pusser's Landing,** Frenchman's Cay, on the West End (☎ **284/495-4554**), you can enjoy grilled fish such as mahimahi, West Indian roast chicken, or an English-inspired dish like shepherd's pie. Try the mango soufflé for dessert. **Quito's Gazebo,** on Cane Garden Bay, is owned by local recording star Quito Rhymer. It's a good place for West Indian fish dishes; Quito performs Thursday to Sunday and Tuesday.

VIRGIN GORDA

Instead of visiting Tortola, some small cruise ships put in at lovely Virgin Gorda, famous for its boulder-strewn beach known as **The Baths.** The second-largest island in the colony, it got its name ("Fat Virgin") from Christopher Columbus, who thought the mountain framing it looked like a protruding stomach. At 10 miles long and 2 miles wide, the island is about 12 miles east of Road Town, so it's easy to take a ferry or boat here if your ship only visits Tortola.

The island was a fairly desolate agricultural community until Little Dix Bay Hotel opened here in the early 1960s. Other major hotels followed, but privacy and solitude still reign supreme on Virgin Gorda.

Frommer's Favorite Virgin Gorda Experiences

- **Visiting The Baths:** House-sized boulders and clear waters make for excellent swimming and snorkeling in a fabulous setting (see "Beaches," and "Shore Excursions," below).
- **Spending a beach day in Spring Bay or Trunk Bay:** Located near The Baths, Spring Bay has one of the best beaches on the island, with white sand, clear water, and good snorkeling. Trunk Bay, a wide sand beach that can be reached by boat or via a rough path from Spring Bay, is another good bet (see "Beaches," below).
- **Taking an island tour:** Open-air safari buses do a good job of showing guests this beautiful island (see "Shore Excursions," below).

COMING ASHORE   Virgin Gorda doesn't have a pier or landing facilities to suit any of the large ships. Most vessels anchor and send small craft ashore, disembarking passengers at Leverick Bay. Many others dock beside the pier in Road Town on Tortola and then send tenders across the channel to Virgin Gorda. A limited number of taxis are usually available at Leverick Bay.

GETTING AROUND   The best way to see the island is to call Andy Flax at the Fischers Cove Beach Hotel (☎ **284/495-5511**). He runs the **Virgin Gorda Tours Association,** which gives island tours for about $40 per couple. Tours leave twice daily. They will pick you up at the dock if you give them 24-hour notice. Taxis are available in limited numbers at Leverick Bay, and if you can get one, will take visitors to Spanish Town (about 20 min. away) or to The Baths and area beaches for about $5 per person each way.

SHORE EXCURSIONS

✪ **The Baths Excursion** ($38, 3–4 hr.): All cruise lines stopping at the island offer this trip. (See "Beaches," below, for details.)

Frommer's Ratings: Virgin Gorda					
	Poor	Fair	Good	Excellent	Outstanding
Overall Experience					✓
Shore Excursions			✓		
Activities Close to Port				✓	
Beaches & Water Sports				✓	
Shopping		✓			
Dining/Bars			✓		

✪ **Island Tour** ($42, 3–4 hr.): The open-air safari buses do a good job of showing guests this beautiful island. You'll get views of the sea, the entire erratically shaped island, and Tortola and St. Thomas, too, as you head across the island from Leverick Bay via North Sound Road, ascending at least partway up 1,370-foot Gorda Peak. Some tours stop at the base of the mountain, where a local guide walks visitors through the national park there to the peak, from where visitors can mount an observation deck and snap photos. After, visitors reboard their bus for a drive to the quaint capital, called Spanish Town. Tours usually include a stop at Copper Mine Point, where visitors can view the ruins of a 19th-century copper mine.

ON YOUR OWN: WITHIN WALKING DISTANCE

Souvenirs and locally produced artwork are available right in Leverick Bay, where most of the island's shopping is located. The Palm Tree Gallery carries jewelry, artwork, books, postcards, and other souvenirs. The water-sports center in Leverick Bay rents two- and four-person dinghies starting at $40 per half day, and visitors can even hire a water taxi here to visit **Bitter End Yacht Club** in the North Sound area, where guests can have a lobster lunch. The taxis pick up guests at Bitter End for the trip back, with a round-trip fare of $25 per person. Snorkel equipment can be rented for $5 per day at the water-sports center. There's also a local branch of the BVI's famous **Pusser's Company Store,** which includes a gift shop, restaurant, and bar serving the famous Pusser's Rum, a locally produced product.

ON YOUR OWN: BEYOND WALKING DISTANCE

The **Virgin Gorda Yacht Harbour** is a taxi ride away from the Leverick Bay pier, and has several restaurants, shops, a bank, and the local office of the B.V.I. Tourist Board. Stores in the Yacht Harbour area include DIVE BVI, which sells diving equipment and offers diving instructions for all ability levels; Margo's Jewelry Boutique, which sells handcrafted gold and silver items; Virgin Gorda Craft Shop, featuring locally made items; and Wine Cellar, which offers oven-baked French bread and pastries, cookies, and sandwiches. Pelican Pouch Boutique, also in the Yacht Harbour area, sells women's swimwear. A gallery and boutique where Virgin Gorda artists display their works can be found at the Olde Yard Inn.

You might also consider cabbing it to the glamorous **Little Dix Bay** resort, established by Laurence Rockefeller in 1965, to enjoy a lunch buffet at an outdoor pavilion that shows off Virgin Gorda's beautiful hills, bays, and sky.

BEACHES

The major reason cruise ships come to Virgin Gorda is to visit ✪ **The Baths,** where geologists believe ice-age eruptions caused house-sized boulders to topple onto one another to form the saltwater grottoes we have today. The pools around The Baths are excellent for swimming and snorkeling (equipment can be rented on the beach), and it's a fun exercise to walk between and among the boulders, which in places are very cavelike. There's a cafe just above the beach, for a quick snack or a cool drink before heading back to the ship. **Devil's Bay** is a great beach near The Baths, and is usually less crowded.

Also near The Baths is ✪ **Spring Bay,** one of the best of the island's beaches, with white sand, clear water, and good snorkeling. Nearby is **The Crawl,** a natural pool formed by rocks that's great for novice snorkelers; a marked path leads there from Spring Bay. ✪ **Trunk Bay** is a wide sand beach that can be reached by boat or via a rough path from Spring Bay. **Savannah Bay** is a sandy stretch north of the yacht harbor, and **Mahoe Bay,** at the Mango Bay Resort, has a gently curving beach and vivid blue water.

A Slice of Paradise: Jost Van Dyke

Covering only 4 square miles, mountainous Jost Van Dyke is truly an offbeat, nearly undiscovered retreat—unless you count the small yachts dotting the Great Harbour. There is no cruise pier, so passengers are shuttled ashore via tender. Small-ship lines like Windjammer Barefoot Cruises will sometimes throw an afternoon beach party on the beach at **White Bay,** with the crew lugging ashore a picnic lunch for a leisurely afternoon of eating, drinking, and swimming. If your ship stays late, don't miss a trip to **Foxy's,** a well-known watering hole at the far end of the Great Harbour that's popular with the yachting set as well as locals. It's your classic island beach bar, with music pounding and drinks flowing into the wee hours.

    Devil's Bay National Park can be reached by a trail from The Baths. The walk to the secluded coral-sand beach takes about 15 minutes through a natural setting of boulders and dry coastal vegetation.

    North Sound, on the island's northern edge and accessible via taxi, is another recommended beach. Water-sports facilities are available from the dive center at the Leverick Bay landing.

SPORTS

WATER SPORTS   **Kilbrides Underwater Tours,** at the Bitter End Resort at North Sound (☎ **800/932-4286** in the U.S., or 809/495-9638), offers the best diving in the British Virgin Islands at 15 to 20 dive sites, including the wreck of the HMS *Rhône.* You can purchase a video of your dive.

GREAT LOCAL RESTAURANTS & BARS

At the end of the waterfront shopping plaza in Spanish Town, **Bath and Turtle Pub,** Virgin Gorda Yacht Harbour (☎ **284/495-5239**), is the island's most popular bar and pub. You can join the regulars over midmorning guava coladas or peach daiquiris and order fried fish fingers, nachos, very spicy chili, pizzas, Reubens or tuna melts, steak, lobster, and daily seafood specials such as conch fritters. **Valley Inn** (☎ **284/495-5639**) serves local specialties, including fried fish, johnnycakes, and curried goat. **Mad Dog** (☎ **284/495-5830**) is a hot-dog stop near The Baths that also serves BLTs, beer, and frozen piña coladas.

9 Cozumel & Playa del Carmen

A very popular cruise port, the island of Cozumel has white-sand beaches and fabulous scuba diving, but its greatest draw is its proximity to the ancient Mayan ruins at Tulum and Chichén-Itzá. Some ships also stop at nearby Playa del Carmen on the mainland of the Yucatán Peninsula, as it's easier to visit the ruins from there than from Cozumel. Generally, you can do tours to the ruins from either Cozumel or Playa del Carmen.

CURRENCY   The Mexican currency is the *nuevo peso* (new peso). Its symbol is the "$" sign, but it's hardly the equivalent of the U.S. dollar. The exchange rate is $9.56 pesos to U.S.$1 ($1 peso = 10¢). The main tourist stores gladly accept U.S. dollars, credit cards, and traveler's checks, but if you want to change money, there are lots of banks within a block or so from the Muelle Fiscal pier.

LANGUAGE Spanish is the tongue of the land, although English is spoken in most places that cater to tourists.

CALLING FROM THE U.S. When calling from the United States, you need to dial "011" before the numbers listed throughout this section.

MAYAN RUINS ON THE MAINLAND

The largest and most fabled of the Yucatán ruins, **Chichén-Itzá** was founded in A.D. 445 by the Mayans, and then inhabited by the conquering Toltecs of central Mexico. Two centuries later, it was mysteriously abandoned. After lying dormant for two more centuries, the site was resettled and enjoyed prosperity again until the early 13th century, when it was once more relinquished to the surrounding jungle. The area covers 7 square miles, so you can see only a fraction of it on a day trip.

The best known of the ruins is the pyramid **Castillo of Kukulkán,** which is actually an astronomical clock designed to mark the vernal and autumnal equinoxes and the summer and winter solstices. A total of 365 steps, one for each day of the year, ascend to the top platform. During each equinox, light striking the pyramid gives the illusion of a giant snake slithering down the steps to join its gigantic stone head mounted at the base.

The government began restoration on the site in the 1920s. Today it houses a museum, a restaurant, and a few shops. Admission is included in shore excursions.

Eighty miles south of Cancún and about a 1 1/2-hour drive from Playa del Carmen, the walled city of **Tulum** is the single most visited Mayan ruin. It was the only Mayan city built on the coast and the only one inhabited when the Spanish conquistadors arrived in the 1500s. From its dramatic perch atop seaside cliffs, you can see wonderful panoramic views of the Caribbean. Tulum consists of 60 individual structures. As with Chichén-Itzá, its most prominent feature is a pyramid topped with a temple to Kukulkán, the primary Mayan/Olmec god. Other important structures include the Temple of the Frescoes, the Temple of the Descending God, the House of Columns, and the House of the Cenote, which is a well. Entrance is included in shore excursions.

A 35-minute drive northwest of Tulum puts you at **Cobá,** site of one of the most important city-states in the Mayan empire. Cobá flourished from 1100 B.C. to A.D. 400, its population numbering perhaps as many as 40,000. Excavation work began in 1972, but archaeologists estimate that only 5% of this dead city has yet been uncovered. The site lies on four lakes. Its 81 primitive acres provide excellent exploration opportunities for the hiker. Cobá's pyramid, Nohoch Mul, is the tallest in the Yucatán. The price of admission is included in shore excursions.

COZUMEL

The ancient Mayans who lived here for 12 centuries would be shocked by the million cruise passengers who now visit Cozumel each year. Their presence has greatly changed San Miguel, the only town, which now has fast-food eateries and a Hard Rock Café. However, development hasn't touched much of the island's natural beauty. Ashore (away from San Miguel) you will see abundant wildlife, including armadillos, brightly colored tropical birds, and lizards. Offshore, the government has set aside 20 miles of coral reefs as an underwater national park, including the stunning Palancar Reef, the world's second-largest natural coral formation.

Frommer's Favorite Cozumel Experiences

- **Visiting the Mayan ruins at Chichén-Itzá or Tulum:** Chichén-Itzá is the largest and most fabled of the Yucatán ruins—and you get to fly in a small plane to get

The Yucatán's Upper Caribbean Coast

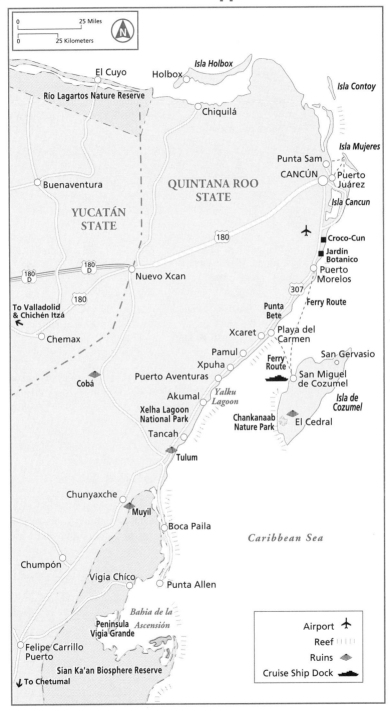

0   25 Miles

0   25 Kilometers

N

El Cuyo

Holbox

Isla Holbox

Isla Contoy

Río Lagartos Nature Reserve

Chiquilá

Isla Mujeres

Punta Sam

CANCÚN

Puerto
Juárez

Buenaventura

QUINTANA ROO
STATE

Isla Cancun

YUCATÁN
STATE

Croco-Cun

Jardín
Botanico

180

Puerto
Morelos

180
D

180
D

Nuevo Xcan

307

Ferry Route

To Valladolid
& Chichén Itzá

180

Punta
Bete

Chemax

Xcaret

Playa del
Carmen

Pamul

San Gervasio

Cobá

Xpuha

Puerto Aventuras

Ferry
Route

San Miguel
de Cozumel

Akumal

*Yalku
Lagoon*

*Isla de
Cozumel*

Xelha Lagoon
National Park

Chankanaab
Nature Park

El Cedral

Tancah

Tulum

Chunyaxche

Muyil

Boca Paila

Caribbean Sea

Chumpón

Vigia Chíco

Punta Allen

*Bahia de la
Ascensión*

Peninsula
Vigia Grande

Felipe Carrillo
Puerto

Sian Ka'an Biosphere Reserve

To Chetumal

Airport ✈

Reef

Ruins

Cruise Ship Dock

133

there! Tulum is perched dramatically above the ocean (and in the middle of "iguana central"—they're everywhere), and tours there often include a stop at the beautiful Xel-Ha Lagoon for some swimming (see "Mayan Ruins on the Mainland," above, and "Shore Excursions," below).

- **Renting a motor scooter:** You can easily see most of the island this way, including its wild and natural side (see "On Your Own: Beyond Walking Distance," below).
- **Signing up for a jeep trek:** Explore Cozumel's jungles and sandy back roads on a fun self-drive caravan-style adventure, and then stop at a beach for lunch and swimming (see "Shore Excursions," below).

COMING ASHORE   Ships arriving at Muelle Fiscal on Cozumel tender passengers directly to the heart of San Miguel. From the downtown pier, the shops, restaurants, and cafes are just a short walk away. Other ships anchor off the well-accoutred International Pier 3 miles from San Miguel (about a $5 taxi ride from town and about a half-hour walk from the heart of San Miguel). The beaches are close to the International Pier.

You can make **telephone calls** in Cozumel from the Global Communications phone center on the International Pier for $2 a minute, or better yet, from a kiosk inside the terminal for $1.50 a minute (keep in mind, there are often lines). In town, try the **Calling Station,** Avenida Rafael Melgar 27 (☎ **987/2-1417**), at the corner of Calle 3 in San Miguel, 3 blocks from Muelle Fiscal.

INFORMATION   The **Tourism Office,** Plaza del Sol (☎ **987/2-0972**), distributes the *Vacation Guide to Cozumel* and *Cozumel Island's Restaurant Guide;* both have island maps. It's open Monday to Friday from 8am to 2:30pm.

GETTING AROUND

The town of San Miguel is so small you can walk anywhere you want to go. Essentially, there's only one road in Cozumel—it starts at the northern tip of the island, hugs the western shoreline, and then loops around the southern tip and returns to the capital.

If you're driving in Cozumel, it's helpful to know that the roads parallel to the sea are called avenues, and these have the right of way. The ones running from the sea are called streets, and you have to stop at each street to give way.

BY TAXI   Taxi service is available 24 hours a day. Call ☎ **987/2-0236.** Cabs are relatively inexpensive, but since it's customary here to overcharge cruise ship passengers, settle on a fare before getting in—remember, the better you bargain, the cheaper the taxi ride. The average fare from San Miguel to most major resorts and beaches is about $8; between the International terminal and downtown it's about $4. More-distant island rides cost $12 and up.

Frommer's Ratings: Cozumel					
	Poor	Fair	Good	Excellent	Outstanding
Overall Experience				✓	
Shore Excursions					✓
Activities Close to Port				✓	
Beaches & Water Sports		✓			
Shopping				✓	
Dining/Bars			✓		

BY RENTAL CAR   If you want to drive yourself, four-wheel-drive vehicles or open-air jeeps are the best rental choice. **Budget Rent-a-Car,** Avenida 5A at Calle 2 N. (☎ **800/527-0700** in the U.S., or 987/2-0903), 2 blocks from the pier at Muelle Fiscal, rents both. A four-door economy car rents for about $35 a day, with a Jeep Cherokee going for $45 and up.

BY MOPED   Mopeds are a popular means of getting about despite heavy traffic, hidden stop signs, potholed roads, and a high accident rate. The best and most convenient rentals are at **Auto Rent** (☎ **987/2-0844**) in the Hotel Ceiba, a block from the pier at Muelle Fiscal. The cost is about $28 per day. Mexican law requires helmets.

BY FERRY   A number of passenger ferries link Cozumel with Playa del Carmen. The most comfortable are the two big speedboats and water-jet catamaran run by **Aviomar** (☎ **987/2-0477**). They operate Monday to Saturday from 8am to 8pm, Sunday from 9am to 1pm. The trip takes 45 minutes. All the ferries have ticket booths at the main pier. One-way fares range from $4 to $5 per person. You'll get a ferry schedule when you buy your ticket.

SHORE EXCURSIONS

It's easier to see the ruins at Chichén-Itzá, Tulum, and Cobá from Playa del Carmen, since it's on the mainland and therefore closer to the ruins sites. Many ships en route to Cozumel pause in Playa del Carmen to drop off passengers who have signed up for ruins tours. After the tours, passengers either take a ferry back to the ship in Cozumel or, if the tour is by plane, get dropped off at the airport in Cozumel, near downtown. See "Mayan Ruins on the Mainland," above, for details about the ruins. If your ship is not dropping passengers off at Playa del Carmen (many don't), keep in mind shuttling back and forth via ferry or tender will add another hour or two to your schedule. If you're more interested in a lazy, relaxing day (and your ship doesn't go to Playa del Carmen) you may want to just hang out in Cozumel.

✪ **Chichén-Itzá Excursion** ($220–$240, 6–7 hours): Founded in A.D. 445, Chichén-Itzá is the largest and most fabled of the Yucatán ruins—and you can even climb up its tallest pyramid for wonderful views of the ancient city, much of which is still covered in foliage and earth. You'll take a 45-minute flight each way on 10- to 20-seater aircraft. The flight there is almost as interesting as the ruins. This tour may leave from Playa del Carmen. (*Note:* It can get hot. Bring water.)

✪ **The Mayan Ruins of Tulum** ($63–$74 adults, $33–$59 kids, 6–7 hours): Very worthwhile. The ruins of this walled city are all the more spectacular because they're located on a cliff, dramatically perched above the ocean. This tour often includes an hour or two stop at the Xel-Ha Lagoon, a beautiful and natural setting for swimming (in this case, the tour is 7 to 8 hours long and costs another $20 or so). The tour leaves from Playa del Carmen.

✪ **Jeep Trek** ($68–$74, 4–6 hours): Hop in a jeep seating four and explore the natural side of Cozumel, its jungle mangroves and sandy back roads. Much of the roller-coaster–like route is off-road, and the jeeps travel in a convoy, with one of you driving. Included is a visit to the La Palma ruin where goddess Ixchel is said to still grant wishes (you make them with your eyes closed, facing the sea), and a stop at a lovely secluded beach for swimming and a picnic lunch of tasty Mexican fare.

Horseback-Riding Tours ($71, 3–4 hours): Worthwhile horseback-riding tours offer a chance to see Cozumel's landscape and the fun of riding a horse, and though they tout visits to Mayan ruins, don't get your hopes up—there are really no authentic ruins to speak of on Cozumel; most are reproductions. The tour includes a guide who discusses Mayan culture and customs while exploring the inside of a cave where the Mayans gathered for ceremonial meetings. A bus transports riders to a ranch, where the ride begins.

ON YOUR OWN: WITHIN WALKING DISTANCE

For walkers, the classic grid layout makes getting around the town of San Miguel easy. Directly across from the docks, the main square—**Plaza del Sol** (also called *la plaza* or *el parque*)—is excellent for people-watching. Avenida Rafael Melgar, the principal street along the waterfront, runs along the western shore of the island, site of the best resorts and beaches. Most of the shops and restaurants are on Rafael Melgar, although many well-stocked duty-free shops line the Malecón, the seaside promenade.

Only 3 blocks from Muelle Fiscal on Agenda Rafael Melgar between Calles 4 and 6 N., the **Museo de la Isla de Cozumel** (☎ **987/2-1434**) has two floors of exhibits displayed in what was Cozumel's first luxury hotel. Exhibits start in the pre-Hispanic times and continue through the colonial era to the present. Included are many swords and nautical artifacts; one display showcases endangered species. The highlight is a reproduction of a Mayan house. It's open daily from 10am to 6pm; admission is $1.75.

ON YOUR OWN: BEYOND WALKING DISTANCE

You can ✪ **rent a motor scooter** and zip around most of the island, including its wild and natural side. Stop for lunch at a beachside, open-air seafood restaurant for some grilled fish and a cool drink. Scooters can be rented from several outfits, including **Auto Rent** (☎ **987/2-0844**) in the Hotel Ceiba, a block from the pier at Muelle Fiscal.

Outside of San Miguel is the **Chankanaab Nature Park,** where a saltwater lagoon, offshore reefs, and underwater caves have been turned into an archaeological park, botanical garden, and wildlife sanctuary. More than 10 countries have contributed seedlings and cuttings. Some 60 species of marine life occupy the lagoon, including sea turtles. Reproductions of Mayan dwellings are scattered throughout the park. There's also a wide white-sand beach with thatch umbrellas and a changing area with lockers and showers. Both scuba divers and snorkelers like examining the sunken ship offshore (there are four dive shops here). The park also has a restaurant and snack stand.

The park is located at Carretera Sur, Kilometer 9 (no phone). It's open daily from 9am to 5pm. Admission is $7; free for children 9 and under. The 10-minute taxi ride from the pier at Muelle Fiscal costs about $5.

Mayan ruins on Cozumel are very minor compared to those on the mainland. **El Cedral** lies 2 miles inland at the turnoff at Kilometer 17.5, east of Playa San Francisco. It's the island's oldest structure, with traces of original Mayan wall paintings. The Spanish tore much of it down, and the U.S. Army nearly finished the job when it built an airfield here in World War II. Little remains now except a Mayan arch and a few small ruins covered in heavy growth. Guides at the site will show you around for a fee.

Another meager ruin is at **San Gervasio,** reached by driving west across the island to the army air base, and then turning right and continuing north 4 miles to San Gervasio. This was once a ceremonial center and capital of Cozumel. The Mayans dedicated the area to Ixchel, the fertility goddess. The ruins cost $3.50 to visit, plus $1 for entrance to the access road. Guides will show people what's left, including several broken columns and lintels, for $12. It's open daily from 8am to 5pm.

SHOPPING

You can walk from the pier at Muelle Fiscal to the best shops in San Miguel. Because of the influx of cruise ship passengers, prices are relatively high here, but you can and should bargain. Silver jewelry is big business here, and it's generally sold by weight. You can find some nice pieces, but again, don't expect to pay peanuts for it. There are wall-to-wall shops along the waterfront in San Miguel, including **Viva Mexico,** for all manner of souvenirs. Also, shops line the perimeter of Plaza del Sol, adjacent to the downtown cruise pier, and there are several shopping arcades accessible from the plaza, including the pleasant, tree-lined **Plaza Confetti. Agencia Publicaciones Gracia,** Avenida 5A, a block from Muelle Fiscal, is Cozumel's best source for English-language books, guidebooks, newspapers, and magazines. **Casablanca,** Avenida Rafael Melgar 33 (located in front of the International Pier), has a fine selection of Mexican jewelry and loose stones, plus a well-chosen collection of Mexican crafts. **Gordon Gilchrist,** Studio 1, Avenida 25 S. 981 at Calle 15 S., produces Cozumel's finest etchings of local Mayan sites. **Rachat & Romero,** Avenida Rafael Melgar 101 has a wide variety of loose stones, which they can mount while you wait. **Ultra Femme,** Avenida Rafael Melgar 341, is one of the most important jewelers in Cozumel, and the exclusive distributor of Rolex watches on the Mexican Riviera. **Unicornio,** 5 Avenida Sur 2 (2 blocks from Muelle Fiscal), has Mexican handcrafts.

If you're docking at the International Pier, there are a bunch of nice shops in the terminal, selling everything from Mexican blankets to jewelry, T-shirts, and handcrafts of all kinds. Again, prices aren't cheap—a roll of film went for $9 at the terminal last time I was there.

BEACHES

Cozumel's best powdery white-sand beach, **Playa San Francisco,** stretches for some 3 miles along the southwestern shoreline. It was once one of the most idyllic beaches in Mexico, but resort development is threatening to destroy its old character. You can rent equipment for water sports here, or have lunch at one of the many *palapa* restaurants and bars on the shoreline. There's no admission to the beach, and it's about a $10 taxi ride south of San Miguel's downtown pier. If you land at the International Pier, you're practically at the beach already.

Many of your fellow cruisers have heard of the fine **Playa del Sol,** about a mile south of Playa del San Francisco, so it's likely to be overcrowded.

Playa Bonita (sometimes called "Punta Chiqueros") is one of the least crowded beaches, but it lies on the east (windward) side of the island and is difficult to reach unless you rent a vehicle or throw yourself on the mercy of a taxi driver. It sits in a moon-shaped cove sheltered from the Caribbean Sea by an offshore reef. Waves are only moderate, the sand's powdery, and the water's clear.

You may want to consider **Parque Chankanaab,** a parklike beach area lined with thatched umbrellas and contoured plastic chaise lounges. While the water is rough here and not ideal for swimming, the beach and scenery are very nice and the place is popular with locals. Admission is $7, and you can swim with dolphins (for a fee, of course) or rent snorkeling equipment. There's also a restaurant and bar. This beach is about a 15-minute, $8 taxi ride from the downtown pier.

If you don't want to go far, there are two hotel beaches a stone's throw north of the International Pier (facing the water, they're on the right) that welcome day visitors. **Le Ceiba** charges $5 per person for the day and includes one tropical drink, and the **Crown Paradise sol Caribe** wants $22 per person for the day (9am to 5pm), including a drink and lunch.

SPORTS

SCUBA DIVING   Jacques Cousteau did much to extol the glory of Cozumel for scuba divers. Here he discovered black coral in profusion, plus hundreds of species of rainbow-hued tropical fish. Underwater visibility can reach 250 feet. All this gives Cozumel some of the best diving in the Caribbean. Cruisers might want to confine their adventures to the finest spot, **Palancar Reef.** Lying about a mile off-shore, this fabulous water world features gigantic elephant-ear sponges and black and red coral, as well as deep caves, canyons, and tunnels. It's a favorite of divers from all over the world. The best scuba outfitter is **Aqua Safari,** Avenida Rafael Melgar at Calle 5, next to the Vista del Mar Hotel (☎ 987/2-0101). A worthwhile competitor is **Diving Adventures,** Calle 51 Sur no. 2, near the corner of Avenida Rafael Melgar (☎ **987/2-3009**).

SNORKELING   Shallow reefs at Playa San Francisco or Chankanaab Bay are among the best spots. You'll see a world of sea creatures parading by, everything from parrot fish to conch. The best outfitter is **Cozumel Snorkeling Center,** Calle Primera Sur (☎ 987/2-0539), which offers a 3-hour snorkeling tour, including all equipment and refreshments. They can also arrange parasailing here. You can also just rent snorkeling equipment at Chankanaab.

GREAT LOCAL RESTAURANTS & BARS

The **local beer** is Sol. On a hot day, a quart bottle of the stuff is manna from heaven.

Right in front of the in-town cruise dock, ✪ **Café del Puerto,** Avenida Rafael Melgar 3, is a local favorite. The kitchen bridges the gap between Mexico and Europe with dishes like a superbly prepared mustard steak flambé, succulent lobster, and Yucatán chicken wrapped in banana leaves. Also on the main drag in town is **Lobster's Cove** and **Palmeras,** just across from the downtown pier, both offering tasty seafood and Mexican dishes. Just north of the ferry pier, **Carlos 'n Charlie's,** Avenida Rafael Melgar 11, is Mexico's equivalent of the Hard Rock Café, but much wilder (especially on Friday nights!). Sawdust litters the floor (to sop up the beer), music blares, and tourists pound back yard-long glasses of beers like they're going out of style. Many cruise passengers have stumbled back from Carlos 'n Charlie's, clutching their yard-long glasses as though they were the Holy Grail—proof that they've been to Mexico. People come here for good times and the spicy, tasty ribs. You can dine surprisingly well on Yucatán specialties, and the best chicken and beef fajitas in Cozumel. Another party spot is the **Hard Rock Cozumel** itself, at Avenida Rafael Melgar 2A, which serves the hard stuff as well as burgers and grilled beef or chicken fajitas. Yet another is the **Fat Tuesday,** at the end of the International Pier, where you'll find lots of crew members on their day or night off (you can even hear their revelry from the ship). Join the fun and guzzle a 16-ounce margarita for $5 a pop or a 24-ounce version for $7. A half block from the pier, **Las Palmeras,** Avenida Rafael Melgar, is ideal for casual eating. If you arrive in time, it serves one of the best breakfasts in town; for lunch, it offers tempting seafood dishes or Mexican specialties.

El Capi Navegante, Avenida 10A Sur 312 at Calles 3 and 4 (5 blocks from Muelle Fiscal), offers the freshest fish in San Miguel with a great lobster soufflé. **La Choza,** Calle Rosada Salas 198 at Avenida 10A Sur (2 blocks from the Muelle Fiscal pier), offers real local cooking that's a favorite of the town's savvy foodies.

PLAYA DEL CARMEN

Some cruise ships spend a day at Cozumel and then another at Playa del Carmen, but most drop off passengers here for tours to Tulum and Chichén-Itzá, and then head on to spend the day tied up at Cozumel.

The famed white-sand beach here was relatively untouched by tourists not many years ago, but today the pleasure-seeking hordes have replaced the Indian families who used to gather coconuts for copra (dried coconut meat). If you can tolerate the crowds, snorkeling is excellent over the offshore reefs. Turtle watching is another local pastime.

Avenida Juárez in Playa del Carmen is the principal business zone for the Tulum-Cancún corridor. Part of Avenida 5 running parallel to the beach has been closed to traffic, forming a good promenade. Most visitors at some point head for **Rincón del Sol,** a tree-filled courtyard built in the colonial Mexican style. It has the best collection of handcraft shops in the area, some of which offer goods of excellent quality, not the junky souvenirs peddled elsewhere.

Frommer's Favorite Playa del Carmen Experiences

• **Having beer and nachos on the beach:** Hang out on the beach for great views of the anchored ships a mile or so out at sea and the tourists coming in off the tenders. A couple of casual beachside restaurants provide all the beer, quesadillas, and nachos you'll need.

• **Taking a tour of Tulum or Chichén-Itzá:** Both of the tours described in the Cozumel section (see above) are also offered here.

COMING ASHORE   Some cruise ships dock at anchor or at the pier of Cozumel, and then send passengers over to Playa del Carmen by tender. Others dock at the new Puerto Calica Cruise Pier, which is 8 miles south of Playa del Carmen. Taxis meet each arriving ship, and drivers transport visitors into the center of Playa del Carmen.

GETTING AROUND

BY TAXI   Taxis are readily available to take you anywhere, but you can walk to the center of town, to the beach, and to most major shops.

BY RENTAL CAR   If you decide to rent a car for the day, try **National,** Hotel Molcas, 1A Avenida Sur 5A (☎ **987/3-0360**), or **Dollar,** Hotel Diamond at Playacar (☎ **987/3-0340**). Cars at either agency usually come with unlimited mileage and most forms of insurance included, and rent for between $50 and $80 a day.

SHORE EXCURSIONS

Most visitors head for the Mayan ruins the moment they reach shore (see "Shore Excursions" in the Cozumel section, above).

Frommer's Ratings: Playa del Carmen					
	Poor	Fair	Good	Excellent	Outstanding
Overall Experience				✓	
Shore Excursions					✓
Activities Close to Port			✓		
Beaches & Water Sports			✓		
Shopping		✓			
Dining/Bars			✓		

Xcaret Ecological Park ($39 adults, $24 kids): Lying 4 miles south of Playa del Carmen on the coast, Xcaret (pronounced "Ish-car-*et*") is a 250-acre ecological theme park where many visitors spend their entire day. It's a great place. Mayan ruins are scattered about the lushly landscaped acres. Visitors can put on life jackets for an underwater river ride, which takes them through currents running throughout a series of caves. You can also snorkel through these flooded caves (this I highly recommend!). There's also a botanical garden and a dive shop. Xcaret is open Monday to Saturday from 8:30am to 8:30pm, Sunday from 8am to 5pm. Buses from Playa del Carmen come here frequently; a taxi costs about $5 one-way. If you sign up for an organized excursion, a shuttle will transport you between ship and park.

ON YOUR OWN: WITHIN WALKING DISTANCE

You can walk to the center of town, to the beach, and to the small shopping district.

ON YOUR OWN: BEYOND WALKING DISTANCE

Other than the beach, there's no major attraction in Playa del Carmen except **Xcaret** (see above). Xcaret is open Monday to Saturday from 8:30am to 8:30pm, Sunday from 8am to 5pm. The easiest way to get there is to sign up for your ship's organized excursion, which includes transportation. Even if you come independently of a tour, general admission is a steep $39 for adults, $24 for children 5 to 11 (free for kids 4 and under). For information, call ☎ **988/3-0654.** Buses from Playa del Carmen come here frequently; a taxi costs about $5 one-way.

GREAT LOCAL RESTAURANTS & BARS

El Chino, Calle 4, Avenida 15 (☎ **987/3-0015**), is a pristine restaurant known locally for its regional Yucatán specialties as well as standard dishes from throughout Mexico. ✪ **Máscaras,** Avenida Juárez (☎ **987/3-1053**), serves great pastas, brick-oven pizzas, and other Italian dishes. The four-cheese pizza is justifiably the most popular. **El Tacolote,** Avenida Juárez (☎ **987/3-1363**), specializes in fresh seafood and the best grilled meats in town, brought to your table fresh from the broiler on a charcoal pan to keep the food warm.

10 Curaçao

As you sail into the harbor of Willemstad, be sure to look for the quaint "floating bridge," the **Queen Emma pontoon bridge,** which swings aside to open the narrow channel (a man actually drives the bridge in and out of place). Bordering the harbor are those much-photographed, picture-postcard pastel rows of gabled Dutch houses. Welcome to Curaçao, the largest and most populous of the Netherlands Antilles, just 35 miles north of the Venezuelan coast.

Curaçao was first discovered by the Spanish around 1499, but in 1634 the Dutch came and prospered. In 1915, when the Royal Dutch/Shell Company built one of the world's largest oil refineries to process crude from Venezuela, workers from 50 countries poured in to the island. Today, Curaçao remains a melting pot, although it still retains a Dutch flavor. A tropical Holland in miniature, this island has the most interesting architecture in the West Indies. Its Dutch-colonial structures give Willemstad a storybook look, but the rest of the desertlike island seems like the American Southwest, with three-pronged cacti, spiny-leafed aloes, and divi-divi trees bent by trade winds.

Since much of this island's surface is an arid desert, its canny Dutch settlers ruled out farming and developed Curaçao into one of the Dutch Empire's busiest trading

Curaçao

posts. Until the post–World War II collapse of the oil refineries, Curaçao was a thriving mercantile society with a capital (Willemstad) that somewhat resembled Amsterdam and a population with a curious mixture of bloodlines (including African, Dutch, Venezuelan, and Pakistani). Tourism began to develop during the 1980s, and many new hotels have been built since.

Frommer's Favorite Curaçao Experiences

- **Visiting Christoffel National Park:** Hike up the 1,230-foot-high St. Christof-felberg, passing cacti, iguanas, wild goats, many species of birds, and ancient Arawak paintings along the way. There's also 20 miles of roads, so you can see the park by car (see "On Your Own: Beyond Walking Distance," below).
- **Gazing into the mirrored waters of Hato Cave:** Stalagmites and stalactites are mirrored in a mystical underground lake in these caves, whose limestone forma-tions were created by water seeping through the coral (see "On Your Own: Beyond Walking Distance," below).

Frommer's Ratings: Curaçao					
	Poor	Fair	Good	Excellent	Outstanding
Overall Experience				✓	
Shore Excursions			✓		
Activities Close to Port				✓	
Beaches & Water Sports		✓			
Shopping			✓		
Dining/Bars			✓		

- **Take the Hato Caves/Curaçao Liqueur Tour:** This is a neat combination. A short bus ride gets you to the caves, and then to a plantation house and the liqueur factory for a tour (see "Shore Excursions," below).

COMING ASHORE   Cruise ships dock at the new $9-million megapier, just beyond the Queen Emma pontoon bridge, which leads to the duty-free shopping sector and the famous floating market. It's a 5- to 10-minute walk from here to the center of Willemstad, or you can take a taxi from the stand. Rumor has it that a private developer plans to build a shopping/entertainment complex in the adjacent historic fort. The town itself is easy to navigate on foot. Most of it can be explored in 2 or 3 hours, leaving plenty of time for beaches or water sports. Although the ship terminal has a duty-free shop, save your serious shopping for Willemstad.

There's a **phone center** at the cruise terminal, which is just beyond the Queen Emma pontoon bridge.

CURRENCY   The official currency is the **Netherlands Antillean florin (NAf),** also called a guilder, which is divided into 100 cents. The exchange rate is 1.78 NAf to U.S.$1 (1 NAf = .56¢). Canadian and U.S. dollars are accepted for purchases, so there's no need to change money. Unless otherwise noted, prices in this section are given in U.S. dollars.

LANGUAGE   Dutch, Spanish, and English are spoken on Curaçao, along with Papiamento, a patois that combines the three major tongues with Amerindian and African dialects.

INFORMATION   For visitor information, go to the **Curaçao Tourist Board,** Pietermaai (☎ 599/9-4616000). It's open Monday to Friday from 9am to 5pm. For information before you go, call the **Tourism Department** in New York at ☎ **800/ 445-8266** or 212/683-7660 or log on to the Web site at www.Curacao-tourism.com.

CALLING FROM THE U.S.   When calling Curaçao from the United States, you need to dial "011" before the numbers listed throughout this section.

GETTING AROUND

BY TAXI   Taxis don't have meters, so settle on a fare before getting in. Drivers are supposed to carry an official tariff sheet. Generally, there's no need to tip. The best place to get a taxi is on the Otrabands side of the floating bridge or call ☎ **599/ 9-8690747.** A fleet of DAF yellow buses operates from Wilhelmina Plein, near the shopping center, and runs to most parts of Curaçao. You can hail a bus at any designated bus stop. Up to four passengers can share the price of an island tour by taxi, which costs about $30 per hour.

BY RENTAL CAR   Driving is on the right on paved roads. If you want to rent a car, try **Avis** (☎ **800/331-2112** or 599/9-681163), **Budget** (☎ **800/527-0700** or 599/9-683420), or **Hertz** (☎ **800/654-3001** or 599/9-868118).

SHORE EXCURSIONS

Many excursions aren't really worth the price here—you can easily see the town on your own and hop a taxi to the few attractions on the island outside of Willemstad (see "Touring Through Local Operators," below).

✪ **Hato Caves/Curaçao Liqueur Tour** ($30, 3 hours): After a short bus ride to the caves and a walking tour through the grottoes, stalactites, and petroglyphs, the tour takes passengers to an old plantation house for a look around, and then to Curaçao Liqueur Factory for a tour and a sample of the popular liqueur, which is made from Laraha orange peels.

Countryside Bus Tour ($31, 2–3 hours): This excursion takes you via bus to sights like the Westpunt, Mount Christoffel, the towering cacti, and the rolling hills topped by *landhuizen* (plantation houses) built more than 3 centuries ago. You'll also stop at a beach, the Curaçao Seaquarium, and Chobolobo, an old colonial mansion where the original Curaçao liqueur is still distilled.

ON YOUR OWN: WITHIN WALKING DISTANCE

Willemstad is the major attraction here, and you can see it on foot. After 10 years of restoration, the town's historic center and the island's natural harbor, Schottegat, have been inscribed on UNESCO's World Heritage List. Be sure and watch the Queen Emma pontoon bridge move (it is motorized and a "driver" actually drives it to the side of the harbor every so often so ships and boats can pass through the channel). It's really neat.

A **statue of Pedro Luis Brion** dominates the square known as Brionplein, at the Otrabanda end of the Queen Emma pontoon bridge. Born in Curaçao in 1782, Brion became the island's favorite son and best-known war hero. He was an admiral of the fleet under Simón Bolívar and fought for the independence of Venezuela and Colombia.

Fort Amsterdam, site of the Governor's Palace and the 1769 Dutch Reformed church, has the task of guarding the waterfront. The church still has a British cannonball embedded in it. The arches leading to the fort were tunneled under the official residence of the governor. A corner of the fort stands at the intersection of Breedestraat and Handelskade, the starting point for a plunge into the island's major shopping district.

A few minutes' walk from the pontoon bridge, at the north end of Handelskade, is the **Floating Market,** where scores of schooners tie up alongside the canal. Boats arrive here from Venezuela and Colombia, and from other West Indian islands, to sell tropical fruits and vegetables, as well as handcrafts. The modern market under its vast concrete cap has not diminished the fun of watching the activity here. Either arrive early or stay late to view these marine merchants setting up or storing their wares.

Between the I. H. (Sha) Capriles Kade and Fort Amsterdam, at the corner of Columbusstraat and Hanchi Snog, is the **Mikve Israel-Emanuel Synagogue.** Dating from 1651, the Jewish congregation here is the oldest in the New World.

Next door, the **Jewish Cultural Historical Museum,** Kuiperstraat 26-28 (☎ **599/ 9-4611633**), is housed in two buildings dating from 1728. They were the rabbi's residence and the *mikvah* (bath) for religious purification purposes.

You can walk from the Queen Emma pontoon bridge to the **Curaçao Museum,** Van Leeuwenhoekstraat (☎ **599/9-4626051**). The building, constructed in 1853 by the Royal Dutch Army as a military hospital, has been carefully restored and furnished with paintings, objets d'art, and antique furniture, and houses a large collection from the Caiquetio tribes. On the museum grounds is an art gallery for temporary exhibitions of both local and international art.

ON YOUR OWN: BEYOND WALKING DISTANCE

Cacti, bromeliads, rare orchids, iguanas, donkeys, wild goats, and many species of birds thrive in the 4,500-acre ✪ **Christoffel National Park,** located about a 45-minute taxi or car ride from the capital near the northwestern tip of Curaçao. The park rises from flat, arid countryside to 1,230-foot-high St. Christoffelberg, the tallest point in the Dutch Leewards. Along the way are ancient Arawak paintings and the Piedra di Monton, a rock heap piled by African slaves who cleared this former plantation. Legend says slaves could climb to the top of the rock pile, jump off, and fly back home across the Atlantic. If they had ever tasted a grain of salt, however, they would crash to their deaths. The park has 20 miles of one-way trail-like roads. The shortest is about 5 miles long, but takes about 40 minutes to drive because of its rough terrain. One of several hiking trails goes to the top of St. Christoffelberg. It takes about $1\frac{1}{2}$ hours to walk to the summit (come early in the morning before it gets hot). There's also a museum in an old storehouse left over from plantation days. Guided tours of the park are available. The park is open Monday to Saturday from 8am to 4pm and on Sunday from 6am to 3pm. Admission is $10 per person.

The **Curaçao Seaquarium,** off Dr. Martin Luther King Boulevard (☎ **599/9-4616666**), displays more than 400 species of fish, crabs, anemones, and other invertebrates, sponges, and coral. A rustic boardwalk connects the hexagonal buildings, which sit on a point near the site where the *Oranje Nassau* broke up on the rocks and sank in 1906. The Seaquarium also has Curaçao's only full-facility, white-sand, palm-shaded beach. In the "shark and animal encounter," divers, snorkelers, and experienced swimmers are able to feed, film, and photograph sharks, stingrays, lobsters, tarpons, parrot fish, and other marine life in a controlled environment. Nonswimmers can see the underwater life from a 46-foot semisubmersible observatory.

Stalagmites and stalactites are mirrored in a mystical underground lake in ✪ **Hato Caves,** F. D. Rosseveltweg (☎ **599/9-8680379**). Long ago, geological forces uplifted this limestone terrace, which was originally a coral reef. The limestone formations were created over thousands of years by water seeping through the coral. After crossing the lake, you enter two caverns known as "The Cathedral" and La Ventana or "The Window." Displayed here are samples of ancient Indian petroglyphs. Professional local guides take visitors through the caves every hour. The caves are open daily from 10am to 4pm. Admission is $7.25 for adults, $5.75 for children 4 to 11 (free for kids 3 and under).

SHOPPING

Curaçao is a shopper's paradise, with some 200 stores lining such streets as Heerenstraat and Breedestraat in the 5-block district called the **Punda.** Many shops occupy the town's old Dutch houses.

The island is famous for its 5-pound "wheelers" of **Gouda or Edam cheese.** Look for good buys in wooden shoes, French perfumes, Dutch blue Delft souvenirs, finely woven Italian silks, Japanese and German cameras, jewelry, silver, Swiss watches, linens, leather goods, liquor, and island-made rum and liqueurs, especially

Curaçao liqueur, some of which has a distinctive blue color. Some stores also offer good buys on intricate lacework imported from everywhere between Portugal and China. If you're a street shopper and want something colorful, consider a carving or flamboyant painting from Haiti or the Dominican Republic. Both are hawked by street vendors at any of the main plazas.

Suggested shops include **Bamali,** Breedestraat 2, for Indonesian-influenced clothing (mostly for women); **Gandelman Jewelers,** Breedestraat 35, Punda, for a large selection of fine jewelry as well as Curaçaoan gold pieces; and **Curaçao Creations,** Schrijnwerkerstraat 14, for Curaçao handcrafts.

BEACHES

Curaçao's beaches are not as good as Aruba's 7-mile strip of sand, but it does have some 38 of them, ranging from hotel sand patches to secluded coves. The seawater remains an almost-constant 76°F year-round, with good underwater visibility. **Taxi** drivers waiting at the cruise dock will take you to any of the beaches, but you'll have to negotiate a fare. To be on the safe side, arrange to have your driver pick you up at a certain time and take you back to the cruise dock.

The **Curaçao Seaquarium** has the island's only full-facility, white-sand, palm-shaded beach, but you'll have to pay the full aquarium admission to get in (see "On Your Own: Beyond Walking Distance," above). The rest of the beaches on this island are public.

A good beach on the eastern side of the island is **Santa Barbara Beach,** on land owned by a mining company between the open sea and the island's primary water-sports and recreational area, known as Spanish Water. You'll also find Table Mountain, a remarkable landmark, and an old phosphate mine. The natural beach has pure-white sand and calm water. A buoy line protects swimmers from boats, and there are rest rooms, changing rooms, a snack bar, and a terrace. You can rent water bicycles and small motorboats. It's open daily from 8am to 6pm. The beach has access to the Curaçao Underwater Park.

Daaibooi is a good beach about 30 minutes from town, in the Willibrordus area on the west side of Curaçao. It's free, but there are no changing facilities.

Blauwbaai (Blue Bay) is the largest and most frequented beach on Curaçao, with enough white sand for everybody. Along with showers and changing facilities, there are plenty of shady places to retreat from the noonday sun. To reach it, take the road that goes past the Holiday Beach Hotel & Casino, heading in the direction of Juliandorp. Follow the sign that tells you to bear left for Blauwbaai and the fishing village of San Michiel.

Westpunt is known for its gigantic cliffs and the Sunday divers who jump from them into the ocean below. This public beach is on the northwestern tip of the island. **Knip Bay,** just south of Westpunt, has beautiful turquoise waters. On weekends, live music and dancing make the beach a lively place. Changing facilities and refreshments are available. **Playa Abao,** with crystal turquoise water, is situated at the northern tip of the island.

Warning: Beware of stepping on the hard spines of sea urchins, which are sometimes found in these waters. While not fatal, their spines can cause several days of real discomfort. For temporary first aid, try the local remedies of vinegar or lime juice.

SPORTS

SCUBA DIVING/SNORKELING/WATER SPORTS
You can see steep walls, at least two shallow wrecks, gardens of soft corals, and more than 30 species of hard corals at **Curaçao Underwater Park,** which stretches 12¹/₂ miles along Curaçao's

southern coastline, from Princess Beach Resort & Casino to East Point, the island's southeasterly tip. The park has placed over a dozen mooring buoys at the best dive and snorkel sites, and a snorkel trail with underwater interpretive markers just east of the Princess Beach Resort & Casino. Access from shore is also possible at Santa Barbara Beach in Jan Thiel Bay. Spearfishing, anchoring in the coral, and taking anything from the reefs except photographs are strictly prohibited. **Seascape Dive and Watersports,** at the Curaçao Casino Resort, Piscadera Bay (☎ 599/9-4625000), specializes in snorkeling and scuba-diving near reefs and underwater wrecks, and offers snorkeling excursions in the underwater park, waterskiing, Sunfish sail boats, and jet-ski rentals. It operates from a hexagonal kiosk set on stilts above the water, just offshore from the hotel's beach. It's open from 8am to 5pm daily.

GREAT LOCAL RESTAURANTS & BARS

Curaçao's **local beer** is the very Dutch Amstel. The **local drink** is Curaçao liqueur, some of which has a distinctive blue color.

De Taveerne, Landhuis Groot Vavelaar, Silena (☎ 599/9-7370669), is actually two restaurants: a French restaurant at street level and a less formal brasserie serving inexpensive international food on its second floor. If you're hot, dusty, and in a hurry, your best bet might be to order a platter of food in the brasserie. **Golden Star,** Socratesstraat 2, at the corner of Dr. Hugenholtzweg and Dr. Maalweg, southeast of Willemstad (☎ 599/9-4654795), is the best place to go on the island for *criollo,* or local food. It's inland from the coast road leading southeast from St. Anna Bay, 8 minutes by taxi from the cruise dock. **La Pergola,** in the Waterfront Arches, Waterfort Straat (☎ 599/9-4613482), is an Italian restaurant where the menu items change virtually every day. **Rijstaffel Restaurant Indonesia and Holland Club Bar,** Mercuriusstraat 13, Salinja (☎ 599/9-4612999), is the best place on the island to sample the Indonesian *rijstaffel,* the traditional "rice table" with all the zesty side dishes. You must ask a taxi to take you to this villa in the suburbs near Salinja, near the Princess Beach Resort & Casino southeast of Willemstad.

11 Dominica

First things first. It's pronounced "Dome-ee-*nee*-ka," not "Doe-*min*-i-ka." And it has nothing to do with the Dominican Republic. The Commonwealth of Dominica is an independent country, and English, not Spanish, is the official language. The only Spanish commonly understood in Dominica is *mal encaminado a Santo Domingo* ("accidentally sent to the Dominican Republic"), the phrase stamped on the many letters that make it to their proper destination only after an erroneous but common detour.

To be sure, Dominica has some rough edges. The island is poor, so don't expect luxury or up-to-the-minute technology around every corner, and not everything man-made is as beautiful as nature's handiwork. Balancing this, though, is the fact that Dominica is the most lush and mountainous island in the Caribbean. Twenty-nine miles long and 16 miles wide, and lying between the French islands of Guadeloupe and Martinique, smack-dab in the center of the arc formed by the Antilles, it's blessed with astonishing natural wonders—crystal-pure rivers (one for every day of the year, they say), dramatic waterfalls, volcanic lakes (one gurgles and boils from the heat and tumult in the earth below), and foliage as gargantuan as any H. G. Wells ever imagined on Venus. Volcanic coral reefs, every bit as biologically complex as the rain forests onshore, ring the island, and a bit farther from land, whales mate and calve.

Dominica

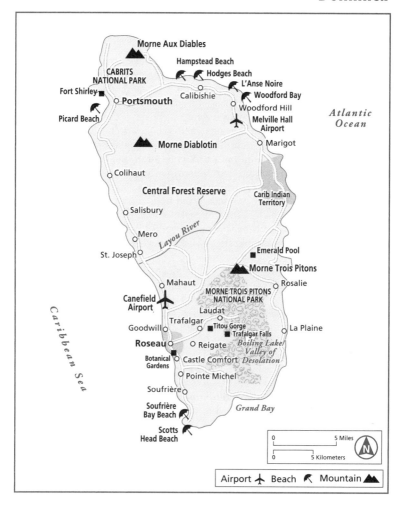

Much of Dominica's beauty is accessible to even the most sedentary visitor. Sitting in a rowboat, you can glide up a river through swampland crowded with mangroves and exotic birds, and impressive waterfalls are minutes from paved roads. You can also wend through astonishingly verdant rain forests along undemanding nature trails.

The island's people—primarily descendants of the West Africans brought over to work the plantations, plus some descendants of Europeans and Indians—are another great natural resource. Friendly and proud of their national independence, Dominica's 71,000 citizens remain for the most part unchanged by tourism, a still-developing industry here. Don't be surprised when you're greeted with a smile and an "OK," the island's equivalent of "hi." By smiling back and by respecting Dominica's culture and natural beauty, you help to perpetuate this congeniality. One portion of the island's population has immeasurable ethnological significance: Concentrated in a territory in the northeast, Dominica's approximately 3,000 Carib Indians are the last remaining members of the people who dominated the region when Europeans arrived.

Make Mine a Chubby Cola

Think before you order that Diet Coke. As the Procter & Gambles and Coca-Colas of the world continue their inexorable conquest of the world's markets, local products and brands disappear. Too bad—local products are part of local color. Dominica has been able to buck the trend in some respects, retaining some of its individuality through homegrown items. Where else on the planet can you get delicious **Kubuli beer** (the name comes from the Carib name for the island)? Or **Café Dominique,** the strong, dark coffee grown in those emerald mountains right ahead of you? Wait until you're back onboard the ship for that Pepsi. While you're onshore, be adventurous—try a distinctively Dominican product.

Bello, Dominica's equivalent of Kraft Foods, markets a variety of products, including guava jellies, bay rum lotion, and tropical fruit juices. If you want to conduct some personal research on the relationship between Cajun and Creole cooking, sample some of Bello's hot sauces. Special Pepper Sauce, a Tabasco-like condiment, has a considerable kick. Classic Yellow Pepper Sauce has the added tang of mustard.

To extinguish that hot-sauce fire in your mouth, try some **Sea Moss.** This beverage, made from sea moss, water, milk, sugar, and spices, is creamy like eggnog but less custardy and more cinnamony. Fans of the drink tout its refreshing healthfulness, but its fame as an aphrodisiac probably does more to boost sales.

As long as we're on the subject of "marital aids," consider *bois bandé* **herbal tea.** From your high-school French class, you know that *bois* means "wood," but did you know that *bandé* is French slang for "erection?" You get the idea. The infusion, made from the bark of a local tree, has a mild flavor, and it's naturally caffeine-free.

For the cigarette after, try a **Hillsborough.** The tobacco actually comes from Africa, but the cigarettes are rolled in a small factory at the corner of Old and Cork streets in downtown Roseau. The red, gold, and white package with its central illustration of three golden tobacco leaves is very 1940s. Of course, "The Minister of Health advises that smoking is hazardous to health."

And alcohol's no treat for your liver, but your Caribbean rum collection is incomplete without a bottle from Dominica. Stronger than the liquors of many other islands, **Macoucherie and Soca rums** have an appealing frontier roughness.

Enough of vices. **Jolly's Pharmacy,** with several branches in Roseau, has its own line of personal-care products. Babylis Nursery Jelly is one of its more popular items. More easily absorbed than Vaseline, Babylis has a darling baby on the label and a pleasant talc scent. It's perfect for baby's behind as well as mommy's chapped hands.

Finally, discerning Dominican children of all ages turn up their noses when offered a Coke or Pepsi; they demand **Chubby Cola.** It's awfully sweet (Duh! It's for kids), but if you're looking for an anti-diet soft drink, this one's up front about it.

Frommer's Favorite Dominica Experiences

- **Hiking to the Emerald Pool:** A 15-minute walk through gorgeous forest brings you to this primeval pool, where you can swim or just take in the beauty of the picture-perfect waterfall, the moss-covered boulders, and the sunlight streaming through branches high overhead. (See "Shore Excursions," below.)

TIMBUKTU   KALAMAZOO

AT&T Direct® Service

The easy way to call home from anywhere.

Global | **AT&T**
connection | direct
with the AT&T | service
Network |

the easy way to call home, take the attached wallet guide.

- **Paddling up the Indian River:** Minutes from Portsmouth, the gentle Indian River drains into the Caribbean from its source in the foothills of the island's tallest mountain, 4,747-foot high Morne Diablotin. As a boatman paddles you up the twisting river, you'll pass through swampland that features giant palms and mango trees with serpentine roots. (See "Shore Excursions," below.)
- **Scuba diving among Champagne bubbles:** Dominica is fast becoming a favorite destination of avid divers. Among the more popular dive sites is Soufrière Crater, a submerged volcanic caldera near Scott's Head on the southwestern coast. Inside the perimeter of the crater, steep walls plummet nearly 1,000 feet, while pinnacles formed by lava flow thrust upward. Gobies and wrasses hang close by as more adventurous butterflies, angels, and parrot fish investigate the pinnacles and canyons. Normally shy blackbar soldierfish are ubiquitous, and yellow-tube and barrel sponges loom over encrusting corals. Thermal underwater vents release thousands of bubbles, giving the Champagne site its name. (See "Shore Excursions," below.)
- **Experiencing Carib culture:** Along a rugged portion of Dominica's northeastern coast, the 3,700-acre Carib Territory is home to the world's last surviving Carib Indians. The Caribs today live like most other rural islanders—growing bananas and coconuts, fishing, and operating small shops. But the sturdy baskets of dyed and woven *larouma* reeds and the wooden canoes carved from the trunks of massive *gommier* trees are evidence of the people's links to the past. A traditional big house, called the Karbet, serves as a cultural and entertainment center. If you're lucky, you'll witness a performance of the Karifuna Cultural Group, whose youthful members are dedicated to the regeneration of Carib spirit and culture. (See "Shore Excursions," below.)
- **Exploring Fort Shirley and the rest of Cabrits National Park:** On Dominica's northwestern coast, right by the cruise ship port of Portsmouth, the 260-acre Cabrits National Park combines stunning mountain scenery, tropical deciduous forest and swampland, volcanic-sand beaches, coral reefs, and the romance of an 18th-century fort. (See "On Your Own: Within Walking Distance," below.)

COMING ASHORE   Dominica has two cruise ship ports. The largest and most frequented is in the heart of **Roseau,** the country's capital and largest town. The other is near the northwestern town of **Portsmouth.** Banks, restaurants, a market, a tourism office, and the excellent Dominica Museum line the road opposite Roseau's harbor. Portsmouth's port boasts a tourist-welcoming center (with an auditorium for speakers and films), shops, and instant access to Fort Shirley and Cabrits National Park.

CURRENCY   Dominica's official currency is the Eastern Caribbean dollar (EC$). The exchange rate is roughly 2.7 EC dollars to U.S.$1. U.S. dollars are accepted

Frommer's Ratings: Dominica					
	Poor	Fair	Good	Excellent	Outstanding
Overall Experience			✓		
Shore Excursions				✓	
Activities Close to Port			✓		
Beaches & Water Sports		✓			
Shopping			✓		
Dining/Bars			✓		

almost everywhere, but you're likely to receive change in the local currency. Several ATMs in Roseau, including one at the port, dispense both U.S. and EC dollars. Credit cards are widely accepted.

LANGUAGE   English is Dominica's official language. Almost everyone speaks Creole as well, a patois that combines elements of French, English, and African languages. Dominica's Creole is the same as that spoken on the neighboring French islands of Guadeloupe and Martinique.

INFORMATION   Dominica's **Division of Tourism** operates branches at the Roseau and Portsmouth cruise ship berths (the Roseau office is located a block from the waterfront at the old post office building on Dame M. E. Charles Boulevard). For information before you leave home, call the Dominica Tourist Office at ☎ **212/949-1711** or log on to www.dominica.dm/travel.htm. Several island businesses, including restaurants, tour operators, and other service providers, have joined forces to create another site, www.delphis.dm/home.htm, which has scores of links and helpful information.

CALLING FROM THE U.S.   When calling Dominica from the United States, you need only dial a "1" before the numbers listed throughout this section.

GETTING AROUND

BY RENTAL CAR   Dominica's road system is extensive and well maintained, but driving is on the left side, and passage through the mountains can be harrowing. You need a valid driver's license and a Dominican driver's permit, which costs about $12 and is available through rental agencies. Don't get annoyed when other drivers sound their horns; honking usually indicates an oncoming vehicle (especially at sharp curves) or is meant as a friendly greeting. **Island Car Rentals** (☎ **888/696-4202** in the U.S., or 767/448-2886) has offices in both Roseau and Portsmouth. So does **Valley Rent-a-Car** (☎ **767/448-3233**). **Wide Range Car Rentals,** in Roseau only (☎ **767/448-2198**), specializes in four-wheel-drive vehicles. Daily rates range from $35 to $75. You can also try **Avis,** which has an office in Roseau (☎ **800/882-8471** in the U.S., or 767/448-2481), and **Budget,** with a bureau at Canefield Airport, outside of Roseau (☎ **800/992-2776** in the U.S., or 767/449-2080).

BY TAXI   Taxis and public minivans are designated by license plates that begin with the letters *H* or *HA.* Fleets of both await cruise ship passengers at the Roseau and Portsmouth docks. Drivers are generally knowledgeable about sites and history, and the standard sightseeing rate is $18 per hour for up to four people. The vehicles are unmetered, so negotiate a price in advance and make sure everyone's talking about the same currency. You can get more information from the **Dominica Taxi Association** (☎ **767/449-8533**). **Mally's Tour and Taxi Service** (☎ **767/448-3114**) and **Julius John's** (☎ **767/449-1968**) are two reputable operators.

SHORE EXCURSIONS

✪ **Trafalgar Falls and Emerald Pool Nature Tour** ($40, 4 hours): Drive to Morne Bruce for a panoramic view of Roseau and learn about local flora and fauna at the Botanical Gardens. Proceed to a lookout point for a majestic view of Trafalgar Falls. After refreshment at a nearby restaurant, drive to the Emerald Pool, where after a 15-minute walk, you can swim in a natural pool surrounded by moss-covered boulders at the base of a picture-perfect waterfall.

Roseau and Indian River Tour ($40, 5 hours): Drive through Roseau and fishing villages along the island's western coast to the town of Portsmouth. Embark on wooden canoes for a guided tour of the Indian River. Ferns, lianas, and reeds cluster between the trees, forming a cool green tunnel of foliage. You'll spot herons, bananaquits, and the occasional iguana. Land crabs shuffle between the roots, and fish occasionally pop out of the water. The relaxing trip features informative commentary by your boatman and a brief stop at a rain-forest refreshment stand, where you can also pick up a fish or bird fashioned origami-style from reed.

Carib Indian Territory ($51, 5 hours): Drive to the Carib Territory, where the tribe's chief will acquaint you with Carib history. Attend a performance by the Karifuna Cultural Group and view local crafts.

Champagne Scuba Dive ($51, 3 hours, equipment included): Certified divers can dive the reef named for the bubbles produced by an underwater geothermal vent. Observe corals, fishes, and other marine life.

D'Auchamps Gardens and Museum ($36, 3 hours): Walk through an impressive collection of exotic plants and flowers and learn about their uses and origins. Along a marked trail through this old coffee estate you'll see cacao, avocado, breadfruit, and citrus trees as well as heliconias, orchids, and other spectacular blooms from around the world. View Trafalgar Falls and a variety of birds. Learn about Dominica's history at the recently completed museum.

TOURING THROUGH LOCAL OPERATORS

Dominica has several excellent tour operators who know the island's many features and intricate terrain like the backs of their hands. One truly outstanding and highly recommended operation is **Ken's Hinterland Adventure Tours,** 10 Old St., Roseau (☎ 767/448-4850; www.kenshinterlandtours.com). Ken's offers a wide variety of tours, some that focus on botany, natural history, bird watching, or whale watching; others feature more vigorous activities like river hiking, waterfall stalking, or mountain climbing. Ken and his team of knowledgeable guides have years of experience with various groups, including botanists and ornithologists—they can tell you the scientific and vernacular names of every bird and plant you encounter—and the company can customize a tour for cruise ship passengers. Just make arrangements in advance. **Dominica Tours** (☎ 767/448-2638) is a good alternative. For trips through the Carib Territory, you might want to make arrangements with **NICE (Native Indigenous Carib Excursions)** (☎ 767/448-2489). You can't miss with the firsthand knowledge of Carib traditions offered by NICE's operator, former Carib chief Irvince Auguiste.

ON YOUR OWN: WITHIN WALKING DISTANCE

IN ROSEAU   The French, in the early 18th century, chose to build their largest settlement at what is now **Roseau** because the area has the largest expanse of flat land on the leeward coast and is well supplied with freshwater from the nearby Roseau River. The town's name comes from the river reeds (*roseaux* in French) that grow profusely around the estuary. As you come ashore, you'll see the **Dominica Museum,** which faces the bay front. Housed in an old market house dating from 1810, the museum's permanent exhibit provides a clear and interesting overview of the island's geology, history, archaeology, economy, and culture. The displays on pre-Columbian peoples, the slave trade, and the Fighting Maroons—slaves who resisted their white overlords and established their own communities—are particularly informative The museum is open Monday to Friday from 9am to 4pm, Saturday from 9am to noon; admission is $2.

Directly behind the museum is the **Old Market Square.** Vendors of vegetables, fruits, and other merchandise have crowded this cobbled square for centuries, and over the years the location has also witnessed slave auctions, executions, and political meetings and rallies. Today it offers primarily handcrafts and souvenirs. The **Public Market Place** at the mouth of the Roseau River, to your left as you leave the ship, is the Old Market Square's successor as the town's center of commercial activity. It's most colorful on Saturday mornings, when farmers and country vendors from the hills artfully display their fruits, vegetables, root crops, and flowers across the courtyards, sidewalks, and stalls of the marketplace.

It took more than 100 years to build the **Roseau Cathedral** of Our Lady of Fair Heaven, on Virgin Lane, which was completed in 1916. Made of cut volcanic stone, its style is Gothic-Romanesque revival. The original funds to build the church were raised from levies on French planters, and Caribs erected the first wooden ceiling frame. Convicts on Devil's Island built the pulpit, and one of the stained-glass windows is dedicated to Christopher Columbus. The **Methodist Church** stands next door to the Cathedral on land that once belonged to Catholics who later converted to Methodism. The Protestant church's location so close to the cathedral on once-Catholic land caused discomfort in the late 1800s that culminated in a street riot. Things are calmer today. One of the church's interior monuments memorializes Charles Gordon Falconer, a newspaper editor and fiery leader of the Mulatto Ascendancy, a politically skillful and powerful group of mixed-race Dominicans in the 19th century.

On the eastern edge of Roseau, the **Botanical Gardens** lie at the base of Morne Bruce, the mountain overlooking the town. The gardens were established at the end of the 19th century to encourage the diversification of crops and to provide farmers with correctly propagated seedlings. London's Kew Gardens provided exotic plants collected from every corner of the tropical world, and experiments conducted to see what would grow in Dominica revealed that everything does. Hurricane David in 1979 destroyed many of the garden's oldest trees. One arboreal victim, an African baobab, still lies on the bus it crushed, a monument to the power of the storm. At the garden's aviary you can see sisserou and jacko parrots, part of a captive-breeding program to repopulate these endangered species. Throughout Roseau, you'll notice wood-and-stone houses with cheerfully painted shutters and roofs. Programs to preserve the town's architectural heritage have led to the restoration of several buildings, including the **Lilac House** on Kennedy Avenue, which features intricate gingerbread fretwork, latticed veranda railings, and several shades of purple paint, and the **J. W. Edwards Building,** at the corner of Old and King George V streets, which boasts a stone base and a wooden gallery on the second floor.

IN PORTSMOUTH   The cruise ship dock at Portsmouth leads directly to 260-acre **Cabrits National Park,** which combines stunning mountain scenery, tropical deciduous forest and swampland, volcanic sand beaches, coral reefs, and the romance of an 18th-century **Fort Shirley** overlooking the town of Portsmouth and Prince Rupert's Bay. Previous visitors to the area include Christopher Columbus, Sir Francis Drake, Admiral Horatio Nelson, and John Smith, who stopped here on his way to Virginia, where he founded Jamestown. Fort Shirley and more than 50 other major structures comprise one of the West Indies' most impressive and historic military complexes.

ON YOUR OWN: BEYOND WALKING DISTANCE

Approximately 15 to 20 minutes from Roseau, **Trafalgar Falls** is actually two separate falls fancifully referred to as the mother and the father falls. The cascading white torrents dazzle in the sunlight before pummeling black lava boulders below.

The surrounding foliage comes in innumerable shades of green. To reach the brisk water of the natural pool at the base of the falls, you'll have to step gingerly along slippery rocks, and the nonballetic are dissuaded from attempting the climb. The constant mist that tingles the entire area beats any spa treatment. The rainbows are perpetual.

Titou Gorge, near the village of Laudat, offers an exhilarating swimming experience. Wending through the narrow volcanic gorge, you struggle against the cool current, which becomes stronger and stronger until you feel like a salmon swimming upstream to spawn. The sheer black walls enclosing you loom 20 feet above. At first, they seem sinister. But worn smooth by the water, they're ultimately womb-like rather than menacing. Rock outcrops and a small cave provide interludes from the water flow, and eventually you reach the thundering waterfall that feeds the torrent. The final approach to this source is like swimming on a treadmill. On the way back to your starting point, recuperate in the adjacent hot-water spring.

Emerald Pool sits deep in the rain forest not far from the center of the island. After walking 15 minutes along a level trail shaded by majestic trees, you reach a 50-foot waterfall that crashes into the pool named for the moss-covered boulders enclosing it. Splash in the refreshing water. Float on your back to see the thick rain-forest canopy and bright blue sky above you.

About 4 miles from Portsmouth, in the midst of orange, grapefruit, and banana groves, the **Syndicate Nature Trail** provides an excellent introduction to tropical rain forests. The easy loop trail meanders through a stunningly rich ecosystem that features exotic trees such as the *lwoyé kaka,* so named because it smells like you know what; the *gommier* (hundreds of feet tall, it supplies the wood preferred by Carib canoe builders; its sap—*gomme* in French—is used to make incense and the chrism used in Catholic confirmations); and the *chantannyé,* whose gnarly roots spread above ground for 30 feet or more, buttressing the base trunk. Giant *fougère* ferns, an array of bromeliads, multicolored anthuriums, and endless varieties of dangling epiphytes compete beneath the tall trees. Don't miss the abandoned aerie built by an ornithologist monitoring the local sisserou and jacko parrots, and don't be surprised if you spot a hawk or two. That furry creature that just hopped across the trail up ahead was probably an agouti.

 Hard-core masochists have an easy choice—the forced march through the **Valley of Desolation** to **Boiling Lake.** Experienced guides say this all-day hike is like spending hours on a maximally resistant Stairmaster; one ex-Marine drill sergeant, a master of understatement, referred to it as "arduous." No joke, the trek *is* part of the Dominican army's basic training (of course, *you* won't have to carry one of your colleagues along the way). Why would any sane person endure this hell? To breathe in the harsh, sulfuric fumes that have killed all but the hardiest vegetation? Because the idea of baking a potato in the steam rising from the earth is irresistible? Maybe to feel the thrill that comes with the risk that you might break through the thin crust that separates you from hot lava? Or could it be the final destination, the 70-foot-wide cauldron of bubbling, slate-blue water of unknown depth. Don't even think of taking a dip in this flooded fumarole: The water temperature ranges from 180° to 197° Fahrenheit. Can we sign you up?

SHOPPING
In addition to the usual duty-free items—jewelry, watches, perfumes, and other luxury goods—Dominica offers handcrafts and art not obtainable anywhere else, most notably **Carib Indian baskets** made of dyed *larouma* reeds and *balizier* (heliconia)

leaves. Designs for these items originated in Venezuela's Orinoco River valley and have been handed down from generation to generation since long before the time of Columbus. Dominican designs and materials are similar to those made today in the Orinoco River valley—amazing considering that there's been no interaction for more than 500 years. The Carib basket you buy, therefore, is more than a souvenir—it's a link to the pre-Columbian Caribbean. You can buy Carib crafts directly from the craftspeople in the **Carib Territory** or at various outlets in Roseau. A small, 12-inch model will cost about $10, and you can get a bell-shaped model about 22 inches high for $30 or $35. Floor mats made from *vertiver* grass are another Dominican specialty.

Here are some other great places for local crafts. At **Tropicrafts,** at the corner of Queen Mary Street and Turkey Lane in Roseau, you can watch local women weave grass mats with designs as varied and complex as those you made as a child with your Spirograph. The large store also stocks Carib baskets, locally made soaps and toiletries, rums, jellies, condiments, wood carvings, and masks made from the trunks of giant *fougère* ferns. The **Rainforest Shop,** at 12 Old St. in Roseau, is dedicated to the preservation of Dominica's ecosystem and offers colorful hand-painted items made from recycled materials such as oil drums, coconut shells, and newspapers. A percentage of proceeds from all sales go to programs designed to preserve the island's coral reefs, rain forests, fishes, iguanas, and other marine and terrestrial life. **The Crazy Banana,** at 17 Castle St., features Dominican arts and crafts, including straw and ceramic items, as well as jewelry and Cuban cigars. For unique and sometimes whimsical objects, try **Balisier's** at 35 Great George St. Local artist Hilroy Fingal transforms throwaway items like aluminum cans, perfume bottles, rocks, and coconut shells into things of beauty. His aesthetic is a little like Keith Haring's and every bit as fun. **Caribana,** at 31 Cork St., is one of the island's oldest craft shops. It offers items as varied as furniture, home accessories, jewelry, books, and skin-care products. It also serves as a showcase for local painters and sculptors and as a gathering place for the local arts community. **Frontline Cooperative,** at 78 Queen Mary St., specializes in books about Caribbean peoples, issues, and cooking. It's the best place to track down works by Dominican authors like Lennox Honychurch, Jean Rhys, and Phyllis Shand Allfrey. Eddie Toulon, the store's owner, is also an authority on Dominica's vibrant music scene. He can recommend CDs from the store's extensive stock. **The Butterfly Boutique** at the Papillote Wilderness Retreat, outside of Roseau on the way to Trafalgar Falls, boasts a fine selection of local arts and crafts that reflect the island's African, Amerindian, and European heritage. Of special note are the mahogany sculptures of local artist Desiré. The store also carries paintings, prints, hand-stitched quilts and doilies, and an impressive selection of books of local interest. Near the Carib Territory in the town of Concord, the **Floral Gardens,** a hotel, restaurant, and garden complex, has an interesting gift shop with an especially good Carib-basket selection. For local products like Chubby Cola, Kubuli beer, Café Dominique, Bello hot sauces, Macoucherie and Soca rums, and bois bandé tea, go to one of the large supermarkets: **A. C. Shillingford** (34 King George V St.) and **Whitchurch Supercentre** (Old Street) are both in Roseau; **Brizee's Mart** is in Canefield, near the airport.

BEACHES

If your sole focus is beaches, you'll find Dominica so-so. Much of the seacoast is rocky, and many sandy beaches have darker, volcanic sand. But there are golden sand beaches as well, primarily on the northern coast. Head for **Woodford Bay,**

L'Ance Tortue, Pointe Baptiste, or **Hampstead Beach;** all have white sand, palm trees, and azure waters protected by reefs or windswept headlands.

SPORTS

FISHING   Dominica is a prime destination for anglers looking to catch marlin, wahoo, yellowfin tuna, or dorado. The island's numerous rivers flow into the Caribbean, providing an abundance of bait fish like bonito, jacks, and small tuna that attract bigger deepwater species. You can drop your line in the water a mere 15 minutes from the dock. **Rainbow Sportfishing** (☎ 767/448-8650) operates a 32-foot Sea Ray while **Game Fishing (Dominica)** (☎ 888/CASTAWAYS in the U.S., or 767/449-6244) has two boats, a 34-foot Luhrs and a 28-foot Pacemaker. Prices start at $50 per person (four-passenger minimum).

HIKING   Dominica offers physically fit hikers some of the most amazing geological sights in the Caribbean—scalding lava covered with only a thin crust, a boiling lake where mountain streams vaporize as they reach superheated volcanic fissures, and a barren wasteland known as the Valley of Desolation. Other areas feature cool, rushing streams and sublime waterfalls, the results of the 300-plus inches of rain that drench the island's mountaintops every year. Ten-foot-tall ferns and hundreds of orchids and other epiphytes create a tangle of underbrush, while insects, birds, and reptiles round out the nature experience. Botanists, geologists, and avid hikers consider climbs through the hills and forests of Dominica among the Caribbean's most rewarding. **Ken's Hinterland Adventure Tours** (☎ 767/448-4850) is universally recommended as the best source of guides and itineraries. Rates depend on the number of people in your group; $30 to $50 per person should cover it for a group of four. Make arrangements in advance.

KAYAKING   Why not paddle lazily along Dominica's western coast in a sea kayak? If the sun gets too hot, you can jump overboard to snorkel or swim. Choose a guided trip or, for perfect solitude, set out on your own. No doubt you'll discover some little cove along the shoreline perfect for a tranquil picnic and for watching frigate birds bomb-dive for fish. **Nature Island Dive** in Roseau (☎ 767/449-8181) is your best bet for advice and equipment rental. The rate for half-day kayak rental is about $25.

SCUBA DIVING   Dominica's lush, beautiful scenery above water is echoed underwater in the surrounding Caribbean and Atlantic. Although the island is drained by hundreds of rivers and streams, the jagged volcanic underseascape prevents runoff sediment from clouding the water. Visibility ranges from 60 to more than 100 feet. Most local dive operations surpass international standards set by PADI, NAUI, and SSI, and small, uncrowded excursions are the norm. **Dive Dominica** (☎ 888/262-6611 in the U.S., or 767/448-2188) is perhaps the island's best operator. You can also try **Anchorage Dive Center** (☎ 800/934-DIVE in the U.S., or 767/448-2638), **Dive Castaways** (☎ 888/CASTAWAYS in the U.S., or 767/449-6244), **East Carib Dive** (☎ 800/867-4764 in the U.S., or 767/449-6575), and **Cabrits Dive Centre** (☎ 767/445-3010). Single-tank boat dives run about $50. First-time dives with instruction run about $100 to $125.

SNORKELING   Dominica offers almost 30 top-notch snorkeling areas. Snorkelers can join a dive-boat party, participate in special snorkel excursions, or explore the coast in a sea kayak, periodically jumping overboard for a look below. The calm water on the island's leeward side is perfect for viewing the riotous colors of sponges, corals, and the 190-plus fish species native to the area. Offshore snorkeling and equipment rental can be arranged through any of the dive operators listed above. Prices start at approximately $25.

WHALE & DOLPHIN WATCHING   How often do you get a chance to befriend cetaceans, our seafaring, mammal brothers? Dominica boasts a resident pod of sperm whales, and during the peak season, from November to June, many more migrating whales arrive in search of food, mates, and a place to give birth. And on any given day, hundreds of spinner, spotted, or bottlenose dolphins might spin, flip, and leap around your boat. Sightings of sperm whales and humpbacks are common; killer orcas, beaked pygmy sperm whales, and fraser dolphins are rarer. You're briefed on what you may see, and identification charts are available. Be sure to bring binoculars. Several operators offer 4-hour boat trips for about $40 to $50 per person, including beverages. Try **Anchorage Dive Center** (☎ 767/448-2638), **Dive Dominica** (☎ 767/448-2188), **Carib Cruises** (☎ 767/448-2489), or **Rainbow Sportfishing** (☎ 767/448-8650).

GREAT LOCAL RESTAURANTS & BARS

Seafood, local root vegetables referred to as "provisions," and Creole recipes are among the highlights of Dominican cuisine. Crapaud (mountain chicken in English—it's really mountain frog) is the national delicacy. For a **local beer,** try Kubuli; for a **local rum,** try Soca.

IN ROSEAU   Try **La Robe Créole,** 3 Victoria St. (☎ 767/448-2896), which gets top marks for its callaloo soup (made from the spinachlike leaves of the local vegetable, *dasheen,* and coconut), lobster and conch crepes, and mango chutney. The decor features heavy stone walls, solid ladder-back chairs, and colorful madras tablecloths. **Guiyave,** 15 Cork St. (☎ 767/448-2930), an airy restaurant on the second floor of a pistachio-colored wood-frame house, features steamed fish, conch, octopus, and spareribs. Take a table on the veranda and cool off with one of the fresh-squeezed juices. How about soursop, tamarind, sorrel, cherry, or strawberry? The downstairs take-out counter offers chicken patties, spicy rotis, and delectable tarts and cakes. **The Sutton Grille,** 25 Old St. (☎ 767/449-8700), in the Sutton Place Hotel, boasts an airy dining area ensconced in 100-year-old stone walls. You can choose a table a few steps up from the bustle of downtown Roseau or one set back from the action. The menu, a veritable primer of Creole and other West Indian cookery, also offers a generous sprinkling of international and vegetarian dishes. Chef Pearl Pinard's robust character makes her the star of **Pearl's Cuisine,** 50 King George V St. (☎ 767/448-8707), but her magic in the kitchen is the real draw. Try the rice and spareribs or the codfish and plantains, two favorites of local patrons. **Cornerhouse Café,** 6 King George V St. (☎ 767/449-9000), is a cozy place for a cappuccino, a cold beer or fruit juice, even a fresh-baked bagel with cream cheese. You can also check your E-mail, get information from the Internet, and bask in the sun on the wraparound veranda. For traditional Creole pastries and dark rum-drenched fruitcake, stop by **Fran's** on Great George Street between King George V Street and Field Lane. If that sounds too heavy after a full day in the heat, sample some homemade ice cream. **Al's,** 5 Great George St., and **Piwi's,** 12 Kings Lane, both scoop up flavors like almond, coconut, peanut, mint, and soursop.

IN PORTSMOUTH   If you disembark in Portsmouth, get a table at the **Coconut Beach Restaurant** at Picard Beach (☎ 767/445-5393). It overlooks the Caribbean and the twin peaks of Cabrits National Park across Prince Rupert's Bay. The fresh seafood and Creole dishes taste even better with the tang of salt in the air.

The **Purple Turtle** (☎ 767/445-5296) is closer to the dock and features lobster and crayfish as well as lighter fare such as rotis, sandwiches, and salads.

FARTHER OUT   Outside of Roseau not far from Trafalgar Falls, the **Papillote Rainforest Restaurant** (☎ 767/448-2287) overlooks the luxuriant Roseau Valley and exotic gardens. Indulge in a "seafood symphony lunch" before relaxing in the hot mineral pools on the premises. After scuba diving in the Scott's Head area, lunch at **The Sundowner Café** (☎ 767/448-7749). Perched feet above the seashore, it offers fish caught hours, maybe only minutes, earlier and, not infrequently, views of frolicking dolphins or passing whales. If you're near the Carib Territory, you can dine in exotic gardens overlooking a rushing river at **Floral Gardens** in Concord (☎ 767/445-7636). Lush mountains, chirping birds, and evanescent rainstorms are included with the great local cuisine.

12 Dominican Republic

Called the "the fairest land under heaven" by some because of its sugar-white beaches and mountainous terrain, the Dominican Republic has, despite a persistent reputation for high crime, poverty, and social unrest, become one of the fastest-growing destinations in the Caribbean. Despite social and political drawbacks, the island still manages to intrigue visitors with its natural beauty and rich colonial heritage, so much so that many return again and again.

Nestled amid Cuba, Jamaica, and Puerto Rico, the island of Hispaniola (Little Spain) consists of Haiti, on the westernmost third of the island, and the Dominican Republic, which has a lush landmass equal to that of Vermont and New Hampshire combined. In the Dominican interior, the fertile Valley of Cibao (rich sugarcane country) ends its upward sweep at Pico Duarte, formerly Pico Trujillo, the highest mountain peak in the West Indies, which soars to 10,417 feet. Puerto Rico sits 54 miles off the Republic's east coast across the Mona Passage, prompting many poverty-stricken Dominicans to risk their lives crossing the channel in hopes of slipping into Puerto Rico and then illegally into the continental United States.

Columbus sighted Hispaniola's coral-edged Caribbean coastline on his first voyage to the New World and pronounced, "There is no more beautiful island in the world." The first permanent European settlement in the New World was founded here on November 7, 1493, and the settlement's ruins still remain near Montecristi in the northeast part of the island. Natives called the island Quisqueya, "Mother Earth," before the Spanish arrived to butcher them.

Much of what Columbus first saw still remains in a natural, unspoiled condition, but that may change: The country is building and expanding rapidly. In the heart of the Caribbean archipelago, the country has an 870-mile coastline, about a third of which is devoted to beaches (the best are in Puerto Plata and La Romana), and near-perfect weather year-round. So, why did it take so long for the Dominican Republic to be discovered by visitors? The answer is largely political. The country has been steeped in misery and bloodshed almost from its beginning, a situation that climaxed with the infamous reign of Rafael Trujillo (1930 to 1961) and the civil wars that followed.

Today the Dominican Republic is being rebuilt and restored, and it offers visitors a chance to enjoy the sun and sea as well as to learn about the history and politics of a developing society. Just exercise caution: Muggings are common (particularly in Santo Domingo); travelers should avoid unmarked taxis at all costs, and be wary of the hustlers in tourist areas.

Frommer's Favorite Dominican Republic Experiences
- **Exploring the Colonial City:** On your own or as part of a shore excursion, this historic section offers a series of firsts for the New World—the first university, hospital, cathedral, and more. The cobblestone streets and restored buildings offer a welcome respite from the bustle of this modern capital (see, "Shore Excursions" and "On Your Own: Within Walking Distance," below).
- **Hitting the beach:** White-sand beaches, blue waters, hotels, restaurants, outdoor cafes, nightclubs, and shops can be found in the seaside resorts of Boca Chica and Juan Dolio. It is worth the trek (see "Shore Excursions" and "Beaches," below).

COMING ASHORE   Ships dock at San Souci, about 3 miles from downtown Santo Domingo. At the terminal are telephones, a bank, a tourist information stand, and shops. The easiest way to get to the city is by taxi. It costs about $10 to go to the Colonial City from the port. Cruise ships also dock at Catalina Island in La Romana, home to one of the Caribbean's most famous resorts, Casa de Campo. Cruise lines offer excursions to the resort and its environs, including Altos de Chavon, a replica of a 16th-century Mediterranean village that boasts an amphitheater, restaurants, cobblestone streets, and artisans' workshops.

At press time, the Dominican Republic was scheduled to start construction in Samana on a project that would create a marina, hotels, villas, shops, residential and commercial areas, and two or three slips for cruise ships.

Credit-card phones are located at the terminal and throughout the city. Prepaid calling cards are available in stores and in Codetel (the country's main phone company) offices in Santo Domingo.

CURRENCY   The **Dominican peso.** The exchange rate is about 15 pesos to U.S.$1 (RD$1 = U.S.7¢). U.S. dollars are accepted by cab drivers and some shopkeepers.

LANGUAGE   The official language is Spanish, but English is also spoken in tourist areas. Knowing a few key Spanish phrases is helpful.

INFORMATION   Located on the corner of Avenida Mexico and Avenida 30 de Marzo is the city's **main tourist office** (☎ 800/OSECTUR or 809/221-4660). The office is open during the week from 9am to 5pm. The staff will give you just the basics. For info before you go, call the Dominican Republic tourist office in the United States at ☎ 888/374-6361 or 212/588-1015 or log on at www.domincana.com.do.

CALLING FROM THE U.S.   When calling Dominican Republic from the United States, you need to dial only a "1" before the numbers listed throughout this section.

Frommer's Ratings: Dominican Republic					
	Poor	Fair	Good	Excellent	Outstanding
Overall Experience		✓			
Shore Excursions			✓		
Activities Close to Port		✓			
Beaches & Water Sports			✓		
Shopping		✓			
Dining/Bars			✓		

Dominican Republic

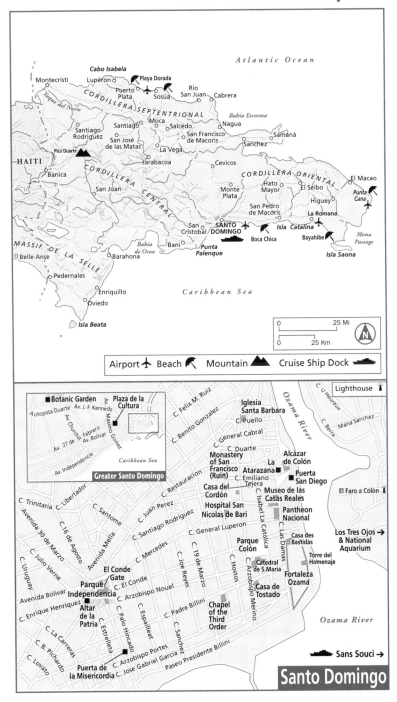

Atlantic Ocean

Cabo Isabela
Montecristi
Lupéron
Playa Dorada
Puerto Plata
Sosúa
Rio San Juan
Cabrera
CORDILLERA SEPTENTRIONAL
Bahía Escocesa
Moca
Salcedo
Nagua
Santiago Rodríguez
Santiago
San Francisco de Macorís
Samaná
San José de las Matas
La Vega
Sanchez
Pico Duarte
Jarabacoa
Cevicos
HAITI
CORDILLERA CENTRAL
Banica
CORDILLERA ORIENTAL
El Macao
San Juan
Monte Plata
Hato Mayor
El Seibo
Higuey
Punta Cana
San Pedro de Macorís
La Romana
San Cristobal
SANTO DOMINGO
Isla Catalina
Bayahibe
MASSIF DE LA SELLE
Bani
Boca Chica
Punta Palenque
Bahía de Ocoa
Mona Passage
Belle Anse
Barahona
Isla Saona
Pedernales
Caribbean Sea
Enriquillo
Oviedo
Isla Beata

Airport ✈ Beach 🏖 Mountain ▲ Cruise Ship Dock 🚢

25 Mi
0
25 Km
0

Lighthouse

Botanic Garden
Plaza de la Cultura
Autopista Duarte Av. J. F. Kennedy
C. Felix M. Ruiz
Iglesia Santa Barbara
Ozama River
C. U Heureux
Av. Churchill
Av. Maximo Gomez
Av. de Febrero
C. Benito Gonzalez
C. Puello
C. Berra
Mana Sanchez
Av. 27 de Febrero
Av. Bolivar
C. General Cabral
Caribbean Sea
Av. Independencia
Greater Santo Domingo
C. Duarte
Monastery of San Francisco (Ruin)
Alcázar de Colón
Atarazana
Puerta San Diego
La
C. Emiliano Tejera
El Faro a Colón
C. Libertador
C. Restauracion
Casa del Cordón
Museo de las Casas Reales
C. Trinitaria
C. Santome
C. Juan Perez
Hospital San Nicolas de Bari
C. Isabel La Catolica
Pantheon Nacional
Avenida 30 de Marzo
C. 16 de Agosto
C. Santiago Rodriguez
C. General Luperon
Casa des Bastidas
Los Tres Ojos & National Aquarium
C. Julio Verne
Avenida Melia
C. Mercedes
Parque Colón
C. Las Damas
C. Uruguay
C. Joe Reyes
C. 19 de Marzo
C. Hostos
Torre del Homenaje
El Conde Gate
Catedral de S.Maria
Avenida Bolivar
Parque Independencia
C. El Conde
C. Arzobispo Nouel
C. Arzobispo Merino
Fortaleza Ozamá
C. Enrique Henriquez
Altar de la Patria
C. Palo Hincado
C. Espaillat
C. Padre Billini
Casa de Tostado
Chapel of the Third Order
Ozama River
C. La Carreras
C. Estrelleta
C. Sanchez
C. B. Pichardo
C. Lovato
Puerta de la Misericordia
C. Arzobispo Portes
C. Jose Gabriel Garcia
Paseo Presidente Billini
Sans Souci →

Santo Domingo

159

GETTING AROUND

BY TAXI   Taxis aren't metered, and you should settle on the fare before you take the ride. The average fare within Santo Domingo is about $6. A cab to Boca Chica and Juan Dolio costs between $20 and $25 one-way. Avoid unmarked taxis. Another option for getting around Santo Domingo is **moto conchos,** which are motorcycle taxis that offer cheaper fares.

BY BUS   Private companies such as **Caribe Tours** (☎ **809/221-4422**) and **Metro Expreso** (☎ **809/566-7126**) operate scheduled service on various routes in air-conditioned buses. The fares are inexpensive (ranging from $3 to $6). Public buses, called **guaguas,** are also cheap (about $1) but are generally crowded, and service is erratic.

RENTAL CARS   Driving here is not for the faint of heart. In Santo Domingo, tailgating is an art form. The main highways are relatively smooth, but the secondary ones have potholes. If you dare, Budget, Hertz, National, and Thrifty have outlets here.

SHORE EXCURSIONS

✪ **Colonial City Walking Tour** ($24, 2$^1/_2$ hours): The tour will take you to the first cathedral in the New World, the earliest fort in the New World, and the oldest street in the New World. There is a stop at the Amber Museum as well as a cigar shop.

Columbus Lighthouse, Amber Museum, and Cathedral Tour ($20, 3 hours): Explore the lighthouse, stop to see amber, and visit the cathedral where Columbus was originally buried.

✪ **Juan Dolio Beach Tour** ($40, 6 hours): You spend the day at a resort's beach with access to its pool, snorkeling equipment, and clubhouse facilities. A buffet lunch and drinks are included.

ON YOUR OWN: WITHIN WALKING DISTANCE

Heading to the beach or discovering the capital's rich history are the best bets for folks visiting by cruise ship. Visitors should head to the **Colonial City** (Zona Colonial), home to the oldest cathedral, monastery, and university in the New World. The heart of the Colonial District is **Calle Las Damas,** the oldest street in the New World. It is named after the ladies of the viceroy's court who would promenade along the street in the afternoons. **Calle El Conde** is the main shopping thoroughfare. The Colonial City is best explored on foot.

Alcazar de Colon (Columbus's Palace), on Calle Las Damas (☎ **809/ 687-5361**), was built for Diego, the son of Christopher Columbus, in 1510. Diego was appointed the first viceroy of the Indies, and the palace served as the center of the Spanish court. Inside, visitors will find furnishings and paintings from that era. The restoration of the palace, which overlooks the Ozama River, first started in 1955 and was completed in the 1990s. Admission is $1, and it's open Monday and Wednesday to Friday from 9am to 5pm, Saturday from 9am to 4pm, and Sunday from 9am to 1pm.

The **Cathedral of Santa Maria de la Encarnacion,** on Calle Arzobispo Merino (☎ **809/689-1920**), was built in stages from 1510 to 1540, although its bell tower was never completed. Pope Paul III declared it the first cathedral in the New World in 1542. A marble mausoleum inside the Spanish Renaissance-style building held the remains of Christopher Columbus until they were transferred to the Columbus

Lighthouse Memorial in 1992. The facade is made of gold coral limestone. Admission is free, and it is open Monday to Saturday from 9am to 4pm.

Next to the cathedral is **Parque Colon** (Columbus Square), which features a larger-than-life bronze statue of the discoverer.

Las Ruinas del Monasterio de San Francisco (The Ruins of the San Francisco Monastery), between Calle Hostos and Calle Emiliano Tejera (☎ **809/682-3780**), has survived hurricanes, earthquakes, the French artillery, and a pillaging by Sir Francis Drake. It was constructed in the early 16th century and is considered—surprise!—the oldest monastery in the New World.

Fortaleza Ozama, on Calle Las Damas, overlooks the Ozama River and is considered the earliest military edifice built in the New World. Inside is **La Torre del Homenaje** (The Tower of Homage) (☎ **809/687-4722**), which served as a prison and fortress well into the 20th century. The fort is open daily from 9am to 5pm, and admission is $1.

ON YOUR OWN: BEYOND WALKING DISTANCE

Outside of the Colonial City is **Faro a Colon** (Columbus's Lighthouse), on Boulevar al Faro (☎ **809/591-1492**). The structure, constructed in the shape of a cross, commemorates the 500th anniversary of Christopher Columbus's arrival in the Americas in 1492 and allegedly houses the discoverer's remains (many other institutions also make this claim), as well as museums and exhibition halls devoted to Columbus. Admission is $2, and it is open Tuesday to Sunday from 10am to 5pm. You'll have to take a cab to get here.

If you're with the kids, visit the **National Aquarium,** on Avenida Espana (☎ **809/592-1509**), which features saltwater and freshwater marine life, including turtles and sharks. Admission is $1, and the aquarium is open Tuesday to Sunday from 9am to 6pm.

Los Tres Ojos (The Three Eyes), on Avenida Las Americas, are three subterranean lagoons that are surrounded by stalagmites and lush greenery. The site is open daily and there is no admission charge. It's located about 15 minutes from Santo Domingo.

Diehard baseball fans will recognize **San Pedro de Macoris,** known as the birthplace of many famous baseball players, including Sammy Sosa and Pedro Martinez. The city is about a 45-minute drive from Santo Domingo, and many tourists head to the local stadium to watch a game and check out future major leaguers.

SHOPPING

The duty-free shopping is below the standard of many other islands, but the Dominican Republic does have plenty of good buys. The main shopping areas are on La Atarazana, Avenida Mella, and Calle El Conde in the Colonial City. The best items to take home include amber or *larimar* (the Dominican turquoise) pieces, coffee, rum, cigars, paintings, woodcarvings, and rocking chairs

The city's marketplace, **Mercado Modelo,** is located on Avenida Mella, and is brimming with stalls selling crafts, paintings, produce, spices, and coffee, among other things. Bargaining is the norm here.

Stop by **Ambar Marie** on Caonabo, **Ambar Nacionale** on Calle Restauracion, and **Ambar Tres** on La Atarazana for amber and larimar. **The Santo Domingo Cigar Club** in the Renaissance Jaragua Hotel, on Avenida George Washington, has the finest selection of cigars in the city. Works of art by Dominicans and Haitians can be found at **Galería de Arte Nader** at Lupero and Duarte. Stop by a local **grocery store** to purchase Café Santo Domingo or Mama Ines/Montana Verde coffee.

BEACHES

The Dominican Republic is known for its great beaches, but you won't find them in Santo Domingo. The main beach areas are **Boca Chica** and **Juan Dolio.** Take a cab: Boca Chica is about 35 minutes east of Santo Domingo; Juan Dolio, about 45 minutes east. Hotels, restaurants, and bars—as well as pesky vendors hawking their wares—are part of the scene. Both seaside resorts offer white-sand beaches, and waters that are calm and shallow, making them ideal for swimming.

While at Boca Chica, stop by **Neptuno's Club,** on Avenida Duarte (☎ **809/ 523-4703**), for a bite to eat. The open-air restaurant serves a variety of seafood dishes.

GREAT LOCAL RESTAURANTS & BARS

Most cruise ship passengers head to the Colonial City or along the Malecon for lunch. There should be a restaurant to suit every visitor's palate, with cuisines ranging from Italian to Japanese to Mexican. The most popular **local beers** are Presidente and Bohemia. The **local rums** are Brugal and Bermudez.

ON THE MALECON   The Malecon is the city's main thoroughfare, which runs along the waterfront. **Vesuvio,** on Avenida George Washington (☎ **809/221-3333**), is the city's best-known Italian restaurant, having opened its doors in 1954. Red snapper, sea bass, and a variety of homemade pastas are on the menu, as well as Dominican specialties. Pizzeria Vesuvio is located next door.

IN THE COLONIAL CITY   Pate Palo Brasserie, on La Atarazana (☎ **809/ 687-8089**), claims to be the oldest pub in the New World. The high ceilings, stone walls, and gracious wait staff create a charming atmosphere. The international menu features seafood and pasta dishes. **La Bricciola,** on Calle Arzobispo Merino (☎ **809/688-5055**), is a restored colonial building that serves delectable Italian cuisine, including lobster medaillons; mushrooms and shrimp; and veal scaloppini with prosciutto, mushrooms, and mozzarella.

For local flavor, **El Conuco,** on Casimiro de Moya (☎ **809/221-3231**), is the place to go. The restaurant, located close to the Colonial City, resembles a hut on a Dominican farm, and serves country-style cooking. There is a great selection of local dishes, including stews, chicken entrees, and the catch of the day.

IN MODERN SANTO DOMINGO   Meson de la Caba, on Avenida Mirador del Sur (☎ **809/533-2818**), is literally an underground experience. Patrons descend a spiral staircase to dine in a natural cave that is 50 feet below the ground. The restaurant is known for its steak and seafood entrees as well as its live entertainment.

13 Grand Cayman

Grand Cayman is the largest of the Cayman Islands, a British colony 480 miles due south of Miami (Cayman Brac and Little Cayman are the others). It's the top of an underwater mountain, whose side—known as the Cayman Wall—plummets straight down for 500 feet before becoming a steep slope that falls away for 6,000 feet to the ocean floor.

Despite its "grand" name, the place is only 22 miles long and 8 miles across at its widest point. Flat and prosperous, this tiny nation depends on Britain for its economic survival and attracts millionaire expatriates from all over because of its lenient tax and banking laws. Relatively unattractive, these islands are covered with scrubland and swamp, but boast more than their share of upscale, expensive private homes and condos. Until recently, Grand Cayman enjoyed one of the most closely

Grand Cayman

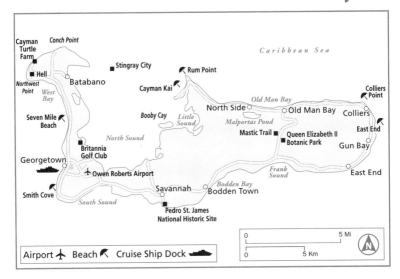

knit social fabrics in the Caribbean, but with recent prosperity, some of this is beginning to unravel. More hotels have begun lining the sands of the nation's most famous sunspot, **Seven Mile Beach,** and the island attracts more than its share of scuba divers and snorkelers.

Grand Cayman is also popular because of its laid-back civility (so civil that ships aren't allowed to visit on Sunday). **George Town** is the colony's capital and its commercial hub.

Frommer's Favorite Grand Cayman Experiences

- **Swimming with stingrays:** At Stingray City, you can hop into the water with dozens of these weird-looking but gentle sea creatures, which swim right into your arms, like dogs (see "Shore Excursions," below).
- **Taking in the scene on Seven Mile Beach:** Grand Cayman's famed stretch of sand is known for its array of water sports and its translucent aquamarine waters (see "Beaches," below).

COMING ASHORE   Cruise ships anchor off George Town and ferry their passengers to a pier on Harbour Drive. Located in the heart of the shopping district, the landing point couldn't be more convenient. There's a tourist information booth at the pier, and taxis line up to meet cruise ship passengers.

Frommer's Ratings: Grand Cayman					
	Poor	Fair	Good	Excellent	Outstanding
Overall Experience					✓
Shore Excursions					✓
Activities Close to Port				✓	
Beaches & Water Sports					✓
Shopping				✓	
Dining/Bars			✓		

There is a **phone center** for credit-card calls on Shedden Road, right in downtown.

CURRENCY   The legal tender is the **Cayman Islands dollar (CI).** The exchange rate is CI.83 to U.S.$1 (CI1 is worth about $1.20). Canadian, U.S., and British currencies are accepted throughout the Cayman Islands. Many restaurants quote prices in Cayman Islands dollars, which can lead you to think that food is cheaper than it is. Unless otherwise noted, prices in this section are given in U.S. dollars.

LANGUAGE   English is the official language of the islands.

INFORMATION   The **Department of Tourism** is in the Pavilion Building, Cricket Square (P.O. Box 67), George Town, Grand Cayman, BWI (☎ **800/346-3313** or 345/949-0623). It's open Monday to Friday from 9am to 5pm. To get info before you go, call the **Grand Caymans Tourism Board** in New York City at ☎ **212/682-5582** or visit its Web site at www.caymanislands.ky.

CALLING FROM THE U.S.   When calling Grand Cayman from the United States, you need to only dial a "1" before the numbers listed throughout this section.

GETTING AROUND

BY TAXI   Taxi fares are fixed; typical one-way fares range from $12 to $20. **Cayman Cab Team** (☎ **345/947-4491**) and **Holiday Inn Taxi Stand** (☎ **345/945-4491**) offer 24-hour service.

BY RENTAL CAR   The roads are good by Caribbean standards, so driving around is relatively easy, as long as you remember to drive on the left side of the road. Reserve a car in advance with **Cico Avis** (☎ **800/331-1084** in the U.S., or 345/949-2468), **Budget** (☎ **800/527-0700** in the U.S., or 345/949-5605), or **Ace Hertz** (☎ **800/654-3131** in the U.S., or 345/949-7861).

BY MOTOR SCOOTER OR BICYCLE   The terrain is relatively flat, so motor scooters and bicycles are another way to get around. **Soto Scooters Ltd.,** Seven Mile Beach (☎ **345/945-4652**), at Coconut Place, offers Honda Elite scooters for about $30 daily, and bicycles for $15 daily.

SHORE EXCURSIONS

Nearly all the shore excursions here are underwater adventures, which you can book on your own or through your cruise ship.

✪ **Stingray City** ($39–$49, 2–3 hours): The waters off Grand Cayman are home to Stingray City, one of the world's most unusual underwater attractions. Set in the very shallow, sun-flooded waters of North Sound, about 2 miles east of the island's northwestern tip, the site was discovered in the mid-1980s when local fishermen cleaned their catch and dumped the offal overboard. They noticed scores of stingrays (which usually eat marine crabs) feeding on the debris, a phenomenon that quickly attracted local divers and marine zoologists. Today, anywhere from 30 to 100 relatively tame stingrays hover in the waters around the site for their daily handouts from hordes of snorkelers (often hundreds of cruise passengers at a time, so don't be surprised if they're not hungry). Stingrays are terribly gentle creatures, but they possess viciously barbed stingers capable of inflicting painful damage to anyone mistreating them. Never try to grab one by the tail. As long as you don't, you can feed and pet these velvet-skinned creatures without incident. Some tours include a quick island tour, including a stop at the Cayman Turtle Farm and a town called Hell (to look at some interesting rock formations and, of course, buy a T-shirt with all manner of Hell logos). The island tour and Stingray City excursion usually runs about 3 hours.

Atlantis **Submarine Excursion** ($76, 1¹/₂ hours): A 45-minute ride in the submarine is usually offered. The "*Atlantis* Expedition" dive visits the Cayman Wall; the "*Atlantis* Discovery" lasts 40 minutes and introduces viewers to the marine life of the Caymans.

Island Tour via Bicycle ($60, 3 hours): A great way to really get a feel for an island—and get some exercise—is via bicycle. You pick up your touring mountain bike at the Beach Club Colony Hotel and then ride along the coastline for views of Seven Mile Beach, then journey inland en route to the north side of the island to ride along the coast again.

TOURING THROUGH LOCAL OPERATORS

Stingray City: If the tours on your ship get booked, about half a dozen entrepreneurs lead expeditions to Stingray City, and there are usually a few tour agents waiting around the terminal in George Town. One well-known outfit is **Treasure Island Divers** (☎ **800/872-7552** from the U.S. or 345/949-4456), which charges snorkelers $30.

Taxi Tours: If you want to see the island, you can grab a taxi in port and take a tour. Taxis should cost about $40 per hour and can hold up to five people, and a 3-hour tour covers all the sights in a leisurely fashion. Make sure to stop in the town called Hell and send a postcard home.

ON YOUR OWN: WITHIN WALKING DISTANCE

In George Town, **Cayman Islands National Museum,** Harbour Drive (☎ **345/949-8368**), is housed in a veranda-fronted building that once served as the island's courthouse and is very worthwhile. Exhibits include Caymanian artifacts collected by Ira Thompson (beginning in the 1930s), and other items portraying the natural, social, and cultural history of the Caymans. There's a gift shop, theater, and cafe (a $5 donation is requested).

ON YOUR OWN: BEYOND WALKING DISTANCE

The only green-sea-turtle farm of its kind in the world, **Cayman Turtle Farm,** Northwest Point (☎ **345/949-3894**), is the island's most popular land-based tourist attraction. Once a multitude of turtles lived in the waters surrounding the Cayman Islands, but today these creatures are an endangered species. The turtle farm's purpose is twofold: to provide the local market with edible turtle meat and to replenish the waters with hatchlings and yearling turtles. You can look into 100 circular concrete tanks containing turtles ranging in size from 6 ounces to 600 pounds, or sample turtle dishes at a snack bar and restaurant.

On 60 acres of rugged wooded land, **Queen Elizabeth II Botanical Park,** off Frank Sound Road, North Side (☎ **345/947-9462**), offers visitors a 1-hour walk along an 8-mile trail through wetlands, swamps, dry thicket, and mahogany trees. You might spot hickatees (the freshwater turtles found only on the Caymans and in Cuba), the rare Grand Cayman parrot, or the anole lizard with a cobalt-blue throat pouch. There are six rest stations along the trail, plus a visitor center and a canteen. There's also a heritage garden, a floral garden, and a lake.

The **Mastic Trail,** west of Frank Sound Road (☎ **345/949-1996**), is a restored 200-year-old footpath through a t2-million-year-old woodland area in the heart of the island. Named for the majestic mastic tree, the trail showcases the reserve's natural attractions, including a native mangrove swamp, traditional agriculture, and an ancient woodland area. You can follow the 2-mile trail on your own, but I recommend taking a 3-hour guided tour. Call to make a reservation first. The trail, adjacent to the Botanical Park, is about a 45-minute drive from George Town.

SHOPPING

There's duty-free shopping here for silver, china, crystal, Irish linens, and British woolen goods, but I've found most prices to be similar to those in the United States. You'll also find cigar shops and international chains like Coach, the leather-goods store. Don't purchase turtle or black-coral products (which you'll see everywhere), since it is illegal to bring them into the United States or most other Western nations.

Some standout shops include **Artifacts Ltd.,** Harbour Drive (on the harbor front, across from the landing dock), for back issues of Cayman stamps; **The Jewelry Centre,** Fort Street, one of the largest jewelry stores in the Caymans; and the **Kennedy Gallery,** West Shore Centre, specializing in watercolors by local artists.

BEACHES

Grand Cayman's ✪ **Seven Mile Beach,** which begins north of George Town, an easy taxi ride from the cruise dock, has sparkling white sands with a backdrop of Australian pines. The beach is really about 5¹/₂ miles long, but the label of "seven mile" has stuck. It's lined with condominiums and plush resorts, and is known for its array of water sports and its translucent aquamarine waters. The average water temperature is a balmy 80°F.

SPORTS

FISHING & GENERAL WATER SPORTS   **Red Sail Sports** (☎ 800/255-6425 in the U.S., or 345/947-5966) has its headquarters in a gaily painted wooden house beside the beach at the Hyatt Regency Grand Cayman on West Bay Road. Its half-day deep-sea fishing excursions for up to eight people depart daily at 7am (returning at noon) and 1pm (returning at 5pm) in search of tuna, marlin, and wahoo (rates are $600 for up to six people; reservations are suggested). Red Sail offers parasailing, waterskiing, and scuba diving for beginners as well as more advanced divers. In addition, it has one of the best-designed sailing catamarans in the Caribbean, berthed in a canal a short walk from the water-sports center. There's a daily sail from 10am to 2pm to Stingray City, with snorkeling equipment and lunch included in the price.

GOLF   The major course on Grand Cayman is at the **Britannia Golf Club,** next to the Hyatt Regency on West Bay Road (☎ 345/949-8020). The course was designed by Jack Nicklaus and is unique in that it incorporates three different courses in one: a nine-hole championship layout, an 18-hole executive set-up, and an 18-hole Cayman course. Nonguests of the club can reserve no more than 24 hours in advance.

SCUBA DIVING & SNORKELING   Coral reefs and other formations encircling the island are filled with marine life. It's easy to dive close to shore, so boats aren't necessary, but plenty of boats and scuba facilities are available, as well as many dive shops renting scuba gear to certified divers. The best dive operation is **Bob Soto's Diving Ltd.,** P.O. Box 1801, Grand Cayman, BWI (☎ 800/262-7686 or 809/949-2022 for reservations, or 345/949-2022), with full-service dive shops at Treasure Island, the SCUBA Centre on North Church Street, and Soto's Coconut in the Coconut Place Shopping Centre. There are full-day resort courses as well as dives for experienced people daily on the west, north, and south walls, plus shore diving from the SCUBA Centre. The staff is helpful and highly professional.

GREAT LOCAL RESTAURANTS & BARS

A favorite **local beer** is Stingray, and a favorite **local rum** is Tortuga.

Abank's by the Sea, on Harbour Drive, is less than a half-mile's walk south of the pier. It's a great open-air seaside cafe for a sandwich, chicken fingers, and a couple of cool Stingray beers. **Cracked Conch by the Sea,** West Bay Road, near Turtle Bay Farm (☎ **345/945-5217**), serves some of the island's freshest seafood, including a succulent turtle steak and the inevitable conch, plus an array of meat dishes, including beef, jerk pork, and spicy combinations of chicken. The **Crow's Nest Restaurant,** South Sound, on the southwesternmost tip of the island, a 4-minute drive from George Town (☎ **345/949-9366**), is one of those places that evokes the Caribbean "the way it used to be." There's no pretense here—you get good, honest Caribbean cookery, including grilled seafood, at great prices. Many dishes are spicy, especially its signature appetizer, fiery coconut shrimp.

The **Hog Sty Bay Café and Pub,** North Church Street, near the beginning of West Bay Road (☎ **345/949-6163**), enjoys a loyal clientele, and is divided into an amusingly decorated pub and a Caribbean-inspired dining room open to a view of the harbor. In the pub, you can order such British staples as fish-and-chips or cottage pie. **Island Taste,** South Church Street (☎ **345/949-4945**), caters more to large appetites than to picky gourmets, and offers great value for the money. Most of the menu is devoted to seafood dishes, such as mahimahi, turtle steak, and spiny lobster. **Ottmar's Restaurant and Lounge,** West Bay Road, side entrance of the Grand Pavilion Hotel (☎ **345/945-5879**), is one of the island's top restaurants, offering such dishes as Bavarian cucumber soup, bouillabaisse, French pepper steak, and Wiener schnitzel. My favorite is chicken Trinidad, stuffed with grapes, nuts, and apples rolled in coconut flakes, sautéed golden brown, and served in orange-butter sauce.

14 Grenada

The southernmost nation of the British Windwards, Grenada (Gre-*nay*-dah) is one of the lushest in the Caribbean. Called the "Spice Island," its extravagant fertility—a result of the gentle climate and volcanic soil—produces more spices than anywhere else in the world: cloves, cinnamon, mace, cocoa, tonka beans, ginger, and a third of the world's supply of nutmeg. The beaches are white and sandy, and the populace (a mixture of English expatriates and islanders of African descent) is friendly. Once a British Crown Colony but now independent, the island nation also incorporates two smaller islands: Carriacou and Petit Martinique, neither of which has many tourist facilities.

St. George's, the country's capital, is one of the most colorful ports in the West Indies. Nearly landlocked in the deep crater of a long-dead volcano, and flanked by old forts, it reminds many visitors of Portofino, Italy. Here you'll see some of the most charming Georgian colonial buildings in the Caribbean, many with red tile roofs (the tiles were brought by European trade ships as ballast) and pastel walls. Churches dot the hillside of the harbor. Frangipani and flamboyant trees add even more color.

Crisscrossed by nature trails, Grenada's interior is a jungle of palms, oleander, bougainvillea, purple and red hibiscus, crimson anthurium, bananas, breadfruit, birdsong, ferns, and palms. The island's lush tropical scenery and natural bounty attract visitors who want to snorkel, sail, fish, hike on jungle paths, or loll the day away on the 2-mile-long, white-sand **Grand Anse Beach,** one of the best in the Caribbean.

Frommer's Favorite Grenada Experiences

- **Picnicking at Annandale Falls:** A 50-foot cascade is the perfect backdrop for a picnic among tropical flora—and you can swim in the falls afterward (see "On Your Own: Beyond Walking Distance," below).
- **Hiking to the Seven Sisters Waterfall:** A hearty walk along a muddy path that winds through the thick, pristine jungle is a blast. At the end of the approximately mile-long trail there's a set of beautiful waterfalls. You can even jump from the tops of two of them into the pools below (see "Shore Excursions," below).
- **Visiting Levera National Park:** With beaches, coral reefs, a mangrove swamp, a lake, and a bird sanctuary, this is a paradise for hikers, swimmers, and snorkelers alike (see "On Your Own: Beyond Walking Distance," below).
- **Taking the rainforest and Grand Etang Lake tour:** Take a bus to an extinct volcanic crater some 1,900 feet above sea level. On the way, drive through rain forests and stop at a spice estate (see "Shore Excursions," below).

COMING ASHORE   Ships either dock at a pier right in St. George's or anchor in the much-photographed harbor and send their passengers to the pier by tender. A tourist information center at the pier dispenses island data. The Carenage (St. George's main street) is only a short walk away from the pier; a taxi into the center of town costs about $3. To get to Grand Anse, you can take a regular taxi or a water taxi (see "Getting Around," below).

You'll find a pair of **credit-card phones** for international calls inside the small cruise terminal and two more just outside of it. There are six more London-style red phone booths midway around the Carenage, less than a half mile from the terminal.

CURRENCY   The official currency is the **Eastern Caribbean dollar (EC$).** The exchange rate is EC$2.70 to U.S.$1 (EC$1 = 37¢). Always determine which dollars—EC or U.S.—you're talking about when discussing a price.

LANGUAGE   English is commonly spoken on this island. Creole English, a mixture of African, English, and French, is spoken informally by the majority.

INFORMATION   Go to the **Grenada Board of Tourism,** on the Carenage in St. George's (☎ **800/927-9554** or 473/440-2279), for maps and general information. Open Monday to Friday from 8am to 4pm. To get information before you go, contact the **Grenada Tourism Board** in New York City at ☎ **212/687-9554** or log on to the Web site at www.grenada.com.

CALLING FROM THE U.S.   When calling Grenada from the United States, you need to only dial a "1" before the numbers listed throughout this section.

Frommer's Ratings: Grenada					
	Poor	Fair	Good	Excellent	Outstanding
Overall Experience					✓
Shore Excursions			✓		
Activities Close to Port				✓	
Beaches & Water Sports			✓		
Shopping			✓		
Dining/Bars			✓		

Grenada

Map legend: Airport ✈ Beach ⚑ Mountain ▲▲ Cruise Ship Dock ⛴

GETTING AROUND

St. George's can easily be explored on foot, although parts of the town are steep as it rises up from the harbor.

BY TAXI   Taxi fares are set by the government. Most cruisers take a cab from the pier to somewhere near St. George's. You can also tap most taxi drivers as a guide for a day's sightseeing. The charge is about $15 per hour, but be sure to negotiate a price before setting out. From the pier to Grand Anse Beach is about $10 per carload.

BY MINIVAN   Minivans, used mostly by locals, charge EC$1 to EC$6 (U.S.40¢ to U.S.$2.20), and the most popular run is between St. George's and Grand Anse Beach. Most minivans depart from Market Square or from the Esplanade area of St. George's.

BY WATER TAXI   An ideal way to get around the harbor and to Grand Anse Beach—the round-trip fare is about $4. A water taxi can take you from one end of the Carenage to the other for another $2.

BY RENTAL CAR   I don't recommend driving here, as the roads are very narrow and windy.

SHORE EXCURSIONS

Because of Grenada's lush landscape, I recommend spending at least 3 hours touring its interior, one of the most scenic in the West Indies.

☼ **Rain Forest/Grand Etang Lake Tour** ($33–$37, 3 hours): This is a great way to experience Grenada's lush, cool, dripping-wet tropical interior. Via bus, you travel past the red-tiled roofs of St. George's en route to the bright blue Grand Etang Lake within an extinct volcanic crater some 1,900 feet above sea level. On the way, you drive through rain forests and stop at a spice estate. Some tours include a visit to the Annandale Falls.

☼ **Hike to Seven Sisters Waterfalls** ($35, 4 hours): After a mile-or-so walk along a muddy path in the lush Grand Etang rain forest, cascading waterfalls and natural pools emerge and passengers are free to take a swim or a hop off a waterfall's edge. It's gorgeous and lots of fun. Don't forget to wear your bathing suit and maybe a pair of Teva-type sandals.

Island Bus Tour ($33, 3 hours): Typical scenic island tours take you through the highlights of the interior and along the coast, including Grand Anse Beach. Along the way you get to see the most luxuriant part of Grenada's rain forest, a nutmeg-processing station, a sugar factory, and many small hamlets. Many cruise lines also book you on a tour ($27, 2 hours) that explores St. George's historical sites and forts before taking you to some of the island's natural highlights, including a private garden where some 500 species of island plants and flowers are cultivated.

Party Cruises ($33, 3 hours): Party cruises are popular here, with no shortage of rum and reggae music. Two large party boats, the *Rhum Runner* and *Rhum Runner II,* designed for 120 and 250 passengers respectively, operate out of St. George's harbor, making three trips daily. The cost includes rum punch, sodas, a beach stop, and sometimes snorkeling.

ON YOUR OWN: WITHIN WALKING DISTANCE

In St. George's, you can visit the **Grenada National Museum,** at the corner of Young and Monckton streets (☎ **473/440-3725**), set in the foundations of an old French army barracks and prison built in 1704. This small but interesting museum houses finds from archaeological digs, including ancient petroglyphs, plus a rum still, native fauna, and memorabilia depicting Grenada's history, including the island's first telegraph. There are also two bathtubs worth seeing—the wooden barrel used by the fort's prisoners and the carved marble tub used by Joséphine Bonaparte during her adolescence on Martinique. The most comprehensive exhibit illuminates the native culture of Grenada. The museum is open 9am to 4:30pm Monday through Friday, and 10am to 1pm Saturdays; admission is $2.

If you're up for a good walk, walk around the historical Carenage from the cruise terminal and head up to **Fort George,** built in 1705 by the French and originally called Fort Royal. (You can pick up a rudimentary walking-tour map from the cruise terminal to help you find interesting sites along the way.) While the fort ruins and the 200- to 300-year-old canons are worth taking a peek at, it's the 360° panoramic views of the entire harbor area—including your ship, the sea, and many of the red-tile-roofed buildings dotting the island—that are most spectacular. Don't forget your camera! Before or after a visit to the fort, be sure to walk along **Church Street** (which leads right to the fort) as far as St. Johns or Juille Street. Along the way, you'll see lots of quaint 18th- and 19th-century architecture framed by brilliant flowering plants: **St. Andrew's Presbyterian Church** built in 1831 with the help of the Freemasons, **St. George's Anglican Church** built in 1825 by the British, the **Houses of Parliament,** and the **Roman Catholic Cathedral** rebuilt in 1884 (the tower dates back to 1818). Along the way you notice examples of

Grenada's **Sedan Porches,** originally open-ended porches used as porte cocheres to keep residents dry when going between house and carriage.

ON YOUR OWN: BEYOND WALKING DISTANCE

You can take a taxi up Richmond Hill to **Fort Frederick,** which the French began in 1779. The British, having retaken the island in 1783 under provision of the Treaty of Versailles, completed it in 1791. From its battlements you have a panoramic view of the harbor and the yacht marina.

Don't miss the mountains northeast of St. George's. If you don't have much time, ✪ **Annandale Falls,** a tropical wonderland where a 50-foot-high cascade drops into a basin, is just a 15-minute drive away, on the outskirts of the Grand Etang Forest Reserve. The overall beauty is almost Tahitian. You can have a picnic surrounded by liana vines, elephant ears, and other tropical flora and spices. Annandale Falls Centre offers gift items, handcrafts, and samples of the indigenous spices of Grenada. Nearby, an improved trail leads to the falls, where you can enjoy a refreshing swim. If you've got more time, the even better **Seven Sisters Waterfalls** is further into Grand Etang, an approximately 30-minute drive and then a mile or so hike along a muddy trail. It's well worth the trip, and you'll really get a feel for the power and beauty of the tropical forest here. The falls themselves are lovely, and you can even climb to the top and jump off into the pool below; be careful, though: It's awfully slippery on those rocks. You may want to skip the jumping and just enjoy a relaxing swim in the cool water after the sweaty hike.

Opened in 1994, 450-acre park ✪ **Levera National Park** has several white sandy beaches for swimming and snorkeling, although the surf is rough. Offshore are coral reefs and sea-grass beds. Inland, the park contains a mangrove swamp, a lake, and a bird sanctuary—perhaps you'll see a rare tropical parrot. It's a hiker's paradise. The interpretation center (☎ **473/442-1018**) is open Monday to Friday from 8am to 4pm, Saturday from 10am to 4pm, and Sunday from 9am to 5pm. The park, about 15 miles from the harbor, can be reached by taxi, bus, or water taxi.

SHOPPING

The local stores sell luxury-item imports, mainly from England, at prices that are not quite duty-free. This is no grand Caribbean merchandise mart, so if you're cruising on to such islands as Aruba, Sint Maarten, or St. Thomas, you might want to postpone serious purchases. On the other hand, you can find some fine local handcrafts, gifts, and art here.

Spice vendors besiege you wherever you go, including just outside of the cruise terminal. If you're finished shopping, a polite no-thank-you usually works ("I just bought some from another vendor" always works for me). But you really should take at least a few samples home with you. The spices here are fresher and better than any you're likely to find in your local supermarket, so nearly everybody comes home with a handwoven basket full of them. Nutmeg products are especially popular. The Grenadians use every part of the nutmeg: They make the outer fruit into either a tasty liqueur or a rich jam, and ground the orange membrane around the nut into a different spice called mace. You'll also see the outer shells used as gravel to cover trails and even parking lots. **Arawak Islands,** Upper Belmont Road, has at least nine different fragrances distilled from such island plants as frangipani, wild lilies, cinnamon, nutmeg, and cloves. You'll also find an all-natural insect repellent that some clients insist is the most effective (and safest) they're ever used. There's also great hot sauce to be found (I only wish I would have bought more than one bottle on my last trip!).

Some worthwhile shops include **Art Fabrik,** Young Street, for batik shirts, shifts, shorts, skirts, T-shirts, and the like; **Creation Arts & Crafts,** the Carenage, for off-island handicrafts (from Venezuela, Sint Maarten, and Cuba); **Sea Change Bookstore,** the Carenage, for recent British and American newspapers; **Spice Island Perfumes,** the Carenage, for perfumes made from the natural extracts of local herbs and spices; and **Tikal,** Young Street, for handcrafts from Grenada and around the world. You'll find that ubiquitous Caribbean chain store, **Colombia Emeralds,** midway along the Carenage.

BEACHES

Grenada's ✪ **Grand Anse Beach,** with its 2 miles of sugar-white sands, is one of the best beaches in the Caribbean. It's long and nice and wide. The water is calm and the views of St. George's make the scene complete. There are several restaurants beachside, including CotBam (see "Great Local Restaurants & Bars," below), and you can also join a banana-boat ride or rent a Sunfish sail boat. From the port, it's about a 10-minute, $10 taxi ride, although you can also take a water taxi from the pier for only $4 round-trip.

SPORTS

SCUBA DIVING & SNORKELING   Grenada offers an underwater world rich in submarine gardens, exotic fish, and coral formations. Visibility is often up to 120 feet. Off the coast is the wreck of the nearly 600-foot ocean liner *Bianca C.* Novice divers should stick to the west coast; the more experienced might search out the sights along the rougher Atlantic side. **Daddy Vic's Watersports,** directly on the beach in the Grenada Renaissance, Grand Anse Beach (☎ **473/444-4371,** ext. 638), is the premier scuba-diving outfit. It also offers snorkeling trips, as well as Windsurfer and Sunfish rentals, parasailing, and waterskiing. It can arrange to pick you up at the pier in a courtesy bus and bring you back to the cruise ship later. Canadian-run **Grand Anse Aquatics,** at Coyaba Beach Resort on Grand Anse Beach (☎ **473/444-4129**), gives Daddy Vic's serious competition, offering both scuba-diving and snorkeling jaunts to reefs and shipwrecks teeming with marine life. Diving instruction is available. (*Warning:* Grenada doesn't have a decompression chamber. In the event of an emergency, divers must be taken to the facilities on Barbados.)

GREAT LOCAL RESTAURANTS & BARS

A favorite **local beer** is Carib; a favorite **local rum** is Clarkecourt.

Your last chance to enjoy food from old-time island recipes, many now fading from cultural memory, is at ✪ **Betty Mascoll's Morne Fendue,** at St. Patrick's (☎ **473/442-9330**), 25 miles north of St. George's. This plantation house was built in 1912 of chiseled river rocks held together by a mixture of lime and molasses. Mrs. Mascoll was born that same year and has lived here ever since, continuing her long tradition of hospitality. You dine as an upper-class family did in the 1920s. Lunch is likely to include a yam-and-sweet-potato casserole or curried chicken with lots of island-grown spices. The most famous dish is Betty's legendary pepper-pot stew, which includes pork and oxtail, tenderized by the juice of grated cassava. Mrs. Mascoll and her loyal, veteran staff need time to prepare, so it's imperative to call ahead. They serve a fixed-price lunch Monday to Saturday from 12:30 to 3pm.

Mamma's, Lagoon Road (☎ 473/440-1459), captures the authentic taste of Grenada. Meals include such dishes as callaloo soup with coconut cream, shredded cold crab with lime juice, freshwater crayfish, fried conch, and rotis made of curry and yellow chickpeas. **The Nutmeg,** the Carenage, located right on the harbor over the Sea Change Shop (☎ 473/440-2539), is a casual hangout for the yachting set and a favorite with expatriates and visitors. The menu is extensive.

Cool breezes that blow in off the port, making **Pierone,** at the extreme northern end of the Carenage (☎ 473/440-9747), a great spot for a midday pick-me-up, with or without alcohol. Menu items include such West Indian dishes as *lambi* (conch) chowder, sandwiches, and the most popular dish on the menu, lobster pando, a form of ragoût. Pubby **Rudolf's,** the Carenage (☎ 473/440-2241), serves the best steaks in the capital. Conch is prepared in several different ways, as are shrimp and octopus. Flying fish and mahimahi deserve the most praise.

Midway along the Grand Anse Beach is the **CotBam** bar and restaurant, overlooking the beach. They serve local specialties like curries and seafood as well as great fruity drinks like piña coladas. Just steps from the cruise terminal is the **007 Bar,** a pleasant dive built on a barge in the harbor and offering good views along with drinks, seafood, and snacks.

15 Guadeloupe

Take the things you love about France—sophistication, great food, and an appreciation of the good things in life—add the best of the Caribbean—nice beaches, a relaxed pace, and warm, friendly people—and combine with efficiency and modern convenience. Voilà!: Guadeloupe. And once you leave the crowded, narrow streets of Pointe-à-Pitre, the commercial center and main port, you'll see that the island is more developed and modern than many others.

Guadeloupe's Creole cuisine, a mélange of French culinary expertise, African cooking, and Caribbean ingredients, is reason enough to get off the ship, regardless of how much you're enjoying the food onboard. And if shopping's your favorite sport, you'll have ample opportunity to stock up on French perfumes, clothes, and other luxury products. For the more adventurous, there's a volcano, scuba diving, surfing, and hiking to spectacular mountain waterfalls. Of course, you can always work on your tan at one of the island's many beaches. Or maybe you just want to sit at a sidewalk cafe, sip your espresso with a copy of *Le Monde,* and watch the world go by.

Guadeloupe, the political entity, is an overseas region of France that includes the islands of St. Barthélemy (St. Barts), St. Martin, Les Saintes, La Désirade, Marie-Galante, and Guadeloupe itself. The name *Guadeloupe,* however, usually refers to two contiguous islands—**Basse-Terre** and **Grande-Terre**—separated by a narrow seawater channel, the Rivière Salée. Nestled between Antigua and Dominica, these two islands are shaped like a 530-square-mile butterfly. The eastern wing, the limestone island of Grande-Terre, is known for its white-sand beaches, rolling hills, sugarcane fields, and resort areas. Pointe-à-Pitre, your port of debarkation, is here. The butterfly's larger, volcanic western wing, Basse-Terre, is dominated by the National Park of Guadeloupe, a mountainous rain forest replete with waterfalls and La Soufrière, a brooding, still occasionally troublesome volcano. The capital of Guadeloupe, also called Basse-Terre, is on this western wing. Almost half of Guadeloupe's population of 410,000 is under the age of 20. About 80% of Guadeloupeans are descended from African slaves, with people of European and East Indian ancestry making up most of the remaining 20%.

Hunter-gatherers from what is today Venezuela inhabited Guadeloupe more than a thousand years before the birth of Christ. By the 9th century, the peaceful Arawaks had been assimilated by the more aggressive Carib Indians, who still inhabited the island when Christopher Columbus landed on Basse-Terre on November 3, 1493. The Caribs called the island Karukera ("island of beautiful waters"). To honor Nuestra Señora de Guadalupe, the patron saint of Spain's Extremadura region, Columbus named the island Guadeloupe. The Spanish never showed an interest in the inhospitable island, concentrating instead on territories with more immediate value. France, eager to establish a toehold in the Caribbean, eventually filled the vacuum. Under grant from Cardinal Richelieu, the first French colonists—mostly farmers from Normandy, Brittany, and Charente—settled Guadeloupe in 1635. Farming was difficult, but eventually, sugar, coffee, and cocoa plantations prospered, largely on the backs of slaves brought from Africa. Disease and land-hungry colonists decimated the Carib population. The Dutch attacked periodically, and the British occupied the island briefly, but the French survived. Gradually, they introduced new crops like cotton and spices.

Reflecting the French Revolution's spirit of "liberté, égalité, fraternité," the Convention of Paris in 1794 voted to abolish slavery and sent Victor Hugues to emancipate Guadeloupe's forced laborers. Estate owners who resisted were guillotined. In 1802, Napoléon reinstated slavery but faced opposition from Louis Delgrès, among others. It was not until 1848 that the fight against slavery, led by Victor Schoelcher, prevailed permanently. The strained relations between former slaves and former masters persisted, though, and workers from India and China were brought over to work the fields. No longer able to rely on free labor and faced with growing competition from other sugar growers, Guadeloupe's planters began to fail. By the second half of the 19th century, many had lost their estates to large foreign companies. The economic crisis led to social upheaval and programs to diversify agricultural production. Cultivation of bananas, pineapples, and rice began after World War II. Today, sugar and rum are the island's main exports.

Frommer's Favorite Guadeloupe Experiences

- **Climbing a volcano:** Draped in thousands of banana trees and other lush foliage, La Soufrière rises 4,800 feet above the surrounding sea and dominates the island of Basse-Terre. You can drive to a parking area at La Savane à Mulets, then hike the final 1,500 feet (two arduous hours) right to the mouth of the volcano. (See "On Your Own: Beyond Walking Distance," below.)
- **Touring the dramatic Atlantic coast of Grande-Terre:** Drive out to Grande-Terre's eastern extreme, La Pointe des Châteaux, to watch the Atlantic and Caribbean vent their fury on the rocky shore. Continue up the coast to La Porte

Frommer's Ratings: Guadeloupe					
	Poor	Fair	Good	Excellent	Outstanding
Overall Experience				✓	
Shore Excursions				✓	
Activities Close to Port					✓
Beaches & Water Sports			✓		
Shopping			✓		
Dining/Bars					✓

Guadeloupe

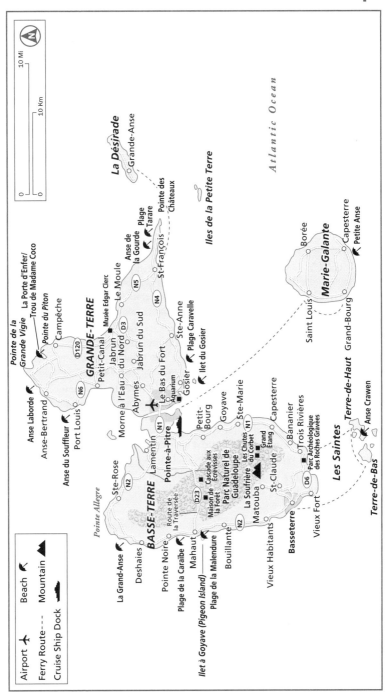

Legend:
Airport ✈
Ferry Route - - -
Cruise Ship Dock
Beach ↙
Mountain ▲

GRANDE-TERRE
Pointe de la Grande Vigie
La Porte d'Enfer/ Trou de Madame Coco
Pointe du Piton
Campêche
Anse Laborde
Anse-Bertrand
Anse du Souffleur
Port Louis
Petit-Canal
Jabrun du Nord
Jabrun du Sud
Musée Edgar Clerc
Le Moule
Anse de la Gourde
Plage Tarare
Pointe des Châteaux
St-François
Morne-à-l'Eau
Abymes
Le Bas du Fort
Aquarium
Gosier
Ste-Anne
Plage Caravelle
Ilet du Gosier
D120
N6
D23
N5
N4

BASSE-TERRE
Pointe Allègre
Ste-Rose
Lamentin
Pointe-à-Pitre
Petit-Bourg
Goyave
Ste-Marie
Capesterre
Bananier
Trois Rivières
Parc Archéologique des Roches Gravées
Route de la Traversée
Maison de la Forêt
Cascade aux Ecrevisses
Les Chutes du Corbet
Grand Etang
Parc Naturel de Guadeloupe
La Soufrière
Matouba
St-Claude
Deshaies
Pointe Noire
Plage de la Caraïbe
Plage de la Malendure
Ilet à Goyave (Pigeon Island)
Bouillante
Mahaut
La Grand-Anse
Vieux Habitants
Basseterre
Vieux Fort
N1
N2
D23
D6

La Désirade
Grande-Anse

Iles de la Petite Terre

Marie-Galante
Borée
Capesterre
Petite Anse
Saint Louis
Grand-Bourg

Les Saintes
Terre-de-Haut
Anse Crawen
Terre-de-Bas

Atlantic Ocean

10 Mi
10 Km

175

d'Enfer and La Pointe de la Grande Vigie for splendid views of limestone cliffs and sparkling aquamarine waters. (See "On Your Own: Beyond Walking Distance," below.)

- **Soaking up the French-Caribbean ambiance:** It's simple but satisfying. Walk the streets of Pointe-à-Pitre or whatever other town you choose. Browse through the stores, and maybe buy some perfume or "thigh-reducing cream" from one of the upscale pharmacies (look for the neon green cross). Pick up a newspaper—it could even be the English-language *International Herald-Tribune*—find a shady table at a sidewalk cafe, order a cold, fresh-fruit juice, and luxuriate in your blessed life.

COMING ASHORE   Cruise ships dock at the modern Centre Saint-John Perse, adjacent to downtown Pointe-à-Pitre, Grande-Terre's main city. The terminal has phones, shops, restaurants, cafes, and a small tourist office.

Phone booths marked TÉLÉCOM require a "télécarte," a discount prepaid phone card that you can buy at post offices and other outlets marked TÉLÉCARTE EN VENTE ICI. Many phones also accept credit cards for long-distance calls. There are phones in the cruise terminal.

CURRENCY   As elsewhere in France, you'll need **French francs.** There are 100 centimes to 1 franc. The exchange rate is roughly 6.4 francs to U.S.1 (1 franc = U.S.15¢). There are numerous ATMs (*distributeur de billets*) in downtown Pointe-à-Pitre that dispense francs. You'll have no trouble using your credit cards.

LANGUAGE   French is the official language, but you'll often hear islanders speaking a local Creole among themselves. Don't expect to get too far with only English unless you're at one of the larger hotels or busier tourist areas. Any attempt you make to speak French will be appreciated, so bring a phrase book.

INFORMATION   The **main tourist office (Office du Tourisme)** in Pointe-à-Pitre is at 5 Square de la Banque, a 5-minute walk from the port (☎ 590/82-09-30). The building, a beautiful colonial mansion, is open Monday to Friday from 8am to 5pm, Saturday until noon. If you want information before you leave home, contact the **Guadeloupe Tourist Office** in New Jersey at ☎ 732/302-1223 or log on to the Web site, www.frenchcaribbean.com.

CALLING FROM THE U.S.   When calling Guadeloupe from the United States, you need to dial the international access code (011) before the numbers listed in this section.

GETTING AROUND

BY TAXI   Metered taxis await cruise passengers at the Pointe-à-Pitre pier. Rates are regulated, but they can be expensive, especially on Sundays and holidays, when fares are 40% higher. Taxis can be hired for private tours, but you'll have a hard time finding a driver who speaks English. Negotiate a price before setting out, and make sure all terms are clear to avoid an unpleasant scene later. One recommended driver is **Alain Narcisse,** an enthusiastic, knowledgeable, and English-speaking guide who offers tours of Grande-Terre, northern Basse-Terre, and southern Basse-Terre. He's often booked, so make arrangements in advance by calling ☎ 590/35-27-29 or 590/83-24-79.

BY MOTOR SCOOTER   Motorbikes are available in Pointe-à-Pitre at **Vespa Sun** (☎ 590/91-30-36) and **Moto Guadeloupe** (☎ 590/82-12-50). Expect to pay about $30 a day, including insurance and a deposit of roughly $150 (credit cards are accepted).

BY BUS   Buses are inexpensive, comfortable, and efficient. Almost all play zouk, an upbeat local music (at reasonable decibel levels), and some have videos. Signs (ARRÊT-BUS) indicate bus stops, but you can wave down a driver anywhere along the road. Pay the driver or the conductor as you get off. The fare from Pointe-à-Pitre to Gosier is just over $1.

BY RENTAL CAR   With a valid driver's license, you can rent a car; almost all have standard transmissions. Reserve a car before leaving home, especially during the high season. **Hertz** (☎ **800/654-3001** or 590/21-09-35), **Avis** (☎ **800/ 230-4898** or 590/82-02-71), **National** (☎ **888/CAR-RENT**), and **Budget** (☎ **800/527-0700**) all have offices on the island. Guadeloupe's road system is one of the best in the Caribbean, and traffic regulations and road signs are the same as elsewhere in France. Driving is on the right. Be forewarned that Guadeloupeans are skillful but aggressive drivers; don't tarry in the passing lane.

BY BICYCLE   You may not be up to completing the entire 800-mile route of the Tour de Guadeloupe, the island's annual bicycle race, but you can rent mountain bikes from **Dingo Location** (☎ **590/83-81-37**) or **Vélo Tout Terrain** (☎ **590/ 97-85-40**), both in Pointe-à-Pitre. They run about $20 a day.

SHORE EXCURSIONS

Carbet Falls ($40, 4 hours): After driving through the banana plantations and rain forests of Basse-Terre's south side, you'll hike 30 minutes to picturesque Carbet Falls, where you're free to swim in the refreshing water. Wear sturdy walking shoes

Pigeon Island ($50, 4^1/$_2$ hours): You'll first pass through Guadeloupe's National Park, a lush and mountainous tropical rain forest, on the Route de la Traversée. At Pigeon Island you'll board a glass-bottom boat for a 90-minute ride around a beautiful coral reef now designated the Cousteau Underwater Reserve. Marvel at the numerous fishes, corals, and other marine life.

TOURING THROUGH LOCAL OPERATORS

Agence Georges Marie-Gabrielle, 21 Rue Alexandre Isaac (☎ **590/820-538** or 590/831-561), and **KPC Petreluzzi,** 14 Place de la Victoire (☎ **590/903-777**), both in Pointe-à-Pitre, have comfortable buses and English-speaking guides. On Basse-Terre, tour operators include **Parfum d'Aventures** (☎ **590/884-762**), **Guadeloupe Découverte** (☎ **590/252-087**), and **Emeraude Guadeloupe** (☎ **590/819-828**).

ON YOUR OWN: WITHIN WALKING DISTANCE

Pointe-à-Pitre's narrow streets and congested sidewalks are bustling with activity, and its markets are among the Caribbean's most colorful. The largest, **Marché St. Antoine,** at the corner of Rues Frébault and Peynier, is well known for its playful, sassy vendors, who sell tropical produce and spices in madras bags. **Marché de la Darse,** on the waterfront at the foot of Place de la Banque, offers exotic fruits,

Insider's Tip: Guadeloupe

The little trolley that meets cruise ship passengers at the port is supposed to provide hassle-free transportation around Pointe-à-Pitre. Unfortunately, it's no match for the city's traffic and narrow roads. Unless you enjoy traffic jams, walk. It's a better way to browse, shop, and visit the museums.

vegetables, and souvenirs. The **Place Gourbeyre Flower Market,** next to the cathedral, is ablaze with tropical blooms, including *roses de porcelaine* and alpinias. Lined
with royal palms, scarlet flamboyants, and travelers palms, the renovated Place de la
Victoire commemorates Victor Hugues' defeat of the English in 1794. It's the
largest public space in town and is bordered with restaurants and cafes. The nearby
Cathedral of St-Pierre and St-Paul, built in 1871, has an iron framework designed
to withstand earthquakes and hurricanes (three churches destroyed by successive
earthquakes form its foundation). The **Musée Municipal Saint-John Perse,** near
the corner of Rues Achille-René Boisneuf and Nozières, (☎ 590/90-01-92) chron-
icles the life of native son Alexis Léger, who won the Nobel Prize for Literature
under the *nom de plume* "Saint-John Perse" in 1960. The museum is housed in one
of the city's most beautifully restored colonial mansions, an urban chalet that
features ornate friezes, voluted consoles, and wrought-iron galleries. Open windows
allow breezes into the main parlor, which is furnished with bourgeois furniture
of the time. In addition to many of the poet's personal effects, the museum boasts
photographs documenting Guadeloupean life from the turn of the century through
the 1930s; you can buy postcards of some of them in the museum gift shop for
about $2.50. It's open Monday to Friday from 9am to 5pm, Saturday until noon.

The **Musée Schoelcher,** 24 Rue Peynier (☎ 590/82-08-04), tells the story of
Victor Schoelcher, the key figure in the move to abolish slavery in Guadeloupe. The
powerful exhibit, housed in a renovated mansion, includes a slave-ship model, a
miniature guillotine, china from Bordeaux with scenes from Uncle Tom's Cabin,
and racist caricatures published in Parisian journals. Particularly moving is an 1845
census document that lists slaves as nothing more than plantation animals. It's open
Monday to Friday from 9am to 5pm; admission is about $1.50.

ON YOUR OWN: BEYOND WALKING DISTANCE

Guadeloupe is too large to tour in 1 day. You'll have to choose among Grande-Terre,
northern Basse-Terre, and southern Basse-Terre.

GRANDE-TERRE

First travel east along the southern coast. The **Aquarium de la Guadeloupe,** near
the Bas du Fort Marina just east of Pointe-à-Pitre (☎ 590/90-92-38), is compact
but has an impressive collection of exotic fish, corals, and sponges from the
Caribbean and the Pacific. Come face-to-face with hugging sea horses, sleeping
nurse sharks, and graceful sea turtles. Don't miss the polka-dot grouper known as
mérou de Grace Kelly. Explanatory markers are in both French and English. The souvenir shop sells hand-painted folk art, jewelry, and fish- and sea-themed trinkets
and T-shirts. It's open daily from 9am to 7pm; admission is $6 for adults, $3 for
children under 12.

Also in Bas du Fort, **Fort Fleur d'Epée** (☎ 590/90-94-61) sits atop a hill overlooking the Bay of Gosier. This bastion was built at the end of the 17th century to
protect the port. In 1794, it witnessed a hard-fought battle between the French, led
by republican leader Victor Hugues, and the British. Aboveground there's a powder
magazine, chapel, and sweeping views. The dungeons and passageways underground are well preserved and evoke a sense of the time. It's open daily from 9:30am
to 5:30pm; admission is free.

The town of **Bas du Fort** is a wealthy enclave of mostly European residents.
Aside from the marina, which every year serves as the terminus of the Route du
Rhum yacht race, the town boasts beautiful homes and gardens and numerous
restaurants and cafes.

Continuing east, you'll come to **Gosier,** the first and largest of the three main resort towns along Grande-Terre's southern coast. The town bears the Creole name for the pelicans that once lived here. Today, resort complexes and hundreds of tourists—the vast majority from "metropolitan" France (meaning European France)—have replaced the birds. The cafes, bakeries, restaurants, beaches, and people give the town the air of a Caribbean Côte d'Azur. Opposite the seafront, the tiny island **Ilet Gosier** has a sandy beach and a small lighthouse. You can take a fishing boat to the island, a 10-minute trip, for about $2.50 round trip.

Ste-Anne, about 8 miles east of Gosier, is the second of the big three resort towns and home to the island's Club Med. A sugar-exporting center in the 18th century, the tidy, relaxed town today is best known for its long white public beaches, seaside promenade, and shady town square. The roadside market sells local fruits, vegetables, and flowers. You can also watch fishermen hawk their morning catch. Seafood stands line the beach area, which is shaded by sea-grape bushes. **St-François,** the final large resort on the southern coast, rivals Gosier in size. The beaches, church, market, and golf course are its major attractions. Once a simple fishing-and-farming community, it now has some of the island's most luxurious hotels.

La Pointe des Châteaux (Castle Point), at Grande-Terre's easternmost point, is an impressive seascape spectacle. Angry Atlantic waves bash black limestone rocks and jagged cliffs with a roughness reminiscent of Brittany's Finistère coast or England's Land's End. Follow the path leading to the point where the land falls off abruptly to the ocean for the best views of the island of La Désirade.

On the way north, you'll pass a large mansion known as **Zévallos.** Aside from the noteworthy architecture—it was once the sugar-plantation home of a colonial family—the place is said to be haunted. **Le Moule,** a port town on the eastern coast, was once Guadeloupe's capital. After hurricanes repeatedly battered the town, the seat of government was moved to Basse-Terre. The church was originally built in 1757, and traditional houses and other wooden buildings line the roads. The lagoon is a top surfing spot.

The **Musée Edgar Clerc,** a few miles north of Le Moule (☎ **590/23-57-57**), is named after an archaeologist and historian. It houses a large collection of Amerindian artifacts in two main halls, one for the Arawak culture, the other for the Caribs. It's open Thursday to Tuesday from 9am to 12:30pm and 2 to 5pm; admission is $1.50.

Farther north, **La Porte d'Enfer** is a quaint little cove and beach protected from the furious Atlantic by an outcrop of limestone cliffs. The name means "Hell's Gate," but swimming close to shore in the turquoise water is usually safe. Don't venture out too far, though; the next cove, **Le Trou de Madame Coco** (Madame Coco's hole), is where the sea stole Madame Coco and her parasol as she promenaded along the edge.

La Pointe de la Grande Vigie, at the northernmost tip of the island, has paths that lead to the edge of spectacular cliffs with dramatic views of Porte de l'Enfer and, on a clear day, the island of Antigua. Cacti and other succulents grow everywhere.

Along the northern coasts of Grande-Terre and Basse-Terre, **La Réserve Naturelle du Grand Cul-de-Sac Marin** is one of the Caribbean's largest marine reserves. It features mangroves, swamp forests, marine herbaceous habitats, and coral reefs. Fishing, boating, snorkeling, and swimming are permitted.

On your way back to Pointe-à-Pitre, stop for a few minutes in the agricultural town of **Morne-à-l'Eau.** The local cemetery is shaped like an amphitheater, with a hodgepodge of black-and-white checkerboard tombs, some the size of small houses. Hundreds of candles bathe the graveyard in a spiritual glow on All Saints' Day (Nov 1).

BASSE-TERRE

Basse-Terre's greatest attraction is the **Parc National de la Guadeloupe,** 74,000 acres of tropical rain forests, mountains, waterfalls, and ponds. UNESCO designated the park a World Biosphere Reserve in 1992. Its 200 miles of well-marked trails make it one of the best places for hiking in the entire Caribbean. Pick up information and maps at park entrances. Thirty minutes from Pointe-à-Pitre, **La Maison de la Forêt** (Forest House) on the Route de la Traversée, which bisects the park, is the starting point for easy walking tours of the surrounding mountainous rain forest. English-language trail guides describe the plant and animal life. Nearby, the **Cascade aux Ecrevisses** (Crayfish Falls), a slippery 10-minute walk from the roadside, is nice for a cooling dip. To the south, the steep hike to the three falls of **Les Chutes du Carbet** (Carbet Falls) is among Guadeloupe's most beautiful excursions (one of the falls drops 65 feet, the second 360 feet, and the third 410 feet). The middle fall, the most dramatic, is the easiest to reach. On the way up, you'll pass Le **Grand Etang** (Great Pond), a volcanic lake surrounded by tree-size ferns, giant vining philodendrons, wild bananas, orchids, anthuriums, and pineapples.

The park's single greatest feature is the still-simmering volcano **La Soufrière.** Ashes, mud, billowing smoke, and tremors in 1975 proved that the volcano is still active. Rising to 4,800 feet, it's flanked by banana plantations and lush vegetation. You can smell sulfurous fumes and feel the heat through the soil as steam spews from the fumaroles. The summit is like another planet: steam rises from two active craters, large rocks form improbable shapes, and roars from the earth make it difficult to hear your companions. Go with an experienced guide. On your way down, don't miss La Maison du Volcan, the volcanology museum in St-Claude.

Gardeners should save a couple of hours to visit the **Domaine de Valombreuse** (☎ 590/95-50-50), a 6-acre floral park with exotic birds, spice gardens, and 300 species of tropical flowers. Created in 1990 and close to the town of Petit Bourg, the park also has a riverside restaurant and a superior gift shop. It's open daily from 9am to 6pm; admission is $6.

Parc Archéologique des Roches Gravées, on Basse-Terre's southern coast in the town of Trois-Rivières (☎ 590/92-91-88), has the West Indies' largest collection of Arawak Indian petroglyphs. The animal and human images etched on boulders date from between A.D. 300 and A.D. 400. Paths and stone stairways meander through the tranquil grounds, which include avocado, banana, cocoa, coffee, guava, and papaya trees. Explanatory brochures are in French and English. It's open daily from 8:30am to 5pm; admission is $1.50.

If you crochet, knit, tat, or make quilts, you won't want to miss the **Centre de Broderie** in Vieux-Fort (☎ 590/92-04-14). Located in the ruins of an old fort, this lace-making center was established by 40 local lace makers in 1980 to preserve, develop, and promote traditional embroidery, which the women of Vieux-Fort have been making for almost 300 years. You can watch the women create intricate handkerchiefs, doilies, and tablecloths. The prices reflect the painstakingly labor-intensive work. It's open daily from 9am to 6pm; admission is free.

Basse-Terre, the town, is Guadeloupe's capital. Its pretty squares, fragrant gardens, and neat narrow streets lie in the shadow of La Soufrière. **Fort Delgrès** (☎ 590/81-37-48), a massive old crumbling fort, has an interesting history museum and great views. It's open Monday to Friday from 8am to 5pm; admission

A Different Kind of Souvenir

One of Guadeloupe's more popular products, *bois bandé* (*bwa bandé* in Creole), is derived from the bark of a tree. It's used to make an herbal tea and to flavor rum and candy. *Bois* means wood, and *bandé* is French slang for "erection." Its allure, as you might now guess, is its reputation as an aphrodisiac. In the words of one excited cruise ship passenger in his late fifties, "It's herbal Viagra; no prescription necessary."

is free. The **Cathedral of Our Lady of Guadeloupe,** a church built in the 1600s, is also of interest.

La Maison du Volcan in St-Claude (☎ 590/78-15-16), has a fascinating exhibit on Caribbean volcanoes, including films on La Soufrière's rumblings in 1975, when 70,000 residents were evacuated for several months. It's on the way to the trail up the volcano. It's open daily from 9am to noon and 2 to 5pm; admission is $2.50.

The northwest coast of Basse-Terre is seldom visited by cruise ship passengers, but it's perfect if you want peace and quiet. The coastal road winds up steep hills lush with vegetation, then descends to salty fishing villages ensconced in bays of deep blue water. Stop in Deshaies (pronounced "day-ay") or Pointe-Noire for lunch or a swim.

If it's your first trip to the Caribbean, you'll want to visit one of the local rum factories. Try the **Domaine de Séverin** in Ste-Rose on the northern coast (☎ 590/28-91-86). A little train takes you around the gardens through cacao, calabash, grapefruit, cinnamon, coffee, and vanilla trees. Lush hibiscuses, birds of paradise, and begonias thrive here. After visiting the distillery and water mill, check out the crayfish farm, the kitchen-size hot-sauce factory, and the souvenir shop, where you can buy rum and other local food products. The factory is open daily from 8:30am to 12:30pm, until 3:30pm during the high season; admission is free. If you have time for lunch, there's also a nice restaurant.

SHOPPING

Parlez-vous Chanel? Hermès? Saint Laurent? Baccarat? If you do, you'll find that Guadeloupe has good buys on almost anything French—scarves, perfumes, cosmetics, crystal, and other luxury goods—and many stores offer 20% discounts on items purchased with foreign currency, traveler's checks, or credit cards. You can also find local handcrafted items, madras cloth, spices, and rum at any of the local markets.

Right at Pointe-à-Pitre's port, the **Centre Saint-John Perse** has about 20 shops that frequently offer lower prices than can be found elsewhere in town. L'Artisan Parfumeur sells French and American perfumes as well as tropical scents. Suzanne Moulin features original African-inspired jewelry and crafts. Jean-Louis Padel specializes in gold jewelry. If you're looking for beach and resort wear, stop by Vanilla Boutique and Brasil Tropique. For something a little more provocative, look through the delicate lingerie at Soph't.

Rue Frébault, directly in front of the port, is one of the best shopping streets for duty-free items. **Rosébleu,** 5 Rue Frébault, offers china, crystal, and silver from Christoffle, Kosta Boda, and other high-end manufacturers. **Phoenicia,** 8 Rue Frébault and 121 bis Rue Frébault, has large selections of French perfumes and cosmetics. For men's and women's fashions, as well as for cosmetics and perfumes, browse through **Vendôme,** 8–10 Rue Frébault. Across the street at the intersection of Rues Frébault and Delgrès, **Geneviève Lethu** is a French version of Williams-Sonoma, with everything for preparing and serving food. If you find yourself over-dosing on froufrou, duck into **Tati,** France's answer to Kmart. It's at the intersection of Rues Frébault and Abbé Grégoire. This venerable old department-store chain, famous for its anti-fashion pink-plaid shopping bags, is great for inexpensive basics.

The French Antilles are where the *beguine* began, so if you're in the market for French Antillean music or French-language books there are a couple of large book-and music stores across from each other on Rue Schoelcher: **Librairie Antillaise** at no. 41 and **Librairie Général** at no. 46. Each has a small selection of English-language books as well. CDs by local zouk musicians make great gifts and are the perfect way to relive your vacation once you're back home. Combining African rhythms and drums with a range of traditional Caribbean influences, Kassav' is the best-known zouk band.

Want to see a French shopping mall? The **Destrellan Commercial Center** in Baie-Mahault (just across the Rivière Salée on Basse-Terre) is the island's biggest. For shopaholics, it warrants a special trip. The 70 boutiques include Roger Albert, Martinique's famous parfumerie, a huge supermarket, and the Galerie de l'Arti-sanat, which showcases the work of the island's best artisans. Here you can buy dolls, lace-trimmed blouses, madras skirts, honeys, and preserved fruit.

BEACHES

Beaches on Grande-Terre's southern coast have soft white sand. Those on the Atlantic coast have wilder water and are less crowded. The convenient **Bas du Fort/Gosier hotel area** has mostly man-made strips of sand with rows of beach chairs, water-sports shops, and beach bars. Changing facilities and chairs are avail-able for a nominal fee. The tiny, uninhabited **Ilet Gosier,** across Gosier Bay, is a quieter option popular with those who want to bare it all. You can take a fishing boat to the island from Gosier's waterfront. The wide strip of white sand at **Ste-Anne,** about 30 minutes from Pointe-à-Pitre, is lined with shops and food stands. **Plage Tarare,** just before the tip of Pointe des Châteaux, is the most popular nude beach. On Basse-Terre, the **Plage de Grande Anse** is a long expanse of ochre sand. A pleasant walk north from Deshaies, it offers changing facilities, water sports, bou-tiques, and outdoor snack bars. Farther south, the gray expanse of **Plage de Mal-endure** is alive with restaurants, bars, and open-air boutiques. It's the departure point for snorkeling and scuba trips to the Cousteau Reserve off Pigeon Island.

SPORTS

BOAT TOURS   King Papyrus (☎ 590/90-92-98) offers 2-hour trips from the Pointe-à-Pitre marina to the Réserve Naturelle du Grand-Cul-de-Sac Marin on Wednesday and Friday ($20 for adults, including refreshments; $10 for children under 12). Based at the marina in Bas du Fort next to the Aquarium, **Bateaux Verts** (☎ 590/90-77-17) offers educational half-day excursions on glass-bottom boats to the same marine reserve.

HIKING   Basse-Terre's **Parc National** has 200 miles of well-marked trails. Some meander through tropical rain forests to waterfalls and mountain pools; others focus on La Soufrière volcano, geology, animals, and vegetation. The **Bureau des Guides de Moyenne Montagne** (☎ 590/81-24-83) offers a range of guided tours. Easy 1-hour hikes are inexpensive; a 4-hour climb up La Soufrière is about $60. Maps and brochures in English can be obtained from the **National Park Office,**

Habitation Beausoleil, Montéran, Boite Postal 13, St-Claude 97120 (☎ **590/ 80-24-25**).

HORSEBACK RIDING   On Grande-Terre, **Le Criolo** in St-Félix (☎ **590/ 83-38-90**) has 30 horses, 10 ponies, lessons, tours, and picnic excursions. **Le Cheval Vert** in Ste-Anne (☎ **590/88-00-00**) also offers lessons and various outings and picnics at prices running from $25 to $90. **Poney Club** in Le Moule (☎ **590/24-03-74**) has horseback trips for children. On Basse-Terre, try **La Martingale** in Baie-Mahault (☎ **590/26-28-39**), priced at $30 to $35 an hour or $55 to $70 for a half day; or **La Manade** in St-Claude (☎ **590/81-52-21**), which makes excursions through the tropical forest in the foothills of La Soufrière, priced from $25 to $80.

SCUBA DIVING   Guadeloupe's premier dive site is the **Cousteau Underwater Reserve** near Pigeon Island, off the western coast of Basse-Terre. Jacques Cousteau once called this one of the world's 10 best diving spots, but skeptics say he made the claim early in his career and that his Gallic pride got carried away. Among the world's best or not, it's certainly one of the most desirable sites in the French-speaking world. The underwater terrain is dramatic, with giant boulders, hot springs, and giant barrel sponges. Visibility averages 100 feet, and you should be able to spot sergeant majors, spiny sea urchins, green parrot fish, and a variety of corals. Malendure, the town closest to the Cousteau Reserve, has several full-service dive shops. **Les Heures Saines** has three boats, its own dock, and several English-speaking staff members (☎ **590/98-86-63**). You might also try **Plaisir Plongée Caraïbes** (☎ **590/98-82-43**), **Aux Aquanautes Antillais** (☎ **590/98-87-30**), or **CIP-Centre International de Plongée** (☎ **590/98-81-72**). Guides and instructors here are certified under the French Confédération Mondiale des Activités Subaquatiques (CMAS), but your PADI or NAUI certification is honored and respected. Boats leave from most shops at 10am, 12:30pm, and 3pm. Expect to pay about $35 for a one-tank dive. Half-hour dives for beginners, referred to as *baptêmes* (baptisms), run about $45.

SNORKELING   Beachside stands at virtually all the resorts on Grande-Terre's southern coast rent snorkeling equipment for about $8 a day. The St-François reef and the Ilet de Gosier are especially recommended. To snorkel in the Cousteau Reserve, contact **Nautilus** (☎ **590/98-89-08**) or **Aquarus** (☎ **590/98-87-30**), both located at the Bouillante town dock, south of Malendure. They make guided tours in glass-bottom boats several times daily; at least 15 minutes is reserved for snorkeling and refreshments (about 90 min., $15 to $25).

SURFING   Le Moule, Port Louis, and Anse Bertrand, all on Grande-Terre, are considered the best surfing spots. Board rental averages a little over $15 a day. Contact Philip Cazé of the **Comité Guadeloupéen de Surf** at ☎ **590/91-77-64.**

WINDSURFING   Guadeloupe hosts several international windsurfing events, including the Ronde du Rhum. Most beachfront hotels offer lessons and equipment rental. Try **Loisirs Nautiques** at the Callinago Hotel at Pointe de la Verdure in Gosier (☎ **590/84-25-25**). Rentals average less than $10 an hour.

GREAT LOCAL RESTAURANTS & BARS

Many restaurants change their hours from time to time and from season to season. Call in advance for reservations and exact hours. Most, but not all, restaurants accept major credit cards. There are no **local beers** made on the island anymore, but locals drink Lorraine, made on the island of Martinique. Similarly,

Creole Cuisine: An Introduction

Like the roots of an old mango tree, Guadeloupe's gastronomic tradition goes deep into the soil, gathering life from every direction. Each of the island's many ethnic groups has contributed something of its own culinary genius—the French passion for perfect technique, African cooking methods and recipes, East Indian spices, and Caribbean ingredients. Lunch at a seaside restaurant could well be one of your best souvenirs of the island. Even if you speak French, though, you might not recognize some of the Creole names on the menu, so here's a brief glossary. Bon appétit.

Accras: Small fritters made with fish or vegetables, often spiced with a trace of hot pepper

Cabri goat: Usually grilled or cooked in a curry sauce

Calalou: A vegetable soup scented with herbs, sometimes served with bits of pork or crab

Chatrou: octopus

Colombo: A curry that includes coriander, cumin, black pepper, mustard, ginger, and hot pepper

Crabes farcis: stuffed land crabs

Féroce: A salad of avocado, cod, manioc flour, and hot pepper

Lambi: Conch

Manicou: The local opossum

Maracudja: Passion fruit

Ouassous: Crayfish

Patate douce: Sweet potato

Souskaï: Green fruit marinated in salt, garlic, and lime

Soudons: Clams

the **local rum,** Bielle, isn't made on Guadeloupe but on the offshore island of Marie-Galante.

ON GRANDE-TERRE

Chez Violetta-La Créole, Perinette, in Gosier (☎ 590/84-10-34), was established by the late Violetta Chaville, the island's legendary high priestess of Creole cookery. Her brother continues the family tradition, serving stuffed crabs, cod fritters, and conch fricasée. It's open daily from noon to 3:30pm.

Les Oiseaux, another wonderful Creole restaurant, is set in a farmhouse made of stucco and stone in Anse des Rochers, about 3¹/₂ miles from St. François (☎ 590/88-56-92). Surrounded by gardens and a scrub-covered landscape, it overlooks the sea and the island of Marie-Galante. Specialties include *entrecôte Roquefort* (shark with coconut); *marmite de Robinson Crusoe* (a stew of dorado, kingfish, tuna, shrimp, and local vegetables), and sea urchins. No lunch Monday to Wednesday; otherwise, open noon to 2:30pm.

About a mile north of Anse Bertrand in northwest Grande-Terre, the relaxed and informal **Chez Prudence** (Folie Plage), Anse Laborde (☎ 590/22-11-17), is especially popular with families on weekends. Children love the pool. Try the fish broth (*court bouillon*) and curried goat. It's open daily from noon to 3pm.

ON BASSE-TERRE

Le Rocher de Malendure, in Bouillante on the western coast (☎ 590/98-70-84), features a fishermen's plate—a sampling of marlin or kingfish, smoked swordfish, crayfish or conch, and local shrimp, most of it caught hours earlier by the owner's husband. Tables are arranged on wooden verandas overlooking a rocky peninsula and the sea. It's open daily from 11am to 3pm.

In Deshaies, Lucienne Salcède's family has run **Le Karacoli** (☎ 590/28-41-17), one of Guadeloupe's best seaside restaurants, for almost 30 years. Sit on the beach-front terrace in the shadow of almond and palm trees and let the waves hypnotize you. In the distance, the island of Montserrat is visible. Try a rum aperitif or two, then bliss out on cod fritters, stuffed christophine, and avocado féroce before moving on to Creole lobster or conch. It's open daily from noon to 2pm; reservations are imperative on weekends.

Ice cream gets the final word. **Chez Monia** at 4 Rue Victor Hugues, off of Rue Nozières in Pointe-à-Pitre, serves ice cream that is pure heaven in the midday heat. Flavors (*aromes*) include pear, lemon, kiwi, guava, and champagne. Three scoops in a homemade waffle cone is about $2. Street vendors also offer superior ice cream, usually flavored with fresh vanilla and coconut, straight from their hand-cranked machines.

16 Jamaica

A favorite of North American honeymooners, Jamaica is a mountainous island rising from the sea 90 miles south of Cuba and about 100 miles west of Haiti. It's the third largest of the Caribbean islands, with some 4,400 square miles of predominantly green terrain, a mountain ridge peaking at 7,400 feet above sea level, and, on the north coast, many beautiful white-sand beaches rimming the clear blue sea.

One of the most densely populated nations in the Caribbean, with a vivid sense of its own identity (among other things, it's one of the most successful black democracies in the world), Jamaica has a history rooted in the plantation economy and some of the most turbulent and impassioned politics in the Western Hemisphere.

Most cruise ships dock at **Ocho Rios** on the lush northern coast, although others are increasingly going to the city of **Montego Bay** ("Mo Bay"), 67 miles to the west. Both ports offer comparable attractions and some of the same shopping possibilities. Don't try to do both ports in 1 day, however, since the 4-hour round-trip ride leaves time for only superficial visits to each.

CURRENCY   The unit of currency is the **Jamaican dollar,** designated by the same symbol as the U.S. dollar ($). For clarity, I use the symbol **J$** to denote prices in Jamaican dollars. There is no fixed rate of exchange. The exchange rate is J$38.80 to U.S.$1 (J$1 = U.S.3¢).Visitors can pay in U.S. dollars, but *be careful!* Always find out if a price is being quoted in Jamaican or U.S. dollars.

LANGUAGE   The official language is English, but most Jamaicans speak a richly nuanced patois that's primarily derived from English but includes elements of African, Spanish, Arawak, French, Chinese, Portuguese, and East Indian languages.

INFORMATION   In Ocho Rios, you'll find **tourist board offices** at the Ocean Village Shopping Centre in Ocho Rios (☎ 876/974-2582); open Monday to Friday from 9am to 5pm. There's also a small information stand right at the dock. In Montego Bay, it's at Cornwall Beach, St. James (☎ 876/952-4425). It's open Monday to Friday from 9am to 5pm. To get info before you go, call the **Jamaica Tourist Office** in New York (☎ **800/233-4582** or 212/856-9727; www.jamaica-travel.com).

CALLING FROM THE U.S.   When calling Jamaica from the United States, you need only dial a "1" before the numbers listed throughout this section.

OCHO RIOS

Once a small banana and fishing port, Ocho Rios is now Jamaica's cruise-ship capital, welcoming about two ships per day during high season. The bay is dominated on one side by a defunct bauxite-loading terminal (some say it loaded sugar or gypsum) and on the other by resort hotels with palm-tree–fringed beaches.

The Ocho Rios area has some of the Caribbean's most fabled resorts and Dunn's River is just a 5-minute taxi ride away, but the town itself is not much to see, though there are a few outdoor local markets within walking distance. Don't expect to shop in the markets without a lot of hassle and a lot of very pushy hawking of merchandise, some of which is likely to be *ganja,* locally grown marijuana. (Remember, although it may be readily available, it's still illegal.) That said, in recent years the government has made an effort to keep things saner. There's an army of blue-uniformed "resort patrol" officers on bikes helping to keep order. At the terminal is an information desk, bathrooms, a telephone center for faxing and postage, and an army of official taxis ready to take you where you want to go. If you want a taxi, it's safest to take one from the pier, and look for the JTB decal (for Jamaican Tourist Board), which ensures they're licensed and trained.

Frommer's Favorite Ocho Rios Experiences
- **Tubing on the White River.** The River Tubing Safari excursion offered by most cruise lines is just a downright fantastic experience (see "Shore Excursions," below).
- **Riding horseback through the surf:** An excursion by horseback includes a stint along the beach and through the surf (see "Shore Excursions," below).
- **Riding a mountain bike to Dunn's River Falls:** This excursion takes you to the top of a mountain, where you hop on your mountain bike and soar downhill to the falls (see "Shore Excursions," below).

COMING ASHORE   Most cruise ships dock at the port of Ocho Rios, near Dunn's River Falls. Only a mile away is one of the most important shopping areas, Ocean Village Shopping Centre; next door, on the second floor, is the main office of the Jamaican Tourist Board. To help you find your way to this shopping center from the cruise ship pier, the route is marked and called the "turtle walk."

There's a telephone center in the cruise terminal.

Frommer's Ratings: Ocho Rios					
	Poor	Fair	Good	Excellent	Outstanding
Overall Experience				✓	
Shore Excursions					✓
Activities Close to Port				✓	
Beaches & Water Sports			✓		
Shopping		✓			
Dining/Bars			✓		

Jamaica

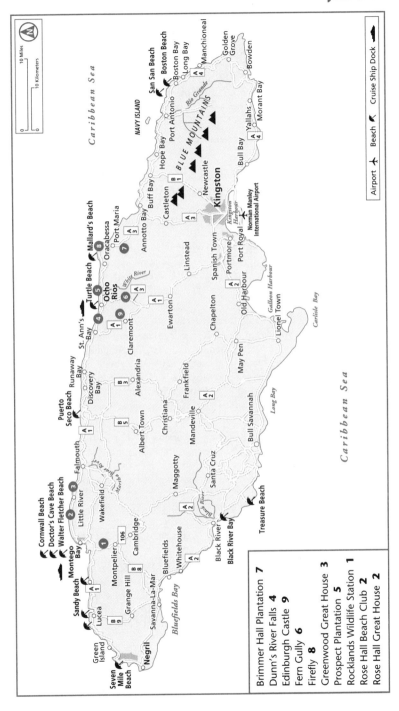

Brimmer Hall Plantation **7**
Dunn's River Falls **4**
Edinburgh Castle **6**
Fern Gully **8**
Firefly **8**
Greenwood Great House **3**
Prospect Plantation **5**
Rocklands Wildlife Station **1**
Rose Hall Beach Club **2**
Rose Hall Great House **2**

Airport ✈   Beach ⚓   Cruise Ship Dock ⚓

Caribbean Sea

Caribbean Sea

NAVY ISLAND

BLUE MOUNTAINS

Rio Grande

White River

Great River

Black River

Martha Brae

Long Bay

Bluefields Bay

Galleon Harbour

Carlisle Bay

Green Island
Negril
Seven Mile Beach
Lucea
Sandy Beach
Montego Bay
Cornwall Beach
Doctor's Cave Beach
Walter Fletcher Beach
Little River
Wakefield
Montpelier
Grange Hill
Savanna-La-Mar
Cambridge
Bluefields
Whitehouse
Black River
Black River Bay
Treasure Beach
Santa Cruz
Maggotty
Albert Town
Christiana
Mandeville
Bull Savannah
May Pen
Frankfield
Chapelton
Ewarton
Claremont
Alexandria
Discovery Bay
Runaway Bay
Puerto Seco Beach
Falmouth
St. Ann's Bay
Ocho Rios
Turtle Beach
Mallard's Beach
Oracabessa
Port Maria
Annotto Bay
Buff Bay
Castleton
Newcastle
Kingston
Spanish Town
Portmore
Port Royal
Norman Manley International Airport
Kingston Harbour
Old Harbour
Lionel Town
Linstead
Hope Bay
Port Antonio
San San Beach
Boston Beach
Boston Bay
Long Bay
Manchioneal
Golden Grove
Bowden
Morant Bay
Yallahs
Bull Bay

10 Miles
10 Kilometers
0

N

187

Getting Around

BY TAXI Taxis are your best means of transport, but always agree on a fare before you get in. Your best and safest bet is to get a taxi from the pier; there will be lots of them waiting. Taxis licensed by the government display JTB decals, indicating they're official Jamaican Tourist Board taxis. All others are gypsy cabs, which you should avoid. Taxi dispatchers are at the pier and fixed rates are posted. Otherwise, if you're getting into a taxi from somewhere else on the island, always agree to the price before getting in.

BY RENTAL CAR I don't recommend renting a car here.

Shore Excursions

Dunn's River Falls Tour ($44, 4 hours): These falls cascade 600 feet to the beach and are the most visited attraction in Jamaica, which means they're hopelessly over-crowded when a lot of cruise ships are in port (the hordes thin out in the afternoon, though, so consider hopping a taxi there yourself later in the day). Tourists are allowed to climb the falls, and it's a ball to slip and slide your way up with the hundreds of others, forming a human chain of sorts. Don't forget your waterproof camera and your aquasocks (most lines will rent you aquasocks for an extra $5). This tour also visits Shaw Park Botanical Gardens, Fern Gully, and other local attractions, with time allocated for shopping. Wear a bathing suit under your clothes.

✪ **River Tubing Safari** ($59, 6 hours): This is one of the best excursions I've ever taken. After a scenic 30-minute-or-so van ride deep into the pristine jungles of Jamaica, the group of 20 or so passengers and a couple of guides get into the White River, sit back into big black inner tubes (they have wooden boards covering the bottom so your butt doesn't scrape the bottom of the river or any rocks you may run into), and begin the 3-mile glide downriver, passing by gorgeous, towering bamboo trees and other lush foliage. It's sometimes peaceful and sometimes exhilarating—especially when you hit the rapids!

✪ **Chukka Cove Horseback-Riding Excursion** ($79, 4 hours): Riders will love this trip, where after a 45-minute ride from the stables through fields you'll gallop along the beach and take your horse bareback into the surf for a thrilling ride through this beautiful sea. *Tip:* Take the morning ride and your horse is bound to be more energetic. (Also, if you book directly with **Chukka Cove, ☎ 876-972-2506,** the same tour, including transportation there and back, runs $60. The Chukka folks also offer a 3¹/₂-hour mountain-biking tour; after being driven up picturesque Lilly-field Mountain, you glide down the 7-mile route drinking in the scenery along the way.)

✪ **Dunn's River Falls Mountain-Biking Trek** ($61–$69, 4 hours): After you're driven up to the summit of 1,500-foot-high Murphy Hill, above Ocho Rios, hop on your mountain bike, strap on your helmet, and enjoy a mostly downhill ride through the natural limestone and ferns, passing the eight springs that form Dunn's River Falls. Once at the bottom, you'll have time to climb the falls before heading back to the ship.

Countryside/Plantation Bus Tour ($54, 5 hours): This tour includes a drive through the Jamaican countryside to Brimmer Hall Plantation, a working plantation property with a Great House and tropical crops, such as bananas and pimiento. On the way back, you pass the estates once occupied by Noël Coward and Ian Fleming.

| **Insider Tip** |

If you step inside of the small cruise "terminal" in Ocho Rios, you'll find a shop called **Cruise Booze,** which sets up a tasting station where you can sample a ton of different rums, including a 150-proof white rum.

Often a stop at Dunn's River Falls is tacked on to the end of the tour. Another variation on this tour ($40, 4–5 hours) stops at the Prospect Plantation instead of Brimmer Hall.

Snorkeling Excursion ($31, 2 hours): A coral reef near the cruise pier is one of the best places in the area for snorkeling, with panoramic underwater visibility. You can also take a 1-hour cruise on a glass-bottom boat for a look at underwater Jamaica.

Martha Brae River Rafting ($50, 5 hours): This tour, in 30-foot, two-seat bamboo rafts, is traditionally one of the most heavily booked tours from both Ocho Rios or Montego Bay. However, most people find it disappointing. I'd recommend the tubing and bicycling excursions instead.

ON YOUR OWN: WITHIN WALKING DISTANCE
Aside from some markets (see "Shopping," below), there's little to do close to the docks.

ON YOUR OWN: BEYOND WALKING DISTANCE
South of Ocho Rios, **Fern Gully** was originally a riverbed. Today, the main A3 road winds up some 700 feet through a rain forest filled with wild ferns, hardwood trees, and lianas. For the botanist, there are hundreds of varieties of ferns, and for the less plant-minded, roadside stands sell fruits and vegetables, carved-wood souvenirs, and basketwork. The road runs for about 4 miles.

Near Lydford, southwest of Ocho Rios, are the remains of **Edinburgh Castle.** This was the lair of one of Jamaica's most infamous murderers, a Scot named Lewis Hutchinson who used to shoot passersby and toss their bodies into a deep pit. The authorities got wind of his activities, and although he tried to escape by canoe, he was captured by the navy and hanged. Rather proud of his achievements (evidence of at least 43 murders was found), he left £100 and instructions for a memorial to be built. It never was, but the 1763 castle ruins remain. To get to Lydford, take the A3 south until you reach a small intersection directly north of Walkers Wood, and then follow the signposts west.

If you're here on a Thursday, the 1817 **Brimmer Hall Estate,** Port Maria, St. Mary's (☎ **876/974-2244**), 21 miles east of Ocho Rios, is an ideal place to spend part of the day. Brimmer Hall is a working plantation where you're driven around in a tractor-drawn jitney to see the tropical fruit trees and coffee plants. Knowledgeable guides tell you about the processes necessary to produce the fine fruits of the island. Afterward, you can relax beside the pool and sample a wide variety of drinks, including an interesting one called "Wow!" The Plantation Tour Eating House offers typical Jamaican dishes for lunch. There's also a souvenir shop with a good selection of ceramics, art, straw goods, woodcarvings, rums, liqueurs, and cigars.

A mile from the center of Ocho Rios, at an elevation of 420 feet, **Coyaba River Garden and Museum,** Shaw Park Road (☎ **876/974-6235**), was built on the grounds of the former Shaw Park plantation. The Spanish-style museum displays artifacts from the Arawak, Spanish, and English settlements in the area. The gardens are filled with native flora, a cut-stone courtyard, and fountains.

Insider Tip: A 1-Day Cultural Exchange

The Jamaica Tourist Board's **Meet the People program** offers a neat way to learn about this country by spending time in the company of its people. And it's free! The JTB matches you with a local person or family who share the same interest you do, even if that happens to be ornithology! Your kids will be introduced to Jamaican playmates. Together you can, say, spend an afternoon at the beach, attend a church service, or share a meal or picnic. You might even do an afternoon of golf or basketball and a beer. Locals are eager to share their perspective of Jamaica, and nearly 1,000 Jamaican families are registered hosts. Contact the tourist board at ☎ **888/ 991-9999** to arrange this in advance of your visit.

At the 600-foot **Dunn's River Falls,** on the A3 (☎ **876/974-2857**), you can relax on the beach, splash in the waters at the bottom of the falls, or climb with a guide to the top and drop into the cool pools higher up between the cascades of water. The beach restaurant provides snacks and drinks, and dressing rooms are available. If you're planning to climb the falls, wear aquasocks or sneakers to protect your feet from the sharp rocks and to prevent slipping. At the prettiest part of Dunn's River Falls, known as the Laughing Waters, scenes were shot for the James Bond classics *Dr. No* and *Live and Let Die.*

Three miles east of Ocho Rios along the A3, adjoining the 18-hole Prospect Mini Golf Course, working **Prospect Plantation** (☎ **876/994-1058**) is often a shore-excursion stop. On your leisurely ride by covered jitney you'll readily see why this section of Jamaica is called "the garden parish of the island." You'll see pimiento (allspice), banana, cassava, sugarcane, coffee, cocoa, coconut, pineapple, and the famous leucaena "Tree of Life," plus Jamaica's first hydroelectric plant. Horseback riding is available on three scenic trails. The rides vary from 1 to $2^1/_4$ hours; you'll need to book a horse 1 hour in advance.

Firefly, Grants Pen, 20 miles east of Ocho Rios above Oracabessa (☎ **876/ 997-7201**), was the home of Sir Noël Coward and his longtime companion, Graham Payn, who, as executor of Coward's estate, donated it to the Jamaica National Heritage Trust. The recently restored house is as it was on the day Sir Noël died in 1973.

SHOPPING

In general, the shopping is better at Montego Bay than here, but if you're not going to Montego, wander around the Ocho Rios **crafts markets.** Literally hundreds of Jamaicans pour into Ocho Rios hoping to peddle something, often something homemade, to cruise ship passengers. Prepare yourself for aggressive selling and fierce haggling. Every vendor asks too much for an item at first, which gives them the leeway to negotiate the price. Shopping in Ocho Rios may not be the most fun you've ever had. You might want to skip it.

There is a handful of main shopping plazas in town, including the **Ocho Rios Craft Park,** a complex of some 150 stalls, **Soni's Plaza,** and the **Taj Mahel.** Word has it Ocho Rios will debut a new crafts market near Soni's by late 2000. An eager seller will weave a hat or a basket while you wait, or you can buy from the mixture of ready-made hats, hampers, handbags, place mats, and lampshades. **Coconut Grove Shopping Plaza** is a collection of low-slung shops linked by walkways and shrubs. The merchandise consists mainly of local craft items. **Island Plaza** shopping

---

Port Tip

Some so-called **duty-free prices** are indeed lower than stateside prices, but then the Jamaican government hits you with a 10% "General Consumption Tax."

---

complex is right in the heart of Ocho Rios. You can find some of the best Jamaican art here, all paintings by local artists. You can also purchase local handmade crafts (be prepared to do some haggling), carvings, ceramics, even kitchenware, and the inevitable T-shirts.

To find local handcrafts or art without the hassle of the markets, head for **Beautiful Memories,** 9 Island Plaza, which has a limited but representative sampling of Jamaican art, as well as local crafts, pottery, woodwork, and hand-embroidered items. I generally ignore hotel gift shops, but the **Jamaica Inn Gift Shop** in the Jamaica Inn, Main Street, is better than most, selling everything from Blue Mountain coffee to Walkers Wood products, and even guava jelly and jerk seasoning. If you're lucky, you'll find marmalade from an old family recipe, plus Upton Pimento Dram, a unique liqueur flavored with Jamaican allspice.

If you'd like to flee the hustle and bustle of the Ocho Rios bazaars, take a taxi to **Harmony Hall,** Tower Isle, on the A3, 4 miles east of Ocho Rios. One of Jamaica's Great Houses, the restored house is now a gallery selling paintings and other works by Jamaican artists. The arts and crafts here are high-quality—not the usual junky assortment you might find at the beach.

BEACHES

Many visitors to Ocho Rios head for the beach. The most overcrowded is **Mallards Beach** at the Jamaica Grand Hotel, shared by hotel guests and cruise ship passengers. Locals may steer you to the good and less-crowded **Turtle Beach,** southwest of Mallards. You might also want to check out the big **James Bond Beach** in Oracabessa, at the east end of Ocho Rios.

SPORTS

GOLF   **Super Club's Runaway Golf Course,** at Runaway Beach near Ocho Rios on the north coast (☎ 876/973-2561), is one of the better courses in the area, although it's nowhere near the courses at Montego Bay. Cruise ship passengers should call ahead and book playing times. The charge is about $60 for 18 holes in winter. Players can rent carts and clubs. **Sandals Golf & Country Club,** at Ocho Rios (☎ 876/975-0119), is also open to the public. The course lies about 700 feet above sea level. To get there from the center of Ocho Rios, travel along the main bypass for 2 miles until Mile End Road; turn right at the Texaco station there, and drive for 5 miles.

GREAT LOCAL RESTAURANTS & BARS

A favorite **local beer** is Red Stripe; a favorite **local rum** is Appleton.

Ocho Rios Jerk Centre, on DaCosta Drive, serves up lip-smacking jerk pork and chicken. Don't expect anything fancy. Just come for platters of meat. For a special lunch out, **Almond Tree Restaurant,** 87 Main St., in the Hibiscus Lodge Hotel, 3 blocks from the Ocho Rios Mall (☎ 876/974-2813), is a two-tiered patio restaurant overlooking the Caribbean, with a tree growing through its roof. Lobster thermidor is the most delectable item on the menu. **Evita's Italian Restaurant,** Eden Bower Road, 5 minutes south of Ocho Rios (☎ 876/974-2333), is run by a flamboyant Italian and is the premier Italian restaurant in Ocho Rios. It serves pastas and excellent fish dishes as well as unique ones like jerk spaghetti and pasta Viagra (don't ask). Lunch with drinks runs about $15. **Little Pub Restaurant,** 59 Main St. (☎ **876/974-2324**), is an indoor-outdoor pub serving such items as grilled kingfish, stewed snapper, barbecued chicken, and the inevitable and over-priced lobster. The cooking is competent and the atmosphere very casual. **Parkway Restaurant,** 60 DaCosta Dr. (☎ **876/974-2667**), couldn't be plainer or less pretentious, but it's always packed. Hungry diners are fed Jamaican-style chicken, curried goat, sirloin steak, fillet of red snapper, and to top it off, banana cream pie. Lobster and fresh fish are usually featured also. The food is straightforward, honest, and affordable.

When you're seated at the beautifully laid tables at the **Plantation Inn Restaurant,** in the Plantation Inn, Main Street (☎ **876/974-5601**), you'll think you've arrived at Tara in *Gone With the Wind.* Jamaican specialties help spice up the continental cuisine in this romantic restaurant.

There are probably more great rum bars on Jamaica than churches. Among the best is **Bibi Bips** in Ocho Rios.

MONTEGO BAY

Montego Bay is sometimes less of a hassle than the port at Ocho Rios, and has better beaches, shopping, and restaurants, as well as some of the best golf courses in the Caribbean, superior even to those on Puerto Rico and the Bahamas. Like Ocho Rios, Montego Bay has its crime, traffic, and annoyance, but there's much more to see and do here.

There's little of interest in the town of Montego Bay itself except shopping, although the good stuff in the environs is easily reached by taxi or shore excursion. Getting around from place to place is one of the major difficulties here, as it is in Barbados. Whatever you want to visit seems to be in yet another direction.

Frommer's Favorite Montego Bay Experiences

In addition to these, my favorite shore excursions from Ocho Rios are also offered from Montego Bay.

- **Visiting Rocklands Wildlife Station:** This is the place to go if you want to have a Jamaican doctor bird perch on your finger or feed small doves and finches from your hand (see "On Your Own: Beyond Walking Distance," below).
- **Spend a day at the Rose Hall Beach Club:** With a secluded beach, crystal-clear water, a full restaurant, two beach bars, live entertainment, and more, it's well worth the $8 admission (see "Beaches," below).

Frommer's Ratings: Montego Bay					
	Poor	Fair	Good	Excellent	Outstanding
Overall Experience				✓	
Shore Excursions					✓
Activities Close to Port				✓	
Beaches & Water Sports			✓		
Shopping			✓		
Dining/Bars			✓		

COMING ASHORE   Montego Bay has a modern cruise dock with lots of conveniences, including duty-free stores, telephones, tourist information, and plenty of taxis to meet all ships.

GETTING AROUND

BY TAXI   If you don't book a shore excursion, a taxi is the way to get around. See "Getting Around" under "Ocho Rios," above, for taxi information, as the same conditions apply to Mo Bay.

BY MOTOR SCOOTER   Montego Honda/Bike Rentals, 21 Gloucester Ave. (☎ 876/952-4984), rents Hondas for about $35 a day, plus a $300 deposit.

SHORE EXCURSIONS

Also see "Shore Excursions" under "Ocho Rios," above.

Croydon Plantation Tour ($55, 4–5 hours): Twenty-five miles from Montego Bay, the plantation can be visited on a half-day tour on Tuesday, Wednesday, and Friday. Included in the price are round-trip transportation from the dock, a tour of the plantation, a tasting of varieties of pineapple and other tropical fruits in season, and a barbecued chicken lunch.

ON YOUR OWN: WITHIN WALKING DISTANCE

Nothing really. You'll have to take a taxi to the town for shopping or sign up for an excursion.

ON YOUR OWN: BEYOND WALKING DISTANCE

These attractions can be reached by taxi from the cruise dock.

Charging a steep admission, the most famous Great House in Jamaica is the legendary ✪ **Rose Hall Great House,** Rose Hall Highway (☎ 876/953-2323), located 9 miles east of Montego Bay along the coast road. The house was built about 2 centuries ago by John Palmer, and gained notoriety from the doings of "Infamous Annie" Palmer, wife of the builder's grandnephew, who supposedly dabbled in witchcraft and took slaves as lovers, killing them when they bored her. Annie also was said to have murdered several of her husbands while they slept, and eventually suffered the same fate herself. The house, now privately owned by U.S.-based philanthropists, has been restored. **Annie's Pub** sits on the ground floor.

On a hillside perch 14 miles east of Montego Bay and 7 miles west of Falmouth, **Greenwood Great House,** on the A1 (☎ 876/953-1077), is even more interesting to some than Rose Hall. Erected in the early 19th century, the Georgian-style building was from 1780 to 1800 the residence of Richard Barrett, a relative of Elizabeth Barrett Browning. On display are the family's library, portraits of the family, and rare musical instruments.

It's a unique experience to have a Jamaican doctor bird perch on your finger to drink syrup, or to feed small doves and finches from your hand, or simply to watch dozens of birds flying in for the evening at **Rocklands Wildlife Station,** Anchovy, St. James (☎ 876/952-2009). Lisa Salmon, known as the "Bird Lady of Anchovy," established this sanctuary. It's perfect for nature lovers and bird watchers, but don't take children 5 and under, as they tend to worry the birds. Rocklands is about a mile outside Anchovy on the road from Montego Bay. It's open daily from 2:30 to 5pm, and charges an admission of J$300 (U.S.$8.55).

SHOPPING

The main shopping areas are at **Montego Freeport,** within easy walking distance of the pier; **City Centre,** where most of the duty-free shops are, aside from those at the large hotels; and **Holiday Village Shopping Centre.**

Old Fort Craft Park, a shopping complex with nearly 200 vendors licensed by the Jamaica Tourist Board, fronts Howard Cooke Boulevard up from Gloucester Avenue in the heart of Montego Bay, on the site of Fort Montego. With a varied assortment of handcrafts, this is browsing country. You'll see a selection of wall hangings, handwoven straw items, and hand-carved wood sculptures, and you can even get your hair braided. Vendors can be extremely aggressive, so be prepared for some major hassles, as well as some serious negotiation. Persistent bargaining on your part will lead to substantial discounts.

You can find the best selection of handmade Jamaican souvenirs at the Crafts Market, near Harbour Street in downtown Montego Bay. Straw hats and bags, wooden platters, straw baskets, musical instruments, beads, carved objects, and toys are all available here. That "jipijapa" hat will come in handy if you're going to be out in the island sun.

One of the newer and more intriguing places for shopping is a mall, Half Moon Plaza, set on the coastal road about 8 miles east of the commercial center of Montego Bay. This upscale minimall caters to the shopping and gastronomic needs of residents of one of the region's most elegant hotels, the Half Moon Club. Also on the premises are a bank and about 25 shops arranged around a central courtyard and purveying a wide choice of carefully selected merchandise.

Ambiente Art Gallery, 9 Fort St., stocks local artwork. At Blue Mountain Gems Workshop, at the Holiday Village Shopping Centre, you can take a tour of the workshops to see the process from raw stone to the finished product available for purchase later. Caribatik Island Fabrics, Rock Wharf on the Luminous Lagoon, Falmouth (2 miles east of Falmouth on the north coast road), is the private living and work domain of Keith Chandler, who creates a full range of batik fabrics, scarves, garments, and wall hangings, some patterned after such themes as Jamaica's "doctor bird." Klass Kraft Leather Sandals, 44 Fort St., offers sandals and leather accessories made on location by a team of Jamaican craftspeople. Things Jamaican, 44 Fort St., stocks Jamaican rums and liqueurs, jerk products, sculpture, handwoven Jamaican baskets, and more.

BEACHES

Cornwall Beach is a long stretch of white-sand beach with dressing cabanas. Daily admission is about $2 for adults, $1 for children. A bar and cafeteria offer refreshment.

Doctor's Cave Beach, on Gloucester Avenue across from the Doctor's Cave Beach Hotel, helped launch Mo Bay as a resort in the 1940s. Admission to the beach is about $2 for adults, half price for children up to 12. Dressing rooms, chairs, umbrellas, and rafts are available.

One of the premier beaches of Jamaica, **Walter Fletcher Beach** in the heart of Mo Bay, is noted for its tranquil waters, which make it a particular favorite for families with children. Changing rooms are available, and lifeguards are on duty. There's also a restaurant for lunch. The beach is open daily, with an admission price of about $1 for adults, half price for children.

You may want to skip the public beaches and head for the ✪ **Rose Hall Beach Club** (☎ **876/953-2323**), lying on the main road 11 miles east of Montego Bay.

It sits on half a mile of secure, secluded, white sandy beach, with crystal-clear water. The club offers a full restaurant, two beach bars, a covered pavilion, an open-air dance area, showers, rest rooms, and changing facilities, plus beach volleyball courts, various beach games, and a full water-sports activities program. There's also live entertainment. Admission fees are about $8 for adults, $5 for children. The club is open daily from 10am to 6pm.

SPORTS

GOLF   Wyndham Rose Hall Golf & Beach Resort, Rose Hall (☎ 876/953-2650), has a noted course with an unusual and challenging seaside and mountain layout. The 300-foot-high 13th tee offers a rare panoramic view of the sea and the roof of the hotel, and the 15th green is next to a 40-foot waterfall, once featured in a James Bond movie. A fully stocked pro shop, a clubhouse, and a professional staff are among the amenities.

The excellent, regal course at the **Tryall** (☎ 876/956-5660), 12 miles from Montego Bay, has often been the site of major golf tournaments, including the Jamaica Classic Annual and the Johnnie Walker Tournament.

Half Moon, at Rose Hall (☎ 876/953-2560), features a championship course—designed by Robert Trent Jones, Sr.—that opened in 1961. The course has manicured and diversely shaped greens.

Ironshore Golf & Country Club, Ironshore, St. James, Montego Bay (☎ 876/953-2800), a well-known, par-72, 18-hole golf course, is privately owned but open to the public.

HORSEBACK RIDING   The best horseback riding is offered by the helpful staff at the **Rocky Point Riding Stables,** at the Half Moon Club, Rose Hall, Montego Bay (☎ 876/953-2286). The stables, built in the colonial Caribbean style in 1992, are the most beautiful in Jamaica.

RAFTING   Mountain Valley Rafting, 31 Gloucester Ave. (☎ 876/956-0020), offers excursions on the Great River. They depart from the Lethe Plantation, about 10 miles south of Montego Bay. Bamboo rafts are designed for two, with a raised dais to sit on. In some cases, a small child can accompany two adults on the same raft, although caution should be exercised. Ask about pickup by taxi at the end of the run. A half-day experience includes transportation to and from the pier, an hour's rafting, lunch, a garden tour of the Lethe property, and a taste of Jamaican liqueur.

WATER SPORTS   Seaworld Resorts Ltd., Cariblue Hotel, Rose Hall Main Road (☎ 876/953-2180), operates **scuba-diving** as well as deep-sea fishing jaunts, plus many other water sports, including sailing and windsurfing. Its scuba dives go to offshore coral reefs that are among the most spectacular in the Caribbean. There are three PADI-certified dive guides, one dive boat, and all the necessary equipment for inexperienced or certified divers.

GREAT LOCAL RESTAURANTS & BARS

The **Pork Pit,** 27 Gloucester Ave., near Walter Fletcher Beach (☎ 876/952-1046), is the best place to go for the famous Jamaican jerk pork and jerk chicken. Many beachgoers come over here for a big lunch. Picnic tables encircle the building, and everything is open-air and informal. Order half a pound of jerk meat with a baked yam or baked potato and a bottle of Red Stripe beer. Prices are very reasonable.

The **Georgian House,** 2 Orange St. (☎ 876/952-0632), brings grand cuisine and an elegant setting to the heart of town. The lunch menu is primarily Jamaican.

The Native Restaurant, Gloucester Ave. (☎ **876/979-2769**), continues to win converts with such appetizers as jerk reggae chicken, ackee and saltfish (an acquired taste), smoked marlin, and steamed fish. Boonoonoonoos, billed as "A Taste of Jamaica," is a big platter with a little bit of everything, including meats and several kinds of fish and vegetables. **Pier 1,** Howard Cooke Boulevard (☎ **876/ 952-2452**), features—among other dishes—fresh lobster, Jamaican soups such as conch chowder or red pea, the juiciest hamburgers in town, and an excellent steak sandwich with mushrooms.

17 Key West

No other port of call offers such a sweeping choice of fine dining, easy-to-reach attractions, street entertainment, and roguish bars as does this heavy-drinking, fun-loving town at the very end of the fabled Florida Keys. It's America's southernmost city at Mile Marker 0, where U.S. Route 1 begins, but it feels more like a colorful Caribbean outpost.

You have only a day, so flee the busy cruise docks and touristy Duval Street for a walk through hidden and more secluded byways, such as Olivia or William streets. Or you might want to spend your day playing golf or going diving or snorkeling.

Frommer's Favorite Key West Experiences

- **Viewing the sunset from Mallory Dock:** More than just a sunset, it's a daily carnival. If your ship is in port late enough, don't miss it (see "On Your Own: Within Walking Distance," below).
- **Taking a catamaran party cruise:** The popular Fury catamarans take passengers snorkeling and then back to shore, with music, booze, and a good time (see "Shore Excursions," below).

COMING ASHORE   Ships dock at Mallory Square, Old Town's most important plaza, or at nearby Truman Annex, a 5-minute stroll away. Both are on the Gulf of Mexico side of the island. Except for esoteric pockets, virtually everything is at your doorstep, including the two main arteries, Duval Street and Whitehead Street, each filled with shops, bars, restaurants, and the town's most important attractions.

CURRENCY   U.S. dollars are used here. You can change other major currencies at **First State Bank,** 1201 Simonton St. (☎ **305/296-8535**), open Monday to Friday from 9am to 3pm. On Friday, it reopens from 4 to 6pm. There's a 2% to 4% exchange fee.

LANGUAGE   Speak English here. You're in the U.S.A., remember.

Frommer's Ratings: Key West					
	Poor	Fair	Good	Excellent	Outstanding
Overall Experience				✓	
Shore Excursions				✓	
Activities Close to Port					✓
Beaches & Water Sports		✓			
Shopping			✓		
Dining/Bars				✓	

Key West

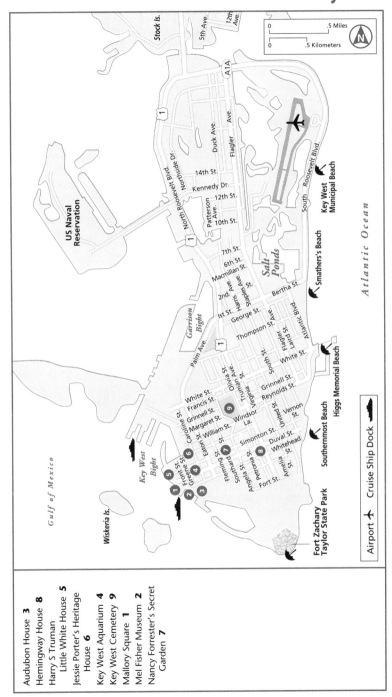

Audubon House **3**
Hemingway House **8**
Harry S Truman
    Little White House **5**
Jessie Porter's Heritage
    House **6**
Key West Aquarium **4**
Key West Cemetery **9**
Mallory Square **1**
Mel Fisher Museum **2**
Nancy Forrester's Secret
    Garden **7**

Airport ✈   Cruise Ship Dock

Gulf of Mexico

Atlantic Ocean

US Naval
Reservation

Stock Is.

Wisteria Is.

Key West
Bight

Garrison
Bight

Salt
Ponds

Key West
Municipal Beach

Smathers's Beach

Higgs Memorial Beach

Southernmost Beach

Fort Zachary
Taylor State Park

5th Ave.
12th Ave.
A1A
Duck Ave.
Flagler Ave.
South Roosevelt Blvd.
North Roosevelt Blvd.
Northside Dr.
14th St.
Kennedy Dr.
12th St.
Patterson Ave.
10th St.
7th St.
6th St.
Macmillan Dr.
2nd St.
1st St.
Harris Ave.
Staples Ave.
George St.
Thompson St.
Bertha St.
Palm Ave.
Flagler Ave.
Laird St.
Atlantic Blvd.
White St.
south St.
south St.
White St.
Francis St.
Grinnell St.
Margaret St.
Caroline St.
Front St.
Greene St.
Eaton St.
William St.
Fleming St.
Southard St.
Angela St.
Petronia St.
Fort St.
Simonton St.
Duval St.
Whitehead St.
Amelia St.
Olivia St.
Truman Ave.
Virginia St.
Windsor La.
Grinnell St.
Reynolds St.
United St.
Vernon St.

1
2
3
4
5
6
7
8
9

0   .5 Miles
0   .5 Kilometers
N

INFORMATION **The Greater Key West Chamber of Commerce,** 402 Wall St. (☎ 305/294-5988), lies near the cruise ship docks. This helpful agency answers questions about local activities, distributes free maps, and assists in arranging tours and fishing trips. Ask for *Pelican Path,* a free walking guide that documents the history and architecture of Old Town, and *Solares Hill's Walking and Biking Guide to Old Key West,* which contains a bunch of walking tours. To get info before you go, call the **Tourism Board** at ☎ 800/733-5397 or log on to the Web site at www.seekeys.com.

GETTING AROUND

The island is only 4 miles long and 2 miles wide, so getting around is easy. Hundreds of people who live here own bicycles instead of cars. The most popular sights, including the Hemingway House and the Harry S Truman Little White House, are within walking distance of the cruise docks, so you're hardly dependent on public transportation unless you want to go to the beaches on the island's Atlantic side.

BY TAXI Island taxis operate around the clock, but are small and not suited for sightseeing tours. They will, however, take you to the beach and arrange to pick you up at a certain time. You can call one of four different services: **Florida Keys Taxi** (☎ 305/294-2227), **Maxi-Taxi Sun Cab System** (☎ 305/294-2222), **Pink Cabs** (☎ 305/296-6666), or **Island Transportation Services** (☎ 305/296-1800). Prices are uniform; the meter starts at about $1.40, and adds 35¢ per quarter mile.

BY TRAM The tram/trolley-car tours are the best way to see Key West in a short time. In fact, the **Conch Tour Train** (☎ 305/294-5161) is Key West's most famous tourist attraction. It's a narrated 90-minute tour, going up and down all the most interesting streets and commenting on 60 local sites, giving you lots of lore about the town. The depot is located at Mallory Square near the cruise ship docks. Trains depart every 30 minutes. The trip is nonstop, unlike tours on the Old Town Trolley (see below), which allow you to get on and off. Most ships sell this as an excursion, but you can also do it on your own; departures are daily from 9am to 4:30pm and cost about $17 for adults, $8 for children ages 4 to 12 (3 and under free).

Old Town Trolley is less popular than the Conch Tour Train, but appeals to visitors who want more flexibility since it lets you get off and explore a particular attraction, and then reboard another of its trains later. Professional guides spin tall tales about Key West throughout the 90-minute route. The trolleys operate 7 days a week from 9am to 4:30pm, with departures every 30 minutes from convenient spots throughout town. You can board the trolley near the cruise docks (look for signposts). Call ☎ 305/296-6688 for more information. Tours cost about $18 for adults, $9 for children ages 4 to 12, free for children under 4.

BY MOTOR SCOOTER OR BICYCLE One of the largest and best places to rent a bicycle or motorbike is **Keys Moped and Scooter Rental,** 523 Truman Ave., about a block off Duval Street (☎ 305/294-0399). Cruise ship passengers might opt for a 3-hour motor-scooter rental for about $12, or all day for $14. One-speed, big-wheeled "beach-cruiser" bicycles with soft seats and big baskets for toting beachwear rent for about $4 for 8 hours.

BY BUS The cheapest way to see the island is by bus, which costs only about 75¢ for adults, and 35¢ for senior citizens and children 6 years and older (kids 5 and under ride free).

BY RENTAL CAR Walking or cycling is better than renting a car here, but if you do rent, try **Hertz,** 3491 S. Roosevelt Blvd. (☎ 800/654-3131 or 305/294-1039), **Tropical Rent-a-Car,** 1300 Duval St. (☎ 305/294-8136), or **Enterprise Rent-a-Car,**

3031 N. Roosevelt Blvd. (☎ **800/325-8007** or 305/292-0222). If you're visiting in winter, make reservations at least a week in advance.

SHORE EXCURSIONS

In Key West, it's definitely not necessary to take an organized excursion since everything is so accessible by foot or tram. If you like the services of a guide, most lines offer walking tours. Also, the trams and trolleys have running narratives about Key West history and culture.

✪ **Catamaran Party Cruises** ($38, 3 hours): The popular Fury catamarans take passenger to a reef for some snorkeling and then finish the trip back to shore with music, booze, and a good time.

Guided Bike Tour ($25, 2 hours): Get the lowdown on Key West's multifaceted history and quirky culture while peddling along a 2^1/$_2$-mile route.

TOURING THROUGH LOCAL OPERATORS

Glass-Bottomed Boat Tours: The MV *Discovery* (☎ **305/293-0099**), a 78-foot motor craft, has 20 large viewing windows (angled at 45°) set below the water line. Passengers can view reef life from safety and comfort below deck. Two-hour tours depart daily at 10:30am, 1:30, and 6pm from Land's End Village & Marina at the western end of Margaret Street, a 6-block walk from the cruise ship docks. The cost is about $20.

ON YOUR OWN: WITHIN WALKING DISTANCE

If the lines aren't too long, you'll want to see the Harry S Truman Little White House and the Hemingway House, but don't feel obligated. If you want to see and capture the real-life mood and charm of Key West in a short time, leave the most-visited attractions to your fellow cruise ship passengers and head for the ones below marked with a star. Each of the sights below is an easy walk from the docks.

Audubon House, 205 Whitehead St., at Greene Street (☎ **305/294-2116**), is dedicated to the 1832 Key West sojourn of the famous naturalist John James Audubon. The ornithologist didn't live in this three-story building, but it's filled with his engravings. The main reason to visit is to see how wealthy sailors lived in Key West in the 19th century, and the lush tropical gardens surrounding the house are worth the price of admission.

Harry S Truman Little White House, 111 Front St. (☎ **305/294-9911**), the president's former vacation home, is part of the 103-acre Truman Annex near the cruise ship docks. The small house, which takes less than an hour to visit, affords a glimpse of a president at play.

There may be long lines at the **Hemingway House,** 907 Whitehead St. (☎ **305/ 294-1575**), where "Papa" lived with his second wife, Pauline. Here, in the studio annex, Hemingway wrote *For Whom the Bell Tolls* and *A Farewell to Arms,* among others. Hemingway had some 50 polydactyl (many-toed) cats, whose descendants still live on the grounds.

Jessie Porter Newton, known as "Miss Jessie" to her friends, was the grande dame of Key West, inviting the celebrities of her day to her house, including Tennessee Williams and her girlhood friend Gloria Swanson, as well as family friend Robert Frost, who stayed in a cottage out back. Today, you can cross her once-hallowed grounds, look at the antique-filled rooms, and inspect her mementos and the exotic treasures collected by six generations of the Porter family at ✪ **Jessie Porter's Heritage House and Robert Frost Cottage,** 410 Caroline St. (☎ **305/296-3575**).

On the waterfront at Mallory Square, the **Key West Aquarium,** 1 Whitehead St. (☎ **305/296-2051**), in operation since 1932, was the first tourist attraction built in the Florida Keys. The aquarium's special feature is a "touch tank," where you can feel a horseshoe crab, sea squirt, sea urchin, starfish, and, of course, a conch, the town's mascot and symbol. It's worth taking a tour, as the guides are both knowledgeable and entertaining, and you'll get to pet a shark, if that's your idea of a good time.

The ✪ **Key West Cemetery** (☎ **305/296-2175**), 21 prime acres in the heart of the historic district, is the island's foremost offbeat attraction. The main entrance is at Margaret Street and Passover Lane. Stone-encased caskets rest on top of the earth because graves dug into the ground would hit the water table. There's also a touch of humor here: One gravestone proclaims "I Told You I Was Sick," and another says, "At Least I Know Where He Is Sleeping Tonight."

Treasure hunter Mel Fisher, who passed away not long ago, used to wear heavy gold necklaces, which he liked to say were worth a king's ransom. He wasn't exaggerating. After long and risky dives, Fisher and his associates plucked more than $400 million in gold and silver from the shipwrecked Spanish galleons *Santa Margarita* and *Nuestra Señora de Atocha,* which were lost on hurricane-tossed seas some 350 years ago. Now this extraordinary long-lost Spanish jewelry, doubloons, and silver and gold bullion are displayed at the ✪ **Mel Fisher Maritime Heritage Society Museum,** 200 Greene St. (☎ **305/294-2633**), a true treasure trove near the docks.

Nancy Forrester's Secret Garden, 1 Free School Lane, off Simonton between Southard and Fleming streets (☎ **305/294-0015**), is the most lavish and verdant garden in town. Some 130 to 150 species of palms, palmettos, climbing vines, and ground covers are planted here, creating a blanket of lush, tropical magic. It's a 20-minute walk from the docks, near Key West's highest point, Solares Hill. Pick up a sandwich at a deli and picnic at tables in the garden.

If your ship leaves late enough, you can take in a unique local celebration: ✪ **viewing the sunset from Mallory Dock.** Sunset-watching is good fun all over the world, but in Key West it's been turned into a carnival-like, almost pagan celebration—a "blazing festival of joy," some call it. People from all over the world begin to crowd Mallory Square even before the sun starts to fall, bringing the place alive with entertainment—everything from a string band to a unicyclist wriggling free of a straitjacket. A juggler might delight the crowd with a machete and a flaming stick. The main entertainment, however, is that massive fireball falling out of view, which is always greeted with hysterical applause.

ON YOUR OWN: BEYOND WALKING DISTANCE

Nothin'. That's the beauty of Key West: Everything worthwhile is accessible by foot.

SHOPPING

Shopping by cruise ship passengers has become a local joke in Key West. Within a 12-block radius of Old Town, you'll find mostly tawdry and outrageously over-priced merchandise—but if you're in the market for some Key West kitsch, this is the neighborhood for you.

Among the less-kitschy alternatives, a few stand out much farther along Duval Street, the main drag leading to the Atlantic, and on hidden back streets. You can reach all these stores from the cruise ship docks in a 15-to-20-minute stroll.

Cavanaugh's, 520 Front St., is a treasure trove of merchandise from all over the world—it's like wandering through the souks in the dusty back alleys of North Africa. **Haitian Art Company,** 600 Frances St., claims to inventory the largest collection of Haitian paintings in the United States. Prices range from $15 to $5,000.

Key West Aloe, Inc., 524 Front St. or 540 Greene St., is aloe, aloe, and more aloe; the shop's inventory includes shaving cream, aftershave lotion, sunburn ointments, and fragrances for men and women based on such tropical essences as hibiscus, frangipani, and white ginger. **Key West Hand Print Fashions and Fabrics,** 201 Simonton St., sells bold, tropical prints—handprinted scarves with coordinated handbags and rack after rack of busily patterned sundresses and cocktail dresses that will make you look jaunty on the deck of an ocean liner. **Key West Island Bookstore,** 513 Fleming St., is well stocked in books on Key West and has Florida's largest collection of works by and about Hemingway. In the rear is a rare-book section where you may want to browse, if not buy. **Michael,** 400C Duval St., stocks coins from sunken wrecks and the Middle East, mounted in various settings.

BEACHES

Beaches are not too compelling here. Most are man-made, often with imported Bahamian or mainland Florida sand. Those mentioned below are free and open to the public daily from 7am to 11pm. There are few facilities, except locals hawking beach umbrellas, food, and drinks.

Fort Zachary Taylor State Beach is the best and the closest to the cruise ship docks, a 12-minute walk away. This 51-acre man-made beach is adjacent to the ruins of Fort Taylor, once known as Fort Forgotten because it was buried under tons of sand. The beach is fine for sunbathing and picnicking and is suitable for snorkeling, but rocks make it difficult to swim. To get there, go through the gates leading into Truman Annex. Watering holes near one end of the beach include the raffish Green Parrot Bar and a booze-and-burger joint called Gato Gordo.

Higgs Memorial Beach lies a 25-minute walk from the harbor near the end of White Street, one of the main east-west arteries. You'll find lots of sand, picnic tables sheltered from the sun, and fewer of your fellow cruise ship passengers. **Smathers Beach,** named in honor of one of Florida's most colorful former senators, is the longest (about 1^1/$_2$ miles), most isolated, and least accessorized beach in town. Unfortunately, it's about a $10 one-way taxi ride from the cruise docks. The beach borders South Roosevelt Boulevard. There's no shade here.

In the 1950s, **Southernmost Beach** drew Tennessee Williams, but today it's more likely to fill up with visitors from the lackluster motels nearby. Except for a nearby restaurant, facilities are nonexistent. The beach lies at the foot of Duval Street on the Atlantic side, across the island from the cruise ship docks. It takes about 20 minutes to walk there along Duval Street from the docks. The beach boasts some white sand, but is not good for swimming. Nevertheless, it's one of the island's most frequented.

SPORTS

FISHING   As Hemingway, an avid fisherman, would attest, the waters off the Florida Keys are some of the world's finest fishing grounds. You can follow in his wake aboard the 40-foot *Linda D III* and *Linda D IV* (☎ **800/299-9798** in the U.S., or 305/296-9798), which offer the best deep-sea fishing here. Arrangements should be made a week or so before you are due in port.

GOLF   Redesigned in 1982 by architect Rees Jones, the **Key West Resort Golf Course,** 6450 E. Junior College Rd. (☎ **305/294-5232**), lies 6 miles from the cruise docks, near the southern tip of neighboring Stock Island. It features a challenging terrain of coral rock, sand traps, mangrove swamp, and pines. The course is a 10- to 15-minute, $15 taxi ride from the dock each way.

SCUBA DIVING The largest dive outfitter is **Captain's Corner,** 0 Duval Street, opposite the Pier House Hotel a block from the dock (☎ **305/296-8865**). The five-star PADI operation has 11 instructors, a 60-foot dive boat (used by Timothy "James Bond" Dalton during the filming of *License to Kill*), and a well-trained staff. To reach the departure point, make a left along the docks, and then walk for about a block to the northern tip of Duval Street.

GREAT LOCAL RESTAURANTS & BARS

RESTAURANTS All the restaurants listed below are within an easy 5- to 15-minute walk of the docks. Several "raw bars" near the dock area offer seafood, including oysters and clams, although the king here is conch—served grilled, ground in burgers, made into a chowder, fried in batter as fritters, or served raw in a conch salad. Even if you don't have lunch, at least sample the local favorites: a slice of Key lime pie with a Cuban coffee. The pie's unique flavor is achieved from the juice and minced rind of the local, piquant Key lime.

Cruise ship passengers on a return visit to Key West often ask for "The Rose Tattoo," a historic old restaurant named for the Tennessee Williams film partially shot on the island. The restaurant is now the **Bagatelle,** 115 Duval St., at Front Street (☎ **305/296-6609**), one of Key West's finest. Look for daily specials or stick to the chef's better dishes, such as conch ceviche (thinly sliced raw conch marinated in lime juice and herbs). **Blue Heaven,** 729 Thomas St. (☎ **305/296-8666**), is a dive that serves some of the best food in town. Some of its finest food is fresh local fish, most often grouper or red snapper, and the hot and spicy jerk chicken is as fine as that served in Jamaica. **Camille's,** 703¹/₂ Duval St., between Angela and Petronia streets (☎ **305/296-4811**), is an unpretentious, hip cafe that serves the best breakfast in town and has the best lunch value. Try a sandwich made from the catch of the day served on fresh bread. Its Key lime pie is the island's best. **El Siboney,** 900 Catherine St. (☎ **305/296-4184**), is the place for time-tested Cuban favorites like *ropa vieja,* roast pork with garlic and tart sour oranges, and paella Valenciana (minimum of two).

Half Shell Raw Bar, Land's End Marina, at the foot of Margaret Street (☎ **305/ 294-7496**), is Key West's original raw bar, offering fresh fish, oysters, and shrimp direct from its own fish market. To be honest, though, I prefer the food at **Turtle Kraals Wildlife Bar & Grill,** Land's End Village, at the foot of Margaret Street (☎ **305/294-2640**). Try the tender Florida lobster, spicy conch chowder, or perfectly cooked fresh fish (often dolphinfish with pineapple salsa or baked stuffed grouper with mango crabmeat stuffing).

Pepe's Café & Steak House, 806 Caroline St., between William and Margaret streets (☎ **305/294-7192**), is the oldest eating house in the Florida Keys, established in 1909. Diners eat under slow-moving paddle fans at tables or dark pine booths with high backs. Cruise ship passengers enjoy the "in between" menu served daily from noon to 4:30pm. You get to choose from zesty homemade chili, perfectly baked oysters, fish sandwiches, and Pepe's deservedly famous steak sandwiches.

If something cool would go down better than a full meal, check out **Flamingo Crossing,** 1105 Duval St., at Virginia Street (☎ **305/296-6124**), which serves the best ice cream in the Florida Keys.

BARS Key West is a bar town. Most places recommended below offer fast food to go with their drinks. The food isn't the best on the island, but usually arrives shortly after you order it, which suits most rushed cruise ship passengers just fine. A favorite **local beer** is Hog's Breath; a favorite **local rum** is Key West Gold (even though it's not actually made on the island).

Heavily patronized by cruise ship passengers, **Captain Tony's Saloon,** 428 Green St. (☎ **305/294-1838**), is the oldest active bar in Florida, and has it ever grown tacky. The 1851 building was the original Sloppy Joe's, a rough-and-tumble fisherman's saloon. Hemingway drank here from 1933 to 1937, and Jimmy Buffett got his start here before opening his own bar and going on to musical glory. The name refers to Capt. Tony Tarracino, a former Key West mayor and rugged man of the sea who owned the place until 1988.

Sloppy Joe's, 201 Duval St. (☎ **305/294-5717**), is the most touristy bar in Key West, visited by almost all cruise ship passengers, even those who don't normally go to bars. It aggressively plays up its association with Hemingway, although the bar stood on Greene Street back then (see "Captain Tony's," above). Marine flags decorate the ceiling, and its ambiance and decor evoke a Havana bar from the 1930s.

Jimmy Buffett's Margaritaville, 500 Duval St. (☎ **305/292-1435**), is the third most popular Key West bar with cruise ship passengers, after Captain Tony's and Sloppy Joe's. Buffett is the hometown boy done good, and his cafe, naturally, is decorated with pictures of himself. And, yes, it sells T-shirts and Margaritaville memorabilia in a shop off the dining room. His margaritas are without competition, but then they'd have to be, wouldn't they?

Open-air and very laid-back, the **Hog's Breath Saloon,** 400 Front St. (☎ **305/ 296-HOGG**), near the cruise docks, has been a Key West tradition since 1976. Drinking is a sport here, especially among the fishermen who come in after a day chasing the big one. Live entertainment is offered from 1pm to 2am.

For a real local hangout within an easy walk of the cruise ship docks, head to ✪ **Schooner Wharf,** 202 William St., Key West Bight (☎ **305/292-9520**), the most robust and hard-drinking bar in Key West, drawing primarily a young crowd, many of whom cater to the tourist industry or work on the town's fleet of fishing boats.

18 Les Saintes

You want charming? The eight islets of Les Saintes (pronounced "lay sant") are irresistibly charming: pastel-colored gingerbread houses with tropical gardens, sugarloaf hills that slope down to miniature beaches, and picturesque bays with pelicans, sailboats, and turquoise water. Only two of the islands in this French archipelago off the southern coast of Guadeloupe are inhabited: Terre-de-Bas and its more populous neighbor, Terre-de-Haut (more populous, in this case, meaning about 1,500 inhabitants). Terre-de-Haut (pronounced "tear d'oh"), with only one village—the straightforwardly named Le Bourg ("town")—is the destination of most visitors. Some say it's what Saint-Tropez was like before Brigitte Bardot. For a U.S. point of reference, think Fire Island, Provincetown, Martha's Vineyard, or Sausalito with a French-Caribbean twist. Nautical and quaint are the watchwords.

But Les Saintes, also known as Iles des Saintes, isn't a fantasy park built to look enchanting. Although tourism is important to the island's economy, most people still make their living from the sea. Les Saintois, as the locals are called, are widely regarded as the best fishermen in the Antilles, and it's this underlying saltiness that keeps the place from being cloyingly sweet.

Christopher Columbus was the first European to sight the islands, November 4, 1493. To commemorate the Feast of All Saints, he named the islands Los Santos. He didn't bother to go ashore, though. The arid, rocky terrain seemed unsuitable for agriculture, and Carib Indians, who had already earned a reputation for fierce resistance, made their presence known.

Europeans didn't seriously attempt to settle the islands until 1648, when the French established a colony to monitor ships passing through the channel between Les Saintes and the more important French colony of Guadeloupe. Carib Indian attacks forced abandonment of the original settlement, but a permanent French presence followed in 1652. Reflecting its strategic significance, Les Saintes became known as the Gibraltar of the West Indies.

In the 17th and 18th centuries, the archipelago witnessed the French and English battle for supremacy of the seas. In 1666, the English took possession of Terre-de-Haut Bay, but within days a terrible storm wiped out their fleet. A week later, on August 15, the French and their Carib Indian allies forced the English to surrender, an event that is still cause for annual celebrations. More than a hundred years later, in 1782, the English had their revenge, decisively defeating the French in the Battle of Les Saintes. Control of the islands didn't revert to France until the signing of the second Treaty of Paris in 1815. To deter any further aggression, the French constructed forts on a couple of the islands, but no violence ensued, and the bastions never fired a shot.

Terre-de-Haut's poor soil precluded the production of sugarcane, a lucrative business on Guadeloupe. Consequently, slaves from Africa were never brought here. The colonists, primarily from the French coastal regions of Brittany, Normandy, and Poitou, turned to the sea for their livelihood. Today their fair-haired, blue-eyed descendants are the primary residents of the island. Motorboats have all but replaced the traditional sailboats (*santois*), and salakos, the bamboo-and-cloth hats that resemble Chinese parasols, are harder and harder to find. You can still see colorful fishing nets drying along the waterfront, though.

Terre-de-Bas, more fertile than its sister isle, is home primarily to descendants of African slaves, who worked the island's sugarcane, cotton, and pepper fields. Coffee grown on this island was served at Napoléon's table.

Frommer's Favorite Les Saintes Experiences

- **Meandering around Fort Napoléon:** The French built this impressive stone fortification after they regained Les Saintes in 1815, and today it houses engaging, detailed exhibits covering the entire history of the islands. (See "On Your Own: Within Walking Distance," below.)
- **Trekking to the top of Le Chameau:** The highest point on Terre-de-Haut, Le Chameau is located in the southern part of the island and offers a tough (though shaded) 30- to 60-minute climb, for which you're rewarded with spectacular views of the entire archipelago, Guadeloupe, and Dominica. (See "On Your Own: Within Walking Distance," below.)
- **Sunbathing on picture-perfect Pompierre beach:** No beach on Terre-de-Haut is nicer than Plage de Pompierre, located only a 15-minute walk from the dock.

Frommer's Ratings: Les Saintes					
	Poor	Fair	Good	Excellent	Outstanding
Overall Experience				✓	
Shore Excursions		✓			
Activities Close to Port					✓
Beaches & Water Sports			✓		
Shopping		✓			
Dining/Bars			✓		

Les Saintes

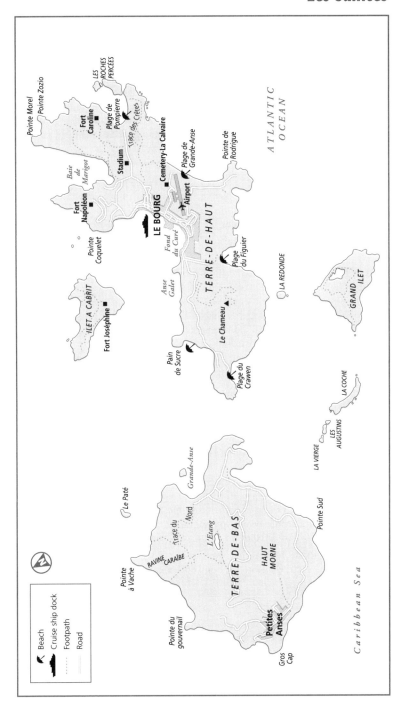

205

Tormented by Love? Have a Pastry

As you disembark from your ship, local women will offer to sell you Les Saintes' signature sweet, tartlets known as *tourments d'amour* (love's torments). Legend has it that young maidens would bake these flaky-crusted, coconut-filled treats to present to their betrotheds as they returned from lengthy fishing expeditions. From time to time, the cruel and heartless sea would claim the life of a beloved, leaving a teary-eyed damsel at the dock with nothing but her pain and pastry. Is it the suffering that makes the tourments d'amour so tasty?

Because the bay is a nature preserve, fishing and anchoring are prohibited. (See "Beaches," below.)

- **Climbing along the Trace des Crêtes:** This trail across the center of Terre-de-Haut offers remarkable views of beaches, cliffs, the island's toylike airport, and neighboring islands. (See "On Your Own: Within Walking Distance," below.)

COMING ASHORE　Cruise ships dock at Le Bourg in Terre-de-Haut. The village has two main streets, both lined with cafes, restaurants, and souvenir shops.

Telephones at the dock require a "télécarte," a prepaid phone card sold at the post office (a 10-minute walk from the dock; take a right) and other outlets marked TÉLÉCARTE EN VENTE ICI. Some phones now accept U.S. calling cards or major credit cards for long-distance calls.

CURRENCY　Les Saintes is part of the larger archipelago of Guadeloupe, an overseas region of France. You'll need **French francs** here. There are 100 centimes to 1 franc. The exchange rate is roughly 6.4 francs to U.S.1 (1 franc = U.S.15¢). An ATM next to the tourism office dispenses them happily.

LANGUAGE　The official language is French. Some islanders speak a local Creole with each other. Few feel comfortable with English, though, so take the opportunity to practice your high-school French. Most everyone is helpful and friendly if you smile and make an effort.

INFORMATION　If you take a right on the main road after you leave the ship, you'll see signs for the tourism office (Office du Tourisme). It's less than a 5-minute walk. Most information is in French, but the maps are helpful even if you don't savvy the lingo. For info before you go, call the **Tourism Board** in in the United States at ☎ **410/286-8310** or log on to the Web site at www.frenchcaribbean.com.

CALLING FROM THE U.S.　When calling Les Saintes from the United States, you need to dial "011" before the numbers listed throughout this section.

GETTING AROUND

If you're reasonably fit, there's no reason you can't walk wherever you want to go. If you're the type who runs 5 miles a day, you can hike up Le Chameau, traipse around Fort Napoléon, head over to Plage de Pompierre, and complete the Trace des Crêtes, with time for a meal or swim before returning to the ship.

BY TAXI　There are a handful of minivans that serve as taxis. Each seats six to eight passengers. You'll find them parked directly in front of the cruise ship dock. Cruise passengers who sign up for shore excursions are transported in similar vans.

BY SCOOTER   Terre-de-Haut is less than 4 miles long and less than 2 miles wide. Aside from tourist vans and the occasional private car, four-wheeled vehicles are rare (at last count, there were less than three dozen). Scooters rule the roads. Scores of them await you just off the dock along Le Bourg's main road. Expect to pay about $36 for a two-seater for the day. A $500 deposit (credit cards accepted) is required.

BY BICYCLE   You can rent bicycles for roughly $15 along Le Bourg's main road. The island is hilly, though. You'd do better to rent a scooter or walk.

SHORE EXCURSIONS
Don't expect any. This is a wander-around-at-your-own pace kind of place.

ON YOUR OWN: WITHIN WALKING DISTANCE
Everything is within walking distance of the dock.

The French built the impressive stone **Fort Napoléon** after they regained Les Saintes in 1815. Sitting atop a hill overlooking the bay, it was completed in 1867. Today it houses engaging, detailed exhibits covering the entire history of the islands—life before Columbus, European expansion into the New World, early French settlements, the Battle of Les Saintes, and the development of the fishing industry. You can wander through barracks, prison cells, and the grounds, which feature an impressive array of cacti and other succulents. If you're lucky, you'll spot iguanas (with names like Victor Hugo and Voltaire), harmless snakes, and turtle doves. Pick up the English-language brochure that describes the vegetation when you purchase your admission ticket (20 francs; about $3). For 5 francs (less than a dollar), you can rent a cassette that provides excellent English commentary as you walk through the museum. The fort is open from 9am till noon, so make it your first destination.

On your way to Fort Napoléon, visit **Jerome Hoff,** a fourth-generation Santois of Alsatian ancestry who paints religious icons in a heartfelt and slightly disturbing style. He has the wild-eyed air of a John the Baptist, but he's a gentle man, retired now, who loves nothing more than talking about his 50 years of singing in the church choir. You can't miss his modest home and studio—they're surrounded by numerous quirky signs that feature colorful saints and passionate prayers. You'll pass **Le Bourg's** stone church on your way to the tourist office. It's humble but worth a moment of your time.

If you're up for some hiking, the **Trace des Crêtes** trail traces the spine of one of Terre-de-Haut's hills just north of the airport and offers remarkable views of beaches, cliffs, and neighboring islands. Although clearly marked, the path is rocky and challenging—you have an advantage if you're part goat. Wear sunscreen and bring water.

Be sure to stop for a few minutes at the **cemetery** next to the airport. You'll notice several graves adorned with conch shells, which signify a sea-related death. On Saturday nights, refrigerator-size speakers are brought in, makeshift food stands are set up, and the cemetery becomes a huge open-air disco. In the same vicinity, **Le Calvaire** is a giant Christ statue at the summit of a hill; numerous steps ascend to great panoramas.

Chameau means camel in French, and with a bit of imagination you can see that **Le Chameau,** the highest point on Terre-de-Haut, looks like the hump of a dromedary. The concrete road to the 1,000-foot summit is off-limits to all motorized vehicles, and, mercifully, it's shaded much of the way. After 30 to 60 minutes of arduous climbing, you're rewarded with spectacular views of the entire archipelago, Guadeloupe, and Dominica. **Tour Vigie,** a military lookout dating from the time of Napoléon, crowns the mountain; unfortunately it's usually locked.

SHOPPING

Little boutiques that sell beachwear, T-shirts, jewelry, and knickknacks line the streets. Stop by **Pascal Foy's Kaz an Nou** Gallery behind the church. You can watch him make Cases Creoles, miniature carved wooden house facades in candy colors. They're becoming collector's items. **Galerie Martine Cotton,** at the foot of the dock, features the work of an artist originally from Brittany who celebrates the natural beauty and fishing traditions of Les Saintes. Beyond the town hall (mairie), **Ultramarine** is a tiny cottage where you can buy unusual dolls, clothes, T-shirts, and handcrafted items from France, Haiti, and Africa. **Galerie Marchande Seaside,** a group of shops around a patio, is just up the street after you turn right from the pier. Art, gifts, antiques, jewelry, lace, beachwear, and ice cream are available.

BEACHES

Beaches with golden sand are tucked away in almost all of the island's coves. Calm, crescent-shaped **Plage de Pompierre** (sometimes spelled Pont Pierre) is shaded by sea-grape bushes and almond and palm trees. A 15-minute walk from the dock, it boasts soft white sand, shade from coconut palms, and quiet seclusion. The gentle water in the cliff-encircled cove is a stunning aquamarine. Because the bay is a nature preserve, fishing and anchoring are prohibited. It's the island's most popular sunbathing spot, so your best bet is to go early or late.

Secluded on the western coast, **Anse Crawen** is the legal nudist beach, which is not to say you won't see nude bodies on other beaches; they're usually found next to the signs that forbid nude bathing—liberté, égalité, nudité! **Grande Anse,** near the airfield, is large, but there's no shade, and the rough surf has a strong undertow. Although swimming is discouraged, the cliffs at either end of the beach and the powerful breakers make for a dramatic seascape. The usually deserted **Figuier,** on the southern coast, has excellent snorkeling.

SPORTS

FISHING Going out to sea with a local fisherman is something you won't soon forget. Most of the local sailors will be delighted to take you out, if you can communicate well enough to negotiate a price. Most fishermen operate from the harbor where cruise ships dock. You'll find most of them to the right of the dock; just follow the waterfront to the fishing boats.

WATER SPORTS For scuba diving and snorkeling, go to **Centre Nautique des Saintes,** at the Plage de la Colline west of town past the market, or **UCPA,** on the other side of Fort Napoléon hill in Marigot Bay. Both also rent sea kayaks and windsurfing equipment.

> ### Insider's Tip
>
> Don't leave anything unattended while swimming at Plage de Pompierre. Savvy goats hide out in the scrub behind the beach, patiently scoping out the action. Once you go into the water, they'll make a beeline for your unattended picnic basket and treat themselves to anything edible. They're especially fond of those tourments d'amour you just bought at the dock. Who's crying now?

GREAT LOCAL RESTAURANTS & BARS

Virtually every restaurant in Terre-de-Haut offers seafood that couldn't be fresher, and many feature Creole dishes. A local favorite is smoked kingfish (*tazard*). **L'Auberge Les Petits Saints aux Anarcadiers** is a hillside veranda restaurant overlooking the bay. The inn, on the Route de Rodrigue, was once the mayor's residence. It boasts a tropical garden and countless antiques. The terrace restaurant at the **Hôtel Bois Joli,** on the island's western tip, offers a view of Pain de Sucre, Les Saintes' petite version of Rio de Janeiro's Sugarloaf Mountain, and is fringed with palm trees. For pasta, pizza, or salad, try **La Saladerie's** seaside terrace on the way to Fort Napoléon. **Le Génois,** yet another waterfront option (100 feet from the dock; turn left), is popular with yachties, who can dock right at the restaurant. The salads here are named after legendary sailboats, while the pizzas pay tribute to local beaches. **Café de la Marine** (on the bay and main street) serves thin-crusted pizzas and seafood. One of the island's best bakeries (*boulangeries*), **Le Fouril de Jimmy,** is on the same square as the town hall, across from the tourist office. If you stop in at the right time, you can get a crusty baguette hot from the oven.

19 Martinique

One of the most exotic French-speaking destinations in the Caribbean, Martinique was the site of a settlement demolished by volcanic activity (St-Pierre, now only a pale shadow of a once-thriving city). Like Guadeloupe and St. Barts, Martinique is legally and culturally French, although many Creole customs and traditions continue to flourish. The Creole cuisine is full of flavor and flair, and the island has lots of tropical charm.

When you arrive at **Fort-de-France,** Martinique's capital, you would never guess that this is one of the most beautiful islands in the Caribbean, but past the port are miles of white-sand beaches along an irregular coastline. Martinique offers some of the most stunning natural wonders in the region.

About 50 miles at its longest and 21 miles at its widest, Martinique is mountainous, especially in the rain-forested northern region where the volcano **Mount Pelée** rises to a height of 4,656 feet. Hibiscus, poinsettias, bougainvillea, and coconut palms grow in lush profusion, and fruit—breadfruit, mangoes, pineapples, avocados, bananas, papayas, and custard apples—fairly drip from the trees.

Frommer's Favorite Martinique Experiences

- **Visiting the Church of Balata:** This colonial-era church was designed as a replica of the Sacred Heart Basilica in Paris.
- **Snorkeling at Anse du Four:** A quaint fishing village with a beautiful sheltered bay, the reef here begins just offshore and overflows with colorful sponge, fish, and other marine animals. The spot is perfect for beginning snorkelers, while deeper sections provide diving opportunities for the more experienced.
- **Touring St-Pierre, site of a volcano eruption:** Mount Pelée erupted in 1902, killing 30,000 people. Today, you can see ruins of the church, the theater, and some other buildings, and tour a volcano museum (see "On Your Own: Beyond Walking Distance," below).
- **Visiting the village of Trois-Ilets:** Tour where Joséphine, the wife of Napoléon I, was born in 1763. There's part of her home, a museum, and a botanical garden (see "On Your Own: Beyond Walking Distance," below).

COMING ASHORE   Cruise ships now dock at the recently built International Pier, which has docking quays for two large-size vessels. As Martinique is a very popular Caribbean port of call, ships also dock at the main harbor, located on the north side of bay, a few minutes' drive from the center of Fort-de-France. Between the two, the International Pier is more convenient as it's adjacent to La Savane, the heart of Fort-de-France and the downtown area. The pier's proximity to La Savane allows passengers to reach the area quickly by foot and avoid a $10 (or more) cab ride or a fairly long, hot walk from the main harbor. Smaller ships also anchor in the bay and ferry passengers to and from shore via tender.

LANGUAGE   French is the official language, but English is spoken in most hotels, restaurants, and tourist facilities.

CURRENCY   The **French franc (F)** is the legal tender here. The exchange rate is 6.29F to U.S.$1 (1F = U.S.16¢). If you're going off on your own or plan to visit the countryside, you might want to exchange some money. A money-exchange service, **Change Caraibes** (☎ **0596/60-28-40**), is at rue Ernest-Deproge 4. It's open Monday to Friday from 7:30am to noon and 2:30 to 4pm.

INFORMATION   The address of the **Office Departmental du Tourisme** (Martinique Tourist Board) is Rue Ernest Deproge, Fort-de-France, 97200 Martinique (☎ **0596/63-79-60**). For info before you go, call the Martinique tourism office in the United States at ☎ **800/391-4909** or log on to the Web site at www. martinique.org.

CALLING FROM THE U.S.   When calling Martinique from the United States, you need to dial "011" before the numbers listed throughout this section.

GETTING AROUND

BY TAXI   Travel by taxi is popular but expensive. Most of the cabs aren't metered, so you have to agree on the price of the ride before getting in. Night fares, in effect from 8pm to 6am, come with a 40% surcharge. For a radio taxi, call ☎ **0596/63-63-62.** If you want to rent a taxi for the day, it's better to have a party of at least three or four people to keep costs down. Taxis are generally available at the cruise pier. Taxi drivers charge approximately U.S.$40 per hour, and passengers should always agree on a fare before stepping into the cab. Check with your ship's port lecturer to determine the current taxi rate. Most taxi drivers do not speak English.

BY BUS   There are collective taxi vans that seat eight and sport A TC sign; they're generally crowded and not the most comfortable. They are widely used by tourists, particularly those who speak some French. The collectives serve Fort-de-France's outlying areas, discharging passengers en route.

BY RENTAL CAR   The scattered nature of Martinique's geography makes renting a car especially tempting. Call **Avis,** rue Ernest-Deproge 4 (☎ **800/331-1212** in the U.S., or 0596/51-17-70); **Budget,** rue Félix-Eboué 12 (☎ **800/527-0700**

Frommer's Ratings: Martinique					
	Poor	Fair	Good	Excellent	Outstanding
Overall Experience				✓	
Shore Excursions			✓		
Activities Close to Port			✓		
Beaches & Water Sports				✓	
Shopping			✓		
Dining/Bars			✓		

Martinique

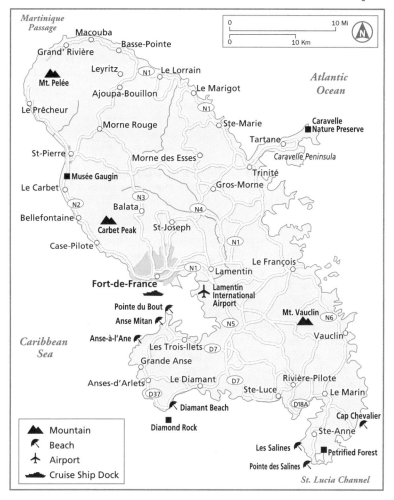

Martinique Passage

Macouba
Basse-Pointe
Grand' Rivière
Leyritz
Le Lorrain
N1
Mt. Pelée
Ajoupa-Bouillon
Le Marigot
Le Prêcheur
N1
Morne Rouge
Ste-Marie

Atlantic
Ocean

Caravelle
Nature Preserve
Tartane
St-Pierre
Morne des Esses
Caravelle Peninsula
Musée Gaugin
Trinité
Le Carbet
Gros-Morne
N2
N3
Bellefontaine
Balata
N4
Carbet Peak
St-Joseph
Case-Pilote
N1
Le François
N1
Lamentin
Fort-de-France
Lamentin
International
Airport
Pointe du Bout
Mt. Vauclin
N6
Anse Mitan
N5
Vauclin
Caribbean
Sea
Anse-à-l'Ane
Les Trois-Ilets
D7
Grande Anse
Anses-d'Arlets
Le Diamant
D7
Rivière-Pilote
D37
Ste-Luce
Le Marin
Diamant Beach
D18A
Cap Chevalier
Diamond Rock
Ste-Anne
Les Salines
Petrified Forest
Pointe des Salines
St. Lucia Channel

- ▲ Mountain
- ⌐ Beach
- ✈ Airport
- ⛴ Cruise Ship Dock

0   10 Mi
0   10 Km

in the U.S., or 0596/63-69-00); or **Hertz,** rue Ernest-Deproge 24, at Lamentin Airport (☎ **800/654-3001** or 0596/60-64-64). Most car-rental rates are about $70 a day, including unlimited mileage. Prices are usually lower if you reserve a car from North America at least two business days before your arrival.

BY FERRY   Take the blue ferry operated by Somatour for $6 per person, round-trip, to reach Pointe du Bout. The schedule is posted at the ferry dock. Pointe du Bout features some of Martinique's best beaches (all beaches here are public). The Méridien Beach Hotel and the Bakoua Resort are good choices as cruise passengers are welcome here and water sports, restaurants, and beach chairs are available.

SHORE EXCURSIONS

Golf at the Country Club of Martinique ($115, 6 hours): The 18-hole, par-71 course here, designed by Robert Trent Jones, is both challenging and picturesque, totaling 6,640 yards of twisting fairways and fast greens. Transportation, greens fees (for 18 holes), and a golf cart are included; lunch is not.

St. Pierre and Rain Forest Drive ($59, 4 hours): Drive through Martinique's lush rain forest and explore the remains of St-Pierre, destroyed by Mount Pelée's eruption in 1902. Passengers stop at the Butterfly Farm, set in a botanical park among the ruins of the island's first sugar plantation, then continue to St-Pierre to visit the ruins. On the drive back to Fort-de-France you'll also visit the Church of Balata, a replica of Paris's Sacred Heart Basilica.

Martinique Snorkeling ($49, 2¹/₂ hours): The reef at Anse du Four offers excellent snorkeling opportunities for experts as well as novices. The reef is filled with marine animals, including French grunts, blackbar soldierfish, and silversides. Equipment is provided, as are instruction, supervision, and transportation.

ON YOUR OWN: WITHIN WALKING DISTANCE

Fort-de-France is a bustling, cosmopolitan town with an unmistakable French air and a little of the flair of the Côte d'Azur—you might say it's a combination of New Orleans and the French Riviera. Narrow streets, pastel buildings, and ornate iron grillwork balconies overflowing with flowers are commonplace. Narrow streets climb up to houses on the steep hills. Almost a third of the island's year-round population of 360,000 lives in the capital, so it's not a small town.

At the center of the town lies **La Savane,** a broad garden with many palms and mangoes bordered by shops and cafes. In this grand square you'll find a statue of Joséphine, "Napoléon's little Creole," carved in white marble by Vital Debray. The statue has seen its share of troubles, having been beheaded in 1991 after Joséphine's role in reinstating slavery in Martinique was brought to light.

A statue in front of the Palais de Justice portrays the island's second main historical figure (after Joséphine), Victor Schoelcher, who worked to free the slaves more than a century ago—you'll see his name a lot in Martinique. The **Bibliothèque Schoelcher** (Schoelcher Library), rue de la Liberté 21, also honors this popular hero. This elaborate structure was first displayed at the Paris Exposition in 1889. The Romanesque portal in red and blue, the Egyptian lotus-petal columns, and even the turquoise tiles were taken apart and reassembled piece by piece here. It's located on the northwest corner of La Savane, and is open Monday to Saturday.

St. Louis Roman Catholic Cathedral, on rue Victor-Schoelcher, was built in 1875. The religious centerpiece of the island, it's an extraordinary iron building, which someone once likened to a Catholic railway station. A number of the island's former governors are buried beneath the choir loft.

Guarding the port is **Fort St-Louis,** built in the Vauban style on a rocky promontory. In addition, **Fort Tartenson** and **Fort Desaix** stand on hills overlooking the port as well.

Musée Départemental de la Martinique, rue de la Liberté 9, is the one place on Martinique that preserves its pre-Columbian past, with relics left from the early Arawak and Carib settlers. The museum faces La Savane and is open Monday to Friday from 8:30am to 5pm, and Saturday from 9am to noon. Admission is 15F ($2.50) for adults, 10F ($1.65) for students, and 5F (85¢) for children.

ON YOUR OWN: BEYOND WALKING DISTANCE

Sacré-Coeur de Balata Cathedral, overlooking Fort-de-France at Balata, is a copy of the basilica looking down from Montmartre in Paris—and this one is just as incongruous, maybe more so. To get there, take the route de la Trace (Route N3). Balata is 6 miles north of Fort-de-France.

A few minutes' taxi ride from Fort-de-France on Route N3, the **Jardin de Balata** (Balata Garden) is a tropical botanical park created by Jean-Phillippe Thoze on land near his grandmother's house. He has restored the house, furnishing it with antiques and engravings depicting life in other days, and with bouquets and baskets of fruit renewed daily. The garden contains flowers, shrubs, and trees. Balata is open daily.

The major goal of all shore excursions, **St-Pierre** was the cultural and economic capital of Martinique until May 7, 1902. That very morning, locals read in their daily newspaper that "Montagne Pelée does not present any more risk to the population than Vesuvius does to the Neapolitans." Then at 8am, the southwest side of **Mount Pelée** exploded in fire and lava. By 8:02am, all but one of St-Pierre's 30,000 inhabitants were dead. St-Pierre never recovered its past splendor. Ruins of the church, the theater, and some other buildings can be seen along the coast.

One of the best ways to get an overview of St-Pierre is to ride a rubber-wheeled "train," the **CV Paris Express,** which departs from the Musée Volcanologique (see below). Tours run Monday to Friday from 10:30am to 1pm and 2:30 to 7pm. In theory, tours depart about once an hour, but actually they leave only when there are enough people to justify a trip.

Musée Volcanologique, rue Victor-Hugo, St-Pierre, was created by American volcanologist Franck Alvard Perret, who turned the museum over to the city in 1933. In pictures and relics excavated from the debris, you can trace the story of what happened to St-Pierre. Dug from the lava is a clock that stopped at the exact moment the volcano erupted. The museum is open daily from 9am to 5pm.

North of Fort-de-France, **Le Carbet** is where Columbus landed in 1502, the first French settlers arrived in 1635, and the painter Paul Gauguin lived for 4 months in 1887 before going on to do his most famous work on Tahiti. Today, the town makes for an idyllic excursion. The landscape looks pretty much as it did when Gauguin depicted the beach in his *Bord de Mer.* **Centre d'Art Musée Paul-Gauguin,** Anse Turin, housed in a five-room building near the beach, commemorates the French artist's stay, with books, prints, letters, and other memorabilia. Of special interest are faïence mosaics made of pieces of colored volcanic rock excavated from nearby archaeological digs. There are also changing exhibits of works by local artists. The museum is open daily from 9am to 5:30pm.

If you're driving yourself around or taking a taxi tour, you will find no better goal than **Hotel Plantation de Leyritz** near Basse-Pointe (☎ **0596/78-53-92**), one of the best restored plantations on Martinique and a good place for an authentic (and expensive) Creole lunch. It occupies the site of a plantation established around 1700 by Bordeaux-born Michel de Leyritz. Sprawled over flat, partially wooded terrain a half-hour's drive from the nearest beach (Anse à Zerot, in Sainte-Marie), it was the site of the "swimming pool summit meeting" in 1974 between Presidents Gerald Ford and Valéry Giscard d'Estaing. Part of the acreage still functions as a working banana plantation. The resort includes 16 acres of tropical gardens. At the core is a stone-sided 18th-century Great House.

Marie-Joséphe-Rose Tascher de la Pagerié was born in the charming little village of **Trois-Ilets** in 1763. As Joséphine, she was to become the wife of Napoléon I and empress of France from 1804 to 1809. She'd been previously married to Alexandre de Beauharnais, who had actually wanted to wed either of her two more attractive sisters. Six years older than Napoléon, she pretended that she'd lost her birth certificate so he wouldn't find out her true age. Although many historians call her ruthless and selfish, she is still revered by some on Martinique as uncommonly gracious. Others, however, blame Napoléon's "reinvention" of slavery on her influence.

To reach her birthplace in Trois-Ilets (pronounced Twaz-ee-*lay*), take a taxi from the pier through lush countryside 20 miles south of Fort-de-France. In la Pagerie, a small museum, **Musée de la Pagerié** (☎ **0596/68-33-06**), sits in the former estate kitchen (the plantation house was destroyed in a hurricane) and displays mementos relating to Joséphine. You'll see a passionate love letter from Napoléon, along with her childhood bed. Here in this room Joséphine gossiped with her slaves and played the guitar. Still remaining are the partially restored ruins of the Pagerié sugar mill and the church where she was christened (the latter is in the village itself). A botanical garden, the **Parc des Floralies,** is adjacent to the golf course Golf de l'Impératrice-Joséphine (see "Sports," below).

Grand'riviere is an old fishing village located on Martinique's isolated north coast. The town is framed by the green cliffs of Mount Pelée, and ringed with palm and breadfruit trees. Many of the town's old customs are still maintained, and visitors can watch village fishermen pull their boats onto the beach as they return with their catches.

Situated on the west side of Route de la Trace (or simply, "The Trace"), a central highland road that winds through Martinique's rain forest, are the **Absalon Mineral Springs.** Near the springs is a hiking trail that begins with a steep climb through the rain forest to a lightly wooded crest along a stream.

Martinique has two casinos located in hotels: the **Casino Trois-Ilets** is in the Le Méridien Hotel on Pointe du Bout, and **La Bateliere** is in La Bateliere Hotel in the Schoelcher region. Both are open from 9pm to 3am.

SHOPPING

Your best buys on Martinique are **French luxury imports,** such as perfumes, fashions, Vuitton luggage, Lalique crystal, or Limoges dinnerware. Sometimes prices are as much as 30% to 40% below those in the United States, but don't count on it. Some luxury goods—including jewelry—are subject to a value-added tax as high as 14%.

If you pay in dollars, store owners supposedly give you a 20% discount; however, their exchange rates are almost invariably far less favorable than those offered by the local banks, so your real savings is only 5% to 11%. Actually, you're better off shopping in the smaller stores, where prices are 8% to 12% less on comparable items, and paying in francs.

The main shopping street in Fort-de-France is **rue Victor-Hugo.** The other two leading shopping streets are **rue Schoelcher** and **rue St-Louis.**

Facing the tourist office and alongside **quai d'Esnambuc** is an open market where you can purchase local handcrafts and souvenirs, many of them tacky. Far more interesting and impressive is the display of vegetables and fruit at the open-air stalls along **rue Isambert.** Gourmet chefs can find all sorts of spices in the open-air markets, and such goodies as tinned pâté or canned quail in the local *supermarchés.*

Shops on every street sell bolts of the ubiquitous, colorful, and inexpensive local fabric, madras. So-called haute couture and resort wear are sold in many boutiques dotting downtown Fort-de-France.

Cadet-Daniel, rue Antoine-Siger 72, competes with **Roger Albert,** rue Victor-Hugo 7-9, to offer the best buys in French china and crystal. Before buying, do some comparison shopping.

Centre des Métieres d'Art, rue Ernest-Deproge, adjacent to the tourist office, is the best and most visible arts-and-crafts store in Martinique. You'll find both valuable and worthless local handmade artifacts for sale, including bamboo, ceramics, painted fabrics, and patchwork quilts suitable for hanging. The owner of **La Belle Matadore,**

Immeuble Vermeil-Marina, Pointe du Bout (midway between the La Pagerié Hôtel and the Méridien Hotel), has carefully researched the history and traditions of the island's jewelry, and virtually all the merchandise sold here derives from models developed during slave days by the *matadores* (prostitutes), midwives, and slaves.

Martinique rum is considered by aficionados to be the world's finest (in *A Moveable Feast*, Hemingway lauded it as the perfect antidote to a rainy day), and **La Case à Rhum,** in the Galerie Marchande, rue de la Liberté 5, offers all the brands. They offer samples in small cups to prospective buyers.

Set on the Route de Lamentin, midway between Fort-de-France and the Lamentin airport, **La Galleria** is, by anyone's estimate, the most upscale and elegant shopping complex on Martinique. On the premises are more than 60 different vendors, from France and the Caribbean. There's also a handful of cafes and restaurants, as well as an outlet or two selling the pastries and sweets for which Martinique is known.

BEACHES

The beaches south of Fort-de-France are white and sandy, but those to the north are mostly gray sand. Outstanding in the south is the 1^1/$_2$-mile **Plage des Salines,** near Ste-Anne, with palm trees and a long stretch of white sand, and the 2^1/$_2$-mile **Diamant,** with the landmark Diamond Rock offshore. The water here is pretty rough, but the beach offers a terrific view of the 600-foot high Diamond Rock, which the British fortified and used as a battlement in their 1804 fight with the French for control of the island. Swimming on the Atlantic coast is for experts only, except at **Cap Chevalier** and **Presqu'ile de la Caravelle Nature Preserve.**

Pointe du Bout is a narrow peninsula across the bay from Fort-de-France, accessible by ferry (see "Getting Around," above). It's the most lavish resort area of Martinique, with at least four of the island's largest hotels, an impressive marina, a golf course, about a dozen tennis courts, swimming pools, facilities for horseback riding and all kinds of water sports, a handful of restaurants, a gambling casino, and boutiques. The area's clean white-sand beaches were created by developers. The sandy beaches to the south at **Anse Mitan,** however, have always been there welcoming visitors, including many snorkelers.

SPORTS

GOLF   The famous golf-course designer Robert Trent Jones, Sr., visited Martinique and left behind the 18-hole **Golf de l'Impératrice-Joséphine** at Trois-Ilets (☎ **0596/68-32-81**), a 5-minute, 1-mile taxi ride from the leading resort area of Pointe du Bout and about 18 miles from Fort-de-France. The only golf course on Martinique, it unfolds its greens from the birthplace of Empress Joséphine, across rolling hills with scenic vistas down to the sea. There's a pro shop, a bar, a restaurant, and three tennis courts.

HIKING   Personnel of the **Parc Naturel Régional de la Martinique** organize inexpensive guided excursions for small groups of tourists year-round. Contact them at the Excollège Agricole de Tivoli, B.P. 437, 97200 Fort-de-France (☎ **0596/64-42-59**). This should be done 2 or 3 days before your ship arrives in Martinique. **Presqu'ile de la Caravelle Nature Preserve,** a well-protected peninsula jutting into the Atlantic Ocean, has safe beaches and well-marked trails through tropical wetlands to the ruins of historic Château Debuc.

HORSEBACK RIDING   **Ranch Jack,** Morne Habitué, Trois-Ilets (☎ **0596/68-37-69**), offers morning horseback rides for both experienced and novice riders.

The daily promenades pass through the beaches and fields of Martinique, and the leaders offer a running commentary of the history, fauna, and botany of the island. Call Ranch Jack for transportation arrangements to and from the cruise dock.

SCUBA DIVING & SNORKELING   Divers come here to explore the Diamond Rock caves and walls and the ships sunk at St-Pierre during the 1902 volcanic eruption. Snorkeling equipment is also available at dive centers. Across the bay from Fort-de-France, in the Hotel Méridien, **Espace Plongée** (☎ **0596/66-00-00**) is a major scuba center and the best in Pointe du Bout. They welcome anyone who shows up. Dive trips leave from the Méridien Hotel's pier. Cruise ship passengers should opt for the morning dives, as afternoon dives may not allow enough time to get back to the ship. The dive shop on the Méridien's beach stocks everything from weight belts and tanks to partial wet suits and underwater cameras.

GREAT LOCAL RESTAURANTS & BARS

A favorite **local beer** is Lorraine; a couple favorite **local rums** are Clement and Saint Jame's.

IN FORT-DE-FRANCE   A La Bonne Viande, 11 rue Lamartine (☎ **0596/ 63-56-93**), is an atmospheric, charming restaurant in the center of town, serving specialties that include tournedos Rossini with foie gras and T-bones with béarnaise sauce. **Le Planteur,** 1 rue de la Liberté, on the southern edge of La Savane, right in the heart of town (☎ **0596/63-17-45**), serves fresh and flavorful menu items such as cassoulet of minced conch. **La Lafayette,** 5 rue de la Liberte (☎ **0596/63-24-09**), is located in downtown Fort-de-France in the hotel of the same name. The flower-laden restaurant features French-Creole selections and a view of La Savane and the bay.

AT POINTE DU BOUT   Pignon sur Mer, Anse-à-l'Ane, a 12-minute drive from Pointe du Bout (☎ **0596/68-38-37**), is a simple, unpretentious Creole restaurant serving island-inspired dishes that might include *delices du Pignon,* a platter of shellfish, or whatever grilled fish or shellfish was hauled in that day. **La Villa Créole,** Anse Mitan (☎ **0596/66-05-53**), is a 3- or 4-minute drive from the hotels of Pointe du Bout and serves reasonably priced set-price menus that offer a selection of such staples as *accras de morue* (beignets of codfish), *boudin creole* (blood sausage), and *un féroce* (a local form of pâté concocted from fresh avocados, pulverized codfish, and manioc flour). **La Belle Epoque,** Route de Didier (☎ **0596/ 64-01-09**), is a small, elegant eatery located on a terrace of a late 19th-century house. The restaurant serves light, creative dishes. **Diamant Creole,** 7 boulevard de Verdun, (☎ **0596/73-18-25**), is a small red-and-white house built in 1927 with a dance studio on the ground floor and a seven-table restaurant upstairs. It serves classic Creole dishes with an updated flair, plus local favorites like soups and vegetables.

ON THE NORTH COAST: TWO "MAMA" CHEFS   Like Guadeloupe, Martinique is famous for its female Creole chefs. If you opted for a taxi tour or a rented car, you can seek out two of the best of these Martinique "mamas" on the north coast.

Chez Mally Edjam, Rte. de la Côte Atlantique, Basse-Pointe, 36 miles from Fort-de-France (☎ **0596/78-51-18**), operates from a modest house beside the main road in the center of town. Grandmotherly Mally Edjam (assisted to an ever-increasing degree by her younger, France-born friend, Martine Hugé) is usually busy in the kitchen turning out her Creole delicacies, like stuffed land crab with a hot seasoning and a classic *colombo de porc* (the Creole version of pork curry).

Yva Chez Vava, Boulevard de Gaulle, west of Basse-Pointe (☎ **0596/55-72-72**), is a combination private home and restaurant, representing the hard labor of three generations of Creole women. It was established in 1979 by a well-remembered, long-departed matron, Vava, whose daughter, Yva, is now assisted by her own daughter, Rosy. Local family recipes are the mainstay of this modest bistro, infused with a simple country-inn style. A la carte menu items include Creole soup, lobster, and various *colombos* or curries. Local delicacies have changed little since the days of Joséphine and her sugar fortune, and include *z'habitants* (crayfish), *vivaneau* (red snapper), *tazard* (kingfish), and *accras de morue* (cod fritters).

20 The Panama Canal

More and more ships are including partial transits of the Panama Canal in their western Caribbean itineraries, plus visits to the area around the Canal. Transiting the Canal is spectacular in itself, but on typical itineraries in this region you get more: on the eastern side, visits to the rain forests of Costa Rica, the Mayan ruins of Guatemala, and the Kuna culture of the San Blas Islands; on the western side (should your ship make a full transit), the beauty of the Mexican Riviera.

The Panama Canal is an awesome feat of engineering and human effort. Construction began in 1880 and wasn't completed until 1914, at the expense of thousands of lives, and the vast majority of the original structure and equipment is still in use. Transiting the canal, which links the Atlantic Ocean with the Pacific, is a thrill for anyone even vaguely interested in engineering or history.

Transiting the canal takes 1 day, generally about 8 hours from start to finish, and it's a fascinating procedure (it often costs ships about $100,000 to pass through; the fee is based on a ship's weight). Your ship will line up in the morning, mostly with cargo ships, to await its turn through the canal. The route is about 50 miles long and includes passage through three main locks, which, through gravity alone, raise ships over Central America and down again on the other side. Between the locks, ships pass through artificially created lakes like the massive **Gatun Lake,** 85 feet above sea level.

While transiting, your ship will feature a running narration of history and facts about the canal by an expert onboard for the day.

Cruises that include a canal crossing are generally 10 to 14 nights long, with popular routes between Florida and Acapulco, visiting a handful of Caribbean islands along the way. A few ports in Central America are also visited, including Panama's

Canal Changes Hands

In compliance with a treaty signed between the United States and Panama in 1977, at the stroke of midnight on December 31, 1999, canal operations were passed from U.S. into Panamanian hands. I'm glad to report that the transition went smoothly. In fact, Panama is pursuing a handful of development projects to keep the canal a major tourism draw. Not only are they intent on hosting as many ships as possible, Panama tourism officials are bent on adding all kinds of additional attractions to lure cruisers. Take the planned Colon Zoo, for example. It's a $45-million private initiative that is to include a duty-free mall, dining and amusements, a 150-room Radisson hotel, and cruise berths. Some dozen shore excursions offered will focus on local history, culture, and nature.

Panama Canal Area

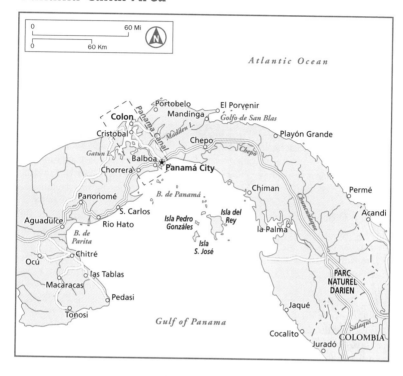

San Blas Islands, Costa Rica's Puerto Caldera, and Guatemala's Puerto Quetzal, in addition to other ports along the coast of Mexico.

SHIPS TRANSITING THE PANAMA CANAL For 2001, ships will be sailing itineraries that include transits of the Panama Canal: American Canadian Caribbean's *Grande Caribe,* Carnival's *Jubilee,* Celebrity's *Zenith,* Crystal's *Harmony* and *Symphony,* Cunard's *QE2,* Holland America's *Maasdam* and *Nieuw Amsterdam,* Mediterranean Shipping's *Melody,* Norwegian's *Norwegian Majesty,* Princess's *Crown Princess* and *Sun Princess,* Radisson's *Radisson Diamond* and *Seven Seas Navigator,* Regal's *Regal Empress,* Royal Caribbean's *Vision of the Seas,* Royal Olympic's *Stella Solaris,* and Seabourn's *Seabourn Legend* and *Seabourn Pride.* See the cruise line notes in chapter 1 for details.

PORTS ALONG THE CANAL ROUTE

The **San Blas Islands** are a beautiful archipelago and home to the Kuna Indians, whose women are well known for their colorful, hand-embroidered stitching. If you get a chance to go ashore, the tiny women, dressed in their traditional *molas* (brightly and intricately embroidered blouses), sell all manner of embroidered molas in square blocks and strips (and don't underestimate their chutzpah—these gals will only bargain so far). The molas make great pillow covers or wall hangings, and cost about $5 to $10 each. When your ship anchors offshore at the islands, be prepared for throngs of Kunas to emerge from the far-off distance, paddling their dugout canoes (a few have motors) up to the ship, where they will spend the entire day calling for money or anything else ship passengers toss overboard. The Kuna seem to enjoy diving overboard to retrieve fruit or coins thrown to them, but of course, it's a sad sight, too, watching entire families so desperate and needy. (Makes you feel damn guilty for rolling in on that fancy cruise ship of yours.)

In **Costa Rica,** many ships call at Puerto Caldera on the Pacific side or Puerto Limón on the Atlantic side. While there's nothing to see from either cargo port, both are great jumping-off points for tours that all visiting ships offer of the country's lush, beautiful rain forests, which are alive with some 850 species of birds, 200 species of mammals, 9,000 species of flowering plants, and about 35,000 species of insects. After a scenic bus ride, tours will take you on a nature walk through the forest.

In **Guatemala,** most Panama Canal–bound ships call at Puerto Quetzal, on the Pacific coast; a few may call at Santo Tomas on the Caribbean side. Both are used as gateways to Guatemala's spectacular Mayan ruins at Tikal. They're the country's most famous attractions and considered the most spectacular yet discovered anywhere in the world, with over 3,000 temples, pyramids, and other buildings of the ancient civilization nestled in thick jungle. Much of it is still uncovered. The setting is surreal. Some of the ruins date as far back as A.D. 300. Excursions here are neither cheap nor easy, but the journey is well worth the effort. A tour involves buses, walking, and a 1-hour flight; expect to pay about $350-plus. Excursions to the less-spectacular Mayan sites in Honduras are also offered from Puerto Quetzal, as are several overland tours of Guatemala's interior.

21 Puerto Rico

When most people think of Puerto Rico, they think of Old San Juan, that beautiful old cobblestoned city stretched over a hilly peninsula surrounded by the sea. Old San Juan is, of course, the main tourist haunt, but there is more to the island. The Commonwealth of Puerto Rico, under the jurisdiction of the United States, is home to over three million Spanish-speaking people. It's the most urbanized island of the Caribbean, with lots of traffic, glittering casinos, its share of crime, and a more-or-less comfortable mix of Latin culture with imports from the U.S. mainland. The island's interior is filled with ancient volcanic mountains and jungly tropical forests, and its coastline is ringed with sandy beaches. In addition to the main island, the Commonwealth includes a trio of small offshore islands: Culebra, Mona, and Vieques. Vieques has the most tourist facilities of the three.

San Juan, Puerto Rico's 16th-century capital, is the Caribbean's most historic port, with some 500 years of history reflected in its restored Spanish colonial architecture. Its shopping is topped by St. Thomas and Sint Maarten, but overall its historic sights, attractions, gambling, and diversions make it number-one in the Caribbean. You'll find some of the Caribbean's best restaurants and hotels here, as well, and it even has a glitzy beach strip, **the Condado.**

The Port of San Juan is the busiest ocean terminal in the West Indies, and second only to Miami for the North America cruise trade. Metropolitan San Juan includes the old walled city and the city center, which contains the Capitol building, on San Juan Island; Santurce, on a larger peninsula, reached by causeway bridges from San Juan Island (the lagoon-front section here is called Miramar); Condado, the narrow peninsula that stretches from San Juan Island to Santurce; Hato Rey, the business center; Río Piedras, site of the University of Puerto Rico; and Bayamón, an industrial and residential quarter.

The Condado strip of beachfront hotels, restaurants, casinos, and nightclubs is separated from Miramar by a lagoon. Isla Verde, another resort area, is near the airport, which is separated from the rest of San Juan by an isthmus.

Frommer's Favorite San Juan Experiences
- **Taking a walking tour of 500-year-old Old San Juan:** Its cobblestoned, narrow streets and Spanish colonial architecture are stunning (see "Shore Excursions," and "On Your Own: A Walking Tour of Old San Juan," below).
- **Taking a hike through El Yunque rain forest:** The forest is home to 240 species of tropical trees, flowers, and wildlife, including millions of tiny coqui tree frogs (see "Shore Excursions," below).

COMING ASHORE   Cruise ships dock on the historic south shore of Old San Juan, within the sheltered channel that was hotly contested by European powers during the island's early colonial days. Each of the piers is within a relatively short walk of the Plaza de la Marina, the Wyndham Hotel, Old San Juan's main bus station, and most of the historic and commercial treasures of Old San Juan. During periods of heavy volume—usually Saturday and Sunday in midwinter, when as many as 10 cruise ships might dock in San Juan on the same day—additional, less convenient piers are activated. They include the Frontier Pier, at the western edge of the Condado, near the Caribe Hilton Hotel, and the Pan American Dock, in Isla Grande, across the San Antonio Channel from Old San Juan. Unless they're up for a long walk, passengers berthing at either of these docks need some kind of motorized transit (usually a taxi or a van supplied by the cruise line as part of the shore-excursion program) to get to the Old Town. For information about the port, contact the **Port of San Juan,** P.O. 362829, San Juan, PR 00936-2829 (☎ **787/723-2260**).

There are **phones** for credit-card calls just outside of the Tourism Information Center at Paseo de la Princesa near Pier 1 in Old San Juan.

CURRENCY   The **U.S. dollar** is the coin of the realm. Canadian currency is accepted by some big hotels in San Juan, but reluctantly.

LANGUAGE   Most people in the tourist industry speak English, although Spanish is the native tongue.

INFORMATION   For additional advice and maps, contact the **Tourist Information Center at La Casita,** Paseo de la Princesa near Pier 1 in Old San Juan (☎ **787/721-2400**). For info before you go, contact the tourism board at ☎ **800/223-6530** or log on to the Web site at www.prtourism.com.

CALLING FROM THE U.S.   When calling Puerto Rico from the United States, you need to dial only a "1" before the numbers listed throughout this section.

GETTING AROUND
Driving is a hassle in congested San Juan. You can walk most of the Old Town on foot or take a free trolley. You can also take buses or taxis to the beaches in the Condado.

Frommer's Ratings: San Juan					
	Poor	Fair	Good	Excellent	Outstanding
Overall Experience					✓
Shore Excursions		✓			
Activities Close to Port					✓
Beaches & Water Sports			✓		
Shopping				✓	
Dining/Bars			✓		

Puerto Rico

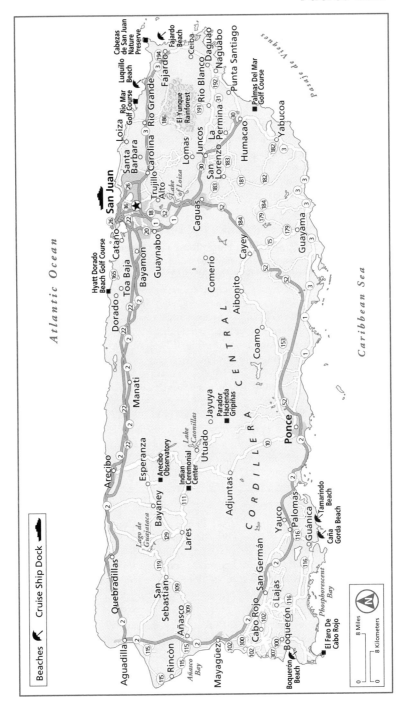

Beaches Cruise Ship Dock

Atlantic Ocean

Caribbean Sea

Pasaje de Vieques

CORDILLERA CENTRAL

San Juan

Ponce

San Juan as a Port of Embarkation

Since a number of cruise ships use San Juan as their port of embarkation and debarkation, you might have the opportunity to spend a night or two here before or after your cruise. If so, here's some information on planning your trip and some picks of the best hotels and nightlife.

GETTING TO SAN JUAN & THE PORT

Visitors from overseas arrive at **Luis Muñoz Marín International Airport** (☎ **787/791-1014**), situated on the city's easternmost side. It's about $7^1/_2$ miles from the port. Taxis will be lined up outside the airport. The fixed fare is about $8 to Isla Verde, $12 to Condado, and $16 to Old San Juan (including the port). The ride to the port takes about 30 minutes, depending on traffic conditions.

ACCOMMODATIONS

NEAR THE DOCKS   **Gran Hotel El Convento,** 100 Cristo St. (☎ 800/ 468-2779 or 787/723-9020), is Puerto Rico's most famous hotel; its third to fifth floors offer large rooms, many with views of the Old Town. **Wyndham Old San Juan Hotel & Casino,** 100 Brumbaugh St. (☎ 800/996-3426 or 787/ 721-5100), is right on the waterfront and the cruise docks. Bedrooms are tasteful and comfortable, and Old San Juan is at your doorstep. **Gallery Inn at Galería San Juan,** Calle Norzagaray 204-206 (☎ 787/722-1808), is a former 1700s Spanish aristocrat's home set on a hilltop with a sweeping view of the sea. It has comfortable and tasteful rooms (although lacking air-conditioning). There's also an on-site artists' studio here. The **Caribe Hilton,** Calle Los Rosales, Puerto de Tierra (☎ 800/HILTONS in the U.S. or Canada, or 787/721-0303), is near the old Fort San Jerónimo. You can walk to the 16th-century fort or spend the day on a tour of Old San Juan, and then come back and enjoy the beach and swimming cove. **Radisson Normandie,** Avenida Muñoz-Rivera at the corner of Calle Los Rosales (☎ 800/333-3333 in the U.S., or 787/729-2929) was built in the shape of the famous French ocean liner *Normandie,* and lies only 5 minutes from Old San Juan in a beachside setting.

IN CONDADO   In this area filled with high-rise hotels, restaurants, and nightclubs, your best bets are the ✪ **Condado Plaza Hotel & Casino,** 999 Ashford

BY TAXI   Taxis are operated by the **Public Service Commission** (PSC), and are metered in San Juan—or should be. The initial charge is $1, plus 10¢ for each one-tenth of a mile and 50¢ for every suitcase. A minimum fare is $3. Taxi companies are listed in the yellow pages of the phone book under "Taxis," or you can call the PSC (☎ **787/756-1919**) to request information or report any irregularities.

BY TROLLEY   When you tire of walking around Old San Juan, you can board one of its free trolleys. Departure points are the Marina and La Puntilla, but you can get on any place along the route. Relax and enjoy the sights as the trolleys rumble through the old, narrow streets.

BY BUS   The Metropolitan Bus Authority operates buses in the greater San Juan area. Bus stops are marked by upright metal signs or yellow posts reading PARADA. Bus terminals in San Juan are in the dock area and at Plaza de Colón. A typical fare is about 25¢ to 50¢. For route and schedule information, call ☎ **787/ 250-6064.**

Ave. (☎ 800/468-8588 in the U.S., or 787/721-1000), and the **San Juan Marriott Resort & Stellaris Casino,** 1309 Ashford Ave. (☎ 800/981-8546 in the U.S., or 787/722-7000). **Aleli by the Sea,** 1125 Sea View St. (☎ 787/725-5313), is a simple but charming small hotel by the sea. Rooms are nothing fancy, but they're clean and the sound of the surf just outside your window and the reasonable rates are big draws (try half what the big hotels charge; an ocean-view room goes for $90 a night).

IN ISLA VERDE   Closer to the airport than the other sections of San Juan, and right on the beach, your best bets are ✪ **El San Juan Hotel & Casino,** 6063 Isla Verde Ave. (☎ 800/468-2818 in the U.S., or 787/791-1000), **The Ritz-Carlton,** 6961 State Rd., no. 187 on Isla Verde (☎ 800/241-3333 in the U.S., or 787/253-1700), and **San Juan Grand Beach Hotel & Casino,** 187 Isla Verde Ave. (☎ 800/443-2009 in the U.S., or 787/791-6100).

SAN JUAN AFTER DARK

If you want to dance the night away, the **Babylon,** in the El San Juan Hotel & Casino, 6063 Isla Verde Ave. (☎ 787/791-1000), attracts a rich and beautiful crowd, as well as a gaggle of onlookers. For action in the Old Town, head for **Laser,** Calle del Cruz 251 (☎ 787/725-7581), near the corner of Calle Fortaleza. Salsa and merengue are often featured.

On the Condado, **Millennium,** in the Condado Plaza Hotel, 999 Ashford Ave. (☎ 787/722-1900), also draws disco devotees. It has a cigar bar on the side. If you just want a drink, **Fiesta Bar,** in the Condado Plaza Hotel & Casino, 999 Ashford Ave. (☎ 787/721-1000), attracts locals and visitors. **Palm Court,** in the El San Juan Hotel & Casino, 6063 Isla Verde Ave. (☎ 787/791-1000), is the most beautiful bar and dance spot on the island.

Stylish and charming, **Violeta's,** Calle Fortaleza 56 (☎ 787/723-6804), occupies the ground floor of a 200-year-old beamed house 2 blocks from the landmark Gran Hotel El Convento (see above). An open courtyard in back provides additional seating. Margaritas are the drink of choice.

BY RENTAL CAR   The major car-rental companies include **Avis** (☎ 800/331-1212 or 787/791-2500), **Budget** (☎ 800/527-0700 or 787/791-3685), and **Hertz** (☎ 800/654-3001 or 787/791-0840).

SHORE EXCURSIONS

In Old San Juan, there's really no need to bother with organized shore excursions, since it's easy enough to get around on your own. But if you prefer a guide to narrate or want to explore the island's El Yunque rain forest, an organized tour is a good idea.

San Juan City and Shopping Tour ($22, 3 hours): In Old San Juan you'll visit the massive El Morro Fortress (built in 1539) and a few other sites. Then after some shopping, move on to the modern city of San Juan.

Juan Carlos and His Flamenco Rumba Show ($43, 1 hour): At the Club Tropicoro at the El San Juan Hotel and Casino, enjoy dance performances of the mambo, rumba, samba, conga, and flamenco.

El Yunque Rain Forest and Bacardi Rum Tour ($32, 4–5 hours): By minibus, travel along the northeastern part of the island and take a short hike in the 28,000-acre El Yunque rain forest, home to hundreds of species of plants and animals. Afterward, tour the Bacardi Rum Plant, which produces something on the order of 100,000 gallons of the stuff daily. (And yes, you get free samples.)

TOURING THROUGH LOCAL OPERATORS

Rain Forest and Bacardi Rum Tour: If your ship doesn't offer it, **Castillo Watersports & Tours,** 2413 Calle Laurel, Punta La Marias, Santurce (☎ **787/791-6195** or 787/726-5752), has tours departing in the morning.

ON YOUR OWN: A WALKING TOUR OF OLD SAN JUAN

The streets are narrow and teeming with traffic, but a walking tour through Old San Juan (in Spanish, *El Viejo San Juan*) is a stroll through 5 centuries of history. The throngs thin out by late afternoon, so you might want to linger to enjoy the charming beauty of Old San Juan sans crowds. Within this 7-square-block landmark area in the city's westernmost part are many of Puerto Rico's chief historic attractions.

Begin your walk near the post office, amid the taxis, buses, and urban congestion of:

1. **Plaza de la Marina,** a sloping, many-angled plaza situated at the eastern edge of one of San Juan's showcase promenades—*El Paseo de la Princesa.*

Walk westward along paseo de la Princesa, past heroic statues and manicured trees, until you reach:

2. **La Princesa,** the gray-and-white building on your right, which for centuries served as one of the most feared prisons in the Caribbean. Today it houses a museum and the offices of the Puerto Rico Tourism Company.

Continue walking westward to the base of the heroic fountain near the edge of the sea. Turn to your right and follow the seaside promenade as it parallels the edge of the:

3. **City Walls,** once part of one of the most impregnable fortresses in the New World and even today an engineering marvel. At the top of the walls you'll see balconied buildings that have served for centuries as hospitals and residences of the island's governors.

Continue walking between the sea and the base of the city walls until the walkway goes through the walls at the (*Note:* At press time, most of the seaside promenade here was closed for constuction, but should reopen by mid-2001. Rejoin the walking tour at the San Juan Gate.):

4. **San Juan Gate,** at Calle San Juan and Recinto del Oeste. This is actually more of a tunnel than a gate. Now that you're inside the once-dreaded fortification, turn immediately right and walk uphill along Calle Recinto del Oeste. The wrought-iron gates at the street's end lead to:

5. **La Fortaleza and Mansion Ejecutiva,** the centuries-old residence of the Puerto Rican governor, located on Calle La Fortaleza.

Now retrace your steps along Calle Recinto del Oeste, walking first downhill and then uphill for about a block until you reach a street called las Monjas. Fork left until you see a panoramic view and a contemporary statue marking the center of:

6. **Plazuela de la Rogativa,** the small plaza of the religious procession.

Continue your promenade westward, passing between a pair of urn-capped gateposts. You'll be walking parallel to the city walls. The boulevard will fork

San Juan at a Glance

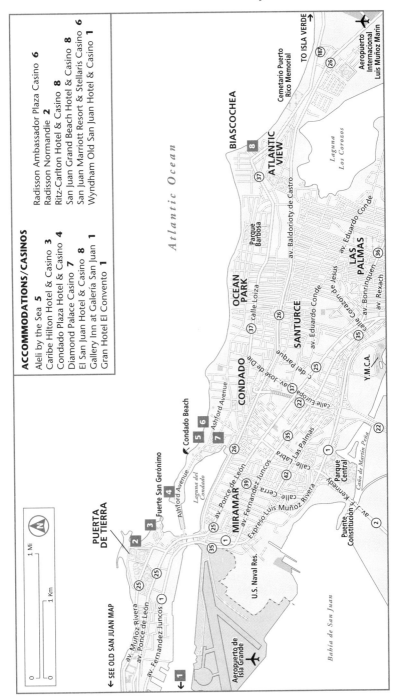

ACCOMMODATIONS/CASINOS

Aleli by the Sea **5**
Caribe Hilton Hotel & Casino **3**
Condado Plaza Hotel & Casino **4**
Diamond Palace Casino **7**
El San Juan Hotel & Casino **8**
Gallery Inn at Galería San Juan **1**
Gran Hotel El Convento **1**

Radisson Ambassador Plaza Casino **6**
Radisson Normandie **2**
Ritz-Carlton Hotel & Casino **8**
San Juan Grand Beach Hotel & Casino **8**
San Juan Marriott Resort & Stellaris Casino **6**
Wyndham Old San Juan Hotel & Casino **1**

(bear to the right); continue climbing the steeply inclined cobble-covered ramp to its top. The views from this part of the walk are awesome. Walk westward across the field toward the neoclassical gateway of a fortress believed impregnable for centuries, the:

7. **Castillo de San Felipe del Morro ("El Morro"),** whose treasury and strategic position were the envy of both Europe and the Caribbean. Here, Spanish Puerto Rico struggled to defend itself against the navies of Great Britain, France, and Holland, as well as the hundreds of pirate ships that wreaked havoc throughout the colonial Caribbean. First built in 1540 and added to in 1787, the fortress walls were designed as part of a network of defenses that made San Juan *La Ciudad Murada* (the Walled City). The fortress sits grandly on a gently sloping, grassy hill, offering some excellent photo ops.

After your visit, with El Morro behind you, retrace your steps through the sunlit, treeless field to the point you stood at when you first sighted the fortress. Walk down the Calle del Morro past the:

8. **Antiguo Manicomio Insular,** originally built in 1854 as an insane asylum. It now houses the Puerto Rican Academy of Fine Arts. Further on, the stately neoclassical building (painted buff with fern-green trim) on your right is the:

9. **Asilo de Beneficencia** ("Home for the Poor"), which dates from the 1840s.

Continue walking uphill to the small, formal, sloping plaza at the street's top. On the righthand side, within a trio of buildings, is:

10. **La Casa Blanca,** built by the son-in-law of Juan Ponce de León to be the great explorer's island home (he never actually lived here, though). Today, this "White House" accommodates a small museum and has beautiful gardens.

Exit by the compound's front entrance and walk downhill, retracing your steps for a half block, and then head toward the massive and monumental tangerine-colored building on your right, the:

11. **Cuartel de Ballajá.** The military barracks of Ballajá evokes the most austere and massive monasteries of Old Spain. On the building's second floor is the **Museum of the Americas.**

After your visit, exit through the barracks's surprisingly narrow back (eastern) door, where you'll immediately spot one of the most dramatic modern plazas in Puerto Rico, the:

12. **Plaza del Quinto Centenario,** a terraced tribute to the European colonization of the New World, and one of the most elaborate and symbolic formal piazzas in Puerto Rico.

Now, walk a short block to the southeast to reach the ancient borders of the:

13. **Plaza de San José,** dominated by a heroic statue of Juan Ponce de León, cast from English cannon captured during a naval battle in 1797. Around the square's periphery are three important sites: the **Museo de Pablo Casals,** where exhibits honor the life and work of the Spanish-born cellist who adopted Puerto Rico as his final home; **Casa de los Contrafuertes** (House of the Buttresses); and **Iglesia de San José,** where the conquistador's coat-of-arms hangs above the altar. Established by the Dominicans in 1523, this church is one of the oldest places of Christian worship in the New World.

Exiting from the plaza's southwestern corner, walk downhill along one of the capital's oldest and best-known streets, **Calle del Cristo.** Two blocks later, at the corner of las Monjas, is:

14. **El Convento,** originally a convent in the 17th century, but now for many decades one of the few hotels in the old city. Recently restored, it's better than

Old San Juan Walking Tour

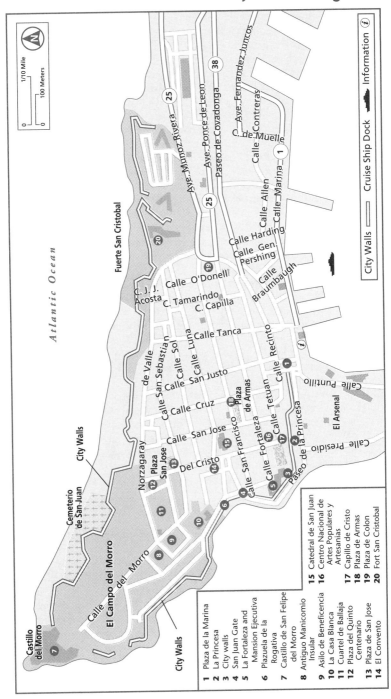

Atlantic Ocean

Castillo del Morro

Cemeterio de San-Juan

El Campo del Morro

Calle del Morro

Fuerte San Cristobal

City Walls

Norzagaray

Plaza San Jose

Del Cristo

Calle de Valle

Calle San Sebastian

Calle Sol

Calle Luna

Calle Tanca

C. J. J. Acosta

Calle O'Donell

C. Tamarindo

C. Capilla

Calle San Justo

Calle Cruz

Plaza de Armas

Calle San Jose

Calle San Francisco

Calle Fortaleza

Calle Tetuan

Calle de la Princesa

Paseo de la Princesa

Calle Recinto

Calle Harding

Calle Gen. Pershing

Calle Braumbaugh

Calle Allen

Calle Marina

Calle Harding

Ave. Munoz Rivera

Ave. Ponce de Leon

Paseo de Covadonga

Ave. Fernandez Juncos

C. de Muelle

Calle Contreras

El Arsenal

Calle Puntillo

Calle Presidio

City Walls

1 Plaza de la Marina
2 La Princesa
3 City walls
4 San Juan Gate
5 La Fortaleza and Mansion Ejecutiva
6 Plazuela de la Rogativa
7 Castillo de San Felipe del Morro
8 Antiguo Manicomio Insular
9 Asilo de Beneficencia
10 La Casa Blanca
11 Cuartel de Ballaja
12 Plaza del Quinto Centenario
13 Plaza de San Jose
14 El Convento

15 Catedral de San Juan
16 Centro Nacional de Artes Populares y Artesanias
17 Capillo de Cristo
18 Plaza de Armas
19 Plaza de Colon
20 Fort San Cristobal

City Walls —— Cruise Ship Dock —— Information ⓘ

227

ever. Across the street from El Convento lies the island's most famous church and spiritual centerpiece, the:

15. **Catedral de San Juan.** Now walk 2 more blocks southward along Calle del Cristo, through one of the most attractive shopping districts in the Caribbean. After passing Calle La Fortaleza, look on your left for the:

16. **Centro Nacional de Artes Populares y Artesanias,** a popular arts-and-crafts center run by the Institute of Puerto Rican Culture.

Continue to the southernmost tip of Calle del Cristo (just a few steps away) to the wrought-iron gates that surround a chapel no bigger than a newspaper kiosk, the:

17. **Capilla de Cristo.** Its silver altar is dedicated to the "Christ of Miracles."

Retrace your steps about a block along the Calle del Cristo, walking north. Turn right along Calle La Fortaleza. One block later, go left onto Calle de San José, which leads to the site of the capital's most symmetrical and beautiful square, the:

18. **Plaza de Armas,** a broad and open plaza designed along Iberian lines during the 19th century. Two important buildings flanking this square are the neoclassic **Intendencia** (which houses certain offices of the U.S. State Department) and **San Juan's City Hall** (Alcaldía).

You can either end your tour here, or forge ahead to two important sites on the east side of Old San Juan. To continue, leave the square eastward along the Calle San Francisco. Eventually you'll come to:

19. **Plaza de Colón,** with its stone column topped with a statue of Christopher Columbus. On the south side of the square is the Tapía Theater, which has been restored to its original 19th-century elegance.

Then continue along Calle San Francisco to its intersection with Calle de Valle, and follow the signs to:

20. **Fort San Cristóbal,** built as part of the string of fortifications protecting one of Spain's most valuable colonies. Today, like its twin, El Morro, it is maintained by the National Park Service and can be visited throughout the day.

When you're through with this walking tour, be sure to just meander about Old San Juan's charming side streets; there are some quaint bars and restaurants that are perfect for a drink or some lunch.

GAMBLING

Casinos are one of the island's biggest draws. Most are open daily from noon to 4pm and again from 8pm to 4am.

The 18,500-square-foot **Casino at the Ritz-Carlton,** 6961 State Rd., no. 187, Isla Verde (☎ **787/253-1700**), is the largest in Puerto Rico. It combines the elegant decor of the 1940s with tropical fabrics and patterns. This is one of the plushest entertainment complexes in the Caribbean. You expect to see Joan Crawford arrive beautifully gowned and on the arm of Clark Gable.

The **San Juan Grand Beach Hotel & Casino,** 187 Isla Verde Avenue in Isla Verde (☎ **800/443-2009** in the U.S., or 787/791-6100), is a 10,000-square-foot gaming facility and an elegant rendezvous. One of its Murano chandeliers is longer than a bowling alley. The casino offers 207 slot machines, 16 blackjack tables, three dice tables, four roulette wheels, and a mini–baccarat table.

You can also try your luck at any of the following:

- **The Caribe Hilton,** Calle Los Rosales (☎ **787/721-0303**)
- **The Wyndham Old San Juan Hotel & Casino,** 100 Brumbaugh St. (☎ **787/ 721-5100**)

- **El San Juan Hotel and Casino,** 6063 Isla Verde Ave., Carolina (☎ 787/ 791-1000)
- **The Condado Plaza Hotel & Casino,** 999 Ashford Ave. (☎ 787/721-1000)
- **The Radisson Ambassador Plaza Hotel & Casino,** 1369 Ashford Ave. (☎ 787/ 721-7300)
- **The Diamond Palace Hotel & Casino,** 55 Condado Ave. (☎ 787/721-0810)
- **The Stellaris Casino** at the San Juan Marriott Resort, 1309 Ashford Ave. (☎ 787/722-7000)
- **The Crowne Plaza Hotel and Casino,** Route 187, Kilometer 1.5, Isla Verde (☎ 787/253-2929)

BEACHES

Beaches on Puerto Rico are open to the public, although you will be charged for use of *balneario* facilities, such as lockers and showers. Public beaches shut down on Mondays; if Monday is a holiday, the beaches are open for the holiday but closed the next day. Beach hours are from 9am to 5pm in winter, to 6pm in the off-season.

Bordering some of the Caribbean's finest resort hotels, the **Condado** and **Isla Verde** beaches are the most popular in town. Both are good for snorkeling and have rental equipment for water sports. **Condado Beach** is the single most famous beach strip in the Caribbean, despite the fact it's not the best beach and can be crowded in winter. Its long bands of white sand border some of the Caribbean's finest resort hotels. Locals prefer to head east of El Condado to the beaches of **Isla Verde,** which are less rocky and better sheltered from the waves. You can reach the beaches of **Ocean Park** and **Park Barboa,** on San Juan's north shore, by bus.

Luquillo Beach, lying about 30 miles east of San Juan, is edged by a vast coconut grove. This crescent-shaped beach is not only the best in Puerto Rico but one of the finest in the entire Caribbean. Coral reefs protect the crystal-clear lagoon from the fierce Atlantic. There are changing rooms, lockers, showers, and picnic facilities. However, the beach isn't as well maintained as it used to be.

Dorado Beach, Cerromar Beach, and **Palmas del Mar** are the chief centers for those seeking the golf, tennis, and beach life. Sometimes they're overcrowded, especially on Saturday and Sunday, but at other times they're practically deserted. If you find a secluded beach, be careful: Solitude is nice, but so is safety in numbers.

SPORTS

DEEP-SEA FISHING   It's said in deep-sea-fishing circles that **Capt. Mike Benitez,** who has chartered out of San Juan for more than 40 years, sets the standard by which to judge other captains. Benitez Fishing Charters can be contacted directly at P.O. Box 5141, Puerto de Tierra, San Juan, PR 00906 (☎ 787/723-2292). The captain offers a 45-foot air-conditioned deluxe Hateras, the *Sea Born.* Fishing tours for parties of up to six cost around $450 for a half-day excursion, and $750 for a full day, with beverages and all equipment included. In the waters just off Palmas del Mar, the resort complex on the southeast coast of Puerto Rico, **Capt. Bill Burleson,** P.O. Box 8270, Humacao, PR 00792 (☎ 787/850-7442), operates charters on his fully customized 46-foot sportfishing boat, *Karolette.* Burleson prefers to take fishing groups to Grappler Banks, 18 nautical miles away. It costs $570 for a maximum of six people for 4 hours, $720 for 6 hours, and $960 for 9 hours. He'll give you a discount if you pay in cash. He also offers snorkeling expe-ditions to Isla de Vieques and other locations.

GOLF   Puerto Rico may be a golfer's dream, but you'll need to sign up for the ship's excursion or rent a car to reach the major courses, which lie 45 minutes to 1¹/₂ hours from San Juan. With 72 holes, the **Hyatt Resorts Puerto Rico at Dorado** (☎ 787/796-1234) offers the greatest concentration of golf in the Caribbean, including the 18-hole Robert Trent Jones, Sr., courses at the Hyatt Regency Cerromar and the Hyatt Dorado Beach, and the par-72 East course at Dorado Beach, with the famous par-5, 5,540-yard 14th hole. The **Golf Club,** at Palmas del Mar in Humacao (☎ 787/852-6000, ext. 54), is 45 miles east of San Juan. The par-72, 6,803-yard course was designed by Gary Player. **Rio Mar Golf Course,** at Palmer (☎ 787/888-8815), is a 45-minute drive from San Juan along Route 187, on the northeast coast. The greens fees at this 6,145-yard course are less expensive after 2pm.

SCUBA DIVING   Puerto Rico offers excellent diving, but most of it is not within easy reach of San Juan. **Caribe Aquatic Adventures,** P.O. Box 9024278, San Juan Station, San Juan, PR 00902 (☎ 787/724-1882), will take you to sites in San Juan. Its dive shop is located in the rear lobby of the Radisson Normandie Hotel. Diving ranges from $45 to $125 for a full-day excursion to Fajardo and $80 for snorkelers.

WINDSURFING, JET-SKIING & SNORKELING   The best place for windsurfing and snorkeling on the island's north shore is along the well-maintained beachfront of the Hyatt Dorado Beach Hotel, near the 10th hole of the hotel's famous east golf course. Here, **Penfield Island Adventures** (☎ 787/796-1234, ext. 3768, or 787/796-2188) offers 90-minute windsurfing lessons and board rentals. Boards designed specifically for beginners and children are available. The school benefits from the north shore's strong, steady winds and an experienced crew of instructors. You can also rent jet skis and Sunfish sailboats.

SHOPPING

U.S. citizens don't pay duty on items bought in Puerto Rico and brought back to the mainland United States. You can find great bargains in San Juan; prices are often lower than those in St. Thomas. The streets of the **Old Town,** such as Calle San Francisco and Calle del Cristo, are the major venues. Most stores in Old San Juan are closed on Sunday. Local handcrafts can be good buys, including *santos* (hand-carved wooden religious figures), needlework, straw work, ceramics, hammocks, guayabera shirts for men, papier-mâché fruit and vegetables, and paintings and sculptures by Puerto Rican artists.

The biggest and most up-to-date shopping plaza in the Caribbean Basin is **Plaza Las Americas,** which lies in the financial district of Hato Rey, right off the Las Americas Expressway. The complex, with its fountains and advanced architecture, has more than 200 shops, most of them upmarket.

El Alcazar, Calle San José 103, is the largest emporium of antique furniture, silver, and art objects in the Caribbean. The best way to sift through the massive inventory is to begin at the address listed above, on Calle San José between Calle Luna and Calle Sol, and ask the owners, Sharon and Robert Bartos, to guide you to the other three buildings, all stuffed with important art and antiques.

Set in a 200-year-old colonial building, **Puerto Rican Arts & Crafts,** Calle Fortaleza 204, is one of the premier outlets on the island for authentic handcrafts. Of particular interest are papier-mâché carnival masks from the town of Ponce; their grotesque and colorful features were designed to chase away evil spirits.

José E. Alegria & Associates, Calle del Cristo 152-154, is half antiques shop, half old-fashioned arcade lined with gift shops and boutiques. **Galería Botello,** Calle del Cristo 208, is a living tribute to the late Angel Botello, one of Puerto Rico's most outstanding artists. Once his home, today the space displays his paintings and sculptures, and also offers a large collection of Puerto Rican antique santos. **Haitian Souvenirs,** Calle San Francisco 206, specializes in Haitian art and artifacts. Its walls are covered with primitive Haitian landscapes, portraits, and crowd scenes, most costing from $35 to $350.

San Juan is also home to some great outlet shops. At **London Fog,** Calle del Cristo 156, and the **Polo Ralph Lauren Factory Store,** Calle del Cristo 201, you can get the famous raincoats and the famous fashions at prices that are often 30% to 40% less than on the U.S. mainland.

GREAT LOCAL BARS & RESTAURANTS IN OLD SAN JUAN

A favorite **local beer** is Medalla; a favorite **local rum** is the famous Bacardi (pro-nounced Bah-carrrr-*di*), in all its various varieties.

Al Dente, Calle Recinto Sur 309 (☎ 787/723-7303), is a relaxed, trattorialike place serving reasonably priced dishes like brochettes of fresh tuna laced with pepper and Mediterranean herbs. ✪ **Amadeus,** Calle San Sebastián 106, across from the Iglesia de San José (☎ 787/722-8635), offers Caribbean cuisine with a nouvelle twist. **El Patio de Sam,** Calle San Sebastián 102, across from the Iglesia de San José (☎ 787/723-1149), is a popular gathering spot for American expatriates, newspeople, and shopkeepers. It's known for having the best burgers in San Juan. Speaking of burgers, the **Hard Rock Café** is at Calle Recinto Sur 253 (☎ 787/724-7625).

La Bombonera, Calle San Francisco 259 (☎ 787/722-0658), offers exceptional food at affordable prices. For decades a rendezvous for the island's literati and Old San Juan families, the food is authentically Puerto Rican, homemade, and inexpensive. **La Mallorquina,** Calle San Justo 207 (☎ 787/722-3261), was founded in 1848, and its chef specializes in the most typical Puerto Rican rice dish: *asopao*. You can have it with either chicken, shrimp, or lobster and shrimp. The nuevo Latino cuisine at ✪ **Parrot Club,** 363 Calle Fortaleza (☎ 787/725-7370), blends traditional Puerto Rican cookery with Spanish, Taíno, and African influences.

22 St. Barthélemy (St. Barts)

Part of the French department of Guadeloupe, lying 15 miles from Sint Maarten, sexy St. Barthélemy (also called **St. Barts** or **St. Barths**) is a small, hilly island with a population of 3,500 people of European and African descent who live on 13 square miles of verdant and dramatically hilly terrain bordered by pleasant white-sand beaches. St. Barts is sophistication in the tropics, an expensive and exclusive stamping ground of the rich and famous, with a distinctive seafaring tradition and a decidedly French flavor—chic, rich, and very Parisian, with a touch of Normandy and even Sweden in its personality. It's quite the European playground, disguised as a Caribbean island.

Forget such things as historical sights or ambitious water sports here. Come instead for white sandy beaches, fine French cuisine, relaxation in ultimate comfort, and the scene. Generally, only small cruise ships can visit this little French pocket of posh.

The island's capital and only town is **Gustavia,** named after a Swedish king. Set in a sheltered harbor, it looks like a little dollhouse-scale port.

Frommer's Favorite St. Barts Experiences

- **Hanging out at the Le Select cafe:** The most popular gathering place in Gustavia is *the* place to get a taste of local life (see "Great Local Restaurants & Bars," below).
- **Heading to the beaches:** There are several utterly gorgeous ones on St. Barts (see "Beaches," below).
- **Touring the Island in a Mini-Moke:** You'll feel totally cool zipping around the island's undulating, hilly roads in one of these open-air vehicles, which are half golf cart and half jeep.

COMING ASHORE   Cruise ships anchor right off Gustavia; tenders then ferry passengers to the heart of town. There are usually shaded refreshment stands onshore. A short walk will get you into Gustavia's restaurant and shopping district.

CURRENCY   The official monetary unit is the **French franc (F),** but most stores and restaurants prefer U.S. dollars. The exchange rate is 6.29F to U.S.$1 (1 F = U.S.16¢). I've used this rate to convert currency throughout this section.

LANGUAGE   St. Barts is technically part of France, so the official language is French. However, nearly everyone speaks English.

INFORMATION   Go to the **Office du Tourisme** in the Town Hall, quai du Général-de-Gaulle, in Gustavia (☎ **590/27-87-27**). It's open Monday to Friday from 9am to 5pm. For info before you go, call the tourist board office in the U.S. at ☎ **410-286-8310** or log on to the Web site at www.frenchcaribbean.com.

CALLING FROM THE U.S.   When calling St. Barts from the United States, you need to dial "011" before the numbers listed throughout this section.

GETTING AROUND

BY TAXI   Taxis meet all cruise ships and aren't very expensive, since no destination is all that far. Dial ☎ **590/27-66-31** for taxi service. The fare is about 25F ($4) for rides up to 5 minutes; each additional 3 minutes is another 20F ($3.20).

BY MINI-MOKE OR SAMURAI   If you're a confident driver, renting one of these open-sided Mini-Mokes or manual-transmission Suzuki Samurais is great fun and the only way to zip around the jagged (and picturesque) hills of this 8-square-mile island in style. It'll cost about $40 a day. Try **Budget** (☎ **800/527-0700** or 590/27-66-30); **Hertz** (☎ **800/654-3001**), which operates through a local dealership, Henry's Car Rental; and **Avis** (☎ **800/331-1084** or 590/27-71-43), whose local name is St. Barts Centre-Auto.

BY MOTOR SCOOTER   You can rent motorbikes and scooters from **Rent Some Fun,** rue Gambetta in Gustavia (☎ **590/27-70-59**). The approximately $30 daily rental fee covers both bike and helmet; a $200 deposit is required.

Frommer's Ratings: St. Barts					
	Poor	Fair	Good	Excellent	Outstanding
Overall Experience				✓	
Shore Excursions			✓		
Activities Close to Port				✓	
Beaches & Water Sports				✓	
Shopping				✓	
Dining/Bars			✓		

St. Barthélemy (St. Barts)

SHORE EXCURSIONS

Many passengers prefer to spend their time ashore walking around and exploring Gustavia, which should take no more than 2 hours.

Minibus Island Tour ($25, 1¹/₂ hours): The duration is so short because there are almost no attractions other than the island's natural beauty and beaches. The minibus goes through the port, and then past the village of St-Jean to an overlook in Salinos, where you can take in the view. On the windward side of the island, you'll notice the different architecture required to withstand the heavy breezes. Next you'll head to Grand Cul-de-Sac for a view of the lagoon, and then have a brief stop at La Savone. You'll be brought back to the ship via Corossol, a tiny fishing village where the locals make straw from lantana palms.

ON YOUR OWN

All the big attractions—beaches, shopping, and people-watching—are covered elsewhere in this section.

SHOPPING

You don't pay any duty on St. Barts, so it's a good place to buy liquor and French perfumes at some of the lowest prices in the Caribbean. In fact, perfume and champagne are cheaper here than in metropolitan France. You'll also find good buys in sportswear, crystal, porcelain, watches, and other luxuries. The only trouble is that selections here are limited.

If you're in the market for **island crafts,** try to find those convertible-brim, fine straw hats St. Bartians like to wear. *Vogue* once featured them in its fashion pages. There are also some interesting block-printed cotton resort clothes on the island.

La Boutique Couleur des Îles, rue du Général-de-Gaulle 8, sells shirts and blouses for about $30 to $50 with hand-embroidered references to the flora and fauna of St. Barts. **Laurent Eiffel,** rue du Général-de-Gaulle, sells imitations of designer items that usually cost 10 times as much. Look for belts, bags, and accessories modeled after Versace, Prada, Hermès, Gucci, and Chanel. **St. Barts Style,** rue Lafayette, near the corner of rue du Port, stocks brightly hued beachwear by Jams World and Vicidomine. **Le Comptoir du Cigare,** rue du Général-de-Gaulle 6, caters to the villa-and-yacht crowd. Its cigars hail from Cuba and the Dominican Republic; connoisseur-quality rums come from Martinique, Cuba, and Haiti. (Remember that Cuban cigars cannot legally be brought into the United States, so you must smoke them abroad.)

Diamond Genesis/Kornérupine, rue du Général-de-Gaulle 12, Les Suites du Roi-Oskar-II, is one of the few shops on the island where jewelry is handcrafted on the premises (and sells for between $20 and $60,000). **La Maison de Free Mousse,** Carré d'Or, quai de la République, is the most unusual gift shop on St. Barts, with wood carvings and handcrafts from throughout Europe, Asia, and South America.

BEACHES

There are 14 white-sand beaches on St. Barts. My favorites (Gouverneur, Saline, Marigot, and Colombier) are pretty secluded, but few beaches here are ever crowded, even during winter. All are public and free, and easily accessible by taxi from the cruise pier. You can also make arrangements to be picked up at a scheduled time. Nude bathing is officially prohibited, but topless sunbathing is quite common.

Gouverneur on the south is gorgeous and offers some waves, but wear lots of sunscreen—there's no shade. Get there by driving or taking a taxi through Gustavia and up to Lurin. Turn at the Santa Fe Restaurant (see "Great Local Restaurants & Bars," below), and head down a narrow road. To get to the beach **Saline,** to the east of Gouverneur, drive up the road from the commercial center in St-Jean. A short walk over the sand dune and you're there. Like Gouverneur, it offers some waves but no shade.

Marigot, also on the north shore, is narrow but good for swimming and snorkeling. **Colombier** is difficult to get to, but well worth the effort for swimmers and snorkelers. You'll have to take a boat or a rugged goat path from Petite Anse past Flamands, a 30-minute walk. You can pack a lunch and eat in the shade.

The most famous beach is **St-Jean,** which is actually two beaches divided by the Eden Rock promontory. It offers water sports, beach restaurants, and a few hotels, as well as some shady areas. **Flamands,** to the west, is a very wide beach with a few small hotels and some lantana palms.

If you want a beach with hotels, restaurants, and water sports, the **Grand Cul-de-Sac** area on the northeast shore fits the bill. There's a narrow beach here protected by a reef.

SPORTS

SCUBA DIVING **Marine Service,** quai du Yacht-Club in Gustavia (☎ **590/27-70-34**), operates from a one-story building on the water at the edge of a marina, across the harbor from the more congested part of Gustavia. The outfit is familiar with at least 15 unusual dive sites scattered at various points offshore, including The Grouper, a remote reef west of St. Barts, close to the uninhabited cay known as Ile Forchue. Almost as important are the reefs near Roche Rouge, off the opposite (i.e., eastern) edge of St. Barts. The island has only one relatively safe wreck dive, to the rusting hulk of *Kayali,* a trawler that sank offshore in 1994. It's recommended only for experienced divers.

WATERSKIING   Marine Service (see above) can also arrange waterskiing, offered daily from 9am to 1pm and again from 4:40pm to sundown. Because of the shape of the coastline, skiers must remain at least 80 yards from shore on the windward side of the island and 110 yards off the leeward side.

WINDSURFING   Try **St. Barth Wind School** near the Tom Beach Hotel on Plage de St-Jean. It's open daily from 9am to 5pm.

GREAT LOCAL RESTAURANTS & BARS

IN GUSTAVIA   The most popular gathering place in Gustavia is ✪ **Le Select,** rue de la France (☎ **590/27-86-87**), apparently named after its more famous granddaddy in the Montparnasse section of Paris. It's utterly simple. A game of dominoes might be under way as you walk in. Tables are placed outside on the gravel in an open-air cafe garden near the port. The outdoor grill promises a "cheeseburger in Paradise." Jimmy Buffett might show up here, or perhaps Mick Jagger. If you want to spread a rumor and have it travel fast across the island, start it here. The place is open Monday to Saturday from 10am to 11pm.

L'Iguane, Carré d'Or, quai de la République (☎ **590/27-88-46**), offers an international menu that includes sushi, American breakfasts, and California-style sandwiches and salads.

AT MORNE LURIN   Santa Fe Restaurant, Morne Lurin (☎ **590/27-61-04**), is a burger house and sports bar that's carved out a niche for itself among the island's English-speaking clientele. It features wide-screen TVs that present American sports events.

IN GRANDE SALINE   Le Tamarin, Plage de Saline (☎ **590/27-72-12**), is an informal bistro isolated amid rocky hills and forests east of Gustavia. Menu items are mostly light, including gazpacho, a *pavé* of Cajun-style tuna with Creole sauce and baby vegetables, and chicken roasted with lemon and ginger.

IN GRAND CUL-DE-SAC   Lunching at **Club Lafayette,** Grand Cul-de-Sac (☎ **590/27-62-51**), located in a cove on the eastern end of the island, is like taking a meal at your own private, very expensive beach club. The menu includes such items as warm foie gras served with apples, and one of the best meal-size lobster salads on the island. **West Indies Café,** in El Sereno Beach Hotel, Grand Cul-de-Sac, 4 miles east of Gustavia (☎ **590/27-64-80**), incorporates aspects of a Parisian cabaret with simple but well-prepared meals such as fish tartare, eggplant mousse, grilled lobster, and grilled tuna and snapper.

23 St. Croix

Though it's now part of the U.S. Virgin Islands, and though seven different flags have flown over St. Croix in its history, it's the 2^1/$_2$ centuries of Danish influence that is most visible in the island's architecture, while the island's population is descended from African and European origins. Some families have been on the island for 10 generations, with roots dating back to colonial times. Today, St. Croix competes with St. Thomas for the Yankee cruise ship dollar. Although it gets nowhere near the number of visitors, St. Croix is more tranquil and less congested than its smaller sibling. The major attraction here is **Buck Island National Park,** a national offshore treasure.

St. Croix boasts some fine beaches as well, including Sandy Point, Sprat Hall, and Rainbow Beach. At the east end of the island (which, incidentally, is the easternmost possession of the United States), the terrain is rocky and arid. The west end is lusher, with a rain forest of mango and mahogany, tree ferns, and dangling lianas. Rolling hills and upland pastures make up much of the area between the two extremes, while African tulips are just one of the many tropical flowers that add a splash of color to the landscape. St. Croix's most prominent landmarks are the ruins of the sugarcane plantations that once covered the islands.

Although large cruise ships moor at **Frederiksted,** most of the action is in **Christiansted,** located on a coral-bound bay about midway along the north shore and featuring more sights and better restaurants and shopping. The town is being handsomely restored, and the entire harbor-front area is a national historic site.

Frommer's Favorite St. Croix Experiences

- **Visiting Buck Island Reef National Monument:** Within this 800-acre preserve, the only underwater national monument in the United States, you can snorkel over a series of unqiue underwater trails and experience some of the best-preserved coral reefs in the Caribbean. A snorkeling instructor guides the excursion.
- **Biking along the coast:** On this tour, you pass through Frederiksted, then past ruins and through forests and rolling grasslands (see "Shore Excursions," below).
- **Gambling:** Try your luck at St. Croix's first casino, which opened in early 2000 at the new Divi Carina Bay Hotel.
- **Strolling through Christiansted:** Because of its well-preserved 18th- and 19th-century Danish architecture (particularly Fort Christiansvaern), Christiansted has been designated a National Historic Site. In the late 1700s, it was a crown colony of Denmark and one of the Caribbean's major ports, and today many street signs are still in Danish.

COMING ASHORE Only cruise ships with fewer than 200 passengers can land directly at the dock at Christiansted. Others moor at a 1,500-foot pier at Frederiksted, a sleepy town that springs to life only when the ships arrive. Both piers have information centers and telephones. I suggest you spend as little time as possible in Frederiksted and head immediately for Christiansted, some 17 miles away. It's easy to explore either Frederiksted or Christiansted on foot (the only way, really), although you might want to consider one of the shore excursions outlined below to see more of the island, especially its underwater treasures.

There are 10 **phone booths** at the end of the pier.

CURRENCY The **U.S. dollar** is the official currency.

LANGUAGE English is spoken here.

Frommer's Ratings: St. Croix

	Poor	Fair	Good	Excellent	Outstanding
Overall Experience				✓	
Shore Excursions				✓	
Activities Close to Port				✓	
Beaches & Water Sports				✓	
Shopping					✓
Dining/Bars		✓			

St. Croix

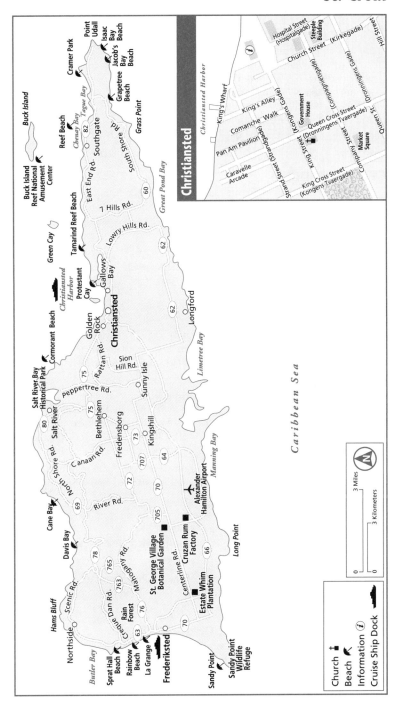

Christiansted

Hospital Street (Hospitalgade)
Steeple Building
Church Street (Kirkegade)
Hill Street
King's Wharf
King's Alley
Comanche Walk
Government House
Pan Am Pavilion
Queen Cross Street (Dronningens Tvaergade)
Caravelle Arcade
King Cross Street (Kongens Tvaergade)
Market Square
Strand Street (Strandgade)
King Street (Kongens Gade)
Company Street (Compagniesgade)
Queen St.
Queen Street (Dronningens Gade)
Christiansted Harbor

Point Udall
Isaac Bay Beach
Jacob's Bay Beach
Cramer Park
Grapetree Beach
Reef Beach
Grass Point
Buck Island
Southgate
East End Rd.
South Shore Rd.
Great Pond Bay
Chenay Bay
Tague Bay
Buck Island Reef National Amusement Center
Green Cay
Tamarind Reef Beach
7 Hills Rd.
Lowry Hills Rd.
60
62
Protestant Cay
Gallows Bay
Gallows
Christiansted Harbor
Longford
62
Cormorant Beach
Golden Rock
Christiansted
Sion Hill Rd.
Sunny Isle
Limetree Bay
Salt River Bay Historical Park
Rattan Rd.
Peppertree Rd.
75
75
Bethlehem
Fredensborg
Kingshill
Salt River
80
Canaan Rd.
73
64
Manning Bay
707
72
70
Alexander Hamilton Airport
North Shore Rd.
69
River Rd.
705
Cruzan Rum Factory
Cane Bay
St. George Village Botanical Garden
Davis Bay
78
765
Centerline Rd.
66
Long Point
Hams Bluff
Scenic Rd.
763
Rain Forest
Mahogany Rd.
76
Estate Whim Plantation
Creque Dan Rd.
63
70
Northside
Butler Bay
Sprat Hall Beach
Rainbow Beach
La Grange
Frederiksted
Sandy Point
Sandy Point Wildlife Refuge

Caribbean Sea

N

3 Miles
3 Kilometers
0
0

Church
Beach
Information
Cruise Ship Dock

INFORMATION   The **U.S. Virgin Islands Division of Tourism** has offices in Christiansted at Queen Cross Street (☎ **340/773-0495**), and at the Customs House Building, Strand Street in Frederiksted (☎ **340/772-0357**). Open Monday to Friday from 9am to 5pm. To get info before you go, contact the tourism board office in the U.S. at ☎ **800/372-USVI** or www.visitstcroix.com. To get up-to-the-minute info on St. Croix, from taxi and bus rates to maps and info on restaurants and the island's history and culture, pick up a free copy of the pink *St. Croix This Week.* (It's a lot more than just ads!)

CALLING FROM THE U.S.   When calling St. Croix from the United States, you need to dial only a "1" before the numbers listed throughout this section.

GETTING AROUND

BY TAXI   Taxis are unmetered, so agree on the rate before you get in. The **St. Croix Taxicab Association** (☎ **340/778-1088**) offers door-to-door service. Taxi tours are a great way to explore the island. For one or two passengers, the cost is about $50 for 2 hours or $70 for 3 hours. I don't recommend renting a car. It costs $20 to take a taxi from Christiansted to Frederiksted.

BY BUS   Air-conditioned buses run daily between Christiansted and Frederiksted about every 40 minutes between 5:30am and 9pm. The fare is $1. For more information, call ☎ **340/778-0898.**

SHORE EXCURSIONS

Although it's possible to get around St. Croix on your own, you also have the option of joining some of the most varied organized shore excursions in the Caribbean, including snorkeling and sailing trips, island tours, golf, catamaran party tours, hikes, and bicycle excursions.

Buck Island National Park Tour/Snorkeling ($50, 4–5 hours): The premier tour in St. Croix takes you to a tropical underwater wonderland of blue water and colorful coral reefs. Transportation is provided from the Frederiksted pier to Christiansted, where a powerboat takes you over to Buck Island. An experienced guide provides snorkel lessons.

Island Tour ($31, 4 hours): For a taste of the whole island, this tour includes a visit to the Whim Great House sugar plantation, Christiansted, and other major sites.

St. Croix Bike Tour ($49, 3 hours): Bike along the coast of St. Croix, passing through the town of Frederiksted before heading out on the Northside Road, past ruins and through forests and rolling grasslands.

Hiking Tour ($40, 2 hours): Hike through the 225-acre Butler Bay preserve and enjoy bird watching and a good hearty walk.

Golf at Carambola ($74–$105): One of the Caribbean's most famous courses is another excursion destination. Your cruise line will probably offer an excursion here, or you can do it on your own (see "Sports," below).

TOURING THROUGH LOCAL OPERATORS

Horseback Tour: On this tour, run by Paul and Jill's Equestrian Stables, Sprat Hall Plantation, Route 58 (☎ **340/772-2880**), you'll pass ruins of abandoned 18th-century plantations and sugar mills and climb the hills of St. Croix's western end. Tour guides give running commentaries on island fauna and history, and on riding techniques. The stables, owned by Paul Wojcie and his wife, Jill Hurd (a daughter of the establishment's original founders), are set on the sprawling grounds of the island's oldest plantation, and are known throughout the

Caribbean for the quality of the horses and the scenic trail rides through the forests. Beginners and experienced riders alike are welcome. Make reservations at least a day in advance.

St. Thomas Hydrofoil or Seaplane Trip: If you want to go to St. Thomas for the day, you can make the 40-mile trip via hydrofoil from Christiansted to Charlotte Amalie in little over an hour for $90 round-trip. A seaplane shuttle between the two is also available for $110 round-trip. Contact **Seaborne Seaplanes** at 34 Strand St. in Christiansted (☎ **340/773-6442**).

ON YOUR OWN: WITHIN WALKING DISTANCE

IN FREDERIKSTED   Frederiksted is nothing great, but if you decide to hang around you should begin your tour at russet-colored **Fort Frederik,** next to the cruise ship pier. Some historians claim it was the first fort to sound a foreign salute to the U.S. flag, in 1776. The structure, at the northern end of Frederiksted, has been restored to its 1840 look. You can explore the courtyard and stables, and examine an exhibit area in what was once the Garrison Room. Admission is free. It's open Monday to Saturday from 8am to 5pm.

IN CHRISTIANSTED   Begin your visit at the **visitor bureau** (☎ **340/773-0495**), a yellow building with a cedar-capped roof near the harbor front. It was built as the Old Scalehouse in 1856 to replace a similar, older structure that burned down. In its heyday, all taxable goods leaving and entering the harbor were weighed here. The scales could once accurately weigh barrels of sugar and molasses weighing up to 1,600 pounds.

Another major attraction is the **Steeple Building** (☎ **340/773-1460**), or Church of Lord God of Sabaoth, which was completed in 1753 as St. Croix's first Lutheran church. It, too, stands near the harbor front; get there via Hospital Street. The building was deconsecrated in 1831 and has served at various times as a bakery, a hospital, and a school. Admission is $2, which also includes admission to Fort Christiansvaern (see below). It's open daily from 8am to 5pm.

Overlooking the harbor, **Fort Christiansvaern** (☎ **340/773-1460**) is the best preserved colonial fortification in the Virgin Islands. The National Park Service maintains the fort as a historic monument. Its original star-shaped design was at the vanguard of the most advanced military planning of its era. It's open Monday to Thursday from 8am to 5pm, Friday and Saturday from 9am to 5pm. Admission is included in the ticket to the Steeple Building (see above).

ON YOUR OWN: BEYOND WALKING DISTANCE

The only known site where Columbus landed in what is now U.S. territory was at Salt River, on the island's northern shore. To mark the 500th anniversary of his arrival, President George Bush signed a bill creating the 912-acre ✪ **Salt River Bay National Historical Park and Ecological Preserve.** The landmass includes the site of the original Carib village explored by Columbus and his men, along with the only ceremonial ball court ever discovered in the Lesser Antilles.

At the Carib settlement, the men of Columbus liberated several Taíno women and children held as slaves. On the way back to their vessels, the Spaniards faced a canoe filled with hostile Caribs, armed with poison arrows. One Spanish soldier was killed, and perhaps six Caribs were either slain or captured. This is the first documented case of hostility between invading Europeans and the native Americans. Sailing away, Columbus named this part of St. Croix "Cape of the Arrows."

The park today is in a natural state. It has the largest mangrove forest in the Virgin Islands, sheltering many endangered animals and plants, plus an underwater canyon attracting scuba divers from around the world. **The St. Croix Environmental Association,** 3 Arawak Building, Gallows Bay, conducts tours of the area. Call them at ☎ **340/773-1989** for details.

The **Cruzan Rum Factory,** West Airport Road, Route 64 (☎ **340/692-2280**), distills the famous Virgin Islands rum, which residents consider to be the finest in the world. Guided tours depart from the visitor pavilion; call for reservations and information.

The **Estate Whim Plantation Museum,** Centerline Road, about 2 miles east of Frederiksted (☎ **340/772-0598**), restored by the St. Croix Landmarks Society, is composed of only three rooms and is unique among the many old sugar plantations dotting the island. Its 3-foot-thick walls are made of stone, coral, and molasses. Also on the museum's premises is a woodworking shop, the estate's original kitchen, a museum store, a servant's quarters, and tools from the 18th century. The ruins include remains of the plantation's sugar-processing plant, complete with a restored windmill.

Note: The **St. George Village Botanical Garden of St. Croix** (☎ **340/692-2874**), the much loved and popular Eden of tropical trees, shrubs, vines, and flowers 4 miles east of Frederiksted, was unfortunately wiped out by Hurricane Lenny in late 1999. At press time, it had not been rebuilt.

SHOPPING

Americans get a break here, since they can bring home $1,200 worth of merchandise from the U.S. Virgin Islands without paying duty, as opposed to a paltry $400 from most other Caribbean ports. And liquor here is duty-free.

A major redevelopment of the waterfront at Christiansted, following the hurricanes of 1995, was **King's Alley Complex,** a pink-sided compound filled with the densest concentration of shopping options on St. Croix.

Worthwhile specialty shops include **Skirt Tails,** Pam Am Pavilion, one of the most colorful and popular boutiques on the island, specializing in hand-painted batiks for both men and women; **The White House,** King's Alley Walk, which stocks women's clothing ranging from dressy to casual and breezy—but all, everything, in white; **Elegant Illusions Copy Jewelry,** 55 King St., which sells credible copies of the baroque and antique jewelry your great-grandmother might have worn, priced from $9 to $1,000; **Larimar,** The Boardwalk/King's Walk, which specializes in larimar—a pale-blue pectolyte prized for its sky-blue color—in various gold settings; **Estate Mount Washington Antiques,** 2 Estate Mount Washington, which is the best treasure trove of colonial West Indian furniture and "flotsam" in the Virgin Islands; **Folk Art Traders,** 1B Queen Cross St., which deals in Caribbean art and folk-art treasures, such as carnival masks, pottery, ceramics, original paintings, and hand-wrought jewelry; and **Many Hands,** in the Pan Am Pavilion, Strand Street, which sells Virgin Islands handcrafts, spices and teas, handmade jewelry, and more.

The Royal Poinciana, 1111 Strand St., looks like an antique apothecary, but is actually the most interesting gift shop on St. Croix. You'll find such Caribbean-inspired items as hot sauces ("fire water"), seasoning blends for gumbos, island herbal teas, Antillean coffees, and a scented array of soaps, toiletries, lotions, and shampoos.

BEACHES

Beaches are the biggest attraction on St. Croix. The drawback is that getting to them from Christiansted or Frederiksted isn't always easy. Taxis will take you, but they can be expensive. In Christiansted, take a ferry to the **Hotel on the Cay,** a palm-shaded island in the harbor.

Most convenient for passengers arriving at Frederiksted is **Sandy Point,** the largest beach in all the U.S. Virgin Islands. Its waters are shallow and calm, perfect for swimming. Sandy Point is the nesting ground for the endangered leatherback and green sea turtles that lay their eggs every year between early April and early June.

Cramer Park, at the northeastern end of the island, is a special public park operated by the Department of Agriculture. Lined with sea-grape trees, the beach has a picnic area, a restaurant, and a bar.

I highly recommend **Cane Bay** and **Davis Bay.** They're both the type of beaches you'd expect to find on a Caribbean island—palms, white sand, and good swimming and snorkeling. Cane Bay attracts snorkelers and divers with its rolling waves, coral gardens, and drop-off wall. It's near Route 80 on the north shore. Davis Beach draws bodysurfers. There are no changing facilities here. It's off the South Shore Road (Route 60), in the vicinity of the Carambola Beach Resort.

Windsurfers like **Reef Beach,** which opens onto Teague Bay along Route 82, East End Road, a half-hour ride from Christiansted. You can order food at Duggan's Reef. On Route 63, a short ride north of Frederiksted, **Rainbow Beach** invites with its white sand and ideal snorkeling conditions. **La Grange** is another good beach in the vicinity, also on Route 63, about 5 minutes north of Frederiksted. You can rent lounge chairs here, and there's a bar nearby.

At the **Cormorant Beach Club,** about 5 miles west of Christiansted, palm trees shade some 1,200 feet of white sands. A living reef lies just off the shore, making snorkeling ideal. **Grapetree Beach** offers a similar amount of clean white sand on the eastern tip of the island. Follow the South Shore Road (Route 60) to reach it. Water sports are popular here.

SPORTS

GOLF   St. Croix has the best golfing in the U.S. Virgins. In fact, guests staying on St. John and St. Thomas often fly over for a day's round on the island's two 18-hole and one nine-hole golf courses. The **Carambola Golf Course,** on the northeast side of St. Croix (☎ 340/778-5638), was designed by Robert Trent Jones, Sr., who called it "the loveliest course I ever designed." The course, formerly the site of "Shell's Wonderful World of Golf," has been likened to a botanical garden. Golfing authorities consider its collection of par-3 holes to be the best in the tropics. Carambola's course record of 65 was set by Jim Levine in 1993. The **Buccaneer,** 2 miles east of Christiansted (☎ 340/773-2100, ext. 738), is a challenging 5,810-yard, 18-hole course with panoramic vistas. Players can knock the ball over rolling hills right to the edge of the Caribbean. A final course is the **Reef,** at Teague Bay on the east end of the island (☎ 340/773-8844), a 3,100-yard, nine-hole course. The longest hole is a 579-yard par 5.

SCUBA DIVING   Divers love St. Croix's sponge life, beautiful black-coral trees, and steep drop-offs near the shoreline. This island is home to the largest living reef in the Caribbean. Its fabled north-shore wall begins in 25 to 30 feet of water and drops—sometimes almost straight down—to 13,200 feet. There are 22 moored diving sites. Favorites among them include the historic **Salt River Canyon,** the coral gardens of **Scotch Banks,** and **Eagle Ray,** filled with cruising rays. **Pavilions** is yet another good dive site, with a pristine virgin coral reef. The best site of all, however, is **Buck Island,** an underwater wonderland with a visibility of more than 100 feet and an underwater nature trail. All the minor and major agencies offer scuba and snorkeling tours to Buck Island. **Dive St. Croix,** 59 King's Wharf (☎ 800/523-DIVE in the U.S., or 340/773-2628; fax 340/773-7400), operates the 38-foot dive boat *Reliance.* The staff offers complete instruction, from beginners' courses through full certification. **S.C.O.R.E./V.I. Divers Ltd.,** in the Pan Am Pavilion on Christiansted's waterfront (☎ 800/544-5911 in the U.S., or

340/773-6045), is the oldest and one of the best dive operations on the island. *Rodales Scuba Diving* magazine rated its staff as among the top 10 worldwide. This full-service PADI five-star facility offers daily two-tank boat dives, as well as guided snorkeling trips to Green Cay.

GREAT LOCAL RESTAURANTS & BARS

A couple favorite **local beers** are Carib and Blackbeard's (made on St. Thomas); a favorite **local rum** is Cruzan.

IN CHRISTIANSTED   **Annabelle's Tea Room,** 51-ABC Company St. (☎ **340/ 773-3990**), occupies a quiet courtyard and serves an assortment of sandwiches, salads, soups, and platters. **Harvey's,** 11B Company St. (☎ **340/773-3433**), features the thoroughly zesty cooking of island matriarch Sarah Harvey. Main dishes are the type of food she was raised on: barbecue chicken, barbecue spareribs (barbecue is big here), boiled fillet of snapper, and even lobster when she can get it. **Indies,** 55-56 Company St. (☎ **340/692-9440**), serves what may be the finest and freshest meal on St. Croix. The swordfish with fresh artichokes, shiitake mushrooms, and thyme has a savory flavor, as does the baked wahoo with lobster curry and fresh chutney and coconut.

Paradise Café, Queen Cross St. at 53B Company St. (across from Government House; ☎ **340/773-2985**), serves New York deli–style sandwiches throughout the day—everything from a Reuben to a tuna melt. Of course, burgers are always featured. **St. Croix Chop House & Brew Pub,** King's Alley Walk (☎ **340/713-9820**), boasts one of the best harbor views in Christiansted, and serves beer, burgers, and sandwiches at street level and a two-fisted menu upstairs that includes garlic-stuffed fillet steak and such fish as wahoo and marlin. **Tutto Bene,** 2 Company St. (☎ **340/ 773-5229**), serves a full range of delectable pastas, plus fish, veggie frittatas, a chicken pesto sandwich, spinach lasagna, and more.

IN FREDERIKSTED   **Le St. Tropez,** Limetree Court, 67 King St. (☎ **340/ 772-3000**), is the most popular bistro in Frederiksted, offering crêpes, quiches, soups, or salads at lunch in the sunlit courtyard. At night it's Mediterranean cuisine. **Pier 69,** 69 King St. (☎ **340/772-0069**), looks like a combination of a 1950s living room and a nautical bar, and is a hangout for Christiansted's counterculture and a place for sandwiches and salads.

AROUND THE ISLAND   **Duggan's Reef,** East End Road, Teague Bay (☎ **340/ 773-9800**), is the most popular restaurant on St. Croix. At lunch, a simple array of salads, crêpes, and sandwiches is offered. At dinner, specialties include Duggan's Caribbean lobster pasta and Irish whiskey lobster. **Sprat Hall Beach Restaurant,** Route 63, 1 mile north of Frederiksted (☎ **340/772-5855**), serves local dishes like conch chowder, pumpkin fritters, tannia soup, and the fried fish of the day. These local dishes have an authentic island flavor, perhaps more than anywhere else on St. Croix.

24 St. Kitts & Nevis

Linked politically if not physically—they form one nation, though they're separated by 2 miles of ocean—St. Kitts and Nevis lie somewhat off the beaten tourist track, south of St. Martin and north of Guadeloupe. Formerly possessions of Britain, the two islands were given self-government in 1967, and in 1983 became a totally independent nation known as the Federation of St. Kitts and Nevis. It's a stormy marriage, however: Nevis's 1998 referendum for separation from its larger partner failed by the slimmest of margins.

CURRENCY   The local currency is the **Eastern Caribbean dollar (EC$).** The exchange rate is EC$2.70 to U.S.$1 (EC$1 = U.S.37¢). Many shops and restaurants

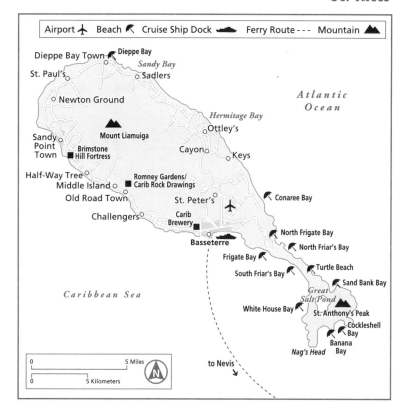

quote prices in U.S. dollars. Always determine which currency locals are talking about. I have used U.S.-dollar prices in this section.

LANGUAGE   English is the language of the island.

CALLING FROM THE U.S.   When calling St. Kitts or Nevis from the United States, you need to dial only a "1" before the numbers listed throughout this section.

ST. KITTS

St. Kitts—or St. Christopher, a name hardly anyone uses—is by far the more populous of the two islands, with some 35,000 people. It was the first English settlement in the Leeward Islands, and during the plantation age its 68 square miles enjoyed one of the richest sugarcane economies in the Caribbean. Of course, the plantation age depended on slave labor for cultivation, and today, though the bulk of the island's revenue still comes from the nationalized sugar industry, the back-breaking and low-paying work of sugar harvesting is shunned by most of St. Kitts's citizens (in their place, Guayanese workers come in for the harvesting season). Cane fields climb the slopes of a volcanic mountain range, and you'll see ruins of old mills and plantation houses as you drive around the island.

St. Kitts is lush and fertile, dotted with rain forests and waterfalls, but it's also extremely poor and has suffered catastrophically in recent years, being hit with several successive hurricanes. In the aftermath of 1998's Hurricane Georges, the country's U.N. Mission released a statement which said, in part, "Initial reports indicate that all productive sectors including sugar and non-sugar agriculture and manufacturing have

Frommer's Ratings: St. Kitts					
	Poor	Fair	Good	Excellent	Outstanding
Overall Experience			✓		
Shore Excursions			✓		
Activities Close to Port	✓				
Beaches & Water Sports			✓		
Shopping		✓			
Dining/Bars			✓		

come to a standstill. Thousands of people are expected to be out of work." A year later, Hurricane Lenny pounded the ravaged country once again, exacerbating its problems. Despite efforts at wooing tourism to bring in badly needed cash, the country lags behind in amenities and infrastructure.

The island is crowned by the 3,792-foot Mount Liamuiga, a crater that, thankfully, has remained dormant (unlike the one at Montserrat). Its most impressive landmark is the **Brimstone Hill fortress,** one of the Caribbean's most impressive. **Basseterre,** the capital city, is full of old-time Caribbean architecture and a few worthwhile landmarks, but overall has little to hold the interest of visitors.

Frommer's Favorite St. Kitts Experiences

- **Visiting Brimstone Hill Fortress:** Begun by the British in 1690 and subsequently changing hands from British to French and back to British again, it's one of the most impressive forts in the Caribbean, with battlement after battlement leading up to a spectacular view of the sea. (See "Shore Excursions," and "On Your Own: Beyond Walking Distance," below.)
- **Hiking Mount Liamuiga:** The hike up this dormant volcano will take you through a rain forest and along deep ravines up to the rim of the crater at a cool 2,625 feet (see "On Your Own: Beyond Walking Distance," below).

COMING ASHORE   In April 1997, the government of St. Kitts and Nevis attempted to replace the older, drab-looking industrial piers of Basseterre by building Port Zante, a pier stretching from the center of town into deep waters offshore, but fate apparently had other plans, and whacked Port Zante hard with successive hurricanes. At press time, Zante sits unused in the middle of several acres of halted construction, and in a November 1999 address on the effects of Hurricane Lenny, Prime Minister Denzil L. Douglas said "It is safe to say at this point that my government will require a huge degree of persuading before we decide to restart this project in its original design and format. I do not wish here to repeat what informed opinion in the engineering field is, but I am mindful at this stage of the particular maxim 'not all errors can be corrected.'" Expect to arrive at those same old industrial piers for the foreseeable future.

INFORMATION   You can get local tourist information at the **St. Kitts/Nevis Department of Tourism,** Pelican Mall, Bay Road, in Basseterre (☎ **800/582-6208** or 869/465-4040). Open Monday to Friday from 9am to 5pm. For info before you go, contact the tourism board office in the United States at ☎ **212/535-1234** or www.stkitts-nevis.com.

GETTING AROUND

BY TAXI   Taxis wait at the docks in Basseterre and in the Circus, a public area near the docks at the intersection of Bank and Fort streets. Since most taxi drivers are also guides, this is the best means of getting around the island. Taxis aren't metered, so before heading out you must agree on the price, and ask if the rates quoted are in U.S. dollars or Eastern Caribbean dollars.

BY RENTAL CAR   I don't recommend renting a car.

SHORE EXCURSIONS

✪ **Brimstone Hill Tour** ($28, 2^1/$_2$ hours): Visit this inspiring 17th-century citadel, which, at some 800 feet above sea level, gives you a panoramic view of the coastline and the island. Tours typically include a visit to the beautiful Romney Gardens, which lie between Basseterre and the fort. You can check out the lush greenery, say "hi" to the cows that graze just across the hill, or shop at Carabelle Boutique, which has its shop on the site.

Rain Forest Adventure Hike ($41, 4 hours): Departing from Romney Gardens, about 5 miles from Basseterre, you'll hike along a loop of trail through lush rain forest. With luck, you'll catch sight of some of St. Kitts's resident monkey population.

Beach Horseback Ride ($38, 1–2 hours): Cruise ship passengers ride well-trained horses along the Atlantic coastline, where trade winds ensure a cool trip.

Sail & Snorkel Catamaran Trip ($46, 3–4 hours): A sailing catamaran takes you to secluded Smittens Bay for snorkeling among the diverse reef fish and coral formations. Complimentary rum punch is served aboard the boat on your return trip.

TOURING THROUGH LOCAL OPERATORS

Taxi Tours: Taxi drivers will take you on a 3-hour tour of the island for about $60. Lunch can also be arranged at one of the local inns. Good choices are **Golden Lemon** at Dieppe Bay (☎ **869/465-7260**) or **Rawlins Plantation,** Mount Pleasant (☎ **869/465-6221**).

ON YOUR OWN: WITHIN WALKING DISTANCE

The capital city of Basseterre, where the docks are located, has typical British colonial architecture and some quaint buildings, as well as shops and a market where the locals display fruits and flowers—but even this description might be overstating the place's appeal. Truth is, it's a very poor town, with few attractions aimed at visitors. Chickens roam the streets, pecking around right outside the headquarters of the government, and it says something (though I'm not sure what) that the most visible component of the town's "skyline" is a Kentucky Fried Chicken. Most businesses are entirely for the local populace (furniture shops, clothing stores, and the like), and there are few charming spots—wherever you go, you're reminded that this is a poor nation that's been dealt a bad hand by Mother Nature over the past several years, getting beaten down again by hurricanes every time it starts to stand up.

Independence Square, a stone's throw from the docks along Bank Street, is pretty, with its central fountain and old church, but there's no good reason to linger unless it's to sit in the shade and toss back a bottle of the local soda, a refreshing (if sweet) grapefruit-based concoction called Ting.

St. George's Anglican Church, on Cayon Street (walk stright up Church Street or Fort Street from the dock), is the oldest church in town and is worth a look.

ON YOUR OWN: BEYOND WALKING DISTANCE

The **Brimstone Hill Fortress** (☎ **869/465-6211**), 9 miles west of Basseterre, is the major stop on any tour of St. Kitts. This historic monument, among the largest and best preserved in the Caribbean, is a complex of bastions, barracks, and other structures ingeniously adapted to the top and upper slopes of a steep, 800-foot hill.

The name of the place derives from the odor of sulfer released by nearby undersea vents.

The structure dates from 1690, when the British fortified the hill to help recapture Fort Charles below from the French. In 1782, an invading force of 8,000 French troops bombarded the fortress for a month before its small British garrison, supplemented by local militia, surrendered. When the British took the island back the next year, they proceeded to enlarge the fort into "The Gibraltar of the West Indies." In all, the fort took 104 years to complete.

Today the fortress is the centerpiece of a national park featuring nature trails and a diverse range of plant and animal life, including green vervet monkeys. It's also a photographer's paradise, with views of mountains, fields, and the Caribbean Sea. On a clear day you can see six neighboring islands. From below, the fort presents a dramatic picture, poised among diabolical-looking spires and outcroppings of lava rock.

Visitors will enjoy the self-directed tours among the many ruined or restored structures, including the barrack rooms at Fort George. The gift shop sells prints of rare maps and paintings of the Caribbean. Admission is $5 for adults, $2.50 for children. The park is open daily from 9:30am to 5:30pm.

Mount Liamuiga, in the northwest of the island, was dubbed "Mount Misery" long ago. This dormant volcano sputtered its last gasp around 1692. Today, it's a major goal for hikers. A round-trip to the usually cloud-covered peak takes about 4 hours—$2^1/2$ hours going up, $1^1/2$ coming down. Hikers usually make the ascent from Belmont Estate near St. Paul on the north end of St. Kitts. The trail winds through a rain forest and travels along deep ravines up to the rim of the crater at a cool 2,625 feet. Many hikers climb—or crawl—down a steep, slippery trail to a tiny lake in the caldera, some 400 feet below the rim.

You can reach the rim without a guide, but it's absolutely necessary to have one to go into the crater. **Greg's Safaris** (☎ 869/465-4121) offers guided hikes to the crater for about $60 per person (a minimum of four hikers required), including breakfast and a picnic at the crater's rim. The same outfit also offers half-day rainforest explorations, also with a picnic, for $35 per person.

SHOPPING

Basseterre is not a shopping town, despite the handout maps you'll likely receive when you arrive, which show a listing of shops that would put St. Thomas's Charlotte Amalie to shame—that is, until you look closer and see entries like "R. Gumbs Electrical," "TDC/Finco Finance Co.," and "Horsford Furniture Store." Turns out they just listed *every* business on every street in town, no matter whether it's of interest to visitors or not. Strength in numbers, I suppose.

The closest thing to high-quality shopping is at **Pelican Shopping Mall,** with over a dozen shops, as well as banking services, a restaurant, and a philatelic bureau where collectors can buy St. Kitts stamps and everyone else can mail letters. Here too, though, don't expect much (and whose idea was it to build a covered mall in the sunny Caribbean, anyway?).

At Romney Manor—now more appropriately named Romney Gardens since most of the manor itself burned down in 1996—you'll find **Caribelle Batik** (☎ 869/465-6253), one of the island's most visible boutiques. Inside, artisans demonstrate their Indonesian-style handprinting amid rack after rack of brightly colored clothes. Brimstone Hill and rain-forest hike shore excursions typically include a stop here. If you're coming on your own, look for signs indicating a turnoff along the coast road, about 5 miles north of Basseterre.

BEACHES

The narrow peninsula in the southeast contains the island's salt ponds and also boasts the best white-sand beaches. You'll find the best swimming at **Conaree Beach,** 3 miles from Basseterre; **Frigate Bay,** with its talcum-powder fine sand; the twin beaches of **Banana Bay** and **Cockleshell Bay,** at the southeast corner of the island; and **Friar's Bay,** a peninsula beach opening onto both the Atlantic and the Caribbean. All beaches, even those that border hotels, are open to the public. However, you must usually pay a fee to use a hotel's beach facilities.

SPORTS

GOLF The **Royal St. Kitts Golf Course,** Frigate Bay (☎ **869/465-8339**), is an 18-hole, par-72 championship course featuring seven beautiful ponds. It's bounded on the south by the Caribbean Sea and on the north by the Atlantic Ocean.

SCUBA DIVING & SNORKELING One of the best diving spots is **Nagshead,** at the southern tip of St. Kitts. This is an excellent shallow-water dive for certified divers starting at 10 feet and extending to 70 feet. You'll see a variety of tropical fish, eaglerays, and lobster here. Another good site is **Booby Shoals,** between Cow 'n' Calf Rocks and Booby Island. Booby Shoals has abundant sea life, including nurse sharks, lobster, and stingrays. Dives here are up to 30 feet in depth, and are good for both certified and beginning divers. **Pro-Divers,** at Turtle Beach (☎ **869/465-3223**), arranges scuba-diving and snorkeling expeditions.

GREAT LOCAL RESTAURANTS & BARS

The favorite **local beer** is Carib, brewed right on the northern edge of Basseterre. There's a local cane sugar drink called CSR (Cane Spirit Rothschild), but it's pretty foul.

If you're looking for that unspoiled, casual beach restaurant, try **The Anchorage,** Frigate Bay (☎ **869/465-8235**), for a rum drink, hamburgers, or a dozen kinds of sandwiches along with fresh fish. **Ballahoo Restaurant** (☎ **869/465-4197**), located in Basseterre's most picturesque intersection, The Circus, right by the cruise dock, serves some of the best chili and baby back ribs in town. Seafood platters, such as chili shrimp or fresh lobster, are served with a coconut salad and rice.

NEVIS

Nevis, though smaller than St. Kitts and lacking a major historical site like Brimstone Hill Fortress, is nevertheless far more appealing and upbeat—perhaps because it hasn't been hit so hard by the hurricanes that have devastated its sister island. It's capital city, Charlestown, has a lovely mixture of port-town exuberance and small-town charm.

Nevis lies 2 miles south of St. Kitts, and when viewed from there appears to be a perfect cone, rising gradually to a height of 3,232 feet. In 1493, Columbus first sighted the island, naming it Las Nieves, Spanish for "snows," because its peak reminded him of the Pyrenees. Settled by the British in 1628, the island became a prosperous sugar-growing island as well as the most popular spa island of the 18th century, when people flocked in from other West Indian islands to visit its hot mineral springs.

Nevis's two most famous historical residents were **Admiral Horatio Nelson,** who married a local woman here in 1787, and **Alexander Hamilton,** who was born here and went on to find fame as a drafter of the American Federalist Papers, as George Washington's secretary of the treasury, and as Aaron Burr's unfortunate dueling partner.

Frommer's Favorite Nevis Experiences

- **Wandering around Charlestown:** The capital city is a fine place to wander around on your own, visiting Alexander Hamilton's birthplace, the small but appealing Nelson Museum, and the 17th-century Jewish cemetery, poking your head into some of the small shops, or greeting the goats and chickens that wander past, evidently taking their own walking tours. (See "On Your Own: Within Walking Distance," below.)
- **Taking some downtime on Pinney's Beach:** It's a little less crowded now that Hurricane Lenny took out the Four Seasons Resort, but Pinney's hasn't otherwise lost any of its charm. Lounge back, have a beer, take a swim in the reef-protected waters, do a little snorkeling, or engage in some beachcombing. Talk about relaxation. (See "Beaches," below.)

COMING ASHORE   Only small ships call on Nevis, docking right in the center of Charlestown and/or dropping anchor off the coast of beautiful Pinney's Bay Beach.

INFORMATION   There's a small tourist board office on Main Street, near the docks. If you want to collect additional information ahead of time, contact the tourism board office in the United States at ☎ 212/535-1234 or www.stkitts-nevis.com.

GETTING AROUND

BY TAXI   The entirety of Charlestown is accessible on foot, but if you want to visit Pinney's Beach or elsewhere on the island, you can hop a taxi in Charlestown. The cost to Pinney's is about $5.55. Taxi drivers double as guides on Nevis, so if you want to take a general tour of the island, negotiate a price with your driver.

BY RENTAL CAR   Driving is on the left side in Nevis and most of the worthwhile sites are within walking distance, so I don't recommend renting a car here.

SHORE EXCURSIONS

Aside from island tours you can arrange through taxi drivers and excursions to Pinney's Beach that are part and parcel of some cruise lines' visits to the island, there are no organized shore excursions offered here.

ON YOUR OWN: WITHIN WALKING DISTANCE

If your ship docks in Charlestown, you're dead center of a perfect walking-tour opportunity. Charlestown is a lovely little place, laid back in somewhat the same manner as St. John, but with some of the really rural character of sister island St. Kitts.

If you head left from the docks and walk a little ways (maybe a quarter mile) along Main Street, you'll come to the **Alexander Hamilton Birthplace,** where the road curves just before the turnoff to Island Road. It's a lovely little two-level house set

Frommer's Ratings: Nevis					
	Poor	Fair	Good	Excellent	Outstanding
Overall Experience				✓	
Shore Excursions	✓				
Activities Close to Port				✓	
Beaches & Water Sports			✓		
Shopping		✓			
Dining/Bars		✓			

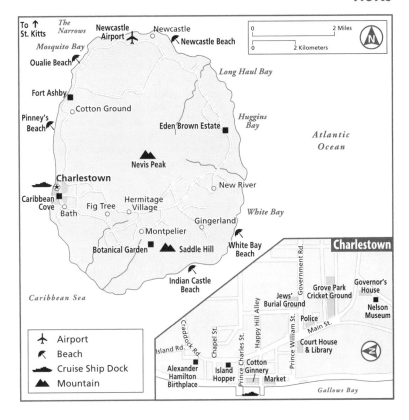

right on the coastline. On the first floor is a small museum and gift shop (admission $2), but in all honesty you'll do just as well to skip it and just appreciate the outside, spending a moment to read the historic plaque. Far be it for me to take a couple dollars out of the island's economy, though, so if you're feeling philanthropic, drop your two bucks and then head on for the rest of your walk.

Backtracking along Main Street you'll pass several serviceable shops (see "Shopping," below). Keep walking through the center of town, saying "hi" to the occasional mama goat and kids you'll pass, then turn left onto Government Road. One block up on the left you'll find the **Jews' Burial Ground,** with graves from 1684 to 1768. Stones left atop the graves attest to the visitors who have been there before you to pay their respects. When I was there, the dead were being entertained with reggae music coming from the doorway of a shop across the street, while a breeze stirred the few trees on the property. All in all, not a bad resting spot.

Backtrack to Main Street, turn left, and continue on past the Grove Park Cricket Ground, bearing left when the road forks. Head up the hill (where you'll see an abandoned hotel and several buildings standing alone on the hill to your right), then turn at the first right, which will bring you back *behind* those buildings, the first of which is the inaccessible Government House and the second of which is the **Nelson Museum.** A very small, very homemade kind of place, it's nevertheless a very interesting and evocative spot, and well worth the $2 admission. The museum traces the history of Admiral Horatio Nelson's career enforcing England's Navigation Acts in the Caribbean, and also houses artifacts from Nevis's Carib, Arawak, and Aceramic peoples, as well as a small display on Nevis today. The timeline of Nelson's Caribbean career includes ship models, ceramic and bronze Nelson figures, paintings of his battles and other scenes, a scrap from the Union Jack under which the admiral was standing when he was shot, a miniature of his casket, and an actual ticket to his funeral, with wax seal. A tiny birdcage with wood enclosing box bears the inscription, "In a number of letters written to Fanny Nisbet [Nelson's wife], Nelson mentioned his search for a traveling birdcage. This bird cage, though not the one Nelson finally procured, is from that period."

The museum's display also includes a number of wonderful clay replicas, including one of the old "Coolie Man's Store," by local artist Gustage "Bush Tea" Williams.

Once back outside, amble slowly off in the same direction you were going (right from the gate). Keep bearing right, and you'll eventually be back on Main Street, in plenty of time to do a little shopping or stop in to one of the local bars or restaurants.

ON YOUR OWN: BEYOND WALKING DISTANCE

Besides Pinney's Beach (see "Beaches," below), there are few other obvious attractions on the island outside of Charlestown. On the east coast, about 1¹/₂ miles from New River, the **Eden Brown Estate** is said to be haunted. Once it was the home of a wealthy planter whose daughter's husband-to-be was killed in a duel at the prenuptial feast. The mansion was then closed and left to the ravages of nature. A solid gray stone still stands. Only the most adventurous, they say, come here on a moonlit night (so it's a good thing you have an excuse—your ship is bound to sail before sunset).

SHOPPING

Nevis is not a shopping hub on the order of St. Thomas or even the much more laid-back St. John. In fact, it's no kind of shopping hub at all. Still, there are a few shops worth poking your head into, all of them along Main Street, right in the port area.

Island Hopper, on Main, one block north of Prince Charles Street, is the best shop for visitors in town, stocking a huge selection of batik clothing. The **Nevis Handcraft Cooperative Society,** at the corner of Main and Prince Charles streets, is pretty sparse, but does carry some folklorically bottled hot sauces and guava jellies, as well as some low-quality craft items. **Pemberton Gift Shop,** across Main Street from Island Hopper, is also sparse, but has a selection of T-shirts, gift items, and a shelf of CSR (Cane Spirit Rothschild), a local cane sugar liquor which, truth to tell, is pretty foul, but cheap enough if you're dead set on exploring all the islands' alcoholic output. **Jerveren's Fashions,** in the Cotton Ginnery complex right at the pier, has a decent selection of T-shirts and gifts.

For stamp collectors, the **Nevis Philatelic Bureau** at the Head Post Office, on Market Street next to the public market (1 block south and 1 block east of the docks) has a range of Nevis stamps.

BEACHES

The name to know on Nevis is **Pinney's Beach,** located north of Charlestown. Though not quite the bustling spot it was before Hurricane Lenny did a number on the adjoining Four Season's Resort (not to mention the backing palm trees, which have seen better days), it's still a lovely spot for swimming, snorkeling, beachcombing, or just sitting back and watching the pelicans dive-bomb into the surf.

Sunshine's Bar and Grill, "Home of the Killer Bee," sits right on the beach, offering beer and other refreshments along with the aforementioned Bees.

GREAT LOCAL RESTAURANTS & BARS

Eddy's, on Main Steet in Charlestown (☎ 869/496-5958), on an upper floor and offering a balcony's-eye view of the slowly bustling town below, is the best place in town. **Muriel's Cuisine,** on Upper Happyhill Alley (☎ 869/469-5920), is in the back of a concrete building whose front houses the Limetree shop. It serves typical local West Indian food. **Cotton House Restaurant and Bar,** on the second floor of the Cotton House complex, right by the cruise dock, is nothing fancy, but makes for a pleasant place to grab a snack and a beer in the shade.

25 St. Lucia

In a turbulent history shared by many of its Caribbean neighbors, St. Lucia (pronounced *Loo*-sha), second largest of the Windward Islands at about 240 square miles, changed hands often during the colonial period, being British seven times and French seven times. Today, though, it's an independent state that's become one of the most popular destinations in the Caribbean, with some of the finest resorts. The heaviest development is concentrated in the northwest, between the capital of Castries and the northern end of the island, where there's a string of white-sand beaches. The interior boasts relatively unspoiled green-mantled mountains and gentle valleys, as well as the volcanic Mount Soufrière. Two dramatic peaks (the Pitons), rise along the southwest coast.

Castries, the capital, has grown up around an extinct volcanic crater that's now a large harbor surrounded by hills. Because of devastating fires, the town today has touches of modernity, with glass-and-concrete buildings, but there's still an old-fashioned Saturday-morning market on Jeremie Street. The country women dress in traditional cotton headdress to sell their luscious fruits and vegetables, while weather-beaten men sit close by playing *warrie,* a fast game played with pebbles on a carved board, or fleet games of dominoes with tiles the color of cherries.

Frommer's Favorite St. Lucia Experiences

- **Riding a catamaran along the coast:** See the lush coast of St. Lucia and the mighty Pitons via catamaran, and then ride a minibus to visit a volcano, the Diamond Baths, and sulfur springs (see "Shore Excursions," below).
- **Exploring a banana plantation:** Bananas are St. Lucia's leading export (see "On Your Own: Beyond Walking Distance," below).
- **Hiking up to Fort Rodney in Rodney Bay:** The beautiful Pigeon Island on Rodney Bay offers the chance to hike up to Fort Rodney, an 18th-century English base that was used as an American signal station during World War II. From the top you can catch site of Martinique. (See "On Your Own: Beyond Walking Distance," below.)

COMING ASHORE   Most cruise ships arrive at the fairly new pier at Pointe Seraphine, within walking distance from the center of Castries. Unlike piers on other islands, this one contains St. Lucia's best shopping. You'll find a money exchange, a small visitor information bureau, and a cable and wireless office. Phone cards are sold for use at specially labeled phones.

If Pointe Seraphine is too crowded, your ship might dock at Port Castries (also called Port Careenage). There's now a shopping terminal here called La Place Careenage, but if you still want to shop in Pointe Seraphine, a water taxi ($1) runs between the two all day. A taxi will cost you around $4. You can also walk between the two. Some smaller vessels, such as Seabourn's, anchor off Soufrière and carry you ashore by tender.

There are **telephones** right outside the port gate at Port Careenage, the town's cargo dock, and at the pier at Pointe Seraphine.

CURRENCY   The official monetary unit is the **Eastern Caribbean dollar (EC$).** The exchange rate is EC$2.70 to U.S.$1 (EC$1 = U.S.37¢).Most of the prices quoted in this section are in U.S. dollars, which are accepted by nearly all hotels, restaurants, and shops.

LANGUAGE   English is the official language.

INFORMATION   The **St. Lucia Tourist Board** is at Point Seraphine in Castries (☎ **758/452-4094**). It's open Monday to Friday from 9am to 5pm. For info before you go, contact the tourism board office in the United States at ☎ **800/456-3984** or 212/867-2950 or www.sluonestop.com.

CALLING FROM THE U.S.   When calling St. Lucia from the United States, you need to dial only a "1" before the numbers listed throughout this section.

GETTING AROUND

BY TAXI   Most taxi drivers have been trained to serve as guides. Their cars are unmetered, but the government fixes tariffs for all standard trips. Be sure to determine if the driver is quoting a rate in U.S. or EC dollars. For touring, expect to pay about $5 per person per hour with a minimum of four passengers; with fewer, it's still $20 an hour. You can hire a taxi to go to Soufrière on your own, too. A taxi for four will cost about $120 for a 3- to 4-hour tour, including a beach stop, photo ops, shopping, and sightseeing. Avoid any driver who is not in uniform (which is really just a light-cotton tropical shirt).

BY RENTAL CAR   Driving is on the left, and is not recommended.

SHORE EXCURSIONS

Because of the difficult terrain, shore excursions are the best means of seeing this beautiful island in a day or less. In addition to the sampling below, most ships typically offer plantation tours, island bus tours, and snorkeling cruises.

✪ **Island Tour by Land and Sea** ($69 to $82, 8 hours): A picturesque journey from Castries via catamaran to the Piton peaks takes you along St. Lucia's verdant coast, docking at La Soufrière, where passengers board minibuses and visit the volcano, the Diamond Baths (see "On Your Own: Beyond Walking Distance," below), and sulfur springs. Lunch is included at a restaurant in Soufrière or on the boat.

Frommer's Ratings: St. Lucia					
	Poor	Fair	Good	Excellent	Outstanding
Overall Experience				✓	
Shore Excursions				✓	
Activities Close to Port			✓		
Beaches & Water Sports				✓	
Shopping		✓			
Dining/Bars			✓		

St. Lucia

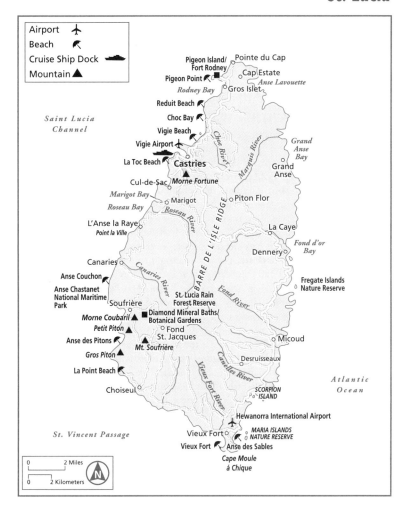

Mountain Ridge Bike Tour ($75, 3¹/₂ hours): From Castries, travel by bus to the top of Morne Fortune where your bike ride begins. You'll pedal through hilltop roads with dramatic views of the harbor on one side and a stunning mountain range on the other. The ride goes past banana plantations, through rural neighborhoods, and through lush valleys.

Morne Coubaril Plantation Tour ($46, 4 hours): By minibus, ride along the island's west coast, between the sea and the rain forest, with views of the Pitons. At the Morne Coubaril Estate, tour the working family plantation, and watch how coconuts, coffee, and cocoa are processed.

Pigeon Island Hike and Beach Swim ($44, 4 hours): A steep walk up to the fort on Pigeon Island where St. Lucians last defeated the French. From the summit, you'll have great views of the Pitons, and sometimes you'll even be able to see Martinique. After the hike, there's a pleasant swim in the island's gin-clear waters and complimentary refreshment in the Captain's Cellar, a rustic pub located in an old fort's Soldier's Mess. Outside are wonderful views of the crashing surf on the Atlantic coast.

Anse Chastanet Snorkel Trip ($18, 3 hours): Travel by jeep to St. Lucia's Anse Chastanet National Marine Park, where you snorkel among an amazing variety of reef fish.

ON YOUR OWN: WITHIN WALKING DISTANCE

First, a tip: In the duty-free marketplaces right at Castries's dock, a guy doles out portable massages for $5 for 5 minutes (this could save you a bundle on those expensive Steiner massages on board!).

The principal streets of Castries are William Peter Boulevard and Bridge Street. A Roman Catholic cathedral stands on Columbus Square, which has a few restored buildings. Also take a gander there at the enormous 400-year-old "rain" tree, also called a "no-name" tree. **Government House** is a late Victorian structure.

Beyond Government House lies **Morne Fortune,** which means "Hill of Good Luck." Actually, no one's had much luck here, certainly not the French and British that battled for **Fort Charlotte.** The fort changed nationalities many times. You can visit the 18th-century barracks, complete with a military cemetery, a small museum, the Old Powder Magazine, and the "Four Apostles Battery"—four grim muzzle-loading cannons. The view of the harbor of Castries is panoramic. You can also see north to Pigeon Island or south to the Pitons. To reach Morne Fortune, head east on Bridge Street.

Definitely don't miss a walk through town. People are very friendly, and Jeremie Street is chockablock with variety stores of the most authentic local kind, selling everything from spices to housewares. Castries's very colorful **Central Market** right near the dock is also worth a visit. The airplane-hangar-size emporium sells local food, trinkets, and produce. Buy some banana ketchup or local cinnamon sticks to take home.

ON YOUR OWN: BEYOND WALKING DISTANCE

Bananas are St. Lucia's leading export, so if you're being taken around the island by a taxi driver, ask him to take you to one of the huge plantations. I suggest a look at one of the three biggest: the **Cul-de-Sac,** just north of Marigot Bay; **La Caya,** in Dennery on the east coast; and the **Roseau Estate,** south of Marigot Bay.

St. Lucia's first national park, **Pigeon Island National Landmark,** was originally an island but is now joined to the northwest shore of the mainland by a very environmentally unfriendly causeway. The 44-acre island got its name from the redneck pigeon, or *ramier,* which once made this island home. It's ideal for picnics and nature walks, and is covered with lemongrass that spread from original plantings made by British light opera singer Josset, who leased the island for 30 years and grew the grass to provide thatch for her cottage's roof. Every few years the grass catches fire and immolates much of the island before it can be put out, due to the volatile oils it contains.

The island's Interpretation Centre is equipped with artifacts and a multimedia display of local history, ranging from the Amerindian occupation of A.D. 1000 to the Battle of Saints, when Admiral Rodney's fleet set out from Pigeon Island and defeated Admiral De Grasse in 1782. Right below the interpretation center is the Captain's Cellar pub.

From the interpretation center you can walk up the winding and moderately steep path to a lookout from which you can see Martinique. In 1780, Admiral

Rodney said of this spot, ". . . This is the post the Governor of Martinique has set his eye on and if possessed by the enemy would deprive us of the best anchorage place in these islands, from which Martinique is always attackable." Remember that when planning your own assault. From the pinnacle you get a wonderful view, and the cannons that ring the space are a nice place to pose for "I was there" pictures.

On Pigeon Island's west coast are two white-sand beaches. There's also a restaurant, **Jambe de Bois** ("Leg of Wood"), named after a peg-legged pirate who once used the island as a hideout.

The park is open daily from 9am to 5pm. For more information, call the **St. Lucia National Trust** (☎ 758/452-5005). The best way to get here is to take a taxi and arrange to be picked up in time to return to the ship.

La Soufrière, a little fishing port and St. Lucia's second largest settlement, is dominated by the dramatic ✪ **Pitons,** two pointed peaks called Petit Piton and Gros Piton, which rise to 2,460 and 2,619 feet, respectively, right from the sea. Formed by lava and once actively volcanic, these mountains are now clothed in green vegetation, with waves crashing around their bases. Their sheer rise from the water makes them such visible landmarks that they've become the very symbol of St. Lucia.

Near the town of Soufrière lies the famous "drive-in" volcano, ✪ **La Soufrière,** a rocky lunar landscape of bubbling mud and craters seething with fuming sulfur. You literally ride into an old crater and walk between the sulfur springs and pools of hissing steam. The fumes are said to have medicinal properties. A local guide is usually waiting nearby; if you do hire a guide, agree—then doubly agree—on what the fee will be.

Nearby are the **Diamond Mineral Baths** (☎ 758/452-4759), surrounded by a tropical arboretum. They were constructed in 1784 by order of Louis XVI, whose doctors told him that these waters were similar in mineral content to the waters at Aix-les-Bains. Their purpose was to help French soldiers fighting in the West Indies recuperate. Later destroyed, they were rebuilt after World War II. The water's average temperature is 106°F. You'll also find another fine attraction here: a waterfall that changes colors (from yellow to black to green to gray) several times a day. For about EC$7 ($2.60), you can bathe and benefit from the recuperative effects yourself.

SHOPPING

Many stores sell duty-free goods; they also deliver tobacco products and liquor to the cruise dock. Keep in mind, you are only allowed to purchase one bottle of liquor here (in St. Thomas, you can buy five). You'll find some good but not remarkable buys in bone china, jewelry, perfume, watches, liquor, and crystal. Souvenir items include designer bags and mats, local pottery, and straw hats—again, nothing remarkable. *A tip:* If local vendors know your cruise also calls in St. Thomas, they may be more amenable to bargaining.

Built for cruise ship passengers, **Pointe Seraphine** has the best collection of shops on the island. You must present your cruise pass when making purchases here. Liquor and tobacco will be delivered to the ship.

Gablewoods Mall, on Gros Islet Highway, 2 miles north of Castries, contains three restaurants and one of the densest concentrations of stores on St. Lucia. Since this mall is near some lovely beaches (and to Sandals St. Lucia), it's possible to plan a day that combines shopping and sunbathing.

At **Caribelle Batik,** Howelton House, Old Victoria Road, The Morne, just a 5-minute taxi ride from Castries, you can watch St. Lucian artists creating intricate patterns and colors through the ancient art of batik. **Eudovic Art Studio,** Goodlands, Morne Fortune, sells wood carvings by Vincent Joseph Eudovic, a native of St. Lucia, and some of his pupils. Take a taxi from the cruise pier. **Choiseul Art & Craft Center,** La Fargue, Choiseul (southwest of Castries), is a government-funded retail outlet and training school that perpetuates the tradition of handmade Amerindian pottery and basketware. Some of the best basket weaving on the island is done here, using techniques practiced only in St. Lucia, St. Vincent, and Dominica. Look for place mats, handbags, woodcarvings (including bas-reliefs crafted from screw pine), and pottery.

BEACHES

If you don't take a shore excursion, you might want to spend your time on one of St. Lucia's famous beaches. A taxi to **Marigot Beach,** for instance, south of Castries Harbour, costs around $20. I prefer the calmer shores along the western coast, since the rough surf on the windward Atlantic side makes swimming potentially dangerous.

Leading beaches include **Pigeon Island,** off the northern shore, with white sand and picnic facilities; **Vigie Beach,** north of Castries Harbour, with fine sands; and **Reduit Beach,** with its fine brown sands, which lies between Choc Bay and Pigeon Point. For a novelty, you might try the black-volcanic-sand beach at Soufrière.

Just north of Soufrière is that beach connoisseur's delight, **Anse Chastanet** (☎ 758/459-7000), with its white sands set at the foothills of lush, green mountains. While here, you might want to patronize the facilities of the Anse Chastanet Hotel.

All beaches are open to the public, even those along hotel properties, but you must pay to use a hotel's beach equipment.

SPORTS

HORSEBACK RIDING   You can go horseback riding at **Cas-En-Bas and Cap Estate Stables,** north of Castries. To make arrangements, call René Trim at ☎ 758/450-8273. Ask about a picnic trip to the Atlantic side of the island, with a barbecue lunch and drinks included. Departures are at 8:30am, 10am, 2pm, and 4pm. Nonriders can also join the excursion; they are transported to the site in a van and pay half price.

SCUBA DIVING   In Soufrière, **Scuba St. Lucia,** in the Anse Chastanet Hotel (☎ 758/459-7000), at the southern end of Anse Chastanet's quarter-mile secluded beach, is a five-star PADI dive center. It offers great diving and comprehensive facilities. Some of the most spectacular coral reefs of St. Lucia—many only 10 to 20 feet below the surface—provide shelter for sea creatures just a short distance offshore. **Rosemond Trench Divers, Ltd.,** at the Marigot Beach Club, Marigot Bay (☎ 758/451-4761), will take both novices and experienced divers to shallow reefs or to some of the most challenging trenches in the Caribbean.

WATER SPORTS   The best center for all water sports except diving is **St. Lucian Watersports,** on Reduit Beach at the Rex St. Lucian Hotel (☎ 758/452-8351).

GREAT LOCAL RESTAURANTS & BARS

A really, really great **local beer** is Piton—very refreshing on a hot day, like Corona but better. A favorite **local rum** is Bounty.

IN CASTRIES   At the **Green Parrot,** Red Tape Lane, Morne Fortune, about 1¹/₂ miles east of the town center (☎ 758/452-3399), there's an emphasis on St. Lucian specialties and homegrown produce. It's trained cruise ship chefs in the use of local products when preparing meals. Try the *christophine au gratin* (a Caribbean squash with cheese) or the Creole soup made with callaloo and pumpkin. One of the newest restaurants on the block is **Café Panache,** located next to the Central Library in Castries, near Derek Walcott Square. It's situated in a century-old family home of Sir Arthur Lewis, St. Lucia's first (and probably only) Nobel Prize winner for economics. The menu features a combo of local, French, and American cuisine. **Jimmie's,** Vigie Cove Marina (☎ 758/452-5142), is known for its fresh-fish menu and tasty Creole cookery. Constructed in the 19th century as a Great House, **San Antoine,** Morne Fortune (☎ 758/452-4660), lies up the Morne hill. You might begin with the classic callaloo soup, and then follow with fettuccine Alfredo, or perhaps fresh fish *en papillote* (baked in parchment). The view and ambiance are more stunning than the cuisine. If you're an aficionado of true local cooking, some of the most authentic varieties can be sampled at the tiny restaurants in the Central Market, which serve plates piled high with local dishes (cow-heel soup anyone?).

AT MARIGOT BAY   Café Paradis, at the Marigot Beach Club (take a ferry across Marigot Bay; ☎ 758/451-4974), is a culinary showplace, the proud domain of a French-trained chef who was eager to escape to the Caribbean. To reach the place, you'll have to take a ferryboat across Marigot Bay. It runs from the Moorings Marigot Bay Resort about every 10 minutes throughout the day and evening. **Hurricane Hole,** in the Moorings, Marigot Bay (☎ 758/451-4357), is the cozy restaurant of the Marigot Bay Resort, which charters yachts to clients from around the hemisphere. The menu is geared to surf-and-turf fans.

IN THE SOUFRIÈRE AREA   Chez Camilla Guest House & Restaurant, 7 Bridge St., 1 block inland from the waterfront (☎ 758/459-5379), which is the only really good place to eat in the village of Soufrière itself, serves sandwiches, cold salads, omelets, and burgers at lunch. **Dasheene Restaurant & Bar,** in the Ladera Resort, between Gros and Petit Piton (☎ 758/459-7323), serves the most refined and certainly the most creative cuisine in St. Lucia. The chef has a special flair for seafood pasta or marinated sirloin steak. Best bet is the catch of the day, likely to be kingfish or red snapper, grilled to perfection. South of Soufrière is a restaurant with a fabulous view, Dasheene. It's perched atop a 1,000-foot ridge and framed by the rising twin peaks of the Pitons. Everything is local, including the furniture. The menu includes yummy dishes like dumpling and callaloo soup, fresh pumpkin risotto with red pepper coulis, and a banana-stuffed pork with ginger and coconut sauce.

IN RODNEY BAY   The Lime, Rodney Bay, north of Reduit Beach (☎ 758/452-0761), is a casual local place specializing in stuffed crab backs and fish steak Creole, and it also serves shrimp, steaks, lamb and pork chops, and rotis (Caribbean burritos). **The Mortar & Pestle,** in the Harmony Marina Suites, Rodney Bay Lagoon (☎ 758/452-8711), offers indoor-outdoor dining with a view of the boats moored at the nearby marina. For something truly regional, try the Barbados souse, with marinated pieces of lean cooked pork, or the frogs' legs from Dominica.

26 Sint Maarten & St. Martin

Legend has it that a gin-drinking Dutchman and a wine-guzzling Frenchman walked around this island one day in 1648 to claim territory for their countries. The Frenchman covered the most ground, but the canny Dutchman got the more valuable real estate. Whether the story is true or not, this island, measuring only 37 square miles, is today the smallest territory in the world shared by two sovereign states. The Dutch side is known as Sint Maarten; the French side, St. Martin. Once you've cleared customs on either side, the only way you'll know you're crossing from

Holland into France is by the BIENVENUE FRANÇAISE signs marking the boundary. Coexistence between the two nations is very peaceful.

Most cruise ships land at **Philipsburg,** capital of the Dutch side, although smaller ships can maneuver into the harbor of **Marigot** on the French side. Don't come to either side to escape the crowds. The 100% duty-free shopping has turned the island into somewhat of a shopper's paradise (more so on the Dutch side), and Philipsburg especially is nearly always bustling with cruise ship passengers.

Although the boom was severely slowed by the hurricanes of 1995, the island quickly rebuilt, and today its 36 white-sand beaches remain unspoiled, if somewhat rearranged by Mother Nature, and the clear turquoise waters are as enticing as ever.

SINT MAARTEN

Founded in 1763 by Comdr. John Phillips, a Scot in Dutch employ, Sint Maarten's capital, **Philipsburg,** curves along the shores of Great Bay. The main thoroughfare is busy Front Street, which stretches for about a mile and is lined with stores selling international merchandise. More shops lie along the little lanes, known as *steegjes,* that connect Front Street with Back Street, another shoppers' mart.

Frommer's Favorite Sint Maarten Experiences

- **Joining the America's Cup sailing regatta:** What an opportunity! You get to race against actual former contenders from the famed America's Cup race (see "Shore Excursions," below).
- **Heading to the beach at Orient Bay:** On the French side, colorful open-air restaurants line this very European beach and its striped umbrellas (see "Shore Excursions," below).

COMING ASHORE   Most vessels land at Philipsburg, docking about a mile southwest of town at A. C. Wathey Pier at Point Blanche. Some passengers walk the distance, but taxis do await all cruise ships. There are almost no facilities at A. C. Wathey Pier except for a few phones. Some ships anchor in the mouth of the harbor, and then take passengers by tender to Little Pier in the heart of town.

There are a few AT&T **credit-card phones** at Philipsburg's A.C. Wathey Pier.

CURRENCY   The legal tender in Dutch Sint Maarten is the **Netherlands Antilles guilder (NAf).** The exchange rate is 1.77 NAf to U.S.$1 (1 NAf = U.S.56¢). However, U.S. dollars are also accepted here. Prices in this section are usually given in U.S. currency.

LANGUAGE   Although the official language is Dutch, most people also speak English.

INFORMATION   For Dutch Sint Maarten, go to the **Tourist Information Bureau,** in the Imperial Building at 23 Walter Nisbeth Rd. (☎ **599/54-22337**).

Frommer's Ratings: Sint Maarten					
	Poor	Fair	Good	Excellent	Outstanding
Overall Experience				✓	
Shore Excursions			✓		
Activities Close to Port				✓	
Beaches & Water Sports			✓		
Shopping					✓
Dining/Bars			✓		

Sint Maarten & St. Martin

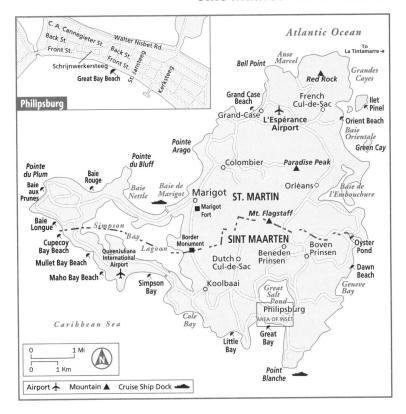

It's open Monday to Friday from 8am to 5pm. For info before you go, contact the tourist board office in the United States at ☎800/786-2278 or 212/953-2084 or www.st-maarten.com.

CALLING FROM THE U.S. When calling Sint Maarten from the United States, you need to dial "011" before the numbers listed in this section.

GETTING AROUND

TAXIS Taxis are unmetered, but Dutch Sint Maarten law requires drivers to list fares to major destinations on the island. There are minimum fares for two passengers, and each additional passenger pays another $2. Call a cab at ☎ 599/54-54317.

MINIBUSES The privately owned and operated minibuses are a reasonable way to get around, if you don't mind some inconveniences and possible overcrowding. They run daily from 7am to midnight and serve most major locations on Sint Maarten. Fares range from about $1 to $2. The most popular run is from Philipsburg to Marigot on the French side.

BY RENTAL CAR Rental cars are a practical way to see both the Dutch and the French sides of the island. **Budget** (☎ 800/527-0700 in the U.S., or 599/54-54030), **Hertz** (☎ 800/654-3131 in the U.S., or 599/54-54314), and **Avis** (☎ 800/331-1212 in the U.S., or 599/54-52847) all have agencies here. If you're calling in advance, you might try **Auto Europe** (☎ 800/223-5555). Rates begin at about $50 per day with unlimited mileage for a subcompact car. Drive on the right-hand side of the road on both sides of the island.

SHORE EXCURSIONS

The beaches and shopping are some of the biggest attractions here. Other typical excursions include snorkeling cruises and island tours.

✪ **America's Cup Sailing Regatta** ($71, 3 hours): Sail on one of the actual former contenders of the America's Cup race, and compete in an actual race. This is a hands-on tour where you'll be grinding winches, trimming sails, and ducking under booms. It's great fun.

Island Tour ($20, 3 hours): By minibus, you'll see both sides, stopping for panoramic views. There's usually a stopover in Marigot for sightseeing and shopping.

Ilet Pinel Snorkeling Tour ($29, 3 hours): After a scenic bus ride to Cul-de-Sac on the French side, take a tender to Ilet Pinel for snorkeling (equipment is included in the price).

Butterfly Farm and Marigot ($28–$38, $3^{1}/_{2}$ hours): After a scenic drive through both the French and Dutch sides of the island, visit a butterfly farm, where a guide points out the different species. End the tour with a short stop in Marigot.

Orient Bay Excursion ($43, 4–5 hours): You'll be driven to the beach in Orient Bay, with the driver narrating the sights along the way. Spend a couple of hours at this wide, colorful beach, often called "the French Riviera of the Caribbean." The excursion includes beach chairs and lunch.

ON YOUR OWN

This is a shopping/beaching/gambling kind of port, and all those attractions are covered in the other sections of this review.

GAMBLING

In the absence of natural wonders or man-made attractions, the biggest onshore lure for cruise ship passengers are the casinos on the Dutch side. They open anywhere between 11am and 1pm daily and operate into the wee hours of the night.

Most of the casinos are in the big hotels. **Casino Royale,** at the Maho Beach Hotel on Maho Bay (☎ **599/54-52115**), which opened in 1975, has six roulette wheels, three craps tables, 16 blackjack tables, and three Caribbean stud-poker tables. It also offers baccarat, mini-baccarat, and more than 250 slot machines. There's no admission, and a snack buffet is complimentary.

Another popular casino is at the **Pelican Resort and Casino** on Simpson Bay (☎ **599/54-42503**), built to a Swiss design incorporating a panoramic view of the water. This Las Vegas–style casino has two craps tables, three roulette tables, nine blackjack tables, two stud-poker tables, and 120 slot machines.

The Roman-themed **Coliseum Casino,** on Front Street in Philipsburg (☎ **599/54-32102**), tries hard to attract gaming enthusiasts, especially "high rollers," and has the highest table limits ($1,000 maximum) on Sint Maarten. Upon the management's approval, the Coliseum also offers credit lines for clients with a good credit rating at any U.S. casino.

SHOPPING

The main shopping area is in the center of Philipsburg. Most stores are on the two leading streets, **Front Street** (*Voorstraat* in Dutch), which is closer to the bay, and

Back Street (*Achterstraat*), which runs parallel to Front. You'll find all the usual suspects—Little Switzerland and a host of jewelry/gift/luxury item shops—as well as some standout local shops. In general, the price marked on the merchandise in the major retail outlets is what you're supposed to pay. At small, personally run shops, however, some polite bargaining might be in order.

Old Street Shopping Center, with entrances on Front Street and Back Street, features more than two dozen shops and boutiques, including branches of such famous stores as Colombian Emeralds. Dining facilities include the Philipsburg Grill and Ribs Co. and Pizza Hut.

The **Guavaberry Company,** 10 Front St., sells the rare "island folk liqueur" of Sint Maarten, which for centuries was made in private homes but is now available to everyone. Sold in square bottles, the liqueur is aged and has a fruity, woody, almost bittersweet flavor. It's made from rum that's given a unique flavor by rare local berries usually grown in the hills in the center of the island. You can blend it with coconut for a unique guavaberry colada or pour a splash into a glass of icy champagne. Don't confuse guavaberries with guavas—they're very different. Stop in at its shop and free-tasting house.

The **Shipwreck Shop,** Front Street, stocks West Indian hammocks, beach towels, sea salt, cane sugar, spices, baskets, handcrafts, jewelry, T-shirts, postcards, books, and much more.

BEACHES

Sint Maarten has 36 beautiful white-sand beaches, so it's comparatively easy to find one for yourself. But if it's too secluded, be careful: There have been reports of robberies on some remote beaches. Don't carry valuables.

You can often use the changing facilities at some of the bigger resorts for a small fee. Nudists should head for the French side, but the Dutch side is getting more liberal about such things.

On the west side of the island, **Mullet Bay Beach** is shaded by palm trees, but can get crowded on weekends. You can arrange water-sports equipment rentals through the Mullet Bay Resort.

Great Bay Beach is best if you'd like to stay near Front Street in Philipsburg. This mile-long beach is sandy, but since it borders the busy capital it may not be as clean as some of the more remote beaches. Immediately to the west, at the foot of Fort Amsterdam, **Little Bay Beach** looks like a Caribbean postcard, but it, too, can be overrun with visitors.

Stretching the length of Simpson Bay Village, white sand **Simpson Bay Beach,** is shaped like a half moon. It lies west of Philipsburg, just east of the airport. You can rent water-sports equipment here.

West of the airport, **Maho Bay Beach,** at the Maho Beach Hotel and Casino, is ideal in many ways, if you don't mind the planes passing overhead. Palms provide shade, and food and drink can be purchased at the hotel.

The sands are pearly white at **Oyster Pond Beach,** near the Oyster Pond Hotel northeast of Philipsburg. Bodysurfers like the rolling waves here. Nearby **Dawn Beach** is noted for its underwater tropical beauty, with reefs lying offshore.

Beyond the sprawling Mullet Beach Resort on the Dutch side, **Cupecoy Bay Beach** lies just north of the Dutch-French border on the western side of the island. It's a string of three white-sand beaches set against a backdrop of caves and sandstone cliffs that provide morning shade. The beach doesn't have facilities, but is nonetheless popular. One section of the beach is "clothing optional."

SPORTS

GOLF   The **Mullet Bay Resort** (☎ 599/54-52801, ext. 1850) has an 18-hole course designed by Joseph Lee that's one of the most challenging in the Caribbean. Mullet Pond and Simpson Bay lagoon provide both beauty and hazards.

HORSEBACK RIDING   At **Crazy Acres,** Dr. J. H. Dela Fuente Street, Cole Bay (☎ 599/54-42793), riding expeditions invariably end on an isolated beach where horses and riders can enjoy a cool postride romp in the water. Two experienced escorts accompany a maximum of eight people on the 2¹/₂-hour outings. Riders of all experience levels are welcome. Wear a bathing suit under your riding clothes. Reservations should be made at least 2 days in advance.

SCUBA DIVING   Underwater visibility runs from 75 to 125 feet in the island's crystal-clear bays and countless coves. The biggest attraction for scuba divers is the 1801 British man-of-war HMS *Proselyte,* which came to a watery grave on a reef a mile off the coast. The PADI-instructed program at **Pelican Watersports,** Pelican Resort & Casino, Simpson Bay (☎ 599/54-42604), features the most knowledgeable guides on the island, each one familiar with Sint Maarten dive sites. Divers are taken out in custom-built 28- and 35-foot boats. Many say that this is the best reef diving in the Caribbean.

GREAT LOCAL RESTAURANTS & BARS

A favorite **local beer** (on both the Dutch and French sides of the island) is Red White and Blue; a favorite **local rum liqueur** is Guavaberry (see "Shopping," above, for the Guavaberry Company's store in Philipsburg.

   ✪ **Cheri's Café,** 45 Cinnamon Grove, Shopping Centre, Maho Beach (☎ 599/54-53361), is the island's hot spot, once voted best bar in the West Indies by *Caribbean Travel and Life* readers. You can get really fresh grilled fish, 16-ounce steaks, and juicy burgers. Some come for the inexpensive food, others for the potent drinks.

   Antoine's, 119 Front St., Philipsburg (☎ 599/54-22964), offers sophistication, style, and cuisine that mainly consists of old continental favorites, almost equally divided between meat and fish dishes. **Chesterfields,** Great Bay Marina, Philipsburg (☎ 599/54-23484), serves platters of fish, grilled steaks and other meats, sandwiches, and salads at lunchtime. **Crocodile Express Café,** Casino Balcony, at the Pelican Resort & Casino, Simpson Bay (☎ 599/54-42503, ext. 1127), serves hearty deli fare, including well-stuffed sandwiches. **Da Livio Ristorante,** 159 Front St. (at the bottom of Front Street), Philipsburg (☎ 599/54-23363), is the finest Italian dining in Sint Maarten. A favorite dish is homemade manicotti della casa, filled with ricotta, spinach, and a zesty tomato sauce. **The Greenhouse,** Bobby's Marina (off Front Street), Philipsburg (☎ 599/54-22941), is a breezy, open-air restaurant serving lunches that include the catch of the day, a wide selection of burgers, and conch chowder.

ST. MARTIN

The St. Martin side of the island is decidedly French. The tricolor flies over Marigot's *gendarmerie,* towns have names like Colombier and Orléans, and the streets are called "rue de la Whatever."

   French St. Martin is governed from Guadeloupe and has direct representation in the French government in Paris. **Marigot,** the principal town, has none of Philipsburg's frenzied pace and cruise ship crowds. In fact, it looks like a French village transplanted to the Caribbean. Not only is there shopping, but some excellent French Creole restaurants as well.

Frommer's Favorite St. Martin Experiences

- **Joining the America's Cup Regatta or heading to Orient Bay:** Both these excursions listed under "Sint Maarten," above, are also available on the French side.
- **Trekking up to the ramparts of Fort St. Louis:** It's a 10- or 15-minute walk from the heart of Marigot to the top, where you're treated to panoramic views of Marigot and beyond (see "On Your Own," below).
- **Having lunch at Madame Claude's Petit Club:** At the oldest restaurant in Marigot you can savor the rich flavors of the Creole and French cuisine served on the restaurant's cozy, colorfully painted upstairs terrace (see "Great Local Restaurants & Bars," below).

COMING ASHORE   Medium-size vessels can dock at the pier at Port-Royale, at the bottom of the Boulevard de France in the heart of Marigot. When you disembark, you'll see a rather lavish marina, the headquarters of the island's tourist office, and arcades of shops nearby. The pier can accommodate only one ship at a time, so if a cruise ship is already docked, any second ship must anchor and send tenders ashore. Large ships generally dock on the Dutch side of the island, but if they call here, passengers must tender in.

CURRENCY   French St. Martin uses the **French franc (F),** although U.S. dollars seem to be preferred. The exchange rate is 6.29F to U.S.$1 (1F = U.S.16¢). Canadians should convert their money into U.S. dollars, not into francs.

LANGUAGE   Although the official language is French, most people also speak English.

INFORMATION   For French St. Martin, go to the **Tourist Information office,** right in front of the pier at Port-Royale in Marigot (☎ **590/87-5721**). It's open Monday to Friday from 8:30am to 1pm and 2:30 to 5:30pm. For info before you go, contact the French St. Martin Tourism Board in the United States at ☎ **212/ 475-8970** or www.st-martin.org.

CALLING FROM THE U.S.   When calling St. Martin from the United States, you need to dial "011" before the numbers listed in this section.

GETTING AROUND

TAXIS   Taxis are the most common means of transport. A **Taxi Service & Information Center** operates at the port of Marigot (☎ **590/87-56-54**). It also books

Frommer's Ratings: St. Martin					
	Poor	Fair	Good	Excellent	Outstanding
Overall Experience				✓	
Shore Excursions			✓		
Activities Close to Port				✓	
Beaches & Water Sports				✓	
Shopping				✓	
Dining/Bars				✓	

2-hour sightseeing trips around the island. Always agree on the rate before getting into an unmetered cab.

BY MINIVAN Local drivers operate a diverse armada of privately owned minivans and minibuses. There's a departure every hour between Marigot and the Dutch side. Because it's sometimes difficult for a newcomer to identify the buses, it's best to ask a local. It's about $1 or $2 per ride.

BY RENTAL CAR Rental cars are a practical way to see the island. **Budget** (☎ **800/527-0700** in the U.S., or 590/87-38-22), **Hertz** (☎ **800/654-3001** in the U.S., or 590/87-73-01), and **Avis** (☎ **800/331-1212** in the U.S., or 590/87-50-60) all have agencies here. Rates begin at $35 per day with unlimited mileage. Drive on the right-hand side of the road.

SHORE EXCURSIONS

All the same excursions offered in Dutch Sint Maarten (see above) are also offered here.

ON YOUR OWN

All of Marigot's shopping is within walking distance, as well as several restaurants and cafes. Don't miss out on a short hike up to Fort St. Louis for lovely, panoramic views of much of the island.

Beyond walking distance, we're mostly talking beaches (see below).

BEACHES

Top rating on the French side goes to **Baie Longue,** a long, beautiful beach that's rarely overcrowded. Chic and very expensive La Samanna, a deluxe hotel, opens onto this beachfront, which is one of the few on the island that grew rather than diminished in size during the 1995 hurricanes. Unfortunately, the storms created unexpected holes offshore, which makes swimming here more hazardous than before. The beach lies to the north of Cupecoy Beach, by the Lowlands road.

If you continue north, you reach the approach to **Baie Rouge,** another long and popular stretch of sand and jagged coral. Snorkelers are drawn to the rock formations at both ends of this beach, many of which were exposed through erosion caused by the 1995 storms. There are no changing facilities, but that doesn't matter for some, who get their suntans *au naturel.*

Orient Beach is one of the Caribbean's most famous clothing-optional beaches. Colorful canvas umbrellas create a European feel, and there are charming beachside cafes for lunch.

On the north side of the island, to the west of Espérance airport, **Grand-Case Beach** is small but select. Despite the many tons of storm debris left in 1995 by the hurricanes, the sands are once again white and clean.

SHOPPING

Many day-trippers come over to Marigot just to look at the collection of French boutiques and shopping arcades. Because it's a duty-free port, the shopping here is some of the best in the Caribbean. Whether you're seeking jewelry, perfume, or St-Tropez bikinis, you'll find it in one of the boutiques along rue de la République and rue de la Liberté. There's a wide selection of **European merchandise,** much of it geared to the luxury trade. Crystal, perfumes, jewelry, and fashions are sometimes 25% to 50% less expensive than in the United States and Canada. You'll also find fine liqueurs, cognacs, and cigars.

Prices are often quoted in U.S. dollars, and salespeople frequently speak English. U.S. dollars, credit and charge cards, and traveler's checks are usually accepted.

At harbor side in Marigot, there's a frisky **morning market** with vendors selling spices, fruit, shells, local handcrafts, and T-shirts galore. Mornings are even more alive at **Port La Royale,** the bustling center of everything. Schooners unload produce from the neighboring islands, boats board guests for picnics on deserted beaches, and a brigantine sets out on a sightseeing sail. The owners of a dozen different little dining spots get ready for the lunch crowd. The largest shopping arcade on the French side is here, with many boutiques that often come and go rapidly.

Galerie Périgourdine, another cluster of boutiques, faces the post office. Here you might pick up some designer wear for both men and women, including items from the collection of Ted Lapidus.

Worthwhile specialty shops include **Gingerbread & Mahogany Gallery,** 4-14 Marina Royale (in a narrow alleyway at the marina), which deals in Haitian art by both "old masters" and talented amateurs; **Havane,** Port La Royale, which offers exclusive collections of French clothing for men, in both casual and high-fashion designs; **La Romana,** 12 rue de la République, which sells chic women's clothing, focusing on Italian styles; and **Oro de Sol Jewelers,** rue de la République, which stocks high-fashion jewelry studded with precious stones, plus gold watches by Cartier, Chopard, Ebel, Patek Philippe, and Bulgari.

Local artist **Roland Richardson,** a gifted impressionist painter known for his landscape, portraiture, and colorful still-life paintings, has an art gallery on the waterfront.

SPORTS

GENERAL WATER SPORTS   Most of St. Martin's large beachfront hotels maintain facilities for jet skiing, waterskiing, and parasailing, often from makeshift kiosks on the beaches. Two independent operators that function from side-by-side positions on Orient Bay, close to the cluster of hotels near the Esmeralda Hotel, are **Kon Tiki Watersports** (☎ **590/87-46-89**) and **Bikini Beach Watersports** (☎ **590/87-43-25**).

SCUBA DIVING   Scuba diving is excellent around French St. Martin, with reef, wreck, cave, and drift dives ranging from 20 to 70 feet. Dive sites include Ilet Pinel for shallow diving; Green Key, a barrier reef; Flat Island for sheltered coves and geologic faults; and Tintamarre, known for its shipwreck. The island's premier dive operation is **Marine Time,** whose offices are in the same building as L'Aventure, Chemin du Port, 97150 Marigot (☎ **590/87-20-28**). Operated by England-born Philip Baumann and his Mauritius-born colleague, Corine Mazurier, this outfit offers morning and afternoon dives in deep and shallow water, to wrecks and over reefs.

SNORKELING   The island's tiny coves and calm offshore waters make it a snorkeler's heaven. The waters off the northeastern shore are protected as a regional underwater nature reserve, **Reserve Sous-Marine Régionale.** This area includes Flat Island (also known as Tintamarre), Ilet Pinel, Green Key, and Petite Clef. The use of harpoons and spears is strictly forbidden. Snorkeling can be enjoyed individually or on sailing trips. You can rent equipment at almost any hotel on the beach.

WINDSURFING   Because of prevailing winds and calmer, more protected waters, most windsurfers gravitate to the island's easternmost edge, most notably Coconut Grove Beach, Orient Beach, and, to a lesser extent, Dawn Beach. The best of the several outfits that specialize in windsurfing is **Tropical Wave,** Coconut Grove, Le Galion Beach, Baie de l'Embouchure (☎ 590/87-37-25), set midway between Orient Beach and Oyster Pond, amid a sunblasted, scrub-covered, isolated landscape. The combination of wind and calm waters here is considered almost ideal.

GREAT LOCAL RESTAURANTS & BARS

As on the Dutch side, a favorite **local beer** is Red White and Blue, while a favorite **local rum liqueur** is Guavaberry.

Madame Claude herself is running the show at the ✪ **Petit Club,** the oldest restaurant in Marigot, located on the main street in the heart of town. Savor the rich flavors of the Creole and French cuisine—like spicy conch stew or fresh fish Creole style—served on the restaurant's cozy, bright-yellow upstairs terrace. **La Brasserie de Marigot,** rue du Général-de-Gaulle 11 (☎ 0590/87-94-43), is where the real French eat, a great choice for good food at good prices. Meals include pot-au-feu, duck breast with peaches, fillet of beef with mushroom sauce, and even chicken on a spit and steak tartare. **La Maison sur le Port,** Boulevard de France (☎ 0590/87-56-38), is a grand, Parisian, and upscale choice, with cookery that's grounded firmly in France, but with Caribbean twists and flavors. At lunch, you can choose from a number of salads as well as fish and meat courses.

27 St. Thomas & St. John

Vacationers discovered St. Thomas right after World War II, and they've been flocking here in increasing numbers ever since. Today, the island is one of the busiest ports in the Caribbean, often hosting more than 10 cruise ships a day during the peak winter season. **Charlotte Amalie,** its capital, has become the Caribbean's major shopping center.

Tourism and U.S. government programs have raised the standard of living here to one of the highest in the Caribbean. The island, 12 miles long and 3 miles wide, is now the most developed of the U.S. Virgins. Condominium apartments have grown up over the debris of bulldozed shacks.

In stark contrast to this busy scene, more than half of nearby St. John, the smallest of the U.S. Virgin Islands, is pristinely preserved in the gorgeous **Virgin Islands National Park.** The wildlife here is admired by ornithologists and zoologists around the world. A rocky coastline, forming crescent-shaped bays and white-sand beaches, rings the whole island. Panoramic views and ruins of 18th-century Danish plantations dot St. John's miles of serpentine hiking trails. Island guides can point out mysterious geometric petroglyphs incised into boulders and cliffs; of unknown age and origin, the figures have never been deciphered.

Most cruise ships dock in Charlotte Amalie on St. Thomas, but a few anchor directly off St. John. Many of those that stop only at St. Thomas offer excursions to St. John. If yours doesn't, it's easy to get to St. John on your own.

CURRENCY   The U.S. dollar is the local currency.

LANGUAGE   It's English.

INFORMATION   The **U.S. Virgin Islands Division of Tourism** has offices at Tolbod Gade (☎ 340/774-8784), open Monday to Friday from 8am to 5pm and Saturday from 8am to noon. Here you can pick up *St. Thomas This Week,* which includes maps of St. Thomas and St. John. There's also an office at the Havensight Mall.

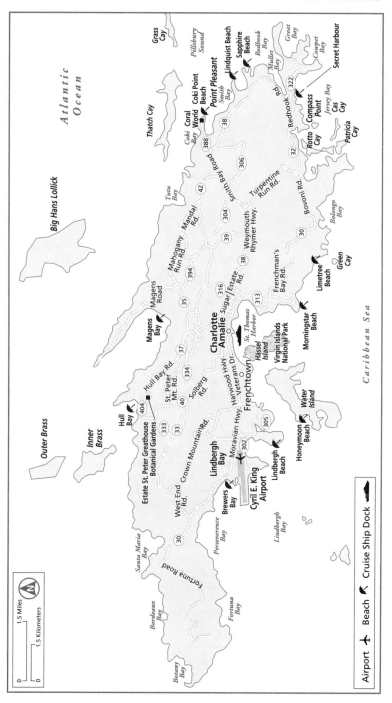

Atlantic Ocean

Grass Cay

Thatch Cay

Big Hans Lollick

Outer Brass

Inner Brass

Pillsbury Sound

Lindquist Beach

Sapphire Beach

Point Pleasant

Coki Point Beach

Coral World

Smith Bay

Coki Bay

388

38

306

Smith Bay Road

42

Mandal Rd.

Tutu Bay

304

Turpentine Run Rd.

Mahogany Run Rd.

394

39

38

Weymouth Rhymer Hwy.

Bovoni Rd.

30

316

313

Frenchman's Bay Rd.

35

Magens Road

Magens Bay

37

Sugar Estate Rd.

Charlotte Amalie

St. Thomas Harbor

Hassel Island

Frenchtown

Virgin Islands National Park

Limetree Beach

Morningstar Beach

Green Cay

Bolongo Bay

Caribbean Sea

Redhook

322

Redhook Rd.

Mullet Bay

Great Bay

Coupet Bay

Secret Harbour

Compass Point

Jersey Bay

Cas Cay

Rotto Cay

Patricia Cay

32

Hull Bay Rd.

St. Peter Mt. Rd.

Solberg Rd.

334

40

404

Hull Bay

Estate St. Peter Greathouse Botanical Gardens

333

33

West End Rd.

Crown Mountain Rd.

Harwood Hwy.

Veterans Dr.

Moravian Hwy.

Lindbergh Bay

302

305

Water Island

Honeymoon Beach

Lindbergh Beach

Cyril E. King Airport

Brewers Bay

Santa Maria Bay

Perseverance Bay

30

Fortuna Road

Lindbergh Bay

Bordeaux Bay

Fortuna Bay

Botany Bay

N

0   1.5 Miles
0   1.5 Kilometers

Airport ✈   Beach ↖   ▲ Cruise Ship Dock

CALLING FROM THE U.S.   When calling St. Thomas from the United States, you need to dial only a "1" before the numbers listed in this section.

ST. THOMAS

With a population of some 50,000 and a large number of American expatriates and temporary sun-seekers in residence, tiny St. Thomas isn't exactly a tranquil tropical retreat. You won't have any beaches to yourself. Shops, bars, and restaurants (including a lot of fast-food joints) abound here, and most of the locals make their living by the tourist trade. Most native Virgin Islanders are the descendants of slaves brought from Africa. In fact, Charlotte Amalie was one of the major slave-trading centers in the Caribbean.

Frommer's Favorite St. Thomas Experiences

- **Biking around the island:** You'll get great views and a great workout, too (see "Shore Excursions," below).
- **Kayaking among the island's mangroves:** You'll learn about the local lagoon-ecosystem and get some exercise to boot (see "Shore Excursions," below).
- **Visiting the colorful village of Frenchtown:** Have lunch in a village settled by French-speaking citizenry uprooted when the Swedes invaded and took over in St. Barts (see "On Your Own: Beyond Walking Distance," below).
- **Taking a nature walk:** The lush Estate St. Peter Greathouse Botanical Gardens has 200 varieties of plants and trees, plus a rain forest, an orchid jungle, a monkey habitat, and more (see "On Your Own: Beyond Walking Distance," below).

COMING ASHORE   Most cruise ships anchor at Havensight Mall, at the eastern end of Charlotte Amalie Harbor, 1¹/₂ miles from the town center. The mall has a tourist information office, restaurants, a bookstore, a bank, a U.S. postal van, phones that accept long-distance credit cards, and a generous number of duty-free shops. Many people make the long, hot walk to the center of Charlotte Amalie, but it's not a scenic route in any way—you may just want to opt for one of the open-air taxis for about $3 per person.

If Havensight Mall is clogged with cruise ships, your ship will dock at the Crown Point Marina, to the west of Charlotte Amalie. A taxi is your best bet—the 30-minute walk into Charlotte Amalie feels longer on a hot day, and isn't terribly picturesque. A taxi ride into town from Crown Point Marina costs about $4.

There are a few AT&T **credit-card phones** at Havensight Mall, at the eastern end of Charlotte Amalie Harbor, 1¹/₂ miles from the town center.

GETTING AROUND

BY TAXI   Taxis are the chief means of transport here. They're unmetered, so agree with the driver on a fare before you get in. The official fare for sightseeing is about

Frommer's Ratings: St. Thomas					
	Poor	Fair	Good	Excellent	Outstanding
Overall Experience				✓	
Shore Excursions				✓	
Activities Close to Port				✓	
Beaches & Water Sports				✓	
Shopping					✓
Dining/Bars			✓		

$30 for two passengers for 2 hours; each additional passenger pays another $12. For 24-hour radio-dispatch service, call ☎ **340/774-7457.** Many taxis transport 8 to 12 passengers in vans to multiple destinations for a lower price.

BY BUS   Comfortable and often air-conditioned, government-run Vitran buses serve Charlotte Amalie and the countryside as far away as Red Hook, a jumping-off point for St. John. You rarely have to wait more than 30 minutes during the day. A one-way ride costs about 75¢ within Charlotte Amalie, $1 to outer neighborhoods, and $3 for rides as far as Red Hook. For routes, stops, and schedules, call ☎ **340/774-5678.**

BY TAXI VAN   Less structured and more erratic are "taxi vans," privately owned vans, minibuses, or open-sided trucks operated by local entrepreneurs. They make unscheduled stops along major traffic arteries and charge the same fares as the Vitran buses. If you look like you want to go somewhere, one will likely stop for you. They may or may not have their final destinations written on a cardboard sign displayed on the windshield.

BY RENTAL CAR   I don't recommend renting a car here.

SHORE EXCURSIONS

In addition to the excursions below, there are plenty of organized snorkeling trips, booze cruises, and island tours offered.

✪ **Island Mountain Bike Adventure** ($59, 3$^1/_2$ hours): For great views of the island and a decent bout of exercise, too, this bike tour starts after a short minivan ride to an elevated part of the island. With a few exceptions, most of the ride is downhill, but you'll definitely work up a sweat. The tour ends at a beach, where there's time for some swimming and relaxing.

✪ **Kayaking the Marine Sanctuary** ($54, 2$^1/_2$ hours): Kayak from the mouth of the marine sanctuary at Holmberg's Marina and spend nearly an hour paddling among the mangroves, while a naturalist explains the mangrove and lagoon ecosystem. At the middle, there's about half an hour to snorkel or walk along the coral beach at Bovoni Point before kayaking back to the starting point.

Island Tour by Minibus and Tram ($30, 3 hours): First drive along the impressive Skyline Drive for panoramic views of St. John and the ship harbor, and then up to the 1,400-foot-high Mountain Top for awesome views of Magens Bay as well as the British Virgin Islands. Then hop in the Paradise Point Tramway for a 15-minute ride to the top of Paradise Point, some 700 feet above the sea.

Atlantis Submarine Odyssey ($70–$74, 2 hours): Descend about 90 feet into the ocean in this air-conditioned submarine for views of exotic fish and sea life.

Virgin Islands Seaplane Exploration ($68, 1$^1/_2$ hours): For great views of these islands, their beaches, old sugar plantations, and lush foliage, there's no better vantage point than from above.

TOURING THROUGH LOCAL OPERATORS

St. John Yachting/Snorkeling Excursion: You can avoid the crowds by sailing aboard *Fantasy* (☎ **340/775-5652**), which departs from the American Yacht Harbor at Red Hook at 9:30am daily. It sails to St. John and nearby islands, carrying a maximum of six passengers, for swimming, snorkeling, beachcombing, or trolling. Snorkel gear with expert instruction is provided, as is a champagne lunch. An underwater camera is also available. There are full-day and half-day tours.

ON YOUR OWN: WITHIN WALKING DISTANCE

The color and charm of a slightly seedy Caribbean waterfront come vividly to life in **Charlotte Amalie.** In days of yore, seafarers from all over the globe flocked to this old-world Danish town. Confederate sailors used the port during the Civil War.

The old warehouses once used for storing pirates' loot still stand and, for the most part, house today's shops. In fact, the main streets (called "Gades" here in honor of their Danish heritage) are now a virtual shopping mall and are usually packed with visitors. Sandwiched among the shops are a few historic buildings, most of which can be covered on foot in about 2 hours.

Before starting your tour, stop off in the so-called **Grand Hotel,** near Emancipation Park. No longer a hotel, it has a restaurant, bar, shops, and a visitor center. Also, from **Hotel 1829** a street farther up, there are views of the harbor below from its wood-paneled pub/restaurant, a great place for a drink or some lunch.

Stray behind the seafront shopping strip (Main Street) of Charlotte Amalie and you'll find pockets of 19th-century houses and, high on the steep sloping Crystal Gade, the truly charming, cozy, brick-and-stone **St. Thomas Synagogue,** built in 1833 by Sephardic Jews. There's a great view from here as well.

Dating from 1672, **Fort Christian** rises from the harbor to dominate the center of town. Named after the Danish king Christian V, the structure has been everything from a governor's residence to a jail. Many pirates were hanged in its courtyard. Some of the cells have been turned into the rather minor **Virgin Islands Museum,** displaying Indian artifacts of only the most passing interest. Admission is free. The fort is open Monday to Friday from 8am to 5pm.

Seven Arches Museum, Government Hill (☎ 340/774-9295), is a 2-century-old Danish house completely restored to its original condition and furnished with antiques. You can walk through the yellow ballast arches and visit the great room with its view of the busy harbor.

The Paradise Point Tramway (☎ 340/774-9809) affords visitors a dramatic view of Charlotte Amalie Harbor at a peak height of 697 feet. The tramways transport customers from the Havensight area to Paradise Point, where riders disembark to visit shops and a popular restaurant and bar.

ON YOUR OWN: BEYOND WALKING DISTANCE

Coral World Marine Park & Underwater Observatory, 6450 Coki Point, off Route 38, 20 minutes from downtown Charlotte Amalie (☎ 340/775-1555), is the number-one attraction in St. Thomas. The $3^{1}/_{2}$-acre complex features a three-story underwater observation tower 100 feet offshore. Through windows you'll see sponges, fish, coral, and other underwater life in their natural state. In the Marine Gardens Aquarium, saltwater tanks display everything from sea horses to sea urchins. An 80,000-gallon reef tank features exotic Caribbean marine life. Another tank is devoted to sea predators, including circling sharks. The entrance is hidden behind a waterfall.

West of Charlotte Amalie, **Frenchtown** was settled by a French-speaking citizenry uprooted when the Swedes invaded and took over in St. Barts. They were known for wearing *cha-chas,* or straw hats. Many of the people who live here today are the direct descendants of those long-ago residents. This colorful fishing village contains several interesting restaurants and taverns. To get there, take a taxi down Veterans Drive (Route 30) west and turn left at the sign to the Admirals Inn.

The lush **Estate St. Peter Greathouse Botanical Gardens,** at the corner of St. Peter Mountain Road (Route 40) and Barrett Hill Road (☎ 340/774-4999), decorates 11 acres on the volcanic peaks of the island's northern rim. It's the creation

Charlotte Amalie

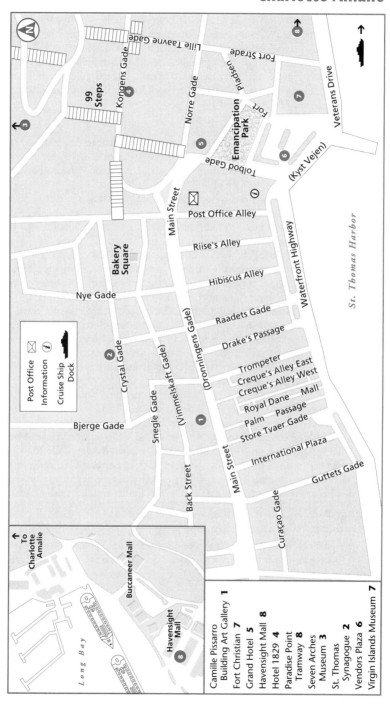

99 Steps

Kongens Gade

Lille Taavne Gade

Fort Strade

Norre Gade

Pladsen

Emancipation Park

Fort

Tolbod Gade

Veterans Drive

(Kyst Vejen)

Main Street

Post Office Alley

Riise's Alley

Hibiscus Alley

Bakery Square

Nye Gade

Raadets Gade

Drake's Passage

Waterfront Highway

St. Thomas Harbor

Crystal Gade

(Vimmelskaft Gade)

(Dronningens Gade)

Trompeter

Creque's Alley East

Creque's Alley West

Royal Dane   Mall

Palm   Passage

Store Tvaer Gade

Snegle Gade

Bjerge Gade

Back Street

Main Street

International Plaza

Guttets Gade

Curaçao Gade

Post Office
Information
Cruise Ship
Dock

To
Charlotte
Amalie

Buccaneer Mall

Havensight
Mall

Long Bay

Camille Pissarro
Building Art Gallery **1**
Fort Christian **7**
Grand Hotel **5**
Havensight Mall **8**
Hotel 1829 **4**
Paradise Point
Tramway **8**
Seven Arches
Museum **3**
St. Thomas
Synagogue **2**
Vendors Plaza **6**
Virgin Islands Museum **7**

271

of Howard Lawson DeWolfe, a Mayflower descendant who, with his wife, Sylvie, bought the estate in 1987 and set about transforming it into a tropical paradise. It's filled with self-guided nature walks that acquaint you with some 200 varieties of plants and trees, including an umbrella plant from Madagascar. There's also a rain forest, an orchid jungle, a monkey habitat, waterfalls, and reflecting ponds. From a panoramic deck you can see some 20 of the Virgin Islands. The house itself is worth a visit, its interior filled with local art.

SHOPPING

St. Thomas is famous for its shopping. As at St. Croix, American shoppers can bring home $1,200 worth of merchandise without paying duty. You'll sometimes find well-known brand names at savings of up to 40% off stateside prices—but you'll often have to plow through a lot of junk to find the bargains.

Many cruise ship passengers shop at the **Havensight Mall,** where they disembark, but the major shopping goes on along the harbor of Charlotte Amalie. **Main Street** (or Dronningens Gade, its old Danish name) is the main shopping area. Just north of Main Street is merchandise-loaded **Back Street,** or Vimmelskaft. Many shops are also spread along the **Waterfront Highway** (also called Kyst Vejen). Running between these major streets is a series of side streets, walkways, and alleys, all filled with shops. All the usual suspects sell all the usual jewelry, watches, perfume, gift items, etc., but there are a number of other interesting shops.

The **Camille Pissarro Building Art Gallery,** Caribbean Cultural Centre, 14 Dronningens Gade, is the house where the impressionist painter Pissarro was born on July 10, 1830. The art gallery is reached by climbing a flight of stairs. In three high-ceilinged and airy rooms, you'll see all the available Pissarro paintings relating to the islands. Many prints and note cards of local artists are available, too, as well as original batiks, alive in vibrant colors.

Street vendors ply their trades in a designated area called **Vendors Plaza,** at the corner of Veterans Drive and Tolbod Gade. Hundreds of them converge under oversize parasols there Monday to Saturday from 7:30am to 5:30pm, and on Sunday if a cruise ship is expected. Food vendors set up on sidewalks outside Vendors Plaza.

Just for fun, you'll want to have a peak in **Lover's Lane,** Raadets Gade 33 (beside Veterans Drive, on the second floor), with its stock of provocative lingerie, inflatable men and women, massage aids of every conceivable type, the largest inventory of vibrators in the Virgin Islands, and all the lace, leather, or latex you'll ever need.

BEACHES

Instead of looking at the minor attractions or going shopping, many cruise ship passengers prefer to spend their time ashore on a beach. St. Thomas has some good ones, and you can reach them all relatively quickly in a taxi (arrange for the driver to return and pick you up at a designated time). If you're going to St. John, you may want to do your beaching there (see "Beaches," under St. John, below).

All the beaches in the U.S. Virgin Islands are public, but some still charge a fee. Mind your belongings at the beach, as St. Thomas has pickpockets and thieves who target visitors.

THE NORTH SIDE   Lying across the mountains 3 miles north of the capital, **Magens Bay** was once hailed as one of the world's 10 most beautiful beaches, but its reputation has faded. Though still beautiful, it isn't as well maintained as it should be and is often overcrowded, especially when many cruise ships are in port. It's less than a mile long and lies between two mountains. Admission is $1 for adults and 25¢ for children under 12. Changing facilities are available, and you can rent snorkeling gear and lounge chairs. There's no public transportation here, so take a taxi. The gates are open daily from 6am to 6pm (you'll need insect repellent after 4pm).

Located in the northeast near Coral World, **Coki Beach** is good, but it, too, becomes overcrowded when cruise ships are in port. Snorkelers come here often, as do pickpockets—protect your valuables. Lockers can be rented at Coral World, next door. An East End bus runs to Smith Bay and lets you off at the gate to Coral World and Coki.

Also on the north side is **Renaissance Grand Beach Resort,** one of the island's most beautiful beaches. It opens onto Smith Bay, right off Route 38, near Coral World. Many water sports are available here.

THE SOUTH SIDE   On the south side, **Morningstar** lies about 2 miles east of Charlotte Amalie at Marriott's Frenchman's Reef Beach Resort. You can wear your most daring swimwear here, and you can also rent sailboats, snorkeling equipment, and lounge chairs. The beach can be easily reached via a cliff-front elevator at the Marriott.

Limetree Beach, at the Bolongo Bay Beach Club, lures those who love a serene spread of sand. You can feed hibiscus blossoms to iguanas and rent snorkeling gear and lounge chairs. There's no public transportation, but it's easy to get here by taxi from Charlotte Amalie.

One of the most popular, **Brewer's Beach** lies in the southwest near the University of the Virgin Islands. It can be reached by the public bus marked FORTUNA heading west from Charlotte Amalie. **Lindberg Beach,** near the airport, also lies on the Fortuna bus route heading west from Charlotte Amalie.

THE EAST END   Small and special, **Secret Harbour** sits near a collection of condos. With its white sand and coconut palms, it's a veritable cliché of Caribbean charm. No public transportation stops here, but it's an easy taxi ride east of Charlotte Amalie heading toward Red Hook.

Sapphire Beach is one of the finest on St. Thomas, set against the backdrop of the Doubletree Sapphire Beach Resort & Marina complex, where you can lunch or order drinks. Windsurfers like this beach a lot. You can also rent snorkeling gear and lounge chairs here. A large reef lies close to the shore, and there are great views of offshore cays and St. John. To get to this beach, you can take the East End bus from Charlotte Amalie, going via Red Hook. Ask to be let off at the entrance to Sapphire Bay; it's not too far to walk from there to the water.

SPORTS

GOLF   Designed by Tom and George Fazio, **Mahogany Run** on the north shore, Mahogany Run Road (☎ **800/253-7103** or 340/777-6006), is one of the most beautiful courses in the West Indies. This 18-hole, par-70 course rises and drops like a roller coaster on its journey to the sea. Cliffs and crashing sea waves are the ultimate hazards at the 13th and 14th holes. The golf course is an $8 taxi ride from the cruise dock.

SCUBA DIVING & SNORKELING   The waters off the U.S. Virgin Islands are rated as one of the "most beautiful areas in the world" by *Skin Diver* magazine. Thirty spectacular reefs lie just off St. Thomas alone. **Dive In!,** in the Doubletree Sapphire Beach Resort & Marina, Smith Bay Road, Route 36 (☎ **800/524-2090**), offers professional instruction, daily beach and boat dives, custom dive packages, underwater photography and videotapes, and snorkeling trips.

GREAT LOCAL RESTAURANTS & BARS

IN CHARLOTTE AMALIE **Beni Iguana's Sushi Bar,** in the Grand Hotel Court, just behind Emancipation Park in downtown (☎ 340/777-8744), is the only Japanese restaurant on St. Thomas. **Greenhouse,** Veterans Drive (☎ 340/774-7998), attracts cruise ship passengers with daily specialties, including much American fare and some Jamaican-inspired dishes. The **Hard Rock Cafe,** 5144 International Plaza (on the second floor of a pink-sided mall), the Waterfront, Queen's Quarter (☎ 340/777-5555), has the best burgers in town, but people mainly come for the good times. ✪ **Virgilio's,** 18 Dronningens Gade, entrance on a narrow alleyway running between Main and Back streets (☎ 340/776-4920), is the best northern Italian restaurant in the Virgin Islands. The lobster ravioli here is the best there is.

IN FRENCHTOWN At **Alexander's,** rue de St. Barthélemy, west of town (☎ 340/776-4211), there's a heavy emphasis on seafood—the menu even includes conch schnitzel on occasion. Other dishes include a mouthwatering Wiener schnitzel and homemade pâté. ✪ **Craig & Sally's,** 22 Honduras (☎ 340/777-9949), serves dishes that, according to the owner, are not "for the faint of heart, but for the adventurous soul"—roast pork with clams, filet mignon with macadamia-nut sauce, and grilled swordfish with a sauce of fresh herbs and tomatoes.

ON THE NORTH COAST **Eunice's Terrace,** 66-67 Smith Bay, Route 38, just east of the Coral World turnoff (☎ 340/775-3975), is one of the island's best-known West Indian restaurants, and oozes with local color. The place made news around the world on January 5, 1997, when Bill and Hillary Clinton showed up unexpectedly for lunch. Surrounded by secret-service men, they shared a conch appetizer, then Mrs. Clinton went for the vegetable plate while the president opted for the catch of the day, which he reportedly loved.

ON SAPPHIRE BEACH **Seagrape,** in the Doubletree Sapphire Beach Resort & Marina, Rte. 6, Smith Bay Rd. (☎ 340/775-6100), is counted among the finest dining rooms along the east coast of St. Thomas. The lunch menu includes the grilled catch of the day and freshly made salads.

NEAR THE SUB BASE **Victor's New Hide Out,** 103 Sub Base, off Route 30 (☎ 340/776-9379), has some of the best local dishes on the island, but first you have to find it—this hilltop perch is truly a place to hide out. Take a taxi. Its dishes have sophisticated flair and zest, as opposed to the more down-home cookery found at Eunice's Terrace (see above).

ST. JOHN

St. John lies about 3 miles east of St. Thomas across Pillsbury Sound. The island, the smallest and least populated of the U.S. Virgins, is about 7 miles long and 3 miles wide, with a total land area of some 20 square miles. When held under Danish control, it was slated for big development, but a slave rebellion and a decline of the sugarcane plantations ended that idea. Since 1956, more than half its land mass, as well as its shoreline waters, have been set aside as the **Virgin Islands National Park.** Miles of winding hiking trails lead to panoramic views and the ruins of 18th-century Danish plantations. Mysterious geometric petroglyphs incised into boulders and cliffs can be pointed out by island guides; of unknown age and origin, the figures have never been deciphered. Since St. John is easy to reach from St. Thomas, many cruise ship passengers spend their entire day here.

St. John

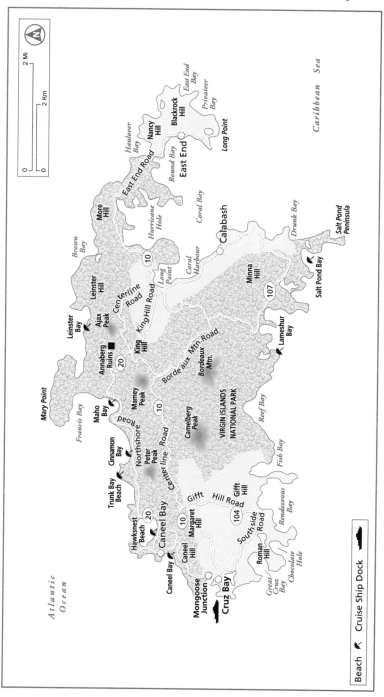

Beach ↙ Cruise Ship Dock ◢

275

Frommer's Ratings: St. John					
	Poor	Fair	Good	Excellent	Outstanding
Overall Experience				✓	
Shore Excursions			✓		
Activities Close to Port				✓	
Beaches & Water Sports				✓	
Shopping		✓			
Dining/Bars		✓			

Frommer's Favorite St. John Experiences

- **Touring the island in an open-air safari bus:** The views are spectacular from the island's coastal road, and you'll visit the ruins of a plantation and one of St. John's excellent beaches (see "Shore Excursions," below).
- **Beaching yourself in Trunk Bay:** Although it can get somewhat crowded, it's a gorgeous beach and there's some decent snorkeling, too (see "Beaches," below).

COMING ASHORE   Cruise ships cannot dock at either of the piers in St. John. Instead, they moor off the coast of Cruz Bay, sending in tenders to the National Park Service Dock, the larger of the two piers. Most cruise ships docking at St. Thomas offer shore excursions to St. John's pristine acres and beaches.

If your ship docks on St. Thomas and you don't take a shore excursion to St. John, you can get here from Charlotte Amalie by ferry. Ferries leave the Charlotte Amalie waterfront for St. John's Cruz Bay at 1- to 2-hour intervals, from 9am until the last departure around 5:30pm. The last boat leaves Cruz Bay for Charlotte Amalie at 3:45pm. The ride takes about 45 minutes and costs $7 each way. Call ☎ 340/776-6282 for more information.

Another ferry leaves from the Red Hook pier on St. Thomas's eastern tip more or less every half hour, starting at 6:30am. It's a 30-minute drive from Charlotte Amalie's port to the pier at Red Hook; the ferry trip to Cruz Bay on St. John takes another 20 minutes each way. The one-way fare is $3 for adults, $1 for children under 11. Schedules can change without notice, so call in advance (☎ 340/776-6282). You can take a Vitran bus from a point near Market Square directly to Red Hook for $1 per person each way, or negotiate a price with a taxi driver.

GETTING AROUND

BY TAXI   The most popular way to get around is by surrey-style taxi. Typical fares from Cruz Bay are $3 to Trunk Bay, $3.50 to Cinnamon Bay, or $7 to Mahoe Bay. For more information, call ☎ 340/693-7530.

BY RENTAL CAR   The extensive Virgin Islands National Park has kept the island's roads undeveloped and uncluttered, with some of the most panoramic vistas anywhere. Renting a vehicle is the best way to see these views, especially if you like to linger at particularly beautiful spots. Open-sided jeep-like vehicles are the most fun of the limited rentals here. There's sometimes a shortage of cars during the busy midwinter season, so try to reserve early. Remember to drive on the left (even though steering wheels are on the left, too—go figure).

The two largest car-rental agencies on St. John are located on St. John: **Avis** (☎ 800/331-1212 or 340/776-6374) charges between $75 and $85 per day, and **Hertz** (☎ 800/654-3001 or 340/693-7580), $60 to $85 per day. Gasoline is seldom included in the price of a rental, and your car is likely to come with just enough fuel to get you to one of the island's two gas stations. Because of the distance between stations, it's never a good idea to drive around St. John with less than half a tank of gas.

BY BICYCLE   Bicycles are available for rent from the **Cinnamon Bay Watersports Center** on Cinnamon Bay Beach (☎ **340/776-6330**). St. John's steep hills and off-road trails can challenge the best of riders, but cyclists in search of more moderate rides can visit the ruins at Annaberg or the beaches at Maho, Francis, Leinster, or Watermelon Bay.

SHORE EXCURSIONS

Island Tour ($39, 4–5 hours): Since most ships tie up in St. Thomas, tours of St. John first require a ferry or tender ride to Cruz Bay in St. John. Then you board open-air safari buses for a tour that includes a stop at the ruins of a working plantation, the Annaberg Ruins, as well as a stop at a beach, like Trunk Bay. The views from the coastal road of the islands and sea beyond are spectacular.

TOURING THROUGH LOCAL OPERATORS

Taxi Tours: Taxi tours of about 2 hours cost from $30 for one or two passengers, or about $12 per person for three or more riders, and are one of the best ways of seeing St. John. Almost any taxi at Cruz Bay can take you on these tours, or you can call ☎ **340/693-7530.**

ON YOUR OWN: WITHIN WALKING DISTANCE

Most cruise ship passengers dart through Cruz Bay, a cute little West Indian village with interesting bars, restaurants, boutiques, and pastel-painted houses. You can browse through **Wharfside Village,** a complex of courtyards, alleys, and shady patios with a mishmash of boutiques, restaurants, fast-food joints, and bars.

Located at the public library, **Elaine Ione Sprauve Museum** (☎ **340/776-6359**) isn't big, but it does contain some local artifacts, and will teach you about some of the history of the island. It's open Monday to Friday from 9am to 5pm. Admission is free.

ON YOUR OWN: BEYOND WALKING DISTANCE

Two-thirds of St. John is national-park land. If you want to explore the **Virgin Islands National Park,** stop off first at the visitor center (☎ **340/776-6201**), right on the dock at St. Cruz. Here you'll see some exhibits and learn more about what you can see and do in the park.

Established in 1956, the park totals 12,624 acres, including submerged land and water adjacent to St. John. You can explore the park on the more than 20 miles of biking trails, or rent your own car, jeep, or Mini-Moke. Make sure you drive on the left. If you want to hike, stop at the office of the park ranger, adjacent to the pier, to watch an 18-minute video about the park. Also pick up maps and instructions before setting out on any of the clearly marked hiking trails. You can take a taxi for about $5 to the starting point of whatever trail you select.

Within the park, try to see the **Annaberg Ruins,** Leinster Bay Road, where the Danes founded a thriving plantation and sugar mill in 1718. You'll find tidal pools, forest lands, hilltops, wild scenery, and the ruins of several Danish plantations. It's located off North Shore Road east of Trunk Bay on the north shore. On certain days of the week (dates vary), guided walks of the area are given by park rangers. Check with the park's visitor center.

SHOPPING

Compared to St. Thomas, there's not a lot of shopping on St. John, but the boutiques and shops at Cruz Bay are generally more interesting. Most of them are clustered at **Mongoose Junction,** in a woodsy area beside the roadway, about a 5-minute walk from the ferry dock.

IN MONGOOSE JUNCTION   **Bamboula** has an unusual and appealing collection of gifts from the Caribbean, Haiti, India, Indonesia, and Central Africa. **The Canvas Factory** produces its own handmade, rugged, and colorful canvas bags. **Donald Schnell Studio** deals in handmade pottery, sculpture, and blown glass. The **Fabric Mill** features silk-screened and batik fabrics from around the world. **R and I Patton Goldsmithing** has a large selection of island-designed jewelry in sterling silver, gold, and precious stones.

IN CRUZ BAY   As you wait at Cruz Bay for the ferry back to St. Thomas, you can browse through the shops of Wharfside Village. **Pusser's of the West Indies** is located here, offering a large collection of classically designed, old-world travel and adventure clothing, along with unusual accessories and Pusser's famous (though not terribly good) rum. A good, cheap gift item is packets of Pusser's coasters, on which is writ the recipe for that classic Caribbean rum specialty, the Painkiller.

BEACHES

For a true beach lover, missing the great white sweep of **Trunk Bay** would be like touring Europe and skipping Paris. Trouble is, the word is out. This gorgeous beach is usually overcrowded, and there are pickpockets lurking about. The beach has lifeguards and offers rentals, such as snorkeling gear. The underwater trail near the shore attracts beginning snorkelers in particular. Both taxis and "safari buses" to Trunk Bay meet the ferry as it docks at Cruz Bay.

Caneel Bay, the stamping ground of the rich and famous, has seven perfect beaches on its 170 acres—but only one open to the public. That's **Hawksnest Beach,** a little gem of white sand beloved by St. Johnians. The beach is a bit narrow and windy, but beautiful. Close to the road you'll find barbecue grills. Safari buses and taxis from Cruz Bay will take you along North Shore Road.

The campgrounds of **Cinnamon Bay** and **Maho Bay** have their own beaches, where forest rangers sometimes have to remind visitors to put their swimsuits back on. Snorkelers find good reefs here. Changing rooms and showers are available.

Salt Pond Bay is known to locals but often missed by visitors. The bay here is tranquil, but there are no facilities. The Ram Head Trail begins here and winds for a mile to a panoramic belvedere overlooking the bay.

SPORTS

HIKING   The network of trails in Virgin Islands National Park is the big thing here. The visitor center at Cruz Bay gives away free trail maps of the park. Since you don't have time to get lost—you don't want the ship to leave without you!—it's best to set out with someone who knows his or her way around. Both **Maho Bay** (☎ 340/776-6226) and **Cinnamon Bay** (☎ 340/776-6330) conduct nature walks.

KAYAKING & WINDSURFING   The most complete line of water sports available on St. John is offered at the **Cinnamon Bay Watersports Center** on Cinnamon Bay Beach (☎ 340/776-6330). The windsurfing here is some of the best anywhere, for both the beginner and the expert. You can also rent kayaks or a 12- or 14-foot Hobie monohull sailboat.

SCUBA DIVING & SNORKELING   Ask about scuba packages at **Low Key Watersports,** Wharfside Village (☎ **800/835-7718** or 340/693-8999). All wreck dives are two-tank/two-location dives. Snorkel tours are also available. The center uses its own custom-built dive boats and also specializes in water-sports gear, including masks, fins, snorkels, and dive skins. It can arrange day-sailing charters, kayaking tours, and deep-sea sportfishing. **Cruz Bay Watersports,** P.O. Box 252, Palm Plaza, St. John, USVI 00831 (☎ **800/835-7730** or 340/776-6234), is a PADI and NAUI five-star diving center. Snorkel tours are available daily.

GREAT LOCAL RESTAURANTS & BARS

Pusser's, Wharfside Village, Cruz Bay (near the ferry dock; ☎ **340/693-8489**), is actually three bars, all serving the famous Pusser's rum and menu choices that include jerk tuna fillet, jerk chicken with a tomato basil sauce over penne, and spaghetti with lobster cooked in rum, wine, lemon juice, and garlic. **The Fish Trap,** in the Raintree Inn, Cruz Bay (☎ **340/693-9994**), is known for its wide selection of fresh fish, but also caters to vegetarians and the burger crowd. The Italian food at ✪ **Paradiso,** Mongoose Junction (☎ **340/693-8899**), is the best on the island—the chicken picante Willie—a spicy, creamy picante sauce over crispy chicken with linguini and ratatouille—was featured in *Bon Apétit.*

28 Trinidad & Tobago

The southernmost islands in the Caribbean chain, Trinidad and tiny Tobago, which together form a single nation, manage to encompass nearly every facet of Caribbean life. Like night and day, one is industrial and the other very natural. Located less than 10 miles east of Venezuela's coast, Trinidad is large (the biggest and most heavily populated Caribbean island) and diverse, with an industrial, cosmopolitan capital city, Port of Spain, and an outgoing, vibrant culture that combines African, East Indian, European, Chinese, and Syrian influences. Little-sister Tobago is the more natural of the two, with rain-forested mountains to spectacular secluded beaches.

Trinidad and Tobago won independence from Britain in 1962 and became a republic in 1976, but some British influences, including the residents' love of cricket, remain. Trinidad grew rich from oil, and the islands are still the Western Hemisphere's largest oil exporters.

Trinidad's music is another local treasure. The calypso, steel-pan, and soca styles originated here have influenced musical trends worldwide. Trinidad's rhythmic, soulful music is a main feature of Carnaval, the Caribbean-wide bacchanalian celebration held across the islands each year on the Monday and Tuesday before Lent. Of all the Carnaval celebrations across the Caribbean islands, Trinidad's is the king.

Trinidad's residents are charming, friendly, and love to talk. With a literacy rate of 97%, the populace is full of well-informed conversationalists. You'll find Trinis (as residents call themselves) happy to socialize with visitors and discuss just about anything.

CURRENCY   The unit of currency is the **Trinidad & Tobago dollar (TT),** sometimes designated by the same symbol as the U.S. dollar ($) and sometimes just by TT. The exchange rate is TT$6.30 to U.S.$1 (TT$1 = U.S.16¢). Vacationers can pay in U.S. dollars, but ask for price quotes in Trinidad *and* U.S. dollars, and try to get change in U.S. dollars. Local ATM machines mainly dispense TT notes.

CALLING FROM THE U.S.   When calling Trinidad and Tobago from the United States, you need to dial "011" before the numbers listed in this section.

LANGUAGE   The official language is English, but like many of their Caribbean neighbors, Trinis speak English with a distinct patois. Hindi, Creole, and Spanish are also spoken amongst various ethnic groups.

TRINIDAD

Trinidad is the one of the most industrialized countries in the Caribbean, and it shows—if you're looking for a sleepy, quiet Caribbean retreat, go to Tobago instead. Trinidad's capital and commercial center, **Port of Spain,** is an energetic, bustling metropolis of 300,000. There are few distinct attractions—Port of Spain isn't necessarily a tourist city—but the central shopping area at the south end of Frederick Street is a colorfully crowded mix of outdoor shopping arcades and air-conditioned mini-malls.

Independence Square, in the heart of Port of Spain, is the place to get a taxi, find a bank, and get good, cheap food. There are mosques, shrines, and temples here and also several travel agencies in the area. Locals gather at Woodford Square to hear impromptu public speakers or attend outdoor meetings.

While Port of Spain is interesting and not threatening by day, it's unsafe at night, and strolling around is not recommended. Panhandlers are likely to approach visitors at times. The cruise-ship complex has a customs hall, shops, car-rental agencies, and a waiting fleet of taxis.

Frommer's Favorite Trinidad Experiences
- **Visiting the Asa Wright Nature Center:** This 200-acre preserve, located in Trinidad's rain forest in the northern hills, features intertwined hiking trails and a bird sanctuary and conservation center. (See "On Your Own: Beyond Walking Distance," below.)
- **Touring the Caroni Bird Sanctuary:** This ecological wonder features dense mangroves, remote canals, and shallow lagoons that are the breeding grounds for spectacular scarlet ibis. Visitors tour the sanctuary in guided boats. (See "Shore Excursions," below.)
- **Trying a drink with Angostura bitters:** This local specialty contains citrus-tree bark and is made from a secret recipe.

COMING ASHORE   Cruise ships visiting Trinidad dock at Port of Spain's 4-acre cruise terminal, built in the early 1990s to accommodate the island's growing cruise traffic. The complex includes a telephone and communications center, a shopping mall, and a branch of the Trinidad and Tobago Tourist Development Authority. Arriving passengers are usually greeted by steel-pan musicians and colorfully dressed dancers. Outside the terminal, there's a craft market with T-shirts, straw items, and other souvenirs.

There is a **telephone** and communications center in the terminal complex.

Frommer's Ratings: Trinidad	Poor	Fair	Good	Excellent	Outstanding
Overall Experience		✓			
Shore Excursions		✓			
Activities Close to Port	✓				
Beaches & Water Sports		✓			
Shopping		✓			
Dining/Bars			✓		

Trinidad

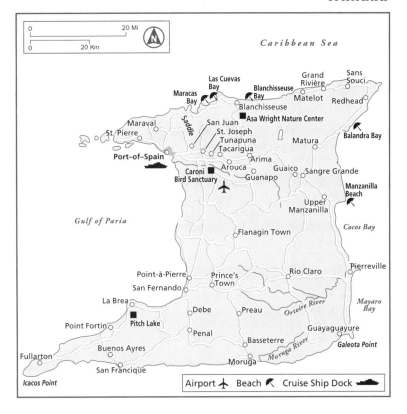

INFORMATION At the terminal in Port of Spain, there's the **Tourism and Industrial Development Corporation of Trinidad and Tobago (TIDCO)** at 10-14 Phillips St., open Monday to Friday from 8am to 4:30pm. For info before you, contact the tourism board office in the United States at ☎ **888/595-4868** or www.visittnt.com.

GETTING AROUND

BY TAXI Taxis are available at the cruise terminal. The Port Authority posts cab fares on a board by the main entrance (the cars don't have meters). Always establish a fare before loading into the taxi and shoving off. Private cabs can be relatively expensive, but maxi-taxis (minivans operating regular routes within specific zones) are lower priced.

BY BUS/VAN Maxi-taxis in Trinidad have a yellow stripe. There are also route taxis, shared cabs that travel along a prescribed route and charge TT$2 to TT$3 (U.S.32¢ to U.S.48¢) to drop you at any spot along the route.

BY RENTAL CAR Driving is on the left. Trinidad has a fairly wide network of roads, and roads in town are generally well marked, but traffic is frequently heavy. There are a few small rental-car companies in Trinidad, but it's probably not necessary to rent a car for a 1-day port call here.

SHORE EXCURSIONS

Caroni Bird Sanctuary ($44, 3 hours): This sanctuary is a pristine network of lush mangroves, quiet canals, and shallow lagoons and is considered a world-class bird-watching preserve. Following a 30-minute drive from the cruise pier, passengers embark for the tour in flat-bottomed boats, which glide through calm-watered canals and lagoons. Guides will point out unique flora and fauna during the ride. Heron, osprey, and scarlet ibis are among the bird species native to this area.

ON YOUR OWN: WITHIN WALKING DISTANCE

Except for the **craft market** right outside the terminal, and a small restaurant across the street, there isn't much to see close to the cruise pier.

ON YOUR OWN: BEYOND WALKING DISTANCE

Among Port of Spain's chief centers of activity, **Independence Square** isn't really a square at all, but parallel streets running east and west and connected at one end by a pedestrian mall. The scene here resembles a Middle Eastern bazaar, with a dense thicket of pushcarts, honking cabs, produce hawkers, and inquisitive shoppers moving constantly to the irresistible beat of soca, reggae, and calypso music blaring from nearby stores and sidewalk stands. Some parts of the square have become run-down in recent years, and some locals consider the area less than safe. Visitors should keep an eye out for pickpockets and petty thieves. **Woodford Square,** laid out by Ralph Woodford, Trinidad's early 19th-century British governor, is among the most attractive areas in Port of Spain, full of large, leafy trees surrounding a rich lawn with landscaped walkways. This area has traditionally served as a center for political debates, discussions, and rallies. The **Cathedral of the Holy Trinity,** built in 1818 by Woodford, lies on the south side of Woodford Square. The church's carved roof is designed as a replica of Westminster Hall in London. Inside of the church is a memorial statue of Woodford.

On the square's western border is **Red House,** an imposing Renaissance-style edifice built in 1906. Red house is indeed red-colored and today houses Trinidad's parliament. The building was badly damaged in 1990 when militants took the prime minister and parliament members hostage. A little farther outside of the city center is **Queen's Park Savannah,** originally part of a 200-acre sugar plantation but now a public park and racetrack with 80 acres of open land and walkways with great shade trees. A depression at the park's northwest section, known as the Hollows, has flower beds, rock gardens, and small ponds. The area has become a popular picnic spot.

There are a number of notable sights along the park's outer edge, including the **Magnificent Seven,** a row of seven colonial buildings constructed in the late 19th and early 20th centuries. The buildings include Queen's Royal College, White Hall, the prime minister's office, and Stollmeyer's Castle, designed to resemble a Scottish castle complete with turrets.

Beyond the northern edge of Queen's Park Savannah lies the **Emperor Valley Zoo,** containing local animals, including tropical toucans and macaws, porcupine, monkeys, and various snakes. But the zoo really emphasizes colorful tropical plants, in evidence all around the zoo's grounds.

The 70-acre **botanical gardens** are east of the zoo. Laid out in 1820, the gardens are landscaped with great trees and attractive walkways. Among the flowering trees here is the wild poinsettia, whose bright red blossom is the national flower. The President's House, built in 1875 as the governor's residence, is adjacent to the gardens.

Near Spring Hill Estate, 30 miles northeast of Port of Spain beside Blanchisseuse Road, the **Asa Wright Nature Center** (☎ 868/667-4655) is known to bird watchers throughout the world. Within its 196 acres, set at an elevation of 1,200 feet in Trinidad's rain-forested mountains, you can see hummingbirds, toucans, bellbirds, manakins, several varieties of tanagers, and the rare oilbird. Hiking trails line the grounds, and guided tours are available. Call for a schedule.

SHOPPING

Shopping in the Port of Spain area means crafts, fabrics, and fashions made by local artists, an array of spices, and colorful artwork. Most of the shopping opportunities lie in the area around Independence Square, particularly Frederick and Queen streets. Art lovers will find a handful of galleries and studios featuring the work of local and regional artists. **Art Creators,** at Seventh Street and St. Ann's Road in the Aldegonda Park section, is a serious gallery offering year-around exhibits from both aspiring and established artists. **Aquarela Galleries,** at 1A Dere St., exhibits the work of recognized and up-and-coming Trini artists and also publishes high-end art books. If you're in the mood for distinctive gift and apparel shopping, hire a cab to the **Hotel Normandie,** 10 Nook Ave. in the St. Ann's section, where the shops feature clothing and jewelry by some of the country's top designers. Officially known as The Village Market, the hotel's shopping plaza features **Greer's Textile Designs,** a boutique carrying colorful batiks and pricey jewelry from designer Jillian Bishop. Also here is **Interiors,** which features all manner of unusual gifts. For craft creations outside of the cruise terminal area, try the **Trinidad and Tobago Blind Welfare Assn.,** at 118 Duke St., which features accessories and gifts of rattan, banana leaves, and other natural substances. All of the products are made by blind craftsmen. **The Trinidad and Tobago Handicraft Cooperative,** at King's Wharf, sells small steel pans, hammocks, and other locally produced items. **Art Potters Ltd.,** located at the cruise terminal, is a pottery specialist.

Music is another of Trinidad's signature products, and the latest soca and reggae styles can be purchased at **Rhyner's Record Shop** at 54 Prince St. in Port of Spain. There's also **Crosby Records,** located in the St. James area.

BEACHES

Unlike its tiny cousin Tobago, Trinidad proper isn't teeming with beautiful beaches. The most popular one is **Maracas Bay,** a scenic, 40-minute drive from Port of Spain. The drive takes vacationers over mountains and through a lush rain forest. As you near the beach, the coastal road descends from a stunning cliff side. The beach itself is wide and sandy, with a small fishing village on one side and the richly dense mountains in the background. There's a lifeguard, changing rooms and showers, and areas for picnics. There's also a small snack stand selling "shark and bake" sandwiches (a local favorite made with fresh slabs of shark and fried bread).

SPORTS

GOLF   The oldest and best-known golf course on the island is 18-hole **St. Andrews Golf Club** in the suburb of Maraval (☎ 868/629-2314). The course, also known as Moka Golf Course, was established in the late 19th century. Trinidad also has a nine-hole public course, **Chaguaramas Public Golf Club,** and courses in Pointe a Pierre and La Brea.

DEEP-SEA FISHING   The Bocas Islands off Trinidad are well known for excellent deep-sea fishing. **Classic Tours** (☎ 868/628-7053) arranges sportfishing excursions to the area.

GREAT LOCAL RESTAURANTS & BARS

A favorite **local beer** is Stag; a favorite **local rum** is Vat 19 Old Oak.

Trinidad is home to some of the most diverse culinary styles in the entire Caribbean, a result of its African, Chinese, English, French, Indian, Portuguese, Spanish, and Syrian influences. **Rafters,** at 6A Warner St. (☎ **868/628-9258**), is an old rum house that still sports brick walls and hand-finished ceilings, and today offers sandwiches, chili, and chicken in its bar. There's also an elegant dining room for more formal meals, and the menu features house specialties. **La Chateau de Poisson,** at 38 Ariapita Ave., is a quality French-Creole restaurant housed in a charming colonial house. There's a lunchtime buffet (11:30am to 2:30pm) priced around TT$50 (U.S.$8). **Solimar,** at 6 Nook Ave. near the Normandie Hotel (☎ **868/624-6267**), features a changing menu of international dishes engineered by owner Joe Brown, a peripatetic Englishman who's a former chef for the Hilton hotel chain. Nightclubs, pubs, and bars run late into the night and almost always feature the island's buoyant musical styles. **Cricket Wicket** at 149 Tragarete Rd., is an after-hours bar with various bands performing on weekends.

TOBAGO

Tobago is the antithesis of its larger cousin, Trinidad, as peaceful, calm, and easy-going as Trinidad is loud, crowded, and frenetic. The island is filled with magical white sandy beaches, languid palm trees, and clear blue waters, and you'll find lots of spots for diving and snorkeling. There are also magnificent rain forests and hundreds of tiny streams and waterways carved into a steep crest of mountains rising 2,000 feet and snaking down the island's center. The bird life and nature trails here are impressive.

Frommer's Favorite Tobago Experiences

- **Visiting Pigeon Point Beach:** One of the most beautiful and distinctive spots in the Caribbean, Pigeon Point is an oasis of white sand, aqua water, and tall palm trees.
- **Snorkeling at Buccoo Reef:** The spot is a must-visit for its exotic fish and impressive underwater coral, which can also be observed via glass-bottom boat.
- **Checking out Nylon Pool:** Named for its crystal-clear water, this small lagoon is located near Buccoo Reef and is filled with tropical fish. It's great for wading and swimming.

COMING ASHORE   Cruise passengers arrive at a small but orderly cruise terminal in central Scarborough, the island's main town. There's usually a fleet of taxis ready to go just outside of the cruise terminal, and cab rates are posted inside the terminal at the main entrance. There's even a detailed taxi rate chart posted inside

Frommer's Ratings: Tobago					
	Poor	Fair	Good	Excellent	Outstanding
Overall Experience				✓	
Shore Excursions			✓		
Activities Close to Port	✓				
Beaches & Water Sports				✓	
Shopping		✓			
Dining/Bars		✓			

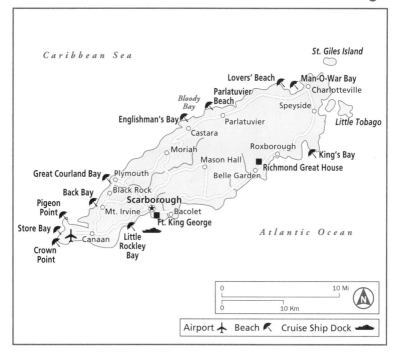

Map of Tobago showing: Caribbean Sea, St. Giles Island, Lovers' Beach, Man-O-War Bay, Parlatuvier Beach, Charlotteville, Bloody Bay, Speyside, Englishman's Bay, Parlatuvier, Little Tobago, Castara, Moriah, Roxborough, King's Bay, Mason Hall, Richmond Great House, Great Courland Bay, Plymouth, Belle Garden, Back Bay, Black Rock, Scarborough, Pigeon Point, Mt. Irvine, Bacolet, Store Bay, Canaan, Ft. King George, Crown Point, Little Rockley Bay, Atlantic Ocean.

Scale: 0–10 Mi, 0–10 Km. Legend: Airport ✈, Beach ⚓, Cruise Ship Dock.

the cruise terminal. Larger ships must anchor offshore and transfer passengers to the terminal via tenders.

There are a number of phones inside the terminal, although last time I was there they weren't taking my AT&T phone card, and I had to buy a local phone card.

INFORMATION There is no official information booth at the small terminal in Scarborough. For info before you go, contact the tourism board office in the United States at ☎ **888/595-4868** or www.visittnt.com.

GETTING AROUND

BY TAXI Taxi is the preferred mode of travel for tourists here; the island is small enough that any location worth visiting can be reached this way. Distances can be deceiving, though, because some of the roads are in very bad shape and others wind along the coast and twist through the mountains. There is no road that completely circles the island. Taxis are normally available at the cruise terminal; rates are posted on a board by the main entrance. It pays to agree on a fare before climbing in.

BY RENTAL CAR There's really no need for a cruise passenger to rent a car on Tobago.

SHORE EXCURSIONS

Pigeon Point Beach Trip ($49, 5¹/₂ hours, including lunch): Via taxi, you head toward Tobago's most popular beach, where you'll find a restaurant, bar, rest rooms, and small cabanas (huts) lining the beach. You have your pick of water sports, including snorkeling and banana-boat rides (for a fee, of course).

Tobago Island Explorer ($59, 7¹/₂ hours, including lunch): Passengers depart the cruise terminal via bus for a trip that starts at Fort King George and the Tobago

Museum. After a tour of the museum, the excursion continues along the Windward Coast Road to the Richmond Greathouse for a guided tour. Continuing to the Speyside lookout, a photo stop is made before the tour proceeds to Jemma's Seafood Kitchen for a tasty lunch.

ON YOUR OWN: WITHIN WALKING DISTANCE

The well-restored, British-built **Fort King George,** dating from 1777, overlooks Scarborough's east side. There's no admission charge to enter the grounds. The fort offers a great view of Tobago's Atlantic coast, and other historic buildings here include St. Andrew's church (built in 1819) and the Courthouse (built in 1825). Scarborough's botanical gardens are situated between the main highway and town center, but it's not much more than a glorified public park with a few marked trees.

Other than this, there aren't many attractions within walking distance of the cruise terminal in Tobago and even the terminal shops are small and limited. It's best to put aside the shopping excursions for another port and enjoy Tobago's relaxed atmosphere and fine beaches.

SHOPPING

There simply isn't much shopping for tourists here, beyond the shops inside the cruise terminal and sporadic craft merchants at the popular beaches at Fort King George.

BEACHES

Pigeon Point, near the southern tip of Tobago on the Caribbean side, is the best beach on an island filled with great beaches. **Store Bay,** south of Pigeon Point, has white sands and good year-around swimming (there's a lifeguard, too). Here you'll find vendors hawking local wares and glass-bottom–boat tours departing to Buccoo Reef. Despite their names, **Parlatuvier** and **Bloody Bay,** on Tobago's Caribbean (west) coast, are tranquil, secluded, and beautiful.

SPORTS

GOLF   There's an 18-hole championship golf course, **Mount Irvine Golf Course** at the Mount Irvine Hotel (☎ **868/639-8871**), about 5 miles from Pigeon Point. It's among the most scenic courses in the Caribbean, and overlooks the sea from gently rolling hills. The clubhouse sits on a promontory and offers great views.

SCUBA DIVING   Tobago is virtually surrounded by shallow-water reefs filled with colorful marine life easily visible through the clear water. The island's reefs offer all kinds of diving experiences, from beginner-level dives at Buccoo Reef to drift diving for experienced divers at Grouper Ground. **Dive Tobago,** at Pigeon Point (☎ **868/639-0202**), is the island's oldest dive operation, offering resort courses and rentals and catering to both beginners and experienced divers.

GREAT LOCAL RESTAURANTS & BARS

There are several moderately priced (U.S.$15 to U.S.$25 per person) restaurants in Tobago, including **The Old Donkey Cart House,** on Bacolet Street in Scarborough (☎ **868/639-3551**), housed in a restored colonial home that once served as Tobago's first guest house. Today it's a bistro serving French wines, light snacks and salads, and specialties like armadillo and opossum (called *manicou*).

The beach at Store Bay is lined with a row of cheap-food stands offering rotis (chicken or beef wrapped in Indian turnovers and flavored with curry), shark-and-bake, crab and dumplings, and fish lunches. **Chrystal's,** on the corner of Store Bay and Milford Road, is another local favorite for flying fish, shark-and-bake, and fruit juices.

Wrapping Up Your Cruise: Debarkation Concerns

4

Hardly anybody likes to get off the ship at the end of his or her cruise, but it's part of the deal. To make matters easier, here's a discussion of a few matters you'll have to take care of before heading back to home sweet home.

1 Tipping

Like waiters and waitresses in the United States, the cruise industry pays its staff low wages, with the understanding that the bulk of their salaries will come from tips. No matter which cabin you occupied or what price you paid for it, if service is satisfactory, you'll be expected to tip a recommended amount (of course, you can always tip more), which comes to about $70 per person (adult or child) for a weeklong cruise. Only some upscale ships, including Radisson's *Radisson Diamond,* forbid tipping altogether.

Tipping is so formally integrated into the cruise experience that it's almost ritualistic, and cruise lines aren't shy about reminding you. Each line has clear **guidelines for gratuities,** which are usually printed in the daily schedule or announced toward the end of the cruise. Likewise, cabin stewards usually leave **little white envelopes** (marked for cabin attendants, dining stewards, and waiters) along with suggested tipping percentages and amounts where you'll be sure not to miss them. Other lines, usually the small, offbeat lines like Windjammer Barefoot Cruises, prefer that a single tip be delivered to a central source; the pooled funds are then equitably distributed to the crew.

Even on lines like Holland America and Windstar, which promote their "tipping not required" policies, tipping really is expected, and the policy is more a way to be diplomatic than to discourage tipping. Granted, if you received truly lousy service, reflect that in the tip you leave as you would at a restaurant shoreside.

Suggested tipping amounts vary slightly with the line and its degree of luxury. As a rule of thumb, however, each passenger should expect to tip about $3.50 per person per day for the **cabin steward** and the **dining room waiter** and about $2 for the dining-room **busboy.** (As a generous tipper and one-time waitress, if service has been good, I generally throw in another $5 or $10 for each at the end of the week, but this, of course, is not mandatory.) Like at any good hotel, feel free to distribute additional tips to anyone else who made your life particularly pleasant during your time onboard.

Wine stewards and **bartenders** are usually rewarded with a 15% surcharge that's added onto a bill every time you sign it; of course, you may want to tip more if you're a barfly. Some lines suggest you tip the **maître d'** about $5 per person for the week and slip another couple of bucks to the **chief housekeeper;** it's your choice (if I've never even met these people, I don't feel obligated to tip them). Some maître d's will appreciate a discreet tip if they've gone to the trouble of reassigning you to a new table at dinner; some will not accept tips for this.

Tip **masseurs** and **masseuses, hair stylists,** and **manicurists** immediately after they work on you; 15% is standard. Tips can be paid in cash or charged to your onboard account (and the Steiner spa-and-salon people will do this for you unless you indicate otherwise; don't feel pressured into giving a tip if your treatment was not satisfactory).

WHEN DO YOU DISTRIBUTE YOUR TIPS?

It's good form to tip your dining stewards during the cruise's final dinner, instead of waiting until breakfast the next morning, when stewards might be assigned other stations or be unavailable. Incidentally, you are expected to tip your waiter and bus-boy for each night of your cruise, even if you did not dine in the main restaurant an evening or two.

SPECIAL TIPPING SITUATIONS

In case you didn't know, tipping the captain or one of the captain's officers is a no-no (they're on full salary, and are—or are expected to be—above all that). If you found someone among the staff to be outstandingly able and helpful, be sure to say so on the **comment card** that's left in your cabin toward the end of your cruise. If you're feeling especially ambitious and kind-hearted, write a brief letter praising this person's performance and send it to the cruise line's director of passenger services.

2 Disembarking

You knew it would finally get to this.

It's a good idea to begin packing before dinner of the final night aboard, and be sure to fill out the **luggage tags** given to you, which might be color-coded, and attach them securely to each piece (if you need more than they leave for you, there are always extras at the purser's desk). You'll be requested to leave your luggage outside your cabin door before you retire for the cruise's final night (by midnight or so), and in the wee hours a crew of deck hands will pick it up and spirit it away. The luggage will be tossed into big rolling carts (like the airlines use) somewhere below deck, and at disembarkation, you'll find your baggage waiting for you at the terminal, organized by the colored or numbered tags you attached to it.

If you've neglected to place any baggage outside your door before the designated deadline, you'll have to lug it off the ship yourself. If you leave something behind, the cruise line might eventually return it to you (if it's ever turned in, of course), but not without a prolonged hassle.

Ships normally arrive in port on the final day of the cruise between 6 and 8am, and need at least 90 minutes to unload baggage and complete dockage formalities. That means no one disembarks much before 9am, and it can sometimes take until 10am before you're allowed to leave the ship.

When disembarkation is announced, get ready for the chaos. No matter how you slice it, departures just aren't graceful, and are, frankly, a blunt return to reality. The staff is distracted and busily preparing for the new group of passengers boarding a

Cruise Tip: Don't Pack Your Booze

Don't pack newly purchased bottles of liquor in the luggage you leave out for the crew to carry off the ship, thinking it's only going 100 yards between your cabin and the terminal before you see it again. A friend absent-mindedly did this and the next morning found her bag sitting in the terminal in a pool of rum. Big mess!

few hours later (the friendly bartender you chatted with every night or the perky social hostess may not have much time for you now); the crew has only about 5 hours to prepare the ship for the next departure.

Since guests are generally asked to vacate their cabins by about 8am so stewards can begin cleaning them for the arriving guests, pooped people by the hundreds, surrounded by their bags, fill virtually every available inch of every public area (stairs and floors not excluded), waiting to hear the numbers they've been assigned so they can finally depart. Remember, **patience is a virtue.**

It's no surprise that this whole process goes much more smoothly on smaller ships with fewer passengers.

Disembarking through the cruise ship terminal is the equivalent of departing from an international flight. You need to claim your luggage and then pass through Customs before exiting the terminal. This normally entails handing the immigration officer your filled-out Customs declaration form as you breeze past, without even coming to a full stop. There are generally **porters** available in the terminals, but you might have to haul your luggage through Customs before you can get to them. It's customary to pay them at least $1 per bag. Alternatively, there may be **wheeled carts** available (for free or no more than $1.50 each) to help you push your possessions out the door.

3 Customs

Customs officers are most interested in expensive, big-ticket items like cameras, jewelry, china, or silverware. They don't care much about your souvenir items unless you've bought so many that they couldn't possibly be intended for your personal use, or they're concealing illegal substances.

U.S. CUSTOMS

The U.S. government generously allows U.S. citizens $1,200 worth of duty-free imports every 30 days from the U.S. Virgin Islands; those who exceed their exemption are taxed at a 5% rate, rather than the normal 10%. The limit is $400 for your regular international destinations such as the French islands of Guadeloupe and Martinique. The limit is $600 if you return directly from the following islands and countries: Antigua and Barbuda, Aruba, the Bahamas, Barbados, Belize, Costa Rica, Dominica, the Dominican Republic, Grenada, Guatemala, Haiti, Honduras, Jamaica, Montserrat, the Netherland Antilles (Curaçao, Bonaire, St. Maarten, Saba, and St. Eustatius), Panama, St. Kitts and Nevis, St. Lucia, St. Vincent and the Grenadines, Trinidad and Tobago, and the British Virgin Islands. If, for instance, your cruise stops in the U.S. Virgin Islands and the Bahamas, your total limit is $1,200 and no more than $600 of that amount can be from the Bahamas. If you visit only Puerto Rico, you don't have to go through Customs at all, since it's an American commonwealth.

U.S. citizens or returning residents at least 21 years of age who are traveling directly or indirectly from the U.S. Virgin Islands are allowed to bring in free of duty 1,000 cigarettes. Duty-free limitations on articles from other countries are generally 1 liter of alcohol, 200 cigarettes (one carton), and 100 cigars (not Cuban). Unsolicited gifts can be mailed to friends and relatives on the U.S. mainland at the rate of $200 per day from the U.S. Virgin Islands or $100 per day from other islands. Unsolicited gifts of any value can be mailed from Puerto Rico. Most meat or meat products, fruit, plants, vegetables, or plant-derived products will be seized by U.S. Customs agents unless they're accompanied by an import license from a U.S. government agency.

Joint Customs declarations are possible for members of a family traveling together. For instance, if you're a husband and wife with two children, your exemptions in the U.S. Virgin Islands become duty-free up to $4,800!

Collect receipts for all purchases made abroad. Sometimes merchants suggest making up a false receipt to undervalue your purchase, but be aware that you could be involved in a "sting" operation—the merchant might be an informer to U.S. Customs. You must also declare on your Customs form all gifts received during your stay abroad.

I've found clearing Customs in Florida to be a painless and speedy process, with Customs officials rarely asking for anything more than your filled-out Customs declaration form as they nod you through the door. Of course, better safe than sorry. It's prudent to carry proof that you purchased expensive cameras or jewelry on the U.S. mainland. If you purchased such an item during an earlier trip abroad, you should carry proof that you have previously paid Customs duty on the item.

To be on the safe side, if you use any medication containing controlled substances or requiring injection, carry an original prescription or note from your doctor.

For more specifics, request the free *Know Before You Go* pamphlet from the U.S. Customs Service, P.O. Box 7407, Washington, DC 20044 (☎ **202/927-6724;** www.customs.ustreas.gov).

CANADIAN CUSTOMS

Canada allows its citizens a $500 exemption if they are out of the country for at least 7 days, and they are permitted to bring back duty-free 200 cigarettes, 200 grams of tobacco, 40 Imperial ounces of liquor, and 50 cigars. In addition, they are allowed to mail gifts valued at $60 (Canadian) or less to Canada from abroad, provided the gifts are unsolicited and aren't alcohol or tobacco. It's a good idea to enclose a gift card and write on the package: "Unsolicited gift, under $60 value." All valuables, such as expensive cameras you already own, should be declared with their serial numbers on the Y-38 Form before departure from Canada.

For more information, write for the *I Declare* booklet, issued by **Revenue Canada,** 2265 St. Laurent Blvd., Ottawa, ON, KIG 4K3, or call ☎ **800/461-9999** or 613/993-0534.

BRITISH CUSTOMS

If you return from the Caribbean either directly to the United Kingdom or arrive via a port in another European Union (EU) country where you and your baggage did not pass through Customs controls, you must go through U.K. Customs and declare any goods in excess of the allowances. These are 200 cigarettes, 100 cigarillos, 50 cigars, or 250 grams of tobacco; 2 liters of still table wine and 1 liter of spirits or strong liqueurs (over 22% alcohol by volume), or 2 liters of fortified or sparkling wine or other liqueurs; 60cc/ml of perfume; 250cc/ml of toilet water; and £145 worth of all other goods, including gifts and souvenirs. (No one under 17 years of age is entitled to a tobacco or alcohol allowance.) Only go through the green "nothing to declare" line if you're sure you have no more than the Customs allowances and no prohibited or restricted goods.

For further information, contact **HM Customs and Excise Office,** Dorset House, Stamford Street, London SE1 9PY (☎ **0171/202-4227**).

Index

General Index

FROMMER'S® COMPLETE TRAVEL GUIDES

Alaska
Amsterdam
Arizona
Atlanta
Australia
Austria
Bahamas
Barcelona, Madrid &
  Seville
Beijing
Belgium, Holland &
  Luxembourg
Bermuda
Boston
British Columbia & the
  Canadian Rockies
Budapest & the Best of
  Hungary
California
Canada
Cancún, Cozumel &
  the Yucatán
Cape Cod, Nantucket &
  Martha's Vineyard
Caribbean
Caribbean Cruises & Ports
  of Call
Caribbean Ports of Call
Carolinas & Georgia
Chicago
China
Colorado
Costa Rica
Denmark
Denver, Boulder & Colorado
  Springs
England
Europe

European Cruises & Ports
  of Call
Florida
France
Germany
Greece
Greek Islands
Hawaii
Hong Kong
Honolulu, Waikiki &
  Oahu
Ireland
Israel
Italy
Jamaica
Japan
Las Vegas
London
Los Angeles
Maryland & Delaware
Maui
Mexico
Miami & the Keys
Montana & Wyoming
Montréal & Québec City
Munich & the Bavarian
  Alps
Nashville & Memphis
Nepal
New England
New Mexico
New Orleans
New York City
New Zealand
Nova Scotia, New Brunswick
  & Prince Edward Island
Oregon
Paris

Philadelphia & the
  Amish Country
Portugal
Prague & the Best of the
  Czech Republic
Provence & the Riviera
Puerto Rico
Rome
San Antonio & Austin
San Diego
San Francisco
Santa Fe, Taos & Albuquerque
Scandinavia
Scotland
Seattle`& Portland
Singapore & Malaysia
South Africa
Southeast Asia
South Pacific
Spain
Sweden
Switzerland
Thailand
Tokyo
Toronto
Tuscany & Umbria
USA
Utah
Vancouver & Victoria
Vermont, New Hampshire
  & Maine
Vienna & the Danube Valley
Virgin Islands
Virginia
Walt Disney World &
  Orlando
Washington, D.C.
Washington State

FROMMER'S® DOLLAR-A-DAY GUIDES

Australia from $50 a Day
California from $60 a Day
Caribbean from $70 a Day
England from $70 a Day
Europe from $60 a Day

Florida from $60 a Day
Hawaii from $70 a Day
Ireland from $60 a Day
Italy from $70 a Day
London from $85 a Day

New York from $80 a Day
Paris from $85 a Day
San Francisco from $60 a Day
Washington, D.C.,
  from $60 a Day

FROMMER'S® PORTABLE GUIDES

Acapulco, Ixtapa &
  Zihuatanejo
Alaska Cruises & Ports of Call
Bahamas
Baja & Los Cabos
Berlin
California Wine Country
Charleston & Savannah
Chicago

Dublin
Hawaii: The Big Island
Las Vegas
London
Maine Coast
Maui
New Orleans
New York City
Paris

Puerto Vallarta, Manzanillo
  & Guadalajara
San Diego
San Francisco
Sydney
Tampa & St. Petersburg
Venice
Washington, D.C.

FROMMER'S® NATIONAL PARK GUIDES

Family Vacations in the
  National Parks
Grand Canyon

National Parks of the
  American West
Rocky Mountain

Yellowstone & Grand Teton
Yosemite & Sequoia/
  Kings Canyon
Zion & Bryce Canyon

FROMMER'S® MEMORABLE WALKS

Chicago
London

New York
Paris

San Francisco
Washington D.C.

FROMMER'S® GREAT OUTDOOR GUIDES

New England
Northern California

Southern California & Baja
Southern New England

Washington & Oregon

FROMMER'S® BORN TO SHOP GUIDES

Born to Shop: China
Born to Shop: France

Born to Shop: Italy
Born to Shop: London

Born to Shop: New York
Born to Shop: Paris

FROMMER'S® IRREVERENT GUIDES

Amsterdam
Boston
Chicago
Las Vegas

London
Los Angeles
Manhattan
New Orleans

Paris
San Francisco
Seattle & Portland
Vancouver

Walt Disney World
Washington, D.C.

FROMMER'S® BEST-LOVED DRIVING TOURS

America
Britain
California

Florida
France
Germany

Ireland
Italy
New England

Scotland
Spain
Western Europe

THE UNOFFICIAL GUIDES®

Bed & Breakfasts in
  California
Bed & Breakfasts in
  New England
Bed & Breakfasts in
  the Northwest
Beyond Disney
Branson, Missouri
California with Kids
Chicago

Cruises
Disneyland
Florida with Kids
Golf Vacations in the
  Eastern U.S.
The Great Smoky &
  Blue Ridge
  Mountains
Inside Disney

Hawaii
Las Vegas
London
Miami & the Keys
Mini Las Vegas
Mini-Mickey
New Orleans
New York City
Paris

Safaris
San Francisco
Skiing in the West
Walt Disney World
Walt Disney World
  for Grown-ups
Walt Disney World
  for Kids
Washington, D.C.

SPECIAL-INTEREST TITLES

Frommer's Britain's Best Bed & Breakfasts and
  Country Inns
Frommer's Britain's Best Bike Rides
The Civil War Trust's Official Guide
  to the Civil War Discovery Trail
Frommer's Caribbean Hideaways
Frommer's Food Lover's Companion to France
Frommer's Food Lover's Companion to Italy
Frommer's Gay & Lesbian Europe
Frommer's Exploring America by RV
Hanging Out in Europe
Israel Past & Present

Mad Monks' Guide to California
Mad Monks' Guide to New York City
Frommer's The Moon
Frommer's New York City with Kids
The New York Times' Unforgettable
  Weekends
Places Rated Almanac
Retirement Places Rated
Frommer's Road Atlas Britain
Frommer's Road Atlas Europe
Frommer's Washington, D.C., with Kids
Frommer's What the Airlines Never Tell You